Marching in Step

Marching in Step

Masculinity, Citizenship,
and The Citadel in
Post–World War II America

ALEXANDER MACAULAY

The University of Georgia Press
Athens & London

Chapter 3 first appeared, in slightly different form, in *Warm Ashes: Issues in Southern History at the Dawn of the Twenty-first Century*, edited by Winfred B. Moore Jr., David H. White, and Kyle S. Sinisi (Columbia: University of South Carolina Press, 2003) and is reprinted by permission of the University of South Carolina Press. Chapter 4 first appeared, in slightly different form, in *Southern Cultures* (Fall 2005). Part of chapter 6 appeared as "Murder and Masculinity: The Trials of a Citadel Man," in *Black and White Masculinity in the American South, 1800–2000*, edited by Lydia Plath and Sergio Lussana (Newcastle: Cambridge Scholars Publishing, 2009) and is published with the permission of Cambridge Scholars Publishing.

Designed by Walton Harris
Set in 10/14 Minion Pro

Printed digitally in the United States of America

Library of Congress Cataloging-in-Publication Data

Macaulay, Alexander, 1972–
Marching in step : masculinity, citizenship, and the Citadel in post-World War II America / Alexander Macaulay.
    p.   cm. (Politics and culture in the twentieth-century South)
Includes bibliographical references and index.
ISBN-13: 978-0-8203-2651-1 (hardcover : alk. paper)
ISBN-10: 0-8203-2651-8 (hardcover : alk. paper)
1. Citadel, the Military College of South Carolina — History — 20th century. I. Title.
U430.C5 M33 2009
355.0071'1757915 — dc22   2009016365

British Library Cataloging-in-Publication Data available

4129469

CONTENTS

ACKNOWLEDGMENTS   *vii*

INTRODUCTION   *1*

CHAPTER ONE. "The Best Chance of Becoming Men and Leaders":
World War II and the Building of Citizen-Soldiers   *9*

CHAPTER TWO. Soaring with the American Eagle: Mark Clark and
Cold War Citizenship   *36*

CHAPTER THREE. Black, White, and Gray: The Racial Integration of
The Citadel, 1963–1973   *61*

CHAPTER FOUR. "An Oasis of Order": Citadel Cadets and
the Vietnam Antiwar Movement   *87*

CHAPTER FIVE. "A *Disciplined College* in an *Undisciplined Age*":
The Citadel and Southern Distinctiveness   *110*

CHAPTER SIX. The Spirit of '76: The South, The Citadel,
and the "New America"   *131*

CHAPTER SEVEN. "Tampering with America": Masculinity, Feminism,
and the Fourth Class System   *147*

CHAPTER EIGHT. Marching Backward: Race and The Citadel
in Reagan's America   *162*

CHAPTER NINE. Save the Males: The Fight over Coeducation   *192*

EPILOGUE   *212*

NOTES   *217*

BIBLIOGRAPHY   *261*

INDEX   *279*

ACKNOWLEDGMENTS

I have been fortunate enough throughout my life to have had family and friends who have helped me, challenged me, humored me, bought me beers, took me home, and welcomed me home. Their kindness and generosity are reflected in everything I do. This book is no exception.

Jane Yates, the archivist at The Citadel, has been involved with this project from the very first day. Although the final product has been over a decade in the making, it would have taken twice that long without her knowledge, diligence, and hard work. She helped track down sources and fulfilled untold number of requests, even when I promised that each one would be the last one. She has done a beautiful job with The Citadel Archives and Museum, cataloguing and organizing a massive amount of material and making it readily accessible to researchers. Whatever they are paying her in Charleston, it isn't enough.

Numerous other Citadel people offered their time, energy, and expertise to this book. Bo Moore taught me as an undergraduate and, despite his increasingly busy schedule, always made time to talk with me, check up on me, and read rough drafts. The dozens of Citadel graduates who agreed to speak with me about their experiences in Charleston have my undying gratitude as well. Of course, it's not all that hard to get Citadel alumni to talk about their alma mater, but they answered my questions and posed some of their own with a candor and enthusiasm that made my job easy and often fun. Two graduates in particular deserve special recognition.

I sat down with Joseph Shine on the floor of his study for well over two hours in December 2007. I left that day with a deep appreciation for his quiet strength and humility. I also discovered that, over the next few weeks, it was easier to get interviews with people who knew him, particularly his Citadel classmates. That as much as anything testifies to his standing among his peers.

I spent the better part of a Saturday morning talking with Frank Mood, a man who knows more about The Citadel than just about anybody else. His insights proved invaluable, and his interest in this study kept my own faith in it from flagging.

Emory Thomas, Robert Pratt, and Tom Dyer read this work in its dissertation form, and their comments improved it immensely. Two other members of that dissertation committee, Bryant Simon and James Cobb, also read this book in its early stages and — rather than run screaming from it — they have shaped it (and its author, for that matter) in positive ways. Like a good historian, Bryant helped me focus on what matters in this story. Like a good friend, he talked me off ledges when I became irrational. Dr. Cobb is everything I could ask for in a teacher and mentor. He demanded my best work and understood how to get it out of me. When he did not get my best effort, he let me know. When he did get it, he also let me know, albeit in more muted tones. Given the great respect I have for Dr. Cobb and his opinions, I find his faith and confidence in me both daunting and encouraging. Besides, as I have said before, if someone from Hartwell, Georgia, can do this job, certainly someone from Walhalla, South Carolina, can excel at it.

My colleagues in the history department at Western Carolina University have helped me out not only by keeping me gainfully employed but also indulging my efforts to steer every conversation to The Citadel, South Carolina, or Kris Kristofferson. Libby McRae, Vicki Szabo, and Richard Starnes read portions of this manuscript under the most onerous conditions possible. When stumped with a particular passage or idea, I would call them or go by their offices, explain my dilemma, and then, out of the blue, read or hand them paragraphs. Each of them are deeply involved in their own lives and work, but they always took the time to help me with mine. Some of the best turns of phrase in the manuscript are Richard's. I haven't cited him in the notes, but I figure this will let him lay claim or deny responsibility accordingly. Vicki mocked me as I agonized over which verbs to use, but she also helped me express my thoughts in ways that made sense. She also kept me supplied with candy, off-brand soft drinks, beer, and horror movies. Libby told me what this book was about, plain and simple. I marvel at the grand way in which she thinks, writes, teaches, and lives.

My family took an interest in me well before I began studying history. My mother and father love, support, and inspire me in ways that I can never repay.

My mother is the strongest person I know. My father is the most honest person I know. Both make it clear that their love for their children is boundless. Even with everything else they do for me, that alone comforts me and drives me to do them proud.

A while back, I was at home with my own children, and to put it euphemistically, we were not having a good day. I started complaining to a friend about this, and he responded, "Yeah, parenting is tough, but who wants boring kids?" I can say without any doubt whatsoever, my children are not boring. I am awed by my eldest daughter Eliza's tenacity and perseverance. If someone tells her she is unable to do something, rest assured she will have completed that task within twenty-four hours. I plan one day to tell her that it is impossible to turn invisible and then sit back and watch what happens. My father calls my son Lee a go-to guy, meaning that he is always up for anything, and his participation can make the most mundane task enjoyable. One day, I hope to be as nice, fun, and enthusiastic about life as he is. A guy I know from Walhalla said he didn't like to talk to his children until they had personality. My youngest daughter Kate abounded in personality from day one. She is what polite parents like to call a "handful," but she is a joyous handful.

I met my wife Eleanor in a bar in Clemson in 1993. We married five years later, and my years with her have been the best of my life. No one in this world means as much to me as she does. I cherish her love and friendship and do my best to be deserving of both. She has not had to live with this project as some authors like to say, but she has lived with me and that is infinitely harder. The best I can do is live my life in a way that makes her happy and proud of me. If this book helps with that, so be it. Either way, I'll keep trying.

Marching in Step

Introduction

 In January 1994, a newspaper reporter approached a senior at The Citadel, the Military College of South Carolina, as he was buying books for the upcoming semester. After months of legal wrangling, Shannon Faulkner, a young woman from Powdersville, South Carolina, was set to attend classes, not wear a uniform or march in formation, alongside the corps of cadets. When asked his opinion on this, the twenty-one-year-old cadet replied, "We can't make her a Citadel man any more than I can have a baby. But we will treat her like a lady, like we were taught to do." This exchange came at a precipitous moment in the history of the school as the one institutional tradition that had truly endured since the antebellum founding of the college, its all-male corps of cadets, was under siege. While this fact alone warranted the attention of the *New York Times* and other national media, what was at stake extended well beyond the admissions policies of a small liberal arts college in Charleston, South Carolina. Indeed, the sound bite provided by this cadet carried with it a larger message, one that drew upon deeply held gendered assumptions about the American body politic. At a school that prided itself on the making of "whole men" who would serve the nation as "citizen-soldiers," this young man evaluated and defined citizenship in a way that was dynamic—as something that could be taught, learned, and constructed—but also gender specific. According to him, men could, should, and would strengthen the nation by learning the lessons of The Citadel and becoming more manly. Such a belief promoted his own masculine civic worth, while confining those who presumably had no chance of meeting such criteria, most notably women, to less public and immutable roles—reproduction, for example.[1]

While not usually articulated in such a straightforward manner, the views expressed by the cadet in the Citadel bookstore were not peculiar to him nor

1

his alma mater.[2] Although many see The Citadel as an isolated outpost that could have arisen and survived only in the South, since the Civil War it has always been a reflection of not only southern but American values, particularly when it comes to conflating masculinity and citizenship. This flies in the face of contemporary popular characterizations of the college as an archaic regional throwback, a quintessentially "southern" institution, immune from shifts and changes in the rest of the country. In his travel guide to the neo-Confederate South, author Tony Horwitz calls The Citadel "arguably the most mummified institution in America." Following a tumultuous and brief tenure as president of the school, an embittered Vice Admiral James Stockdale grumbled "the place is locked in pre–Civil War concrete." Historian Tim Tyson has called the college "perhaps the most hidebound institution in tradition-steeped South Carolina." A former faculty member claims that "perhaps more than any other institution of higher education The Citadel best reflects the cultural values of the Old South."[3]

Writer Susan Faludi counters such conclusions, finding that although "institutions that boast of their insularity, whether convents or military academies, are commonly pictured in the public imagination as static, unchanging abstractions, impervious to the ebb and flow of current events," such places have "functioned more as a barometer of national anxieties than as a stalwart garrison against them." The post–World War II history of The Citadel supports this interpretation. In *Stiffed: The Betrayal of the American Man*, Faludi contends, "The United States came out of World War II with a sense of itself as a *masculine* nation." A prosperous, aggressive America, she adds, "claimed an ascendancy over the world, men an ascendancy over the nation, and a male persona of a certain type ascendancy over men." Nowhere was this more evident than at The Citadel, where school officials, students, and alumni touted a special breed of ascendant male as the college's "only product." In the process, they adopted, defended, and promoted a deeply gendered assessment of citizenship, one that not only reflected broader cultural and political shifts but one that resonated with many Americans and promised "Citadel men" a prominent place in the country's civic hierarchy.[4]

Since the school's inception, Citadel officials had devoted themselves to the training of "citizen-soldiers," men who, as historian Rod Andrew explains, would bolster the "internal health of society" as much as they would "contribute to society's external defense." School publications confirmed that the primary purpose of the college was to prepare men for "civil pursuits" through "a sound education reinforced by the best features of military training." Citadel cadets embraced this ideal, yoking their success and stature to that of the nation. In the wake of the Second World War, one member of the corps described his alma mater as a "staunch Citadel of opportunity, an imperturbable Citadel of progressive training. If ever it becomes anything else, it will be when the country has ceased to be a citadel for the democratic way of life."[5]

With their fate tied directly to the present and future strength of the country, Citadel cadets and school officials adopted an image of the ideal American citizen that mirrored the predominantly white, all-male environment where they studied, lived, and labored. Strong, tough, disciplined, conservative white men became the masculine standard by which Citadel men judged one another and the rest of the nation. Committed to instilling in young men the values that presumably set the corps of cadets, the college, and the country apart from the rest of the world, Citadel students and alumni marketed their alma mater as a "factory," one that "built" the type of exceptionally manly citizens best suited to lead the nation to prosperity and glory. In the process, they gendered a constellation of physical and abstract attributes from toughness to integrity to patriotism, regarding each as singularly manly traits that were not just desirable, but vital to the country's success.

Such beliefs took firm root in the highly politicized atmosphere of the early Cold War, a time when men at The Citadel joined countless other Americans in glorifying physical strength, exhibiting a passionate yet uncritical patriotism, and promoting a decidedly white, exclusively male image of the ideal American, southerner, and Citadel graduate as one and the same. During this period, obedience to authority stood as a pillar of the institution's ideology, an article of faith that fit nicely within the larger national environment. Obsessed with "holding the line," a term that encompassed the dual goals of containing communism abroad and preserving the economic and social status quo at home, many Americans regarded any criticism of the United States and its policies as subversive and dangerous. It should come as no surprise then that The Citadel flourished in an era when "faith was strengthened in the institutions of authority," and many people looked to the military and conservative politicians as the most qualified arbiters and defenders of American values.[6]

This authoritarianism did not last as World War II had unleashed the potential for change, not just the rhetorical weapons to stifle it. Wartime scarcities and necessities opened doors for African Americans and women, while post-war demands for order fueled a backlash against civil rights activists and the symbolism of Rosie the Riveter. Once opened, though, these doors could not be shut, and shifting cultural and social expectations left many Americans hopeful, anxious, anticipatory, and resentful.[7] The American South proved especially ripe for what historian Pete Daniel has dubbed the "interlocking revolutionary components" of "rural change, urbanization, science, technology, racism, and popular culture" that promised to reconfigure the region's politics, society, and culture. Morton Sosna describes the entire post–World War II South as "an arena where the forces of good and evil, progress and reaction, rapid change and seemingly timeless continuities were about to engage in a battle of near mythical proportions." Clarence Mohr has argued that for southern colleges and universities in particular, the war set "in motion forces that would permanently reorder their priorities, remake their institutional culture, and alter their relationship with society at large."[8]

Citadel men responded to these revolutionary forces by absorbing, accommodating, and abrogating key societal shifts, all with an eye toward keeping their institution relevant and preserving their own place atop the civic ladder. In the decades following World War II, conflicting internal and external assessments of the college drew upon larger debates over not only who was worthy of the rights and privileges of full citizenship but how such qualifications were determined and evaluated. The events of the 1960s proved crucial as social, cultural, and political forces pushed some students and alumni to reevaluate their duties as cadets and Americans. The erosion of racial barriers and the reevaluation of sociopolitical mores that came as a result of the modern civil rights movement, the anti–Vietnam War movement, and the student movement prompted a limited alteration of cadets' racialized concepts of manliness and citizenship. Still, African Americans' status as citizen-soldiers depended upon their unquestioning acceptance of the school's "southern" traditions. A persistent lack of racial diversity on the college's campus enabled a large segment of the corps to perpetuate a lily-white assessment of the school's heritage and product, guaranteeing the continued existence of a racialized view of America, the South, and The Citadel.

The willingness of Citadel men to expand their definition of masculinity to include African Americans and student protestors underscores the artificial and protean nature of socially proscribed gender roles. At the same time, however, a great number of cadets and alumni refused to rethink their gendered evaluations of honesty, courage, patriotism, and citizenship. For them, graduating from an institution that embodied such qualities confirmed their status as model men and thus model citizens. Having staked their reputation, identity, and civic worth on the belief that their college imbued them with the manly qualities essential to superior citizenship, they regarded any challenge to their own gender ideals and the school's masculine purpose as a direct threat to The Citadel and Citadel men.

When it came to defending the environment and system that produced the type of manly citizen they believed the country needed, Citadel cadets and alumni often mixed popular notions of American exceptionalism and egalitarianism with typically southern appeals to stability and tradition. Despite its reputation as an institution for South Carolina elites, Governor Ben Tillman famously labeled the college a "military dude factory," The Citadel began as a school for the "poor but deserving boys of the state." The campus housed its share of wealthy scions, but by keeping tuition low and having the state foot the bill for a large number of "beneficiary" cadets, the school offered the sons of white working-class families academic as well as social opportunities that they might not have been able to afford otherwise. School boosters promoted as a "distinctive feature" of the college the meritocratic nature of an institution whose students lived in the same barracks, ate the same food, subjected themselves to the same regulations, and dressed in the same uniforms. In an early history of The Citadel, Oliver J. Bond, a former student, faculty member, and president of the college, claimed that once cadets donned their uniforms, "All distinctions which might arise from difference of dress are obliterated at once, thus promoting the democracy which rests upon merit alone." This held true up to a point, so long as one's vision of democracy did not include the many women and African Americans who for decades were not allowed to join the corps of cadets. It was precisely this blindness that led many people to highlight the egalitarian spirit of an institution that erased markers of economic class, but upheld racial and gender barriers. At times, Citadel personnel would present their college as a true meritocracy as a means of shoring up its American credentials or blunting criticism that they discriminated against women and black men.[9]

School personnel also deflected challenges to their rules and regulations in stereotypically "southern" fashion, evoking "time-honored traditions" and casting certain changes as fatal to the college's vaunted distinctiveness. Just as many white southerners bemoaned any threat to "the southern way of life" in their efforts to sustain segregation, weed out "troublemakers," and preserve the status quo, Citadel cadets often regarded any questioning of their customs and codes as a danger to the "Citadel system." While Citadel alumni, students, and administrators responded to the social changes sweeping America, their reform impulse was tempered by a regional and institutional fear that "too much change" would cost the school and its graduates their unique identity. Challenges to its rules, regulations, and practices met frequent resistance from those who worried that The Citadel would "become another Clemson."[10]

Such beliefs manifested themselves in the often visceral defense of The Citadel's "plebe" or "fourth class system." Widely regarded as the crucible in which boys were forged into Citadel men, the fourth class system played an essential role in fulfilling the college's manly mission.[11] As such, it offers the clearest expression of how those at The Citadel linked manliness and citizenship. A series of written guidelines and unwritten customs designed to test the physical and mental limits of Citadel freshmen, the fourth class system supposedly infused young recruits with the masculine qualities associated with superior citizenship. Admirers credited the system with developing and nurturing manly traits such as discipline, obedience, loyalty, and toughness. They believed that the rigors of plebe year set Citadel men apart from other, less masculine, Americans.

Despite claims to the contrary, however, not all Citadel freshmen labored under the same standards and expectations. In fact, many of the fourth class system's most venerated "traditions" were modern reactions to contemporary developments. By the late 1950s and early 1960s, what had been a relatively sedate method of military instruction had evolved into a grueling test of a cadet's masculinity. With so much resting on their school's ability to build exceptional men, most Citadel cadets and alumni refused to listen to anyone who questioned the benefits or implementation of the fourth class system. Instead, they cast the process as timeless and sacrosanct, shouting down reform efforts as the work of "outsiders" whose tampering would not only hurt The Citadel but cost the nation a reliable source of successful, dependable, and powerful leaders of men.

It is important to remember, though, that with their reliance on conveniently selected interpretations of the past and carefully tailored definitions of citizenship, the arguments of many defenders of The Citadel reflected rather than stood apart from prominent national values. Although some find it convenient and even reassuring to depict the military college as timeless and out of touch with mainstream America, such assessments fuel distorted views of the South and the United States, downplaying significant regional changes while at the same time overestimating national support for these changes. Like the South in many ways, The Citadel has been cast as both the repository for all the nation's historic ills or as a shining example of what does, or once did, make America great. Like most institutions, The Citadel is neither as glorious nor as depraved as its proponents and detractors attest. Still, popular perceptions of the college are linked to larger misconceptions about the South that "not only ignore the social, political, and economic advances in Dixie" but mistake "crusading liberalism and hunger for social justice" as American trademarks.[12]

Although Citadel men mounted a spirited defense of their single-sex traditions and faith in manly citizenship, the most effective method of preserving their environment and worldview was to deny "outsiders" access to the institution. Cadets and alumni found it easier to believe that their distinctive manliness elevated them above less manly Americans so long as these "others" could be ignored or denied the opportunity to prove themselves equally worthy citizen-soldiers. Of course, Citadel men were not the first to realize this or adopt this approach. Michael Kimmel for one has documented "the traditional way that men had defined their manhood — against an other who was excluded from full humanity by being excluded from those places where real men were real men." Historian Gary Gerstle has also examined the tensions that arose when women "entered territory designed for men and joined in activities meant to enhance male fellowship, the sinew of nationhood." Indeed, The Citadel represents one of many "material and symbolic resources" that have helped create and preserve a potent national identity, one built around and sustained by exclusion.[13]

Ultimately, the post–World War II history of The Citadel showcases in their most concentrated, unadulterated form, debates over who deserved full-fledged recognition as an American citizen. Notions of citizenship and freedom feature prominently in our national consciousness, with Eric Foner connecting the latter to "a set of practical rights and entitlements that go along with being an American." This holds true for the former as well, albeit with an added dimension that citizens not only qualify for certain freedoms, but they also assume responsibility for defining, protecting, extending, and limiting those freedoms. It seems that Americans are constantly jockeying for position within the nation's social and political hierarchy, formulating and defending ideas of what America stands for and how "good" citizens look, act, and think. Some take an expansive view; others do not, choosing to validate their place in society by privileging those who look, act, and think like they do. Such constructions harden over time, becoming accepted "facts" that keep countless "others" on the margins of American life. Such efforts have contributed to what many historians recognize as the "racialized tradition" and "gendered character" of American nationalism.[14]

Certainly race factored heavily into the traditions of an institution founded in the wake of an 1822 slave revolt, whose students still brag about their predecessors firing the first shots of the Civil War. At the same time, gender proved crucial to the character of those at a college described as the "last bastion of masculinity," "a repository of antebellum southern male culture," and the "very symbol of South Carolina manhood." A close examination of what it meant to be and what it took to become a Citadel man substantiates the theory that although social constructions based on race and gender tend to "represent relationships of power as innate, fixed or biologically rooted," historians have the power to "make transparent the human agency behind these 'natural' relationships."[15] This study proposes to do just that, uncovering how and why the boundaries of citizenship and civic nationalism were drawn and redrawn in the decades following World War II while at the same time highlighting the hopes and frustrations that marked this process.

CHAPTER ONE

"The Best Chance of Becoming Men and Leaders"

World War II and the Building of Citizen-Soldiers

 In the spring of 1943 The Citadel, the Military College of South Carolina, celebrated its one hundredth birthday. That March the *Saturday Evening Post* ran an article by South Carolina native Herbert Ravenel Sass commemorating the event and offering the school's "militant Americanism" as proof of the country's strength and patriotism. Disappointed that "the great majority of Americans know little or nothing" about The Citadel, Sass declared "it would be hard to find a more inspiring demonstration of the basic strength and soundness of the Republic than this military college in Charleston, South Carolina, most loyal of all Southern cities to the memory and ideals of the Confederacy." Glorifying cadets' roles in both sundering and serving the Union, the author pointed out that Citadel graduates had fought in every major U.S. conflict since the Civil War, proving that "a Confederate stronghold can be a hornet's nest of aggressive and hard hitting Americanism." In 1943 over a quarter of the student body came from outside the South, prompting Sass to note that by serving as valiantly in World War II as they had in the Civil War, The Citadel's "Yanks and Rebs are giving one of the finest exhibitions of Americanism conceivable." Having linked the school's Confederate heritage with its patriotic loyalty to the United States, Sass concluded that The Citadel's story "might even be called an American epic."[1]

A couple of years earlier, with World War II looming on the horizon, another South Carolina native, W. J. Cash, predicted that "in the coming days and probably soon, [the South] is likely to have to prove its capacity for adjustment

far beyond what has been true in the past." The Citadel found its capacity for
adjustment sorely tested as the school struggled to make ends meet following the Great Depression and subsequent wartime conscription of almost the
entire student body. Reeling and unsure immediately following the war, the
college regained its footing with the federal government's help and by opening the school to new students, performing new functions, and providing new
services. In the process, school officials and cadets modified certain rules and
customs but at the same time upheld certain long-standing ideals that they believed had served the college well in the past and would serve the nation well
in the future. As a hot war ended and a cold war began, cadets and school officials made a point of preserving an institutional emphasis on order, discipline,
and obedience dating back to the college's founding.[2]

The history of The Citadel stretches back to 1822 when Denmark Vesey
staged an unsuccessful slave revolt in Charleston, South Carolina. Despite
Vesey's failure, his attempt alarmed white Charlestonians. Rumors abounded
that Vesey and his followers planned to "indiscriminately" kill white men,
while white women "were to have been reserved to fill their — Haram's [sic]."
Following the mass hanging of the conspirators, one Charlestonian warned,
"Let it never be forgotten, that our Negroes are truly the Jacobins of our country, the barbarians who would, IF THEY COULD, become the DESTROYERS of
our race." As the hysteria grew, white vigilantes roamed the streets assaulting
black people. Law enforcement officials arrested large numbers of slaves or
free blacks and locked them in the Workhouse — an edifice where up to twelve
prisoners were chained to a rail and forced to march on a treadmill. The treadmill powered two large wheels that ground corn, and should the prisoners' legs
falter, a "cat o' nine tails" forced them to continue.[3]

These legal and extralegal forms of racial oppression did not pacify white
citizens as they petitioned the state legislature to establish a garrison to "protect
and preserve the public property . . . and safety." The South Carolina General
Assembly responded accordingly, passing "An Act to Establish a Competent
Force to Act as a Municipal Guard for the Protection of the City of Charleston
and Its Vicinity." The new facility designated to house this guard was named
"The Citadel." In his biography of Vesey, Douglas Egerton describes the forbid-
ding structure as "the most impressive symbol of racial control" erected after
the rebellion.[4]

Later, as tensions escalated between the northern and southern states,

Governor John Richardson sought to create an institution that would provide military training to the state's youth as well as offer an education in science and the liberal arts. The South Carolina legislature conceded the "advantages of combining the military duties of the guards at The Citadel with a system of education for the poor but deserving boys of the State," and on December 20, 1842, The Citadel became a military college.[5]

Before two decades had passed, Citadel cadets would allegedly fire the first shots of the Civil War. Many of the school's alumni fought with distinction in the Confederate Army. More than two-thirds of the school's 240 graduates served as officers, including four generals and nineteen colonels. Forty-three Citadel alumni and over two hundred former students died in battle. The current flag of the Corps of Cadets prominently displays nine battle streamers recognizing The Citadel's contribution to the southern war effort.[6]

Following the war, The Citadel served as the headquarters of Lieutenant Colonel Augustus G. Bennett and his Twenty-first United States Colored Regiment. With slavery abolished, black Charlestonians held an Emancipation Day celebration on the school grounds, an event Kathleen Clark lists as one of many "local skirmishes" waged throughout the region as blacks and whites appropriated symbolically charged southern landmarks as a means of promoting their versions of the antebellum past and postbellum present. As African American tradesmen, militia members, teachers, and schoolchildren assembled on the Citadel Green and marched proudly through the city's streets, their actions and demeanor "stressed both the memory of slavery and the evolution of black progress." The efforts of African Americans to carve out and defend their place in the local and national landscape angered and frightened white Charlestonians who bristled at "liberty loving freedmen . . . bearing war like instruments upon their shoulders, [who] looked terribly patriotic as they formed the line."[7]

When federal occupation of The Citadel ended in 1879, state legislators delayed reopening the school for financial reasons. Complicating matters further, many whites in the postbellum South seemed to suffer a generational crisis as Civil War veterans betrayed a distinct lack of confidence in the region's "untested" youth. Urbanization, industrialization, New South boosterism, and challenges to the region's racial mores sparked concerns among veterans that "their successors, soon to take leadership in the society, would fail to understand their achievements . . . and might violate their precedents." Within this charged social environment, southern colleges stressed their cultural function as much as their educational one. Southern progressives defended higher education as an "instrument of material and social control," while college and university officials promoted their schools as defenders of the region's political and social institutions.[8]

As Rod Andrew points out in *Long Gray Lines*, southern proponents of military schools had long stressed the value of such institutions in disciplining the region's youths and ensuring their "submission to lawful authority." During the sectional crisis, military preparedness eclipsed or equaled curbing delinquency as the primary purpose of these schools. Following the Civil War, promoters of military education again couched their arguments in terms of building character and producing respectful, orderly citizens. In *Ghosts of the Confederacy*, Gaines Foster argues that the Lost Cause owed much of its appeal to white southerners' attempts to maintain social order and the status quo. Andrew agrees, noting that "particularly after the Civil War, the South's Confederate past and the powerful appeal of the Lost Cause made southerners apt to equate military service and martial valor with broader cultural notions of honor, patriotism, civic duty and virtue." Andrew adds that "the most compelling and unchallenged tenet" of the Lost Cause remained "the notion that soldierly virtues were the marks of an honorable man and a worthy citizen."[9]

While emphasizing stability and societal order, the southern military tradition also carried with it a message of rebellion and resistance to tyranny. Student uprisings and walkouts occurred periodically at schools such as The Citadel where "the examples of their ancestors taught the cadets that if the citizen-soldier were being treated unfairly, the only honorable thing to do was revolt." School officials often took a different view of such behavior, regarding it as antithetical to institutions devoted to maintaining order and instilling obedience. Many administrators and some alumni found cadet unruliness embarrassing, alarming, and even threatening to schools whose reputation and livelihood hinged on the production of disciplined, law-abiding citizens.[10]

This certainly held true at The Citadel, where, in 1881, a group of alumni launched a statewide campaign to generate public support for their alma mater's resurrection. They peppered newspapers with articles titled "Results of Military Training on the Bearing, Character and Spirit of the Cadet" and "Military Training Useful Principally in the Formation of Character and the Maintenance of Discipline, and Not to Make Professional Soldiers." The focus on character building appealed to legislators and the general public, but the backing of influential alumni helped The Citadel as well. Following the war, many of the college's graduates parlayed their Confederate wartime service into political power, and Andrew notes that "as proof of the school's usefulness, supporters pointed to the large number of Citadel alumni who were then respected leaders in the state." Johnson Hagood, class of 1847, and Hugh Thompson, class of 1856, later served as governors of South Carolina. Several other alumni held positions of power at the local, state, and national levels. In 1882, with a Citadel graduate sitting in the governor's chair, the South Carolina General Assembly approved state funding and The Citadel reopened as a military college. Andrew calls the college's rebirth "an example of how the legacy of the military school's Confederate service and the postwar prestige of many of its graduates helped keep the southern military tradition alive."[11]

Over the next four decades, The Citadel expanded its educational programs, and in 1922, the campus was moved from the center of Charleston to a one-hundred-acre site on the banks of the Ashley River. Unfortunately, excitement over the new location did not last long as The Citadel languished during the economic crises of the late 1920s. Debts mounted, enrollment plummeted, and buildings deteriorated. Dusty, unpaved campus roads circled an unkempt parade ground. During the day, cadets took classes from overworked and underqualified faculty members. At night, they studied in a library that was "crammed into a dark and dusty barracks room." Conditions grew so dismal that, in 1930, The Citadel's outgoing president worried that the South Carolina legislature would cut the school's funding altogether.[12]

With this in mind, Citadel officials searched for a new president who would attract students, publicity, and most of all, money to the college. The man they chose, General Charles Pelot Summerall, seemed ideal for the job. The highly decorated World War I veteran brought immediate national attention to The Citadel. A North Carolina newspaper rejoiced that "one of the world's most distinguished soldiers and leaders . . . will not rust out, but train youth." Summerall devoted himself to improving the college's financial status. He cut salaries, fired workers, limited electrical and water use, disconnected phones, and reduced the number of lightbulbs in classrooms and the library. He prowled the grounds regularly to ensure that everyone followed his directives. In 1932, the *Chicago Tribune* lauded Summerall as a "depression statesman" who proved "that all men of character and purpose . . . can turn the trick." In the process, the writer added, Citadel cadets "learned that honorable men do not live beyond their means, however limited and they have learned fortitude."[13]

While Summerall's authoritarian measures helped, The Citadel did not ride out the Depression on "character and purpose" alone. New Deal programs, private contributions, and legislative appropriations funded campus improvements that helped attract and house new students. State-approved bonds and grants from the Works Progress Administration paid for a new mess hall, a new chapel, a new barracks, and new faculty apartments. Enrollment rose steadily over the next eight years, and one historian notes that by 1940, "The Citadel had become a vibrant and viable institution."[14]

Circumstances soon changed when the United States entered the Second World War. Despite Herbert Sass's 1943 proclamation that The Citadel's "thoughts are focused with an absorbed intensity on its vigorous present," the college struggled during the war. In 1942, almost 2,000 students had attended the institution. Due largely to the draft, that number had fallen to 485 by the following year. At the war's end, enrollment had bottomed out at 427. School officials again cut salaries and fired workers. Between the 1943 and 1944 school years, the size of The Citadel's faculty had shrunk from 104 to 32.[15]

Wartime deprivations and demands forced Citadel officials to overhaul many of the school's policies. The year after the draft claimed almost the entire junior and senior class, The Citadel's governing body, the Board of Visitors, made it possible for students to graduate in three years by dividing the school year into quarters rather than semesters. Still, the most pressing problem and the one with the most far-reaching implications remained the low number of students on campus. Declining enrollments meant declining revenues, and school administrators scrambled for ways to fill The Citadel's barracks, classrooms, and bank accounts.[16]

The U.S. Army came to the school's rescue. In 1942, General Summerall and the Board of Visitors signed a contract with the War Department agreeing to offer army recruits "specialized training along technical lines." Through two main programs, the Army Specialized Training Program (ASTP) and the Specialized Training and Reassignment (STAR) program, soldiers received advanced academic and military instruction at The Citadel, and then, based on their performance, either went on to Officer Candidate School or returned to the enlisted ranks. The War Department set the soldiers' curricula and agreed to cover all expenses relating to the programs, including building upkeep and faculty compensation. At a time when the college was firing teachers by the handful and running low on cash and students, this offer promised to solve The Citadel's immediate problems. Still, several school officials questioned the government's proposal, and their concerns reveal conflicting ideas about The Citadel's purpose, its value, and its constituency.[17]

Debates over how to keep the college solvent without diminishing its manly product dominated campus discussions. Some feared that using Citadel facilities to house and train large numbers of actual soldiers would sully the college's academic reputation. School personnel, cadets, faculty, and administrators alike appreciated The Citadel's mix of military and educational instruction, but worried that the school's obvious military trappings fed the "erroneous assumption that the institution exists to prepare men for war." School boosters claimed that the military aspects of Citadel life simply complemented its educational purpose by making "academic training more complete and effective through the development of soldierly virtues." These virtues included honesty, integrity, discipline, and organization "woven into the lives of men" in such a way that "will produce results for good irrespective of the field in which they are applied."[18]

The primary objection to implementing ASTP and STAR at The Citadel stemmed from fears about the impact such programs might have on the customs and traditions of the school and the corps of cadets. School publications aimed at prospective and new cadets cited obedience and discipline as essential components of a Citadel education. The 1942 *Guidon*, a handbook for freshmen written by cadets, defined The Citadel's mission in part as "To make available to the country young men with alert minds and sound bodies who have been taught high ideals, honor, uprightness, loyalty, and patriotism, who possess that obedience which goes with trained initiative and leadership." The same publication described the college's "military code" as "the law of honor and duty, so closely and intimately blended that no violation of its principles, how small soever [sic], can be permitted either with safety or honor and there is no principle inculcated by the code more imperious or necessary than obedience, prompt, immediate and respectful obedience to every command emanating from proper authority." Explaining "The Citadel Code," General Summerall wrote that anyone claiming the "honor of being a 'Citadel Man'" must first "revere God, love my country, and be loyal to The Citadel."[19]

Many people feared that non-Citadel personnel lacked this fealty and that their presence would have a corrosive impact on the discipline and behavior of the corps. In his preliminary outline of how The Citadel would incorporate ASTP into its regular academic routine, Summerall assured the Board of Visitors that his first priority was to preserve the Citadel "system." He promised that "present regulations and customs would be imposed on the contract cadets and regular cadets alike," and he drew special attention to the fact that cadets and army trainees would live on opposite ends of the campus. The 1943 Citadel *Catalogue* affirmed the corps' role as keeper of school traditions, noting that, "Faced with the added responsibility of growing numbers, the college seeks to preserve in the corps of cadets those ideals and traditions that it has cherished from the beginning, in order that those who enroll for its education and training, who bring to the college the benefits of many backgrounds, may be nevertheless influenced and strengthened by the noble code of The Citadel."[20]

Despite these claims to uphold sacred school traditions, the 1943–1944 school year witnessed a major change in The Citadel's method of building men. More than ten thousand soldiers received some sort of specialized training on the school campus. Due to the "unusual circumstances with the various types of students on campus," General Summerall officially suspended the fourth class system.[21]

Prior to 1943, freshmen — or fourthclassmen as they are known at The Citadel — had to address upperclassmen as "sir" or "mister." When outside their room, all plebes had to appear in full uniform. They were required to learn and recite the history of The Citadel and all the school's cheers and songs. During their first few weeks on campus, fourthclassmen saluted all senior cadet officers. At meals, plebes had to sit without touching the back of their chair and serve all upperclassmen before serving and eating their own food. In the barracks, they had to "square corners," meaning they turned left and right at ninety-degree angles. In both the barracks and the mess hall, freshmen were required to "brace," an exaggerated form of attention whereby the cadet pushed his chin into his chest, rotated his forehead straight back, pulled his shoulders back and down, and locked his arms to his sides.[22]

After Summerall's decision, new *Guidons* replaced "Freshman Regulations" with "A Guide to Your General Conduct and Wellbeing." Under this new "guide," the rigid demands of the fourth class system gave way to a series of hints and suggestions that first-year cadets ought to follow. These suggestions included addressing upperclassmen as "sir" and carrying out orders from senior cadets "with the utmost speed." Bracing was replaced by the urging to "maintain a correct posture and take pride in your military appearance at all times." Instead of reciting the school's history, songs, and cheers on demand, cadets were encouraged to keep abreast of current events and "always yell your best at football games and other contests." With upper-class control over the plebes relaxed, the authors of the *Guidon* asked new cadets to discipline themselves. They reminded freshmen that "griping only makes matters worse," and added, "The cadet who continually gripes is seldom popular. Always show a smile: it will make you feel better and make life more livable in general."[23]

Such changes did not sit well with cadets. In 1944, upperclassmen warned incoming freshmen that the environment that produced Citadel men "cannot be modified. It cannot be absorbed. To transfer it is to kill by transplanting what flourishes in its congenial soil. To modify it is to break its symmetry. To absorb it is to lose its peculiar essence." Decrying the loss of "customs which have made the College what it has been for more than a hundred years," the corps registered their protest through a brief hunger strike. On a day when the Board of Visitors planned to eat in the mess hall with the cadets, the corps filed in silently, sat down, refused to eat, and then walked out as quietly as they had entered. One cadet wrote a letter to a local newspaper protesting "the abolition of certain traditions and regulations which have connected with our school for the past one hundred years, and . . . proven necessary in the training of an officer measuring up to Citadel standards." The protest prompted the suspension of about twenty cadets, and while the Board of Visitors later revoked their suspensions, the fourth class system was not officially reinstated until after the war.[24]

Despite such tensions, The Citadel's contract with the War Department sustained the school when it desperately needed outside assistance. By November 1943, The Citadel had received $495,000 in government checks, and although the school survived on federal largesse during the last two years of the war, the relationship between The Citadel and the War Department was often a frustrating one. General Summerall badgered army officials to pay their bills on time, warning the commanding general of the Fourth Service Command that without prompt and full payments, the school could not continue to train ASTP inductees. In a long exchange of bitter and angry letters, Summerall accused the War Department of welshing on their debts, and the War Department accused The Citadel of inflating its expense accounts. In April 1944, an exasperated Summerall announced that he would never sign another contract with the federal government. The next month, he ordered the commandant to bar ASTP trainees from the mess hall, barracks, and all other campus facilities until the War Department paid its bills. When the U.S. Army severed its contract with The Citadel shortly thereafter, Summerall threatened to sue the Fourth Service Command for the money he claimed it owed. The two sides eventually settled out of court for $86,700. Despite the acrimonious relationship, ASTP and the STAR program proved a much-needed windfall for The Citadel, filling barracks and classrooms that would have stood empty, and allowing the school to receive a sizable state appropriation from the South Carolina legislature.[25]

While wartime exigencies sparked key policy changes at The Citadel, joining the august fraternity of Citadel men still required strict "obedience to authority" and "love of order." Freshmen handbooks continued to inform potential Citadel graduates that their present and future success depended "in large measure, on the extent to which you accept and adhere to the Code of The Citadel Man and the ideology of the institution." The immediate postwar period did produce a great deal of anxiety among the corps and school officials concerning the importance of maintaining these standards. The Cold War and the enrollment of veteran students in particular played key roles in pushing cadets and administrators to define more precisely the type of citizens they believed the nation needed and how The Citadel could best produce such citizens.[26]

Despite General Summerall's lingering reservations about accepting federal money to educate noncadets, the Board of Visitors realized that The Citadel could not survive without outside help. Thus, in 1944, they agreed to accept "such veterans as may seek admission under the GI Bill of Rights." In his study of the University of North Carolina at Chapel Hill, William Link notes that the GI Bill launched a "revolution in higher education" as colleges "underwent a period of sustained expansion in enrollments, faculty and facilities." The Citadel and other military colleges worried that they would miss out on the government-sponsored boom because "men who have been under fire will not wish to return to the military confinement" of such schools. Although school officials decided to "cooperate with these men and allow them to attend college not as cadets, but as civilian students," dramatic postwar growth bypassed The

Citadel for a number of reasons. Physically, the small, confined campus would not permit a vast expansion of school facilities. More importantly, much as they had when it came to the ASTP and STAR program, Citadel cadets and administrators worried about the presence of "an unconventional student body" composed largely of older, less compliant veterans.[27]

In a history of The Citadel published in 1994, D. D. Nicholson claims that immediately following World War II, "the influx of students admitted under the GI Bill rejuvenated the college and sped it on the road to greater service." The fees paid by veterans, or civilian students as Citadel personnel categorized them, did keep the school afloat in the immediate postwar years. At the same time, Nicholson's positive evaluation obscures the cadets' and the administrations' lack of appreciation for the sacrifices and contributions of the veterans. Citadel personnel depended upon the veterans' money to pay the bills and improve campus facilities, but seethed at the civilian students' supposed indifference to the institution's traditions and looked forward to the day when these "outsiders" would no longer be allowed within the Citadel's gates.[28]

In 1945, with a great deal of campus space still unoccupied, school officials allowed noncadet students to live in the barracks and eat meals in the mess hall separate from the corps. The first full year of the plan saw a decrease in the number of cadets, but an overall student increase due to the enrollment of 245 veterans. In his annual report to the Board of Visitors, Summerall expected both cadet and veteran figures to climb and predicted an enrollment of "near capacity" for the upcoming year. Based on this, he asked the state legislature for $2,405,000 to fund an ambitious campus beautification and building program. The General Assembly approved only $350,000 amid rumors that The Citadel "had deteriorated into a second-class college."[29]

Stung by these criticisms, The Citadel's administration relied on the money generated by veteran students to meet its goals. The 1946–1947 school year saw cadet enrollment jump to 743, while the number of veterans skyrocketed to 1,340. As a result, Citadel revenues more than tripled, the size of its faculty more than doubled, and the school began "permanent improvements" to the campus, such as construction of a carillon and bell tower next to the Citadel chapel. This financial and structural growth was directly attributable to the enrollment of veteran students, prompting one observer to note that "by mid-1946, it was apparent that the inflow of veteran students could be the bridge over which The Citadel marched towards post-war success."[30]

As The Citadel marched forward, however, it tried to leave the veterans behind. At colleges such as UNC–Chapel Hill, school officials recognized that older students "grew impatient with the closely supervised traditions of student life" and "wanted their afternoon beers." While other institutions tried to accommodate these needs, at The Citadel, "closely supervised traditions" took precedence over "afternoon beers." As a condition of their acceptance, the civilians were expected to "conduct themselves in a satisfactory manner in conformity with the character of The Citadel." In June 1946, the commandant reported various discipline "problems which were being created by the veteran students" living on campus. Summerall responded by threatening to ban civilian students from the barracks and mess hall "when in his judgment they were not complying with regulations." The Board of Visitors restated its policy "that as few restrictions as possible be placed upon veteran students attending the college in civilian status," provided they adhere to "the requirements of gentlemanly conduct and good behavior and the recognition of constituted authority." The board required all veterans to sign an oath pledging to "obey all regulations or orders" and to "act in an orderly manner and conform to the standards of deportment required at The Citadel." They warned that failure to do so jeopardized "the continuation of the veterans program at The Citadel." That same year, the commandant's office selected certain veteran students to monitor their peers' behavior in the barracks. These measures appeared to work, as a few months later, Summerall reported that "there seemed to be a much better group of veterans enrolled than previously."[31]

Enrollments and revenues continued to rise, as 1,046 cadets and 1,225 veterans enrolled for the 1947–1948 school year. That same year, the South Carolina Budget and Control Board appropriated five hundred thousand dollars to The Citadel for the building of new faculty apartments, a new laundry, and a new academic building. Twenty-eight new faculty members were hired, and the federal government chipped in to help renovate thirteen classrooms. Even with these increases in state and federal funding, the largest source of the school's income still came from the fees paid by civilian students attending regular and summer academic sessions.[32]

Civilian students' contributions extended beyond the increased revenues that helped build new buildings and refurbish old ones. Owing primarily to the infusion of veterans' money and participation, The Citadel revived athletic programs it had suspended during the war. In April 1946, the college hired an athletic director and head football coach, and fielded football, basketball, baseball, boxing, and golf teams. Over the next few years, tennis, wrestling, and track were added to the school's list of varsity sports.[33]

The rising number of students "strained the capacity of the faculty," but spurred the college to improve the quality and quantity of courses offered at The Citadel. In the nine years following World War II, the number of teachers with postgraduate degrees increased steadily, and in 1951, the *Wall Street Journal* recognized the scholarly contributions and superior instruction of The Citadel's Business Department. As the college's academic credentials improved, school administrators worried that the students' scholarly accomplishments had not kept pace. The 1947–1948 school year saw a large number of cadets and an even larger number of civilian students leave school for academic reasons. Summerall lamented that "the problem of the backward student is one of the most baffling at the college," and he urged faculty advisors and senior cadets to offer new students academic and personal guidance. He reduced the teaching loads of department heads so that they could use the extra time to set up tutoring programs for struggling students. By 1950, these initiatives had produced "excellent results," and over the years, the college and individual departments expanded the one-on-one instruction received by the students.[34]

While noncadets underwrote The Citadel's resurgence, prompting reforms that benefited the entire student body, the corps and veterans bickered over the latter's effect on the school's goals, customs, and traditions. Despite the veterans' past military experience, many members of the corps viewed their civilian counterparts as distractions who not only lacked the same discipline and commitment as those who had survived The Citadel's system, but whose presence actually diminished the school's ability to produce superior citizens.[35]

It bothered many cadets that veteran students did not have to wear uniforms, undergo inspections, and stand in daily formations. Members of the corps also grumbled when veterans crossed the parade ground during drill periods, regarding such acts as proof of the latter's disdain for The Citadel's military customs. In April 1947, school officials revived the practice of having cadets march to class. A writer for the student newspaper pointed out that the practice had been discontinued due to the large influx of civilian students, and he announced that "the revival of this custom is just one more step towards the restoration of the excellence of the pre-war Citadel."[36]

Veterans countered cadet criticisms through a recurring column in the school newspaper entitled "Clippings From The Ruptured Duck." The debut article set the tone for those that followed. In it, the author reminded readers that most veterans had faced death and endured grueling wartime struggles. Claiming they just wanted "to lead the normal everyday life," he noted "it is not exactly practical for men who have mental anguish, war nerves, and other physical handicaps to place themselves under a rigid program of military regulations and discipline." The Ruptured Duck reversed the charge that veterans had it easier than cadets by reminding the corps "we have been around a bit, and probably have seen more than most of those who are coming to college and who are away from home for the first time." The author also refuted the "consensus of opinion . . . that the veteran student does not have the proper school spirit" by pointing out that The Citadel's athletic teams "are dominated by the physical and mental superiority that the veteran is supposed to offer."[37]

Later installments blasted away at the cadets' and administration's treatment of veterans as bothersome intruders. The author defied those who "feel that the veteran should conform uniformly to the purpose of The Citadel." He continued, "Of course, these people are not individuals who have seen enough of all parts of the earth, fought at a place where someone fought back, or had anyone drop a bomb on them, even a little bomb." Addressing Citadel cadets and officials directly, he declared, "Many people will be much happier here as students . . . when we can be made to feel that we are part of the institution."[38]

Members of the corps tended to ignore these concerns, continuing instead with calls for more rigid regulations and duties. In June 1946, a reporter for the school newspaper, *The Bulldog*, asked cadets what "traditions or privileges that The Citadel had before the war would you want readopted?" The answers included weekend leave opportunities, longer library hours, and the adoption of a formal honor system. The most common reply recommended the reinstatement of "fourth class restrictions." The respondents saw this as a way to restore "the high standard of discipline for which the corps is well known." In the same issue, another article described the fourth class system as a way to "preserve in the corps of cadets those ideals and traditions it had cherished from the beginning." Without such a system, the author continued, the college could not build leaders "influenced and strengthened by the noble code of The Citadel."[39]

When school officials revived the fourth class system in the fall of 1947, cadets, most of whom had not labored under such restrictions, discouraged freshmen from questioning "the principles of a policy which has paid worthy dividends since 1842." The fourth class system of 1947 was not the same, though, as the one of 1842 or even 1942. The new regulations continued such practices as having plebes address upperclassmen as "mister" or "sir" and restricted their movements on campus. They also required freshmen to brace in the barracks, demanded they memorize school songs and cheers, ordered them to serve upperclassmen at meals, and prohibited "familiarity" between plebes and the rest of the corps. Several of the more demanding regulations from the previous system were missing, however. New cadets were not required to sit at rigid attention during meals. Strict rules concerning plebes' appearance were eliminated with no stated rule demanding that they remain in "complete prescribed uniform" when out of their rooms. Furthermore, college publications contained no hard-and-fast rules governing how freshmen "reported" to upperclassmen's rooms.[40]

The 1947 regulations reinstated the practice of freshmen living apart from the corps for about the first six weeks of the school year. During this time, a select "cadre" of cadets would indoctrinate the new recruits into the Citadel system. When the cadre period ended in November 1947, *The Bulldog* exulted "what a wonderful feeling it was to know that now you 'belonged' to the finest group of cadets in the world." Freshmen were reminded though that membership in this group carried with it the responsibility of instilling and passing down the core beliefs of Citadel men, namely "the value of discipline" and "the importance of obedience."[41]

As members of the corps welcomed back the fourth class system, the Board of Visitors worked to reduce the number of civilian students at The Citadel. New regulations required all physically fit, unmarried veterans under the age of twenty-six with less than six months service in the armed forces to enroll as freshmen cadets. Men who met the same criteria but had served between six to twelve months in the military had to enter the corps by their sophomore year. Those with one year, but less than two years service had to become a cadet by their junior year. Over the next five years, the number of veteran students fell from 858 to 109. Corresponding figures for the corps saw an increase of 1,141 to 1,291.[42]

Declining civilian enrollment fueled college officials' hopes of finally ending the veterans program. Even with The Citadel not operating at full capacity, school administrators waited anxiously for the number of veteran students to dwindle and eventually dry up. In 1951, General Summerall noted a sharp drop in veteran student numbers and predicted "it will be very small in the future." That same year, the Board of Visitors banned civilians from living in the barracks. Even though veteran enrollment actually increased in 1955 and 1956, the board ended the program by refusing to accept civilian students regardless of military service.[43]

Historian Robert Nye and others have noted that "historically societies have valued military masculinity and the personal characteristics of manliness that it comprises more highly than civic virtue and its masculinities." Such was not the case at The Citadel during this time, and while it may seem bizarre for those at a military school to resent the presence of men with actual military experience, such attitudes offer a glimpse into the nation's broader Cold War priorities and guidelines for citizenship. Certainly, Citadel cadets and school officials of this era should not be considered antimilitary. In fact, in response to post–World War II concerns about the militarization of U.S. society, one cadet laid out his defense of the "professional soldier" in stark terms. The writer criticized the "masses" and the "uniformed man on the street" for supposedly treating military officers as "moss-backed, short sighted creatures, who are hopelessly behind the times." Blasting "the intellectuals (and the stupid)" and "would be intellectuals" for stereotyping military officers as "arrogant, warmongering, curt and undemocratic," he argued that despite the "low pay, insults, apathy," and political scapegoating, U.S. officers commit themselves to defending the country at a time "when workers won't even give their employers ten minutes of their time." The cadet praised the devotion, hard work, and loyalty of military officers, predicting they will "still be there when the civilians start the next war."[44]

At the same time, it should be remembered that The Citadel's primary goal was the preparation of citizen-soldiers for civil pursuits, not the training of professional soldiers for military endeavors. While wartime service had traditionally offered a fairly straightforward means of proving one's manliness and civic worth, cadets and school officials believed that The Citadel's system, particularly the fourth class system, offered a better way of instilling young men with the devotion, discipline, and deference central to Cold War citizenship. It was not that cadets viewed the veterans on campus as unmanly or unworthy citizens. The difference between the two groups seemed to be one of degree. Citadel cadets were more beholden to institutional rules and traditions than noncadets, and it was the depth of their willingness to conform to such standards that distinguished Citadel men from other citizens. In January 1949, a writer for *The Bulldog* rebuked members of the corps who complained about the school's military regulations. The author contended that polishing brass and military drilling "instills discipline" and creates "a sense of order and method." He warned the corps that failure to learn these lessons could cost people their lives in times of war. Beyond that, he noted "the ideals for which Americans have fought and died for generations are in your hands. The future of this nation does not belong entirely to the ramrod-backed professional officer. It belongs to the citizen soldier . . . TO YOU."[45]

The importance attached to obedience and order highlights a key aspect of The Citadel's and the nation's post–World War II mission. In *Imperial Brotherhood*, Robert Dean examines the gendered concepts of leadership that guided the nation's Cold War policy from the 1940s through the Vietnam era. Beginning with the Truman administration, U.S. politicians and diplomats emphasized manly courage and toughness as essential to beating back the Soviet threat. According to Dean, such attitudes "squelched independent thought and challenges to perceived wisdom" by equating manliness with "conformity to Cold War orthodoxy." This mind-set was certainly not confined to the White House and State Department as cadets at The Citadel placed a higher civic and gendered value on a citizen's willingness to defend the status quo than they did on a soldier's service in combating international foes. Persistent on-campus tensions between cadets and civilian veteran students indicate that many at the military college believed maintaining internal order through a disciplined, obedient citizenry outweighed military proficiency as the key to winning the Cold War.[46]

Stephen Whitfield agrees that calls for discipline and order resonated in a national Cold War atmosphere that demanded "uncritical patriotism" from its citizens. Fueled by what historian David Caute refers to as "the Great Fear," many Americans spent the decade following World War II signing loyalty oaths, hunting down homegrown Communists, and ferreting out "un-American activities." Popular culture leaped into the fray with Hollywood cranking out films such as *The Red Menace*, *The Red Snow*, and *The Red Danube*.[47]

The Citadel swam along with the current as the corps of cadets presented themselves as precisely the type of disciplined, loyal, and obedient citizens that the nation needed in such troubled times. As more and more Americans put their faith "in the institutions of authority as the best preservatives of national values," Citadel cadets stood ready to assume their role as future leaders of the country where, as a writer for *The Bulldog* put it, "Christian brotherhood reigns supreme." Acknowledging the various fronts on which the Cold War was waged, members of the corps assured one another that at The Citadel "our moral, mental, social, and military leadership qualities are being developed to the utmost." When the federal government increased funding to college ROTC programs, it confirmed one student's belief that "as members of a senior unit of the ROTC, cadets at The Citadel will form one of the largest assets which the government will possess."[48]

As proof of how seriously the corps took their Cold War duties and responsibilities, the editor of the student newspaper assured his "faithful readers that there is no danger of *The Bulldog* letting any valuable military information slip through into our printed sheet." Possibly exaggerating the paper's circulation, he boasted that faculty advisors pored over each story to determine if they contained any "information whatsoever" that might help "an enemy or potential enemy." Once deemed safe, the story was "then quickly and forcefully released for the benefit of the Corps of Cadets." General Summerall took similar precautions in 1947, ordering all "Communistic works purged from the library." That same year, during the school's annual Religious Emphasis Week, he announced that "the person engaged to conduct the services diverted them to un-American political and economic ideologies, and it was necessary to stop him after the first two talks."[49]

The showdown with Soviet communism encouraged many cadets to showcase the democratic nature of the Citadel system. The only type of class distinctions that supposedly mattered among the corps were those that identified you as a firstclassman, secondclassman, thirdclassman, or fourthclassman. Year after year, school publications reminded cadets and prospective cadets, "It is not considered in keeping with the democratic ideals of The Citadel to encourage the formation of exclusive societies or fraternities, membership in which is based on other requirements than individual worth or achievement." Some presented this presumed leveling of socioeconomic status as part of The Citadel's "American heritage."[50]

Embracing America's Cold War mantle as the global "champion of liberty and democracy," cadets found room to criticize U.S. foreign policy only when it failed to intervene aggressively enough in international affairs. Convinced that the United States must "insure [*sic*] that countries are free to choose their own form of government and have economic stability," a writer for the student newspaper pleaded with military officials to protect Latin America from Soviet threats to "the democratic way of life." Commenting on the 1948 presidential campaign, a cadet reported "we know that [Henry Wallace] is being supported by the communists" who hoped the candidate's "isolationist" program would topple America's economic and political systems.[51]

The Bulldog also pushed for a heavy U.S. military presence in Europe to protect "all that our country fought for, and all that we, as a victorious nation are now obligated to uphold." Almost all cadets supported the Truman Doctrine and Marshall Plan, although they did not do so blindly. One acknowledged that Truman's policy provided military aid to Greece and Turkey but solicited "very little advice" from either country. He recognized the dangers of devoting unlimited aid to a vaguely defined cause, but defended the action as an "honest and sincere attempt to alleviate the problem." As for the Marshall Plan, the writer dismissed Soviet accusations of economic imperialism as "fallacious" and compared the plan favorably to the New Deal. Although such sentiments demonstrate that not all cadets were expected to agree on every issue, the author concluded that regardless of any practical or ideological reservations, all Americans had to support these policies if "peace and harmony" were to prevail.[52]

In October 1950, The Citadel received its first report that an alumnus had been killed in Korea. That list would grow over the next several months. As the 1950–1951 school year ended, *The Bulldog* reminded the graduating seniors that "The United States is now in the throes of a fight for its very existence," and charged them with leading the nation to victory, calling it a "definite mistake to sit back and try to analyze the present world situation and search for your reason for fighting a certain government." Later articles in *The Bulldog* lashed out at anyone who dared question U.S. Cold War policies. One author warned that Americans must "cease listening to the sweet resounding lies of the 'Communist Peace Dove' and prepare to accept the possibility of World War III."[53]

Student debates over U.S. domestic policies acknowledged differences of opinion, but remained within the ideological confines of Cold War America. One student endorsed Truman's doomed national health-care plan, citing, "How can people govern themselves, unless they are . . . secure?" A writer for

The Bulldog preached that "a free nation, free to disagree, free to discuss and free to criticize . . . will eventually triumph over the force of any aggressor." His critiques of society referenced organized crime, unarticulated "questions of foreign policy," and ambitious politicians, ignoring heated debates over civil rights and McCarthyism. Following the racially charged presidential campaign of Strom Thurmond and the Dixiecrats, the editor of *The Bulldog* pleaded with Americans to put aside "sectional or regional bias" and "work together." He accused "rabble rousing" politicians of giving "comfort to our enemies who see a division in our ranks," concluding, "whether or not the poll tax, segregation, fair employment, and anti-lynch laws are constitutional or unconstitutional is not for us to say."[54]

Cadets and school officials applied similar restrictions to their discussions of The Citadel's customs and policies. In the fall of 1952, General Summerall informed a group of graduating seniors that The Citadel had prepared them "to conform to the highest standard of conduct," instilling them with moral strength, integrity, responsibility, self-reliance, and efficiency. In return, he added, the cadets owed a deep, uncritical allegiance to their alma mater. Most cadets agreed, reassuring one another that "through instruction, exercise, and obedience to army given standards, you are acquiring the materials to build a strong life." When a writer for *The Bulldog* claimed "the world over Citadel men are looked upon with respect and envy," he reminded cadets that it took decades for The Citadel to earn this reputation and "it could be destroyed easily." To prevent this, the author added, "each individual must abide by the regulations and give his undivided cooperation to the making of a better school."[55]

In some cases, this stifling of dissent took on a distinct regional tone. One cadet noted the sizable number of northerners at The Citadel who "while retaining their own views as to the War Between the States, respect the traditions of the school to which they voluntarily came." He warned them, however, that should any of them "under the cover of rank or class, degrade or disrespect the traditions of The Citadel, they should go to a school where the traditions are more to their liking."[56]

At the same time, corps spokesmen reaffirmed the link between Cold War conformity and masculinity. A writer for *The Bulldog* editorialized on the "Obligations of Manhood," the central of these being obedience to authority. "If you work for a man, in heaven's name, work for him; speak well of him and stand by the institution he represents. . . . If you must growl, condemn, and eternally find fault, resign your position, and when you are on the outside, damn to your heart's content, but as you are a part of the institution, do not condemn it."[57]

Under the headline "The Citadel Speaks," the editor of *The Bulldog* assumed the persona of the college and let The Citadel describe its value to society. The Citadel offered its production of "many good men" as the prime reason for its existence. Despite its sterling record in this regard, the school cast itself as fragile and vulnerable. "I feel that my very existence is in jeopardy, therefore, I feel that I should speak out before I am silenced forever." The voice of The Citadel chastised underclassmen for wanting privileges "without first either working for them or proving themselves worthy of them." It blasted those who broke the rules, complained about the punishment, and then "ridicule[d] their classmates for carrying out their duties." The Citadel predicted that if cadets abandoned the "intimate qualities" of duty and honor, the institution would crumble. Despising the "poor quality of manhood" it housed, The Citadel preferred "a small group of good men than a large group of poor men." The author demanded the corps "be constantly vigilant of that one man who deviated from the true course" and threatened to turn the school into a "degenerated and degraded institution."[58]

"The Citadel Speaks" received rave reviews from cadets and alumni. One condemned "the general disregard for duty which is becoming prevalent in the Corps," and he hoped The Citadel's words would convince cadets to appreciate the school's customs and traditions. Another respondent implored cadets to "uphold the high standards" of the past in honor of the men "who have fought and died to keep The Citadel where it is today — in a free country."[59]

Whether one defined The Citadel's purpose as producing men of honor, integrity, loyalty, or leadership, the key component of all these remained that The Citadel produced men. Insisting that "No country without able men has ever remained at the top for long," school personnel tied the college's uniqueness and worth to its production of not just citizens, but manly citizens. According to members of the corps, "the kind of leader you are depends upon the kind of man you are," and it was The Citadel that produced men with the knowledge, tact, enthusiasm, decisiveness, boldness, and sense of justice found in good leaders. General Summerall praised cadets as "the best type of American manhood," whose alma mater "stands as a beacon for the nation." A writer for *The Bulldog* argued that the "soul of the corps" is the "end product: honorable men of training and strength in a world where these qualities are rare and essential." Another cadet claimed that "Duty to God and to the country have always been the watchword of this institution," adding "none can break these deep traditions of Duty and Honor and remain a Citadel man." The 1952 *Guidon* preached that "in a world of changing and declining moral values, one trait distinguishes men from one another more clearly than race, creed or color: Honor. Today, more than at any other time in history, the destiny of the world rests in the high hope we take from the honorable men among us."[60]

As part of their efforts to define what sort of men America needed and The Citadel manufactured, cadets also determined what type of women America needed. In an era when "sex roles achieved a new level of polarization," Citadel students held strong opinions about how women should look, act, and live. These ideals hardly matched reality, but they were shaped by real changes in women's lifestyles. The corps' concepts of proper feminine behavior reflected a larger trend whereby Americans expected women to be helpless and independent, demure and demanding, hard working and pampered. Most of all, women were expected to defer to men.[61]

Despite all the changes wrought by World War II, for women "the unshaken claim of wifehood and family remained." The restoration of traditional gender roles whereby men worked outside the home and brought home a paycheck while women tended house and raised children took on added importance as the United States sought any edge it had over the Soviet Union. According to Susan Douglas, media images conveyed the message "If the United States was going to fight off contamination from [Communism] then our women had to be very different from their women." Not only were American wives and mothers expected to be more attractive than their Soviet counterparts, but "their women worked in masculine jobs and had their kids raised outside the home in state-run child care centers that brainwashed kids to become good little comrades." As a result, "Our kids had to be raised at home by their moms if we were going to remain democratic and free."[62]

Scholars of this era have recognized that "the effort to reinforce traditional norms seemed almost frantic, as though in reality something very different was taking place." This was certainly the case as dissatisfied, disenchanted housewives found suburbia home to the "feminine mystique" not the American Dream. Even the stay-at-home ideal of American womanhood proved difficult to achieve as millions of females continued to attend college and work outside the home. Even with their increased public presence and the obvious dividends it brought to them and their families, working women were still treated with suspicion and relegated to inferior pay and jobs.[63]

At The Citadel, many cadets took a somewhat dismissive attitude toward women. College officials opened summer school to females in 1949 when the school desperately needed money, but this caused no big stir among the corps. A headline in the school newspaper announced "girls" would take summer classes and added "no living accommodations will be provided on campus for female students." Later when The Citadel made barracks space available to women attendees, General Summerall informed the Board of Visitors each year that "no women occupied rooms in the barracks." One explanation for this general lack of interest is that female summer school students posed no threat to the school's customs and traditions, especially its military and fourth class systems. Excluded from these crucial elements of the man-making process, women had no opportunity to prove that they could compete with men in The Citadel's normal environment. With a female presence limited only to the classroom in an informal summer session, cadets had no reason to fear that these women might withstand the rigors of The Citadel and threaten the school's underlying purpose and design: the production of men.[64]

Just three months after reporting that women would attend summer school, the student newspaper printed a photo of three young children, one boy and two girls, dressed in military uniforms and toting rifles. The caption underneath read "Shades of things to come?" and claimed the image evoked "not entirely unpleasant visions of a future corps complete with WAC units." To underscore the supposed ludicrousness of such an idea, the writer followed his observation with a derisive "seriously though . . ." Six years later, a lampoon edition of the paper mocked the notion again with a front-page headline "Citadel to turn coed." Aware on some level of the consequences of allowing women the chance to become Citadel men, the corps refused to entertain the idea.[65]

The cadets' take on the perfect woman mixed large doses of traditional femininity with brief flashes of the actual shifts taking place in American society. Each edition of the student newspaper featured a "Beauty of the Week." A cadet would nominate a woman for the award, and if chosen, the winner's picture and a brief biographical sketch would appear in the paper. Each installment followed a similar pattern, and the personal information reveals clearly what qualities Citadel men valued in a woman. The column offered stereotypes for all tastes; from "party girls" and "lovelies" to a demure "Southern Belle" who was not only "good looking, but she can sew beautifully and cook those always good southern dishes — and loves a good time."[66]

The columns offered some indication of the increased opportunities women enjoyed, but they pushed these qualities to the background by promoting more domesticated examples of feminine behavior. Almost every "Beauty" attended college, planned to attend college, or worked outside the home. Some exhibited an aggressive sexuality as they enjoyed "cattin around" and living like "real party girls." Reflective of the notion that American women should also be alluring, dutiful, and nonthreatening, the write-ups emphasized physical standards of beauty over intellectual or civic accomplishments. Each entry contained a woman's "vital statistics," which the editor defined as her height and weight. Many captions referred to their subjects as "kitten," "cream queen," "our baby," and the "Queen of all our dreams."[67]

The cadets made no bones about what they considered the most important quality in a woman: her willingness and ability to serve men. One Beauty from a nearby college supposedly spent her time studying "when she was not bringing food out here for him." Another was a husband-hunting registered nurse "who prefers taking care of electrical engineering majors." Several Beauties earned special praise for their cooking prowess. A longing for "one of those rare girls who not only looks good, but cooks that way too" remained a common theme of the column.[68]

While the corps lauded examples of traditional femininity, changes in the fourth class system reflected the ever strengthening bond between the corps' manliness and The Citadel's continued prosperity. These changes also attest to the encroachment of Cold War politics into almost every aspect of American society as a "cult of toughness" took root in American society that equated good citizenship with physical and mental strength. Physical endurance and mental toughness became vital weapons in America's arsenal as pundits declared that U.S. citizens must be prepared to undergo grueling hardships in order to prove their ideological and moral superiority. Aggressive attitudes toward masculinity joined with The Citadel's particular evaluation of Cold War imperatives to increase the demands upperclassmen placed on freshmen. The progression followed that with strong, tough, American men needed to protect the world, and with The Citadel producing the finest models of American manhood, and with plebe year as the fire that forged Citadel men, the fourth class system became the first line of defense against the Soviets.[69]

Warning of the "temptation inherent in a land of plenty, to grow fat and lazy," members of the corps found the rigors of the Citadel system essential to assuring that "the fairheaded favorites of destiny stay physically tough and mentally sharp." They reminded one another that after overcoming the challenges presented by the college, "You will find that wherever you go, you can say with pride, I AM A CITADEL MAN." One freshman rejoiced that "Behind every regulation, every demerit, there is some lesson to be learned, some purpose to be served. We will be made men!" Another student argued that through all the bracing, shoe shining, and brass polishing, "The dross is worn away and the 'Citadel Man' emerges . . . erect and firm of step, alert and proud."[70]

Charges of hazing accompanied this glorification of the Citadel man. A very favorable account of The Citadel's history admitted "any serious study of cadet life since 1937 will convince a discerning researcher that complete elimination of hazing at The Citadel remains Utopian." Alumni from earlier eras admit that physical violence formed a part of their fourth class system, but they characterize these acts as more rambunctious than malicious. Still, at some point, according to a 1938 graduate of the college, "The whole place down there got mean," and while the hazing of the 1940s and early 1950s paled in comparison to later years, the ideological justifications for abuses of the fourth class system grew out of this era.[71]

Since at least 1943, The Citadel had issued stern warnings against hazing. School officials required all cadets to sign an oath pledging not to "engage in hazing in any form" while at the college. By 1951, the emphasis had shifted from expecting students not to harm freshmen physically to expecting freshmen to distinguish between illegal hazing and necessary "military discipline." According to the *Guidon* from that year, the latter was enforced "with fairness, constancy, and rigidity," and must be accepted with the "correct attitude." The 1950 *Guidon* advised freshmen not to question the tenets of the fourth class system. "As time passes, you will not only become more clearly aware of their value, but will find yourself continually falling heir to their increased rights." Ignoring the fact that the system had changed significantly over the past ten years, the authors assured new cadets, "You are not being subjected to anything which has not been included in the training of the hundreds who have gone before you."[72]

An increase in the number of freshmen leaving school shortly after their arrival provides some indication that the fourth class system had taken on a harder edge. In 1950, 179 cadets withdrew from The Citadel, an exodus that drew the attention of school officials. When this trend repeated itself the next year, General Summerall noted the concern of the Board of Visitors in his annual report. He attributed the high attrition to the "inability of those cadets to adjust to military discipline," but his solution involved keeping the freshmen away from the rest of the corps until after the winter break. This remedy appeared to work as the dropout rate soon returned to pre-1950 levels.[73]

In later years, Summerall grew concerned with the poor academic performance of the freshmen class, and he informed the board, "Military training must be adjusted to academic requirements." Most of the new policies Summerall enacted reduced the interaction between freshmen and upperclassmen with an eye toward minimizing potential hazing situations. He extended the cadre period, had freshmen eat meals separate from the rest of the corps, and limited the amount of time devoted to "drill or military instruction." He specifically ordered that plebes should use their evenings to study; not to shine shoes, polish brass, or learn "plebe knowledge" per upperclassmen's demands.[74]

School officials coupled these changes with a harsher attitude toward those who failed to meet the demands of The Citadel. In his contribution to *The Guidon*, the head of the Civil Engineering Department informed freshmen, "If you fail and another man succeeds, the chances are a hundred to one that he is a better man than you. He could take it and you couldn't." The Citadel's president echoed these sentiments. He told new cadets, "It has been our experience that some, too weak to make the effort, fall helpless. Our hearts go out more in sorrow than regret, for they have had the best chance of becoming men and leaders and have failed."[75]

This emphasis on manly vigor and strength as well as the college's regional affiliation benefited The Citadel greatly in the early years of the Cold War. In *Media-Made Dixie*, Jack Temple Kirby argues that before 1954 and the *Brown* decision, the region cashed in on its image as a land of strong, white, macho men to such an extent that the South "became chic." The Citadel seemed to epitomize all the traits that Kirby lists, and while it may not have become chic, the college certainly did not suffer.[76]

Indeed, The Citadel's immediate post–World War II trials and eventual resurgence sharpened ideas about whom the college served and how it best served them. Confronted with certain changes that left many of them uneasy, Citadel cadets rested their claims to superior citizenship upon notions of their exceptional manliness, which they defined in Cold War terms of discipline, obedience, and conformity. According to them, a man's willingness to submit to "lawful authority" trumped all other criteria, including military service, as the key to building and maintaining a strong citizenry, and the fourth class system instilled the devotion and discipline found not just in men, but leaders of men.

CHAPTER TWO

Soaring with the American Eagle

Mark Clark and Cold War Citizenship

 In June 1952, Charles Summerall was eighty-five years old and in unsteady health. He had been hospitalized earlier that year, and despite the general's claim to be as "young as I ever was," the Board of Visitors began urging him to retire. Summerall resented this pressure, but agreed to step down as president on March 31, 1953. As he had for much of his twenty-two-year tenure at The Citadel, Summerall spent his last days in office lobbying the South Carolina legislature for increased state appropriations to the college.[1]

Just like his arrival, Summerall's departure garnered national attention. *Time* magazine remarked that when the general took over at The Citadel, "There was not a soldier or cadet in the land who had not heard of him." School officials heaped praise upon the old soldier. Noting that he saw the college through the crises of the 1930s and early 1940s, the Board of Visitors predicted Summerall's accomplishments "will through the years be a guide to hold the sons of The Citadel unerringly to the path of honor, integrity, and patriotism." They arranged for Summerall to live out his retirement on a Citadel-owned estate in Aiken, South Carolina, and in May, the board renamed the school's chapel the Charles Pelot Summerall Chapel. In his farewell address, the outgoing president proclaimed, "I have loved The Citadel as I have loved no other institution."[2]

While General Summerall's influence on The Citadel was considerable, the man who replaced him would have a more lasting impact on the institution. College officials started searching for Summerall's successor before he left office. Their first two choices, General Lucius Clay and General James Van Fleet, declined the offer. On the recommendation of General Clay and with considerable help from South Carolina Governor James Byrnes, the Board of Visitors contacted General Mark Wayne Clark, then commander in chief of the U.N. forces fighting in Korea, and offered him the position. After negotiating an armistice in Korea and consulting with his close friend President Dwight Eisenhower, Clark accepted the job.[3]

A West Point graduate, Clark had seen limited action as a battalion commander in World War I. During World War II, he had served as General Eisenhower's top aide, and he later commanded the Fifth Army in North Africa and Italy. His successes in both these theatres won him national and global acclaim. Lauded as "the liberator of Rome," Clark had received the Distinguished Service Cross from President Roosevelt, and Winston Churchill had nicknamed him "the American Eagle." After the war, he had served as commander in chief of the U.S. Occupational Forces in Austria. Upon completion of his duties in Korea, Clark retired from the army on October 31, 1953.[4]

General Clark brought even more publicity and excitement to The Citadel than his predecessor. Upon his return to the United States, New York honored him with a ticker-tape parade. Newspaper and magazine articles praised him as "a defender of America and a battler against tyranny." Some people considered the general a worthy candidate for the presidency of the United States. When Clark came to Charleston in October 1953, front-page headlines in the *News and Courier* announced "CLARK GETS HERO'S ACCLAIM/DUE TO VISIT CITADEL TODAY." Later that month, the headlines rejoiced "CLARK ACCEPTS PRESIDENCY OF THE CITADEL."[5]

Over the next few months, The Citadel would bask in the reflected glory of its new president. A *Time* magazine report on Clark's new assignment listed the college's Civil War past, its illustrious alumni, and its fourth class system as proof of its vitality and rich heritage. With a theatrical flourish, the author added, "In time, the new president will also be something to remember: His name Mark Clark, General U.S.A." An article in *The Brigadier*, The Citadel's newly renamed student newspaper, printed a brief biography of Clark, highlighting his awards, honors, and accomplishments. The list appeared alongside numerous photos of the general meeting with presidents, leading his troops, and enjoying a "hero's welcome in New York." The piece ended with "All Citadel Men everywhere can be proud of the unselfish devotion to duty shown by General Clark for the same traits of leadership that won military victories for the nation will now be exerted for the betterment of The Citadel." At Clark's inauguration, Secretary of the Army Robert T. Stevens described The

Citadel as "a symbol of the basic strength, determination, and solidarity of the American people." Lauding the school for offering "a complete and generous education . . . which fits a man to perform justly, skillfully, and magnanimously all of the offices of a citizen," Stevens noted that "today, men of The Citadel are providing an impressive measure of the leaven of great leadership, capability, and moral stamina upon which our national strength largely depends." Buoyed by such praise, a Citadel alumnus predicted that "as The Citadel grew strong under Summerall it will grow great under General Mark Clark."[6]

This remark proved prescient, as the college did indeed thrive under Clark. Due in no small part to the general's reputation and influence, the college prospered financially, reached maximum enrollment, and enjoyed a great deal of favorable publicity. Like his predecessor, Clark tapped into the dominant ideology of the Cold War, touting Citadel graduates' discipline, loyalty, obedience, and patriotism. With Mark Clark at the helm, however, the college did more than drift along with the political and cultural mainstream; it surged forward on waves of anticommunist, anti–civil rights and antiliberal sentiment. Operating within a national and regional environment that privileged such traits, Clark and other school personnel marketed Citadel cadets as the embodiment of "true Americanism" that William Chafe listed as "machismo, patriotism, belief in God, opposition to social agitation, hatred of the Reds."[7]

Historian K. A. Cuordileone, among others, has studied the "excessive preoccupation with — and anxiety about — masculinity in early Cold War American politics," citing observers from the era who commented on a "political culture that put a new premium on hard masculine toughness and rendered anything less than that soft and feminine and, as such, a real or potential threat to the security of the nation." Spurred on by public expressions of "exaggerated masculinity" that accompanied national calls for military preparedness and visceral anticommunism, Citadel personnel laid even greater claim to their school's ability to build the ideal Cold War citizens: tough, white men.[8]

No one person played a larger role in this amplification of the school's gendered civic mission than General Mark Clark. He intensified the institutional emphasis on discipline and order, adding physical toughness to the mix of manly ingredients that elevated Citadel graduates above their contemporaries. Throughout his tenure, Clark expounded regularly on the virtues of proper manly behavior, reminding the corps that The Citadel's purpose was "turning out well rounded, thoroughly educated men" and informing the world that

"America's elite manhood comprises our Corps of Cadets." Clark would eventually coin the term that became the school's mantra, describing The Citadel's system as "inextricably tied to our 'whole man' concept of education," a concept "which we emphasize above all else at The Citadel," whereby Citadel cadets are trained "mentally, physically, morally, and militarily." In the process, Clark established an enduring image of Citadel men, one that emphasized the corps' whiteness, conservatism, and toughness. Given the school's undeniable growth during this period, many came to view these traits as the cornerstone of the institution's and conversely the nation's prosperity.[9]

Clark faced considerable challenges upon entering office since General Summerall's tenure had not ended on a high note. Numerous construction projects remained unfinished, and enrollment stood well below full capacity. General Clark began his revitalization efforts by "clearing house," replacing Summerall's administrative staff with younger men of his own choosing. In a manner befitting the new president's domineering personality, Clark replaced Summerall's spartan office furnishings with his own, adding a large, imposing desk as the room's centerpiece. The Board of Visitors got into the act as well, providing the general and his wife with new on-campus living quarters and putting a shiny Citadel-owned Cadillac at the couple's disposal.[10]

With his people and furniture in place, Clark set out to address the major problems facing The Citadel, which he identified as "enrollment, athletics and construction." Viewing a successful sports program as a way to boost student morale and draw favorable publicity to the college, the general took a keen interest in football. After reviewing the team's prospects for the upcoming year, he concluded, "The Citadel had a very sick patient on its hands, and its only hope for recovery was by means of a drastic remedy." As part of the cure, Clark fired the entire coaching staff and hired a new head coach and assistants. He upped the number of athletic scholarships awarded by The Citadel, urged coaches to keep better track of high school talent, and dropped "powerhouses" such as Georgia Tech and the University of Florida from the team's schedule. These efforts paid off, as the 1954 squad won five games and gave The Citadel its first winning football season since 1942. Over the next six years, the Board of Visitors noted "a remarkable change has occurred in the morale of all of our athletic teams." In 1960, the Citadel football team won its first bowl game, crushing Tennessee Tech in the Tangerine Bowl, 27-0.[11]

Clark achieved similar results when it came to financing new construction projects and completing old ones. In a report to the South Carolina legislature in June 1954, the general asked that the state appropriate $1,631,649.62 for the college, an increase of $624,623.62 from the previous year. He justified this jump as necessary to repair dilapidated buildings, modernize antiquated equipment, improve educational facilities, and increase the number of on-campus services available to cadets. The General Assembly did not match Clark's request, but they did increase the amount of money The Citadel received.[12]

In his first year as president, Clark used state funds, private contributions, and student fees to build a new laundry for use by the corps as well as Citadel faculty and their families. In 1955, he oversaw the completion of a bell tower and carillon and began work on affordable on-campus housing for professors. Construction crews rebuilt the main entrance to The Citadel, making it, in Clark's estimation, "appropriate to the dignity and beauty of the campus." Convinced that "cadets at The Citadel should live in the neatest and most attractive surroundings possible," Clark approved funding to renovate all four barracks, with every cadet room receiving new beds, new mattresses, and new metal closets. At the same time, the corps enjoyed expanded on-campus parking as well as a new canteen, barber shop, post office, student lounge, and outdoor patio. In 1960, cadets ate meals in a refurbished mess hall and sat through religious services in a renovated chapel; both buildings came complete with air conditioning. Three years later, a new library, a new student activities building, a new military science building, and sixty new faculty apartments adorned The Citadel's campus.[13]

Filling these new buildings remained Clark's top priority, and he added a student procurement officer to his administrative staff and urged alumni to intensify their recruiting efforts. Convinced that "our cadets are the best salesmen for The Citadel we have," the general looked to increase the corps' public presence, allowing cadets to appear weekly on a local television program in order to "let the inhabitants of the Charleston area become more familiar with The Citadel." Reaching beyond the South Carolina Lowcountry, cadets visited high schools across the nation while school officials distributed a recruiting video that played on movie screens and television sets nationwide. Finally, Clark used his own celebrity to enhance the college's reputation, attracting national attention when he convinced President Eisenhower to visit The Citadel's campus in October 1954. Clark himself often appeared on television shows and in national publications, promoting the school and its students in glowing terms.[14]

After his first full year in office, Clark's friend Henry Luce published an article on The Citadel in *Life* magazine. The article mixed praise for the institution with adulation for its president. Entitled "Cheers at The Citadel: General Clark Spruces Up a Historic School," the piece opens with a photo of Clark standing confidently on the quadrangle of one of The Citadel's barracks while a large group of cadets cheer in the background. The general is featured in nine of the essay's thirteen photos, with captions detailing how Clark inspired the corps, beautified the campus, and reenergized the school. The writer noted that prior to Clark's arrival, "The Citadel had lost considerable of its old luster and the cadet corps had lost a measure of its old morale." The new president stepped in and "intensified spit-and-polish on the campus, brought about a resurgence of athletics, and lifted the spirits" of the student body. In doing so, the author noted, Clark led "The Citadel back into the national limelight."[15]

Such exposure paid huge dividends for the college. In June 1955, the number of applicants doubled that of the previous year. The number doubled again a year later as school officials prepared for the "largest peacetime freshman class in the history of The Citadel." By 1958, the corps had reached its full capacity of twenty-two hundred men. With The Citadel's reputation on the rise, Clark lobbied the state legislature for more money in hopes of improving the quality of instruction that cadets received. Acknowledging that "The Citadel stands or falls fundamentally as an academic institution, not as a military institution," he used this money to hire an academic dean and to attract new, highly qualified faculty.[16]

Thrilled with this growth, the Board of Visitors thanked the general formally for boosting the college's image and "providing for the physical comforts of the Cadets, the Instructors, and the Administrative Staff." At the same time, these accomplishments gave the president a fair amount of influence over these groups, influence Clark would use to shape what kind of citizens The Citadel produced. With the college's resurgence seeming to validate the new president's worldview, Clark projected his image of the ideal Citadel man into the barracks and the classrooms, and beyond the school's gates.[17]

While he raised teachers' salaries, made it easier for them to further their education, and helped obtain funding for their research, Clark reserved the right to choose which professors were hired or promoted, raising salaries only for those he deemed "deserving personnel." The general opposed tenure for professors because it prevented him from "weeding out" troublemakers. A vocal opponent of school desegregation, he informed potential faculty members, "If you've got any ideas on — private ideas — on integration and all that stuff that you want to publish and identify The Citadel [with], we don't want you. You got any ideas on the military[,] that you don't like [it], then we don't want you." Despite these warnings, Clark conceded "occasionally they'll get a bum, particularly in the political science end of it."[18]

In 1958, Citadel officials caved to pressure from the Southern Association of Colleges and adopted a "policy of Academic Freedom and Tenure." For years, though, Clark omitted this policy from school regulations. The new guidelines still allowed Citadel officials to revoke tenure for "conduct prejudicial to the best interest of the college, which may include such things as public utterances of an unprofessional nature designed to discredit the college or which are inconsistent with the moral beliefs of the community." Other offenses included "membership in or allegiance to organizations whose tenets are incompatible with the American way of life." According to Clark, professors were free to teach whatever they wanted as long as their lessons remained "consistent with the fundamental principles of Americanism." Not surprisingly, The Citadel had no faculty senate or even an American Association of University Professors chapter while Clark was president.[19]

Clark employed subtle and not-so-subtle methods of shaping the image, ideals, and composition of the student body. In 1956, Clark and the Board of Visitors refused to allow filming of the movie version of the Calder Willingham novel *End As a Man* on campus. Willingham had attended The Citadel from 1940 to 1941, and his book deals with life at a southern military college. The work contains strong homoerotic undertones, describes incidents of gruesome hazing, and depicts cadets drinking and gambling in darkened back rooms. The producer, Sam Spiegel, asked for Clark's permission to use the school as the setting, assuring him "they would look to The Citadel for advice on all parts of the production." He promised to let school officials view the movie before its official release and vowed to make "a very wonderful film about The Citadel and Charleston."[20]

After reading the script, Clark, two members of the Board of Visitors, and "a small group of [Clark's] most intimate staff associates" voted unanimously against allowing Spiegel to film on campus. In a long letter to the producer, Clark informed Spiegel that the committee found the film so offensive "that any such identification, however nebulous, would be definitely harmful to a fine military college, which does have national stature, militarily and academically." Specific complaints included the depiction of "a sordid and sullen barracks life, accented by drinking, gambling and ugliness" with no indication that the corps ever "drills, or attends classes, or cracks a book." The reviewers regretted that in addition to a bevy of "unsavory" characters, "the only female character in the script is a tramp." Clark denied that any cadet would associate with such a woman, informing Spiegel that "The Citadel's social life is famous" with dances attended "not only by the finest young men in Charleston, but by girls of the same high characters [*sic*]." Keeping with his overall emphasis on enrollment, Clark worried that "the absence of any scenes or incidents portraying the decent — and I assure you normal — aspects of life here" would discourage young men from applying to the college.[21]

While he guarded their image closely, the general endeared himself to the corps by granting them more freedoms, giving them more responsibilities, and promoting them as the college's main attraction. In a regular column for *The Brigadier*, Clark praised the corps for their patriotism, discipline, character, and "honorable conduct." He formed a Presidential Advisory Committee comprising the five highest-ranking members of the senior class and met regularly with this group to hear and address student concerns. Based largely on the committee's recommendations, Clark authorized the reissue of the cadets' full dress uniforms, set up recreation rooms in the barracks, and instituted a "come as you are" policy for Citadel pep rallies. He lifted the ban on off-campus consumption of alcohol, and he granted each class a set number of weekend and overnight leaves per year. He gave senior cadets more authority by restructuring the college's rank system and allowing all seniors, not just cadet officers, to serve periodically as Officer of the Guard.[22]

Clark and the student body cemented their bond further by devising and adopting a formal honor system at the school that grew into and remains an integral part of cadet life. School personnel had long considered honor an essential component of a Citadel education, but since 1925, the school had no official honor code nor any systematic process for dealing with students who lied, cheated, or stole.[23]

The old honor system had been abandoned after some cadets and school officials began using it as a tool to punish students for disciplinary infractions such as skipping class, missing formations, breaking barracks, drinking, or not cleaning one's room. Wary that such conditions might reemerge, the corps asked that the board couple the reinstatement of an honor system with certain changes to existing college regulations. Believing that the severity of certain punishments and restrictions tended to "encourage lying," cadets suggested that reducing penalties for missing classes or formations along with expanded leave privileges would better "permit a man to live as his honor dictates." They also asked the board to no longer require students to sign a no-hazing pledge, thereby making hazing "solely a violation of military regulations, not the honor code."[24]

In February 1953, the student body took the initiative and presented the Board of Visitors with a framework for uncovering and punishing dishonorable behavior. Over 70 percent of the entire corps and 93 percent of upperclassmen backed the proposal. Under their plan, cadets from all four classes would make up an Honor Committee to prosecute, defend, and judge students accused of an honor violation. A set group of ten Honor Committee members would serve on an Honor Court that would hear and decide every case. An acquittal required three members of the court to render not-guilty verdicts. A guilty verdict meant immediate expulsion.[25]

Once in office, General Clark took up the students' cause. Envisioning the honor system as a means to guarantee that Citadel graduates "will have strength of character as well as intellectual and physical rigor," he asked that their plan be reviewed by the board as well as faculty, alumni, and student committees. In September 1954, Clark printed and distributed the committees' revisions to the board and the corps. The modified Honor Code read simply, "A cadet will not lie, cheat or steal nor tolerate those who do." In the preface to the new manual, Clark allayed students' fears by assuring them that "the honor system is not a means for disciplining the Corps of Cadets" nor for "discovering violations of regulations." He admitted, though, that the adoption of the plan would radically change some aspects of cadet life since practices once regarded as part of a "battle of wits" between cadets and the commandant would constitute honor violations. For example, the code defined lying as "an official statement . . . written or oral made to a commissioned officer of the staff or faculty of the college, a member of the guard on duty, or any cadet required to use the statement as a basis for an official report in any form." Clark noted that "under this criteria, any AWOL cadet, if caught, would face only demerits or punishment tours so long as he neither told an official nor signed a document saying he was not AWOL."[26]

Changes from the original plan allowed only seniors to serve as members of the Honor Committee. Each cadet company would elect an honor representative, and these men, along with the five highest-ranking seniors, would serve on a rotating Honor Court and also defend and prosecute cadets accused of honor violations. If 75 percent of the sitting court members found the defendant guilty, there was "only *one* punishment; *withdrawal from The Citadel.*" The authors of the new plan decided that the proceedings of each trial would remain confidential, with school officials doing all they could to help expelled students continue their education elsewhere. Such measures reaffirmed claims that "the system is designed solely to rid the corps of those cadets who lie, cheat or steal. It is not designed to punish them for the rest of their lives."[27]

In keeping with his pledge that the fate of the honor system rested with the corps, Clark informed the board he would not ask them to vote on the proposed plan until three-fourths of the student body had approved it. When handing the proposed plan over to the corps, Clark reminded them that "the honor code is bigger than any individual or any personal friendship." As a result, he added, all cadets must "freely and zealously guard the honor of the corps" by reporting any violation. Despite this admonition, opponents of the system called it unworkable because they thought nothing could persuade a cadet to snitch on his friend or classmate. Others, mostly seniors, complained that the honor code infringed upon the already limited freedoms cadets enjoyed. Editorials and letters in *The Brigadier* answered these complaints forcefully. One correspondent declared, "It must be the paramount concern of each and every cadet to see the corps an honorable one, and every person, classmate or not, is not worthy of being harboured [*sic*], even by his brother, if he violates the trust of his fellow cadets." He asserted, "We must believe in this system as we have never believed in anything before . . . for we, the individual cadets of the corps, are the greatest beneficiaries of honor."[28]

The more aggressive proponents of the honor system tapped into a Citadel nerve, wrapping their arguments around notions of manly behavior. After failing to convince 75 percent of the corps to approve the plan, a writer for *The Brigadier* railed against the "slothful ones" who "wanted more privileges, more ways to get away with breaches of regulations." He attacked those who balked when "called upon for extra effort" that would serve the "common good." Demanding that "we must have the desire to place honor before all else," he challenged the collective manhood of the corps, asserting "a man who can maintain his devotion to a cause although the temptation is to heckle, is a good man." He regretted that "there were not enough men of this type present to carry out the voting of the Honor System."[29]

Such arguments eventually won out, for in April 1955, 94.4 percent of the corps voted for a modified version of the proposed honor system to take effect the next school year. One change required all guilty verdicts to be unanimous. Also, a convicted cadet could appeal the decision to the college president. Reflecting a persistent concern of the corps, the new regulations clearly prohibited "the Honor Code from being used as an investigative tool." A proviso was added that "no commissioned officer of the staff or faculty, member of the guard, or any cadet in an official position will ask a question which might incriminate a cadet unless the asker has *prima facie* evidence that the cadet has committed a reportable offense." Following its first full year in effect, the corps made allowances for unintentional violations of the honor code.[30]

The new system assumed an almost deified position within the corps. One writer for the student newspaper rejoiced that "a greater show of confidence in us by the Board of Visitors, the President, and the faculty of The Citadel than that of giving us the opportunity to adopt the honor system could not have been manifested." Another cadet claimed the code "increased the esteem of a Citadel graduate," setting him apart from his peers at other colleges. One stated bluntly, "The honor system will make you even more of a Citadel man."[31]

Paul Harvey featured The Citadel and its honor system on his nationally syndicated radio program, describing the code as "a simple condensation of the Ten Commandments." Turning this praise into a Cold War lesson of right and wrong, he applauded cadets for policing themselves, explaining, "If this seems like 'tattling' it is only because our own code of morals and ethics has been so corrupted that Americans have come to attach some 'honor' to the silent criminal; to the Communist who refuses to name his co-conspirators, who hides behind the Fifth Amendment; and to the jurists and politicians who cover up for their colleagues." A U.S. congressman from Charleston echoed Harvey in a speech before the House of Representatives as he lauded The Citadel and its honor system for "making young men from every part of America — better Americans."[32]

With student applications and the school's reputation on the rise, Citadel officials could not only be more discriminating in who they accepted but they could also demand more of those students already enrolled. In 1956, the same year Clark decided to discontinue the veterans program, he announced publicly that slots in The Citadel's summer school were severely limited due to campus construction and faculty shortages. To the Board of Visitors, however, Clark admitted that the previous manner "in which registrations were handled for the summer school were such as to make possible the enrollments of undesirable persons"; thus, he had issued the press release to discourage such people from applying.[33]

Concerned about the poor academic performance of Citadel freshmen, Clark ordered that more rigorous academic criteria be applied. He asserted "that for a long time, we were perhaps too soft with a small number of students who either through sluggishness or lack of capacity or preparation simply were not able to measure up to minimum academic standards." As he "acted to eliminate incompetence from among the existing student body," Clark urged the corps to help in this endeavor by driving out lazy individuals who deprived "a better man of the chance to get a Citadel education." The general viewed stronger educational requirements as a way to ensure the "indolent and shiftless students will have to make way for those who will perform." By June 1959, Clark reported proudly, "We have really cleaned out most of those students who were just hanging on by their teeth, never demonstrating a real industry or desire to measure up to the traditional quality of Citadel men."[34]

While culling out the "indolent and the shiftless students," Clark worked to instill those who remained with his Cold War conservatism. Clark believed wholeheartedly that "being taken for a good American" meant "demonstrating a gut hatred for the commies." In Charleston, a city he described as "all-American," he found a receptive audience for his views and vowed to prepare cadets for the "eventual showdown with communism." In addition to requiring all freshmen and most seniors to read J. Edgar Hoover's *Masters of Deceit*, Clark established the Greater Issues lecture series as a way to familiarize Citadel students "with the complex problems of our world today." Each Greater Issues speaker was chosen by Clark, and they reflected his arch-conservative views when it came to the Cold War. The first four speeches dealt exclusively with the Red Peril. In the fall of 1954, the "Cardinal of the Cold War," Francis Spellman, discussed the "menace of communism in our land," pointing out that America's duties as protector of the free world increased the need for and value of Citadel graduates. General Matthew Ridgway followed Spellman, warning that the U.S. armed forces were ill prepared to counter "the continued menace of Communism." Over the next few years, cadets would listen on a monthly and sometimes weekly basis to men such as Billy Graham, Herbert Hoover, Paul Harvey, and General Maxwell Taylor "condemn communism, praise Clark for his patriotic leadership, and commend [the corps'] preparation to defend civilization."[35]

The Greater Issues series had an almost immediate effect on the student body. *The Brigadier* expanded its coverage of global events with student editorials often echoing the ideas and sentiments of the latest speaker. Writers for a recurring column entitled "Globally Speaking" reminded students "that there is another world beyond the campus" and criticized those who remained ignorant of the "world's problems." Worried about America's declining influence in a destabilized world, cadets warned that "continued complacency could spell disaster for the West." Echoing Eisenhower's domino theory, one student called Soviet maneuvering in Vietnam part of "a strategy to realize complete control of Southeast Asia," while another described the region as economically and strategically vital in "the global struggle between Communism and the free world."[36]

Maintaining a united domestic front against the Soviets remained a major concern, and the corps took their responsibility in this regard very seriously. In 1955, the editor of *The Brigadier* published a "Defense of Censorship," in which he called the administration's control over the paper desirable and necessary. Concluding that "the status quo must be maintained," he decided that the newspaper's primary function was to "present a unified front and extol the virtues and objectives of The Citadel." Welcoming the activism of students in Poland and Hungary, one student favored a "revolution in the thinking of our cohorts," but yoked such a transformation to a defense of the status quo. With massive resistance to school desegregation in full swing, he suggested "we might begin by considering our own government — and whether modern interpretation of our Constitution has gone far enough — or too far."[37]

The entire corps did not march in lockstep, but most kept their critiques of society within acceptable Cold War limits. One student compared the ongoing House Un-American Activities Committee investigations to Stalin's purges and ridiculed the public "redemption" of former Communist Party members who named names. A staunch anticommunism colored his analysis as he complained that the trials allowed the most dangerous enemies of the United States to exonerate themselves by turning in their "politically naïve contemporaries." He questioned a system whereby men and women who had "never considered the overthrowing of the United States government or setting up Communist rule" were punished while those who supposedly did advocate such things were allowed to "reform" themselves by testifying publicly. Regarding communism as a mortal crime, the student reasoned, "The commission of a great sin does not give the perpetrator the right to roundly condemn sinners of an infinitely smaller dimension."[38]

Few Citadel students and administrators disagreed when it came to defining the school's primary purpose: the production of manly citizens. In one of their annual tours of the campus, the Board of Visitors "were delighted to note that with a Cadet Corps expanded to the limits of our capacity, and with many additions and improvements made in our college plant, the customs and traditions of The Citadel have been preserved." Prominent among these customs was the "manly bearing" of the students. As the school continued to grow, the board continued to commend the cadets for "their manly conduct, their devotion to duty, their high moral character, and their outstanding leadership." At the same time, the board reminded the senior class that ensuring "The Citadel remains true to its traditions and lives up to its national reputation largely depends upon their character, loyalty, wisdom, dignity, self-restraint, and leadership."[39]

General Clark described successful Citadel alumni as those who "bore the reputation of solid, well-rounded men; conscientious students, if not always of Gold Star quality; energetic in extracurricular affairs, usually with a love of camaraderie." He drew repeated attention to the school's mission of "turning out well-rounded, thoroughly educated men," informing new cadets that "the measure of your willing conformity with discipline, both academic and military, will very likely be the measure of your success as a Citadel man."[40]

Members of the corps joined in the chorus, with one student declaring, "The Citadel's only product is men and Citadel Men are our very best advertisements." Another described the college as "a factory for turning out men, and I mean men, with better posture and manners, more maturity, sincerity, and loyalty, and a greater devotion to responsibility." He then asked, "What goes into the making of the 'desired man' if not these traits?" He praised the

Citadel "treatment," which made "men out of boys, thinkers out of misfits, aggressors out of passives, leaders out of followers." He concluded, "No school, and I mean no school, on the face of the earth better prepares a man for his future responsibility than does My Citadel." Other members of the corps echoed such sentiment, boasting "here, as in few other American colleges, the aim is to train leaders: leaders of thought and action, leaders of opinion, leaders of men."[41]

Cadets often evoked the sanctity, importance, and effectiveness of the Citadel "treatment" as a way to stifle criticism of their alma mater. One writer for *The Brigadier* asked his peers, "Are You a Bad Apple?" reminding them that "upon donning the uniform, we each became Citadel men in every respect" and "knew the rules which had been a tradition of this institution and pledged our obedience to them." To those colleagues who believed the school's customs and traditions denied them the "full value of a college education," one student warned, "Let him speak and I assure you the authorities will rectify the situation immediately."[42]

While confident that their school produced men, cadets differed as to the manufacturing process. Some saw engagement in intellectual and cultural activities as the best way to become "well-rounded" men. A writer for *The Brigadier* rebuked the corps for its anti-intellectualism, regretting that "the thought of the slightest change in the status quo seems to fill everyone with terror." He attributed this fear to "the thought that some privilege is going to be lost," but added, "By following this line of thought, many new privileges are lost."[43]

In contrast to those who viewed intellectual pursuits as essential to the development of whole men, others pushed for a more stringent mode of production. As Stephen Whitfield writes, "In an era that fixed rigidly the distinction between Communist tyranny and the free world, and which prescribed that men were men and women were housewives, perhaps only one peril seemed, if anything, worse than communism. The overwhelming fear of every parent was that a son would become a sissy." In nationally syndicated articles entitled "Our Unfit Youth" and "Toughening Our Soft Generation," well-known politicians, pundits, and authors targeted weak, unfit Americans as threats to global and national security. They argued that the country needed strong, aggressive, tough citizens to counter the lingering "softness" and "decadence" brought about by New Deal liberalism. Only men such as these could help America to win "converts around the world and to stand as the champion of world society's future."[44]

General Clark endorsed such beliefs wholeheartedly, warning "when the Communist enemy sees weakness, as he has too much in the past, that is when he exploits." As chief of Army Field Forces, Clark had promised to "strip basic training of any gentle aspects," finding such changes necessary if the United States was to defeat the "Communist murderers we're up against in Korea and may have to face in other parts of the world before this is over." In the fall of 1954, *The Brigadier* ran an article from a North Carolina newspaper announcing that the army planned to toughen basic training even more "in the knowledge that in another war the enemy will be tough, cruel, and barbarous."[45]

Worried that "in a nation where luxuries abound and necessities flow even more abundantly, society tends to be a little on the soft side," Citadel personnel marketed the school as having "as tough a Plebe System as exists anywhere in the United States." General Clark took this pledge a step further. Citadel graduate Pat Conroy remembers General Clark boasting "that the school would have the toughest plebe system in the world," with the novelist adding, "I personally attest that he succeeded admirably." The teaching of "prompt and willing obedience to authority" remained a cornerstone of the fourth class system, a focus many cadets viewed as essential to preserving the well-being of The Citadel and American society. Linking "success in the society in which we live" to the qualities instilled at The Citadel, school publications touted obedience and discipline as the key characteristics of successful citizens. By maintaining "discipline in the new class," the fourth class system protected the school's customs, while at the same time, prepared a group "of proud self-respecting men" for the duty of running "the Corps and later the nation."[46]

Responding to "cries of protest" that characterized Citadel upperclassmen as "sadistic monster[s] taking great joy in using [their] authority over a plebe," cadets defended the trials of freshmen year as "the *only* way in which a group of high school civilian students can be molded into a group of well-disciplined, well-trained cadets in so short a period of time." They appreciated that "it is the Corps who enforces the discipline" that produced "well adjusted citizens capable of responsibility." Erroneously treating the system as a static institution, the students suggested that outsiders "leave the running of a system as old as the school to the Corps and those who are *competent* to give advice and *constructive* criticism." Citing the "goal of The Citadel is to provide leaders, both civic and military," other members of the corps asked, "What better leadership training laboratory can be utilized than a cadet-run corps?"[47]

When the student dropout rate increased, however, Citadel officials began to question the upperclassmen's overzealous implementation of the fourth class system. In October 1955, General Clark briefed the Board of Visitors on "the hazing situation at The Citadel," and the Board "pledged support to him in his efforts to prevent hazing." Clark would later remember speaking to the corps at this time about "things in the fourth class system that shouldn't have been there." After cadets on the Presidential Advisory Committee alerted him of practices "that had no useful purpose at The Citadel" and of "things that were perpetrated on the cadets that they shouldn't have had," Clark informed the student body that he "would not tolerate the upperclassmen interfering with the sleeping, eating, or studying of freshmen." The 1956 edition of The Citadel's *Catalogue* contained a stern condemnation of hazing, claiming "individuals who are obsessed with the idea that beatings and indignities are a part of a student's education" were not wanted at The Citadel.[48]

Rigid definitions of "proper" feminine behavior complemented this national and institutional obsession with masculine virility. The acceleration of the Cold War intensified the immediate post–World War II campaign to drive women back into the home, and the Citadel "Beauties" of this period delivered the same mixed messages as the previous one, whereby college-educated, sexually vibrant, gainfully employed women were expected to act as subservient, adorable, gorgeous wives and mothers. Rejoicing that "the Corps' supply of beautiful women is inexhaustible," *Brigadier* columnists portrayed their subjects as "110 pounds of pure sweetness" and "102 pounds strategically located over her five foot two inch figger." Rather than present a biology major as a future doctor, a cadet smirked, "*The Brigadier* can't think of anyone more qualified for teaching Comparative Anatomy."[49]

Not surprisingly, Citadel students continued to view coeducation as little more than a joke. After learning that Winthrop, an all-female college in Upstate South Carolina, and Clemson University had dropped their single-sex admissions policies, a writer for *The Brigadier* wished both schools luck in their "new ventures." In regards to Winthrop, he concluded, "The girls there are a bit restless and need a 'general perking up' all the way around" and offered a "little of our 'brotherly' help to remedy their situation."[50]

An interesting new feature also cropped up around this time, one that testifies to the corps' unassailable belief in their own masculinity. In his study of the South in the 1950s, Pete Daniel notes that many southerners "flirted with transgressive behavior" by participating in "womanless weddings" and other events that featured white men posing as women or African Americans. According to Daniel, these events confirmed that "in a society that placed a premium on masculinity and whiteness . . . white men could violate and enforce barriers with impunity." Around this same time at The Citadel, the newspaper began profiling cadets in drag as the "Beasts of the Week." Despite names like "Miss Stomach Turner" and "Thada Belch," the Beasts' biographical sketches included much of the same information as the women's; without photos, one might even have trouble telling the two apart. Instead of being "a real 'doll,'" one beast was an "enchanting captivating senorita." One columnist used the term "figger" when describing both a Beast and a Beauty. Congruent with the corps' racialized concept of beauty, all the featured women were white, while several of the Beasts were caricatures of nonwhite peoples.[51]

Cadets expressed other racial sentiments less subtly. When the 1954 *Brown v. Board of Education* decision "moved desegregation into the most sensitive zone of white fears," Citadel personnel, like many other southerners, asserted their whiteness as dogmatically as they did their manliness. One of the school desegregation cases that would eventually be incorporated into *Brown* originated in Clarendon, South Carolina. In anticipation of the Court's ruling, South Carolina Governor James F. Byrnes reserved the right to close the state's schools and formed a fifteen-member committee instructed to devise antidesegregation strategies. Unofficially, the committee took the name of its chairman, L. Marion Gressette, and one proposal of the Gressette Committee relieved the state of its constitutional obligation to fund public schools.[52]

Governor Byrne's successor, George Bell Timmerman, continued down this path, signing both an interposition resolution and an appropriations bill that would close any South Carolina college or university required to admit students by court order. According to the chairman of the Gressette Committee, "The people of South Carolina intend to operate their schools in accordance with their own wishes so long as they are allowed to do so. When this right is denied to them, they will close the public schools." Some Citadel officials balked at such a "drastic proposal," with the rising chairman of the Board of Visitors explaining to Clark, "We don't want to give the impression that we would be willing to admit negroes [*sic*] to The Citadel lying down, and at the same time we don't want to burn the barn in order to get rid of the rats."[53]

Evoking "the doctrine of States' Rights," Clark opposed attempts to, as he put it, "force indiscriminate racial integration upon the South," believing instead that "problems of this kind should be left for solution to the people who understand them and know best how to solve them." He claimed that although "the American Negro is demanding 'equality' in every phase of life . . . the blunt fact is that he has been reluctant to accept full responsibility." When making this argument, Clark would often refer back to World War II where he had seen members of the black Ninety-second Division wither under a German assault at the Serchio Valley in December 1944. He blamed the unit's deficiencies not on poor training or demoralizing policies, but on a "general reluctance to accept responsibility for the hard routine discipline that is essential in wartime." Given the high priority Clark and the corps placed on discipline when it came to assessing one's masculinity, this presumed "reluctance" rendered any African American soldier or citizen incapable of becoming a Citadel man. As a means of denying any black person the opportunity to challenge this theory, Citadel officials passed a resolution requiring all in-state applicants to submit two letters of recommendation from Citadel graduates still living in South Carolina. Although these letters were supposed to help the registrar decide if a prospective cadet "is a person of good moral character, and as a student will be adaptable and will conform to the student life, ethical standards and strict discipline of the college," other southern colleges had adopted similar policies as a means of delaying integration.[54]

Just as he used Citadel functions as forums for his anticommunism, Clark invited well-known segregationists to speak on campus. In 1955, he bestowed honorary degrees on Governor Timmerman and Marvin Griffin, a Citadel graduate and then governor of Georgia. That same year, Griffin delivered a Greater Issues speech in which he announced, "We set up our school system, we financed our education program, and we intend to operate our schools." In 1959, Clark honored the arch-segregationist editor of the *Charleston News and Courier*, Tom Waring, who "with the advent of the Era of Bewilderment and Strife following the Supreme Court's segregation decision of May 17, 1954, he became through his editorials, articles, and speeches, one of the nationally known defenders and interpreters of the South."[55]

In *The Politics of Rage*, Dan Carter explains that among southern whites, "any flexibility, and, particularly, any capitulation in the face of black resistance — was perceived as a sign of weakness that would lead to the total collapse of segregation." Citadel men took this to heart, drawing a correlation between one's manliness and one's support for segregation. One writer for *The Brigadier* compared the Supreme Court to "an irksome, destructive child visiting in our home with his mother." In contrast to these bothersome children, one student praised the members of the segregationist Citizens Councils as the only "men of the South who are capable of thinking and reasoning." He looked to such men for protection from "this onslaught of 'social legislation' from a tribunal determined to carry on a policy offensive to many and ruinous to harmonious relations among all people in the South and the nation as well."[56]

The students' angst reached a fever pitch in 1956, the same year Virginia Senator Harry Byrd issued the call for "massive resistance" and Strom Thurmond and other southern politicians penned the "Southern Manifesto." After whites rioted to prevent Autherine Lucy from enrolling at the University of Alabama, *The Brigadier* published a long-winded diatribe blaming "integrationists," not rioters, for taking "a path of forceful belligerence against fellow citizens." Denouncing Lucy, the NAACP, and the Supreme Court for fomenting discord, he welcomed "the spirit of resistance which Alabama students displayed against unwarranted interference by the courts in decreeing whom the university must accept as students." He accused black civil rights activists, not white racists, of causing the "deterioration of race relations that may well cost Negroes in the South more than all the victories in the courts are worth." Inadvertently making a strong case for federal intervention, the author warned, "Alabama, like much of the South, will not willingly accept integration." Deeming reformers "abysmally ignorant of the true situation" due to their "unwarranted assumption that the Negro wants integration," he added, "You cannot legislate morals, especially preconceived interpretations of them which war with millions of citizens' views."[57]

Abandoning the regional perspective, the columnist turned to Cold War issues raised by integration. He believed "the present struggle is weakening America" at a "time of world crisis when other nations of the free world look to us for strength." He soon reversed field, however, asking, "Is it not more

important what we think of each other in America, than it is what the rest
of the world thinks of us in part or in whole?" Finally, he linked communism and desegregation, accusing civil rights activists of entering into a "bar-
gain" with the Soviets in order to split "America over an American way of life
which has been proven through demonstration to be the best under present
conditions."[58]

That same issue of *The Brigadier* alerted readers to "Dangerous Meddling by
the Liberals" in the form of increased federal aid to public schools. The author
of the article accused unspecified "experts" of not only ruining the American
educational system, but for having "almost no faith in the people and almost
total faith in government." While denouncing federal intervention, the student unveiled the ugly racial politics behind his protest. At a time when most
Americans and certainly President Eisenhower were, as Robert Weisbrot put
it, "reluctant to extend federal authority for any purpose, let alone to upset
established racial patterns," he posed the question, "Does anyone believe for a
moment that a federal government dominated by a left-wing, NAACP and other
radical interests will give any school its share of the national tax receipts if it is
not integrated to the limit?"[59]

Adding fuel to the fire, Arizona Senator Barry Goldwater addressed the
corps later that month, confirming their fear of "'pseudo-liberals' acceleration
of the recently developed trend whereby the federal government ignores the
Tenth Amendment to the Constitution and unnecessarily invades the rights
reserved to the states and the people." The senator labeled this trend "un-
American" and the product of "subtle, alien propaganda." The corps cheered
when Goldwater railed against "the socialization of America" and condemned
liberals as a threat to American "freedom."[60]

Not all cadets feared "big government" and some appreciated federal aid,
but none stepped forward publicly to support integration. In *The Brigadier*,
two students wrote letters to the editor outraged at their peer's earlier diatribe
against federal funding of education. Both accused the editor of "sensational-
ism." One was "ashamed" of how poorly the editorial reflected on the corps,
noting that "editorials should act as a mirror for the Corps, and they should
not reflect the opinions and views of the editor or just a few students." Pointing
out inconsistencies in his opponent's argument and recognizing, but not condemning, the federal government's dismal support of civil rights, the student

argued correctly, "A good number of buildings on our campus are the result of federal aid. Have we been ordered to integrate our school?"[61]

The corps' overall attitude toward integration revealed just how deeply race factored into the regional identity of many white southerners. Bemoaning the Supreme Court's efforts to "strike down that which is natural in the South" and accusing the justices of betraying "a marked lack of understanding and sympathy for its problems . . . despite the fact that two so-called 'Southerners' sit on that formerly distinguished bench," one cadet made hatred of integration endemic to all southern whites.[62]

Certain members of the corps demanded such a high level of commitment to segregation that they found many of their fellow South Carolinians wanting. A writer for *The Brigadier* regretted that students across the state had succumbed to "propaganda by subversive organizations" and "swallowed the dangerous and to us obnoxious doctrines of the racial 'integrationists.'" Reaffirming the presumed benefits of a rigorous, disciplined environment, the cadet hoped that once his colleagues at other schools "remove themselves from the impractical idealism they acquire in certain 'arts' courses and face the realities of life, they will realize that the tried and true practice of segregation is best for this day and age."[63]

The corps embraced Confederate symbols and icons as part of their urgent desire to block the "ultimate destruction of the Southern pattern of life," their timing suggesting that white southerners' ostentatious displays of the Confederate flag stemmed from a desire to maintain segregation rather than a longing to celebrate their Civil War heritage. Upon learning that the Georgia legislature had incorporated the Confederate flag into its state flag, members of the corps asked school officials to acquire one of the new banners immediately. *The Brigadier* applauded the "noble sentiments" of a Peach State politician's pledge to "uphold what we stood for, do stand for, and will fight for."[64]

Not content to let their southern neighbors lead the fight, three cadets snuck across campus one night and painted a huge Confederate flag on the water tower overlooking the Citadel grounds. A reporter for *The Brigadier* snickered, "College authorities have smiled and promised that until the tank has to be painted, the honorable flag will continue its vigilance atop The Citadel campus." Calling the painting an act of "love for a cause and lost nation that is kindled within the heart of every true Citadel man," the writer seized the opportunity to reaffirm the southernness of The Citadel and its graduates.[65]

Indicative of the corps' soaring confidence, cadets championed The Citadel as the most southern of all Dixie's schools. Viewing the student body's conservative social and political leanings as the source of their southernness, one student argued that although cadets hailed from all over the country, The Citadel "has never become an amalgamation as have some other southern colleges." At The Citadel, he remarked, Yankees "tend to become converted, in some degree, to the Southern way of thinking." He boasted that when "many other colleges (even Southern colleges) call us 'conservative old fogies' — we reply by telling them that we are not conservative, but rather reactionary." He found that other schools envied the corps' "active feeling of loyalty to a departed nation as opposed to their compartmentalized respect for history" and vowed to "speak forth in these columns from the Southern viewpoint while our liberal friends wrap and twist themselves in a cloak of confused ideals."[66]

While criticizing their peers for selectively interpreting the past, the corps conveniently excised slavery from any discussion of the Confederacy. By evoking Confederate icons and the Lost Cause in their defense of segregation, they made it clear that theirs was a lily-white view of the southern past and present. The corps' one-sided racial politics tainted their sense of humor as well. A photo from the 1958 yearbook shows a group of cadets — some in uniform, others in sweaters and collared shirts — smiling at the camera. A couple of the students are holding up a Confederate flag with a patch attached to it identifying the cadets as members of "Kleen Kut Kompany."[67]

At the close of the 1950s, Clark declared, "Unlike most institutions of higher learning in our country, we approach the vexing educational decade 1960–1970 with equanimity." As the decade ended, though, there were indications that the next ten years might be more troublesome than Clark predicted. Greater Issues speakers continued to focus on containing communism, building up the military, and defending the free world, but by 1958, Clark found it "more and more difficult to get the kind of speakers we wanted."[68]

A subtle shift occurred in cadets' attitudes as well. The late 1950s witnessed a brief thawing in the Cold War with "de-Stalinization" and the signing of the 1959 Camp David Accords. That same year, the new author of The Brigadier's "Globally Speaking" column, Tony Motley, abandoned the apocalyptic tones of his predecessors. While Khrushchev applauded the "spirit of Camp David,"

Motley commended the premier's "honesty," asserting "Mr. Khrushchev has made clear his desire for peace and understanding. He has preached peaceful means, now let him practice them."[69]

Editorials in *The Brigadier* continued to admonish members of the corps for turning a blind eye to classmates who broke the rules, shirked their responsibilities, and slacked off academically, but some cadets loosened their ideological shackles on certain domestic issues. One student wrote a favorable review of a book, claiming, "In an effort to combat the principles of Communist Russia, we are gradually becoming more and more like that police state." Closer to home, the corps began to publicly question some of the college's rules and regulations. In October 1960, the editor of *The Brigadier* penned a satirical protest of the administration's censorship of the paper. Griping about the number of "nitpicky" regulations under which the corps labored, others sought ways to "increase our rights, privileges, and precious moments of comparative freedom." Even the Honor System came under greater scrutiny as some cadets worried that the Honor Court handed down guilty verdicts too readily. While none of these developments qualify The Citadel as a hotbed of youthful dissatisfaction and student unrest, they indicate a somewhat more open, more critical attitude among the student body.[70]

As with much of America in the 1950s, Cold War imperatives shaped the corps' views on racial equality, personal liberties, gender roles, and the responsibilities of citizenship. Disquieted by international instability, many turned to oversimplified evaluations of the world's and the nation's problems. For some, a blind hatred of communism determined the extent of one's patriotism. For most white southerners, a frenzied opposition to integration established one's regional identity. For most Citadel cadets, graduating made one a "whole man." Defining their responsibilities as Americans, southerners, Citadel men, and citizens in such narrow, formulaic terms left the corps ill prepared to accommodate social change. Whether stressing their patriotism, their southernness, or their manliness, their goal remained preservation of the status quo.

While General Clark and other Citadel personnel endorsed such trends, they themselves did not simply conjure up definitions of citizenship designed to bolster the institution's reputation. A national emphasis on the importance of tough, manly leadership as a key to winning the Cold War strengthened many people's belief that Citadel men served a crucial, indeed an essential, role in the country's current and future success. Clark and other Citadel personnel tapped into these broader cultural and political currents, promoting an image of the college that resonated with many Americans who endorsed and submitted themselves to the school's man-building process. Many accepted General Clark's contention that by churning out "whole men," The Citadel turned "cadets into the kind of leaders who will ensure that America fulfills her destiny." In tying U.S. Cold War superiority to the institution's ability to manufacture manly citizens, Citadel cadets, alumni, and administrators equated any challenge to the college's system of building such citizens as a threat to America. Long after Clark had left The Citadel, many Citadel men clung to the notion that "weakening" their alma mater would weaken the nation's citizenry, an attitude that would have a profound impact on how they responded to certain challenges to the school's "traditions."[71]

Cadets' characterization of "true" southerners proved especially far-reaching, with their frantic defense of segregation testifying to how deeply race factored into the regional identity of many white southerners. To much of the corps, being southern had less to do with one's birthplace and hometown than it did with one's political or cultural inclinations. According to the most vocal cadets, "true" southerners were white, voted conservative, revered the Confederacy, resented the federal government, and, most importantly, despised integration. By their standards, Americans from Oregon to Maine might qualify as southern, but by declaring integration an attack on the southern way of life, the corps confirmed Jim Crow's place at the center of the region's political, social, economic, and cultural existence.

CHAPTER THREE

Black, White, and Gray

The Racial Integration of The Citadel, 1963–1973

 Growing up in Charleston in the 1920s, J. Arthur Brown would glare angrily at Citadel cadets as they walked past his house. He resented not being allowed to attend the college simply because "my skin was the wrong color." The sight of three Japanese cadets in Citadel uniforms compounded his frustration since "I only had to travel across town to get to The Citadel while they had to travel half-way around the world." Even on weekends, Brown could watch Bulldog football games only if he agreed to clean the stadium afterward. If the home team started losing, though, disgruntled stadium officials forced him to leave. These experiences left an indelible impression on him, and decades later, as president of the Charleston branch of the National Association for the Advancement of Colored People (NAACP), he made desegregating the city's schools and other public facilities his primary goal.[1]

South Carolina was one of the last southern states to integrate its public colleges and universities, holding out until January 1963 when Harvey Gantt enrolled as the first African American student at Clemson University.[2] After witnessing the ugliness at Ole Miss and other campuses across the region, South Carolina political and business leaders made preserving order and avoiding federal intervention their number-one priority. Devising "probably the most complete and carefully thought out [plan] ever drawn up in the United States to meet the threat of racial violence," state and university officials planned Gantt's first day on campus with the "precision of an astronaut shot." Security guards accompanied him wherever he went. Highway patrolmen set up roadblocks where they screened everyone entering and leaving campus. Students had to wear name tags, and school officials threatened to expel anyone who caused a disturbance. Gantt enrolled without incident, an outcome that a writer for the *Saturday Evening Post* described in an article titled "Integration with Dignity."[3]

A few months later, the University of South Carolina desegregated with the registration of Henrie Monteith, Robert Anderson, and James Solomon. According to a history of the university, college administrators and members of the South Carolina Law Enforcement Division (SLED) mapped out the students' movements "down to the last detail." Several SLED agents escorted Monteith, Anderson, and Solomon around campus. Others stood watch on every street corner surrounding the university. Still more patrolled the grounds disguised as students.[4]

Three years later, in the fall of 1966, Charles DeLesline Foster enrolled as the first African American cadet at The Citadel amid little fanfare.[5] The number of black cadets increased over the next ten years, but by 1976, they still constituted scarcely more than 1 percent of the student body. With the college's unique traditions and military structure, the first African American students at The Citadel faced challenges far different from their peers at other schools. Many at the college refused to reconsider certain practices and traditions that evoked The Citadel's role in buttressing white social, political, and economic dominance. At the same time, a handful of cadets, both black and white, took the lead when it came to meeting the challenges of integration as they strove to overcome a recalcitrant and often hostile administration in an attempt to change their alma mater.

As noted earlier, the president of the college and other school officials opposed integration, but rather than stand in direct defiance of the law, they chose to ignore or obscure the college's exclusionary practices. One way of doing so was to draw attention to the equal opportunities The Citadel promised white men regardless of social class. A year after the *Brown* decision, General Clark alleged, "At The Citadel, you are measured by what you are and what you do, not by any of the more superficial standards of human achievement which we find so often in modern society." In July 1963, President John F. Kennedy sent a letter to the Board of Visitors asking for the school's help in alleviating the nation's racial strife by encouraging all students to further their education. In their reply, the board mentioned The Citadel's high student retention rate, but sidestepped the issue of recruiting or admitting African Americans.

The board's chairman ended his response with the disclaimer, "Since I feel we are already fulfilling the President's wishes and are carrying out the extra programs as outlined in this letter, this will be our only report."[6]

Months before the passage of the 1964 Civil Rights Act, The Citadel received an application request from an African American student at South Carolina State College. At that time, The Citadel did not accept transfer students, and the registrar informed the young man of this policy. When the student replied that he intended to enroll as a freshman, the Board of Visitors declared that his application would "be processed exactly as all applications received from residents of South Carolina regardless of race." On November 11, General Clark addressed the board concerning the "application of the Civil Rights Act on ROTC programs." Four months later, he signed a certificate of compliance.[7]

Clark retired as the president of The Citadel in 1965, and by the time he stepped down, school officials claimed that no black applicants had met the school's admission standards. Several had requested application materials; a few had begun, but not completed, the application process; and one had been rejected for scoring below the school's minimum requirements on the college entrance exam. Clark did not avoid integration completely, however. His assistant, Colonel Dennis Dewitt Nicholson Jr., remarked that the general's "final days were complicated when Negro applicants were found qualified for admission to The Citadel Summer School for the first time." According to Nicholson, the enrollment of African Americans in the summer school program went "without incident . . . and was scarcely noticed by the news media."[8]

Meanwhile, Citadel cadets continued to view integration with a mixture of resentment, resignation, and racism. In the wake of Harvey Gantt's enrollment at Clemson, *The Brigadier* asked cadets their opinions on the desegregation of South Carolina's public schools. A freshman conceded the inevitability of integration, but insisted that a "peaceful, gradual settlement with time for adjustment is the only answer." One student disapproved of the Supreme Court's efforts to "force" social change, while a Charleston native believed segregation should continue "until the Negroe [sic] race has improved its moral standards and its living standards." Attitudes seemed relatively unchanged a year later when a student editorial condemned the pending Civil Rights Act for subverting the American ideals of "private property and self-determination."[9]

The same year Clark retired, The Citadel received six applications from African Americans and approved three of them. Of these three, only Charles

Foster, a Charleston native and high school honors student, enrolled for the upcoming school year. The imminent enrollment of a black cadet piqued the student body's interest. Professors sparked numerous debates by asking cadets their opinions on the impending integration of the college. Many cadets wondered if Foster would operate as a tool of the NAACP and try to cause trouble on campus. Several doubted that African Americans could withstand the rigors of the fourth class system and worried about the consequences should Foster quit. Other students welcomed African Americans based on the stereotypical assumption that it would improve the school's athletic program. Most men assumed that the first black student would look "like superman, earn a 4.0, and go on to attend Harvard." A situation peculiar to The Citadel arose over how upperclassmen would address black freshmen. At that time, cadets commonly referred to individual plebes as "boy," and while many wondered how a young, African American male would respond to this label, most refused to abandon the designation. Several students discussed how a black cadet's classmates should react if an establishment refused to serve African Americans. A majority of them claimed they would walk out, a pledge that would be tested a few years later.[10]

Such debates intensified when Charles Foster reported to The Citadel alongside 658 other freshmen on September 6, 1966. An article in *The State* newspaper described him as "a face in a faceless crowd," while the *New York Times* announced, "Citadel Enrolls First Negro; Entrance Virtually Unnoticed." As he walked with his brother across campus, William Foster sensed an undercurrent of resentment, noting that although "people didn't want him there . . . they treated him as any other plebe coming into the system."[11]

Foster entered The Citadel not long after the college had introduced a new president. General Hugh P. Harris, a native of Anderson, Alabama, had served thirty-four years in the armed forces, retiring as commanding general of the U.S. Continental Army Command. Although he was the third straight four-star general to serve as president of the college, Harris did not generate the same enthusiasm as Summerall and Clark. As a matter of fact, Harris dealt with declining enrollments and decreased public support for the college throughout his five-year presidency.[12]

Thus, while Harris did not share his predecessor's stubbornness regarding integration, an emphasis on public opinion and expediency determined his commitment to civil rights. A black Charlestonian once thanked Harris for his hospitality at a dinner party, adding, "I admire your courage and sense of values very much, and I hope you know that it has made it easier for some of the others of us to do likewise." As president of The Citadel, the general contributed an article to a brochure published by a black college in South Carolina affirming the state's "legal and moral obligation to provide equal opportunity for education to all regardless of race, color, or national origin." At the same time, Harris submitted a deposition in support of a military school in Alabama that was trying to qualify for federal money without admitting African American students. When Charleston Mayor J. Palmer Gaillard requested that The Citadel hire more African Americans to ensure "continued peace and tranquility in Charleston," Harris reaffirmed the school's equal-opportunity employment policies. While the general boasted that blacks constituted half of The Citadel's workforce, most served as janitors, wait staff, or in the laundry and physical plant. He entertained the idea of hiring black faculty members, but never made a concerted effort to do so.[13]

Harris took a similar tack when overseeing the integration of The Citadel. Six months after Charles Foster had enrolled, Harris received a letter from Alderman Duncan, a 1927 graduate, who expressed concern over rumors that the college recruited African American football players. The thought appalled Duncan, who favored "doing away with intercollegiate athletics altogether rather than have Negro players on our teams." He threatened to stop donating money to the Citadel athletic department, informing Harris that other alumni shared his views. The general explained that the college's ROTC affiliation forced it to sign the compliance agreement, but denied any attempt to recruit black athletes, assuring Duncan that only one African American attended the school at that time and "there is little indication that any substantial numbers of Negroes will apply to The Citadel in the near future."[14]

Five months after this declaration, General Harris informed the Board of Visitors that the U.S. Department of Education planned to investigate South Carolina's colleges to determine if they awarded athletic scholarships on a nondiscriminatory basis. According to Harris, The Citadel's policies had not been questioned. The board responded by reaffirming the apparently hollow pledge that "the principle of non-discrimination shall apply equally to the recruitment of athletes by the Athletic Department of The Citadel as it does in all other operational phases of the institution."[15]

Despite their misgivings, Citadel authorities wanted Charles Foster to succeed. Increasingly preoccupied with keeping the school afloat amid a rising tide of Vietnam-related antimilitarism, school administrators sought to avoid any potentially negative publicity. Colonel Nicholson asked local media to minimize their coverage of Foster's arrival, a request that they seemed to respect. A local television station declined a $125 offer from CBS to interview Foster, and even Thomas Waring, the arch-conservative editor of the *Charleston News and Courier* remained uncharacteristically quiet. The day after informing the public of Foster's acceptance, he penned a brief editorial grumbling that "under existing social pressures, racial integration of The Citadel was inevitable," but predicted that the change would occur without any complications.[16]

School officials were not so confident. Hoping to head off potential trouble, one administrator made the student body aware of the importance of Foster's success. Lieutenant Colonel T. Nugent Courvoisie served as assistant commandant of cadets from 1961 until 1968, developing a rapport with the students unlike any person before or since. Cadets nicknamed him "the Boo," and in his first book, Pat Conroy described Courvoisie as the "father of the Corps . . . dutiful and humane, stern and merciful, fierce and infinitely kind." Conroy claims that "had the full destructive energies of the Corps ever been released in a full-scale riot, Mark Clark would have been trampled. Courvoisie could have met the charge head on, issued a command, and stopped two thousand men in their tracks." Before Charles Foster reported as a freshman, the Boo made it known that he would be checking on him throughout the year. He delivered no specific guidelines or special edicts, but as cadet Philip Hoffmann observed, "Anyone with a modicum of intelligence would have realized that laying a hand on [Foster] would get you a one-way ticket to Clemson."[17]

School administrators intervened directly when it came to Foster's room assignment. In 1966, cadets were assigned to their home companies based on height. By this criteria, Charles Foster should have reported to second battalion, F Company. The cadet regimental commander suggested that Courvoisie place Foster in G Company instead for a variety of reasons. For one, the cadets of F-Troop had earned a corps-wide reputation for hazing that did not bode well for the success of any freshman. The regimental commander noted that Golf Company possessed a strong cadet chain of command, one that could be relied upon to guide Foster through the pitfalls of plebe year. Based on this endorsement, Courvoisie assigned Foster to second battalion, G Company. As a further precaution, school officials selected a northerner, Dave Hooper, from Cherry Hill, New Jersey, as Foster's roommate.[18]

The G Company commander, cadet William Riggs, and the cadre platoon leader, cadet Michael Bozeman, also prepared for Foster's arrival. Placing him in a room adjacent to theirs, the two seniors spent the year trying to watch over Foster without setting him apart from the other plebes. While several fourthclassmen suspected that Lieutenant Colonel Courvoisie and cadet officers kept a close eye on Foster, they never noticed any special supervision. One admits that he never saw anyone looking after Foster; he and others "felt it, we suspected it, but it was not blatant." A few times Riggs or Bozeman pulled an overly aggressive junior or sophomore away from Foster, but as one of Foster's classmates recalls, "For the entire freshman year Charlie was one of us and he caught it just the same as we did."[19]

Still, problems encountered regularly by white cadets took on added importance when they affected Foster. Like most freshmen, he considered quitting school on more than one occasion. Citadel personnel feared that if Foster left for any reason, the federal government would accuse them of a civil rights violation. Whenever Foster discussed resigning, various members of Golf Company offered counseling and reassurance that plebe year was demanding but ultimately rewarding.[20]

Another crisis arose when the company had to assign Foster a new roommate. Hooper and Foster had developed an "amicable" relationship, and while Hooper encountered less animosity than Foster, he did achieve a certain notoriety. Hooper and his family received mail praising and condemning him for rooming with The Citadel's first African American cadet. Some upperclassmen referred to him as Foster's "nigger-loving roommate," and they singled him out for extra push-ups and other hardships. Some cadets told Hooper that Foster would live longer with a Yankee roommate. One individual asked Hooper repeatedly, "Did you kill him yet?" Hooper's father expressed concern for his son's welfare to Colonel Courvoisie, and after a personal disagreement between Hooper and Foster, the company assigned Foster another roommate. Company officers screened each freshman, scratching from their list several who flat-out refused to live with an African American. The search took five weeks, but eventually, a new roommate was found.[21]

Many of Foster's classmates contend that in addition to the efforts of cadet officers, Foster's impressive physical stature, his easygoing personality, and the school's demanding lifestyle helped him establish interracial loyalties and friendships. A telling incident occurred after the first week on campus. Henry Kennedy was a G Company freshman from Charleston who decided to go home for the day. Foster opted to spend the day at his parents' house as well, but some upperclassmen refused to allow the two men off campus without proper shirt tucks. Administering a shirt tuck according to Citadel standards required two people. The person who received the shirt tuck first had to unbutton and unzip his pants, and then unfasten the top three buttons of his shirt. While the first cadet pulled the sides of his shirt out to resemble wings, the other cadet stood behind him and ran his hand down the portion of the wing along the classmate's rib cage. The assistant then folded the shirt back tightly, and while the other cadet held the first tuck, he repeated the process on the other side. Finally, the first cadet buckled, buttoned, and zipped his pants back up while the second cadet kept the tuck in place. Kennedy and Foster had to repeat this process several times before meeting the upperclassmen's approval. Such harassment may seem trivial, but it formed an integral part of freshman year at The Citadel, and in this instance, forced a black man and a white man to rely on each other in a rather intimate way not found in other settings. Most whites at other southern colleges ignored the first African American students, but this did not and could not happen to Charles Foster at The Citadel. Within a week of his arrival, he was thrust into a position of interdependence with a white man he had just met. As Foster and his classmates sweated in formation, did push-ups in the barracks, and struggled during long training runs, many white cadets came to view Foster as another plebe trying to survive the year rather than as the man who broke The Citadel's color barrier.[22]

This acceptance was not universal. Many whites expected Foster to be a Herculean segregation buster and complained when he turned out to resemble an average cadet. Upon hearing these grumblings, one professor asked his white students to describe the ideal black cadet. After noting their criteria, he pointed out that the cadets wanted Bill Cosby to integrate The Citadel. During inspections, Foster received noticeably more demerits than his white classmates. As he walked to and from class, white cadets shouted racial epithets out their windows. One day, as the G Company freshmen stood in formation, Foster braced in horror as cadets from another company dressed in white sheets and raced toward him screaming and yelling. Dave Hooper remembers that early in the year, a group of freshmen called him into a room and told him that they planned to run Foster off. Hooper noticed a homemade noose looped over an exposed pipe in the ceiling and left the room immediately. He never told Foster about the incident, and the cadets never carried out their threat.[23]

Foster persevered, emerging from his first year with a great deal of confidence and little resentment. When asked about returning as a sophomore, Foster replied, "I feel like I'm lucky and I'm part of the school and the military. Sure I'm going back, I wouldn't miss it." General Harris congratulated Riggs for the successful completion of Foster's indoctrination, acknowledging, "The Citadel is much in your debt for the effective manner in which you handled all the details associated with this matter."[24]

As an upperclassman, Foster developed close friendships with a few of his peers. He attended Citadel parties and on one occasion even carried a drunken classmate into the barracks. A former roommate recalls several occasions when he went home with Foster or the two socialized in Charleston. Philip Hoffmann participated in a field training exercise with Foster, and the two men shared a foxhole for three days. Hoffmann had not known Foster personally prior to this exercise, but afterward they spoke on a regular basis. According to Hoffmann, "We had camped together. We had peed on the same bush. Now we were buddies."[25]

Foster graduated in May 1970, and his cadet career appears to parallel that of numerous past, present, and future cadets. He posted average grades and never rose above the rank of private. He survived plebe year, put on weight, harassed freshmen, and went to bars. In actuality, though, Foster's Citadel career differed vastly from that of other cadets. One white alumnus described his first day at The Citadel as "walking into Hades itself." Another added, "I was a big hard-nosed football player who could take things in stride and could do push-ups all day long, and [The Citadel] scared me. How would you like to be a black man coming into the place that fired the first shots of the Civil War?" A friend of Foster's commented, "I don't think Charlie was ever comfortable at that place." A white Charlestonian remembers community members predicting that Foster would fail, that cadets would "run him out or they'll give him blanket parties." Living in Charleston, Foster probably heard these same comments, and every night he lay in bed, in a room without locks, knowing that some men hated the very idea of a black man in a Citadel uniform. The anxiety he must have felt when he heard footsteps or voices outside his door cannot be measured in push-ups or demerits.[26]

Unlike other freshmen, Charles Foster did not have the luxury of quitting. To do so would have validated the belief that African Americans could not "stand the gaff." His resignation would have stigmatized "his" race, making it especially difficult for the black cadets who followed. A friend of Foster observed that "Charles would have died, but he would not have given up." Courvoisie praises Foster for having "the guts to stick it out, and that's what got him through."[27]

The uncertainty and constant pressure of Foster's Citadel experience took its toll. He realized some of his peers were waiting to pounce when he committed the smallest infraction. Foster's indiscretions drew a great deal of criticism, and while some cadets saw him as "Charlie," others saw him as "the first black graduate" and expected more. One high school classmate described Foster as "macho," adding that he seemed to internalize many of his troubles. Riggs mentions that Foster "didn't seem outwardly depressed, but he was pretty quiet. There seemed to me like there was a lot of passion within him that we never got to see." William Foster called The Citadel his brother's "toughest challenge. He won, but he never got the prize or recognition. But he's still a Citadel man."[28]

During Charles Foster's sophomore year, Joseph Shine reported to Kilo Company as The Citadel's second African American cadet. Shine lived in Charleston, and respected The Citadel's academic reputation. Also, with the Vietnam War in full swing, he knew that "if I had to go in the military, then I wanted to be an officer." Shine's arrival sparked fewer debates than Foster's, but it still aroused considerable interest. Shine stood five feet eight inches tall and weighed 118 pounds; many cadets wondered if he would survive. One upperclassman feared, "They're going to run this kid out of here in three weeks, and the world's going to come to an end."[29]

No noticeable procedural or administrative adjustments occurred between the enrollments of Foster and Shine. If anything, school officials took a smaller role in Shine's assimilation into the corps with a personal appearance inspection by General Harris marking the extent of Shine's interaction with Citadel authorities. As for Charles Foster, he introduced himself to Shine early in the school year, but never checked on him with any regularity.[30]

Shine did not recall much racial animosity his first few days on campus, but admits that as a freshman, "You're treated lower than dirt anyway." Still, as the year progressed, the bigoted attitudes of several cadets subjected him to more physical and psychological harassment than his white classmates encountered. Men in other battalions urged freshmen to alienate Shine and force him to leave. Others yelled racial slurs out their windows as Shine walked by. On several occasions, Shine returned from mess with shins bloodied where an upperclassman had been kicking him underneath the table. One night, some cadets poured fingernail polish remover in the shape of a cross in front of his room. They lit it, knocked on Shine's door, and scurried off.[31]

According to Shine, his classmates' attitudes ranged from "supportive" to "outright racists." James Lockridge, an Ohio native, roomed with Shine for almost their entire Citadel career, and the two developed a lasting friendship. Shine benefited also from the fact that several K Company freshmen had come from military backgrounds and had attended integrated high schools. While those who disliked Shine avoided him, he formed close relationships with many of his peers.[32]

Many of these bonds were forged in the fires of the fourth class system. Shine struggled physically his freshman year, and when his shortcomings resulted in longer runs or extra "training" sessions, some classmates questioned his motivation and complained that he should have prepared himself better for plebe year. Rather than abandoning Shine, several of his classmates helped him rise to the challenge. Referring to the trials of the fourth class system, Shine learned, "When people feel that you shared that experience with them and you've come through that experience with them, then they're more inclined to accept you into the brotherhood." Shine's classmate Larry Gantt put it another way, pointing out, "Whether you were black or white, you both had the same goal; trying to get through there." Gantt's statement rings true for most cadets, but the plebe experience differed for black and white cadets due largely to the racially charged overtones of the hazing Shine, Foster, and other African American cadets endured. It is doubtful that a white knob had ever been screamed at by Klan-clad upperclassmen or had a cross burned outside his door, but even if one had, the experience would not carry with it the same threatening historical connotations as it would for most African American cadets. One classmate noticed this, claiming that Shine "went through ten times more than we ever went through, both physically and emotionally."[33]

Shine's energy, sense of humor, and intellect overshadowed his physical shortcomings. He earned academic honors, achieved the rank of cadet captain, served on regimental staff, received an air force scholarship, and won recognition as an exemplary air force ROTC student. In his senior year, an incident at a local bar solidified his standing in the class of 1971. Under the headline "Rights Denied," the editor of *The Brigadier*, James Lockridge, informed the corps that a local bar had refused to serve Shine because of his race. Earlier that week, Shine had entered Raben's Tavern with a group of cadets. When he ordered a beer, the proprietor told Shine that he would not serve him unless he moved to a back room. In response, the group of cadets walked out, and for the rest of the year, many members of the corps carried out an informal boycott of the bar. Lockridge vowed never to return until Raben's Tavern learned that "black is just as beautiful as white."[34]

The incident drew the attention of Citadel alumni as well. A 1969 graduate blasted Lockridge for criticizing an establishment "which has been serving cadets for half a century." The alumnus endorsed Raben's as a place "where cadets are served with a smile and treated with special care," adding "right or wrong, some people like to have a place where they can drink beer and talk about problems of the times without looking over their shoulder to see if they are offending the person behind them." Other alumni wrote in praising Lockridge and The Citadel. Neill Macaulay, a 1956 graduate, congratulated the cadets for striking "a blow for human decency." One member of the class of 1971 called Raben's refusal a "turning point" as the strong show of support by white cadets won over a few men who still harbored prejudices against Shine. Even Shine's "chief antagonist" left Raben's with the other cadets and joined in the boycott.[35]

The graduation of Joseph Shine in May 1971 marked another milestone in The Citadel's history. While Charles Foster proved that a black man could survive at The Citadel, Shine proved that a black man could excel there. In a school with no black faculty members and few black administrators, Shine served as a role model for future African American cadets. His hard work resulted in an exemplary cadet career, and like Foster, he won the acceptance of many men predisposed to reject him based on his race. This respect did not come suddenly or easily, but growing up in a segregated society, Shine had expected the cadets' attitudes "to reflect society in general." Overall, Shine approached his Citadel career believing if "you deal with people honestly and fairly and if they are human beings and can get beyond . . . the color of one's skin, then if they enjoy you as an individual, then they will like you."[36]

Shine's most tangible legacy proved to be the African American studies group that he helped to found at The Citadel. While many school officials questioned the necessity of such an organization, Shine worked hard to obtain a charter. He overcame the administration's obstinacy, and the Afro-American Studies Club held its first meeting on February 9, 1971. Open to all students, the club hoped to promote "dialogue between black and white cadets and to introduce features which will promote understanding." As the number of African American cadets at The Citadel grew, the society provided a forum for black freshmen and upperclassmen to relay shared experiences and to air grievances. In later years, it became a vehicle through which black cadets discussed and sought redress for discriminatory school policies. This activism did not endear the group to the majority of white cadets or Citadel officials. The members' suggestions were often ignored as Citadel officials consistently refused to take a proactive role in the school's integration.[37]

In September 1968, General Harris alerted the Board of Visitors to a pending civil rights inspection by the federal government and outlined the school's policies regarding the awarding of scholarships as well as the recruitment and acceptance of minority students. He documented the number of African Americans in The Citadel's Evening and Summer School, and after reviewing HEW reports and civil rights legislation, Harris concluded that The Citadel had fulfilled the federal government's basic requirements concerning integration. Thus, rather than use the investigation as an opportunity to address and correct flawed policies, the administration settled upon a perfunctory assessment of the college's obligations to its students. This attitude resulted in turmoil and controversy as black enrollment increased. Even moderate efforts to heighten racial awareness on campus faced resistance from various forces within The Citadel, and the black members of the class of 1973 bore the brunt of the backlash.[38]

Of the nine African American students who entered The Citadel in 1969, six graduated. The three who did not resigned as upperclassmen, not during their freshman year.[39] One of the six, Herbert Legare, grew up in Charleston and entertained thoughts of a military career. The Citadel's academic and military reputation appealed to him, and in the summer of 1969, he reported to first battalion, D Company. Norman Seabrooks arrived from Florida as The

Citadel's first African American scholarship athlete. George Graham was a self-described "hot-headed kid" from South Carolina who sought the discipline of a Citadel education. Larry Ferguson was a Charleston native who earned a full academic scholarship to the college. When he reported to Regimental Band Company, he fulfilled his father's wish of having a son integrate The Citadel.[40]

As was the case with Foster and Shine, the nature of the fourth class system intensified the racial abuse some of these men endured, but also helped erode stereotypes held by both black and white cadets. As a freshman, Legare encountered some racial hostility, but overall he spoke positively of his relationships with his classmates whose attitudes seemed to range from acceptance to avoidance. Ferguson was subjected to racial slurs throughout his first year, and in an environment where keeping a low profile is definitely preferable, he would later gain a degree of notoriety as his efforts to heighten the administration's awareness of racial injustices earned him the reputation as a "militant radical."[41]

From the moment George Graham arrived on campus, he "understood one thing early on, there were a lot of people . . . that did not want me there." White cadets screamed racial epithets at him, and one junior questioned African Americans' right to come to "his school." A sophomore required Graham to sleep with a Confederate flag to prove he belonged at The Citadel. Another upperclassman declared Graham "culturally deprived" and made him eat cottage cheese to broaden his experiences. One night, a white cadet burst into Graham's room and shouted that The Citadel "was built with the blood of his ancestors and the audacity of a nigger to go there was unbelievable to him." Two upperclassmen approached Graham, claiming the Department of Health, Education, and Welfare had asked them to keep tabs on him. They said if he witnessed any racist acts, he should contact them immediately. Soon afterward, a cadet walked behind Graham and threatened to run him out of school. When Graham reported the incident, the two "agents" forced him to run in place, do push-ups, and hold a fourteen-pound rifle out at arms' length. Graham fared little better with his roommate as the two men butted heads over who would get the top bunk, with both equally determined not to let a black man or white man sleep above him.[42]

Having grown up in a segregated society, Graham entered The Citadel suspicious of white upperclassmen as well as white freshmen. Eventually he understood that his classmates "were just like me, they were having a unique experience. They had never really been around a black person. I had never really been around a white person in close quarters." When Graham saw another freshman faint from exhaustion, he broke ranks to help him. While this outraged the training cadre, his classmates noticed and appreciated it. Once white cadets realized that Graham lacked, as he put it, "horns and a tail," they formed friendships based on character and ability, not skin color. Later that year, when a local bar refused to serve Graham, his white companions walked out.[43]

Such shifts came gradually, though, as throughout the 1960s and into the 1970s, black students suffered racial affronts. At a home football game between The Citadel and George Washington University, the opposing team's African American quarterback wreaked havoc on The Citadel's defense. Frustrated white cadets yelled "get the nigger" until their classmates quieted them down. In 1968, a *Brigadier* article blamed the unrest following the assassination of Martin Luther King Jr. on the opportunist "seeking revenge on 'whitey' to whom he owed money."[44]

Offensive articles such as these faded with the increased enrollment of African American cadets and a heightened activism within the student body. Unhappy with the administration and benefiting from the increased interaction between white and black cadets, members of the corps worked to improve campus race relations through education and communication. An article in the March 7, 1970, edition of *The Brigadier* asked black cadets, "Is The Citadel Biased?" Describing how African Americans adjusted to life on an overwhelmingly white campus, the interviewees credited The Citadel's military environment and small student body for facilitating the formation of relationships across racial lines.[45]

The initiation of a black studies program and the incorporation of black history into courses taught by the faculty became a major issue for *The Brigadier*. After running an article on a University of South Carolina professor who taught a class on "the Negro in American history," the editor volunteered to gauge the corps' interest in instituting a black studies group and to see whether the school had sufficient resources to support the endeavor. Declaring that "now is the time to search our own campus for a way to eradicate interracial misunderstandings which thrive on prejudicial ignorance," the newspaper staff solicited opinions from faculty members, quoting one Citadel professor who stressed that "efforts should be made to get more about the black man into American history courses."[46]

Outside The Citadel's gates, cadets denounced the racist policies of some of Charleston's businesses. In 1969, forty students from South Carolina State and The Citadel held an informal debate on race and racism. A year later, Citadel cadets served in the South Carolina student legislature that passed a resolution condemning discrimination and urging the state to take a firm stand in support of civil rights.[47]

Meanwhile, Citadel officials plodded forward with a stated goal of "conservative progress" and "change where change is desirable and has been proven necessary." In April 1970, HEW officials conducted a civil rights inspection to ensure The Citadel's adherence to federal guidelines. The agents evaluated the school's efforts to attract African American students and involve them in every aspect of Citadel life. They found that black cadets at The Citadel enjoyed many of the same privileges and opportunities as their white peers, but that the school failed to offer African American students "a feeling of belonging or being a part of the college." The absence of black faculty members and administrators meant that black cadets had few opportunities to discuss sensitive racial matters with a sympathetic older person. Furthermore, the school needed to compensate for the extreme numerical discrepancy between black and white students by enacting "an affirmative action program to begin to disestablish past patterns of racial segregation." Noting that few pictures of black students appeared in Citadel films, brochures, or other publications, the inspectors suggested that addressing this oversight might help remedy enrollment disparities.[48]

General Harris concurred with many of the inspectors' proposals, pointing out that the school had either already implemented the changes or planned to do so in the near future. He claimed the institution awarded financial assistance on a nondiscriminatory basis and that school activities remained open to all cadets. When outlining his reply to the Board of Visitors, however, Harris concluded "we should not turn The Citadel into a HEW . . . instrument of social reform" and opposed any measure "to build up the population of any specific ethnic group." Ignoring the cadets' calls for an increased focus on African American history, he decided that because the report made no mention of black studies, "We should not announce our intent on this at this time."[49]

Certain school-sponsored events offer more evidence that the school had failed to take meaningful steps toward integration. During the school year, the administration held formal tea dances and made attendance mandatory for freshmen. College officials arranged for female students from nearby schools to provide companionship for the awkward and unrefined cadets, and as the freshmen in the class of 1973 ambled in, they realized the school had only invited white women. Since attendance was required, the black cadets spent the entire time standing around and drinking punch in excruciatingly uncomfortable conditions. This oversight left a lasting impression on them. As Norman Seabrooks observed, "You can't take a young black man in 1969, force him to go to a tea dance, and then not have anyone for him to dance with." The scene repeated itself the next year when school officials invited only white women to accompany new freshmen on their annual trip to the Citadel beach house.[50]

In 1970 and 1971 only fourteen new black cadets enrolled at The Citadel, meaning that out of a student body of 1,817, about 1 percent were black. A few of these new recruits came from Charleston, and almost all had grown up in South Carolina. Hometown alumni and the prestige and challenge of a Citadel education attracted some, while others were enticed with scholarships.[51]

As with all cadets, their experiences differed. Ken Feaster played baseball, and years later, he would become the first African American Citadel graduate to attain the rank of colonel. He remembered encountering little overt racism, but conceded the difficulty of distinguishing racial hatred from freshman abuse. John McDowell recalls a couple of isolated racial confrontations, but for the most part, "We got our company assignments, got our room assignments, and we continued to march at that point." McDowell drew upon his white classmates for support and vice versa, but he does remember kicking a white cadet who uttered a racial slur in his presence.[52]

Reginald Sealey was the first African American in Hotel Company, and even though he felt isolated at times, he depended upon his classmates and they relied on him. Keith Jones followed Sealey as the second black member of Hotel Company, and he recalled a few times when upperclassmen singled him out due to his race. One Friday afternoon, a sophomore entered Jones's room and ordered him to perform a variety of arduous physical activities. The cadet claimed that he was trying to overcome his animosities toward African Americans, but blamed Sealey and Jones for reinforcing his past prejudices. This confusing monologue ended after an hour, and Jones reported the incident to Sealey. Cadet officers handled the situation within the company, but the offenders received light punishments.[53]

In his first year, Patrick Gilliard faced a terrifying situation in Alpha Company. He encountered racial resentment from his first day on campus, but as one of the first black Charlestonians to integrate the city's public schools, he expected such confrontations. One night, a group of cadets pulled Gilliard from his bed and led him to an upperclassman's room. They blindfolded him, put him on top of a chair, and tied a noose around his neck. While screaming threats and racial slurs, they looped the noose over an exposed pipe in the ceiling, but left the end unsecured. When they pulled the chair out from under him, Gilliard suffered "the longest second of my life." Rather than report the incident to school authorities, Gilliard told his cousin, a junior cadet in an adjacent company, who contacted other African American cadets. These men visited the A Company commander and the cadets involved to make sure this incident would not be repeated. Gilliard's assailants were punished, but details of the incident never reached beyond the battalion tactical officer. Gilliard contends that by keeping the news of this assault at the company and battalion level, he earned the respect of the cadets in his company, including a few of his tormentors. Later that semester, a group of cadets left a bar in protest after the proprietor refused to serve Gilliard.[54]

In the classroom, the black cadets' relationship with the faculty varied according to the teacher and sometimes according to the subject. Norman Seabrooks appreciated the fact that his professors challenged him and allowed him to question their opinions. On the other hand, some African Americans believed that certain professors held black students to a higher standard while other teachers were outright racists. When George Graham called a professor on the phone to protest a grade, the instructor advised him "not to sound like a black man" because it hurt his chances of changing the professor's mind. A recurring problem faced by black cadets stemmed from the fact that their classes rarely contained more than one black student. Ken Feaster felt particularly isolated when he was the only student in a roomful of white cadets to question a history professor's benign depiction of slavery.[55]

Black cadets' relationships with Citadel alumni also differed from the ones enjoyed by white cadets. Citadel graduates typically maintain fierce loyalties to the school, returning to campus frequently where they relive past exploits and tell current cadets "how hard it was when I was a knob." African

American cadets lacked this spontaneous camaraderie with most alumni, but they formed ties with individuals who knew them previously or with whom they shared common experiences. Graham found that most alumni ignored him, while a hometown alumnus helped Reginald Sealey raise enough money to attend The Citadel.[56]

Outside The Citadel's gates, the sight of African American cadets elicited mixed responses from white observers. Joseph Shine noticed some stares, "but no one really approached me one way or the other." Whatever their reception in the white community, African American cadets enjoyed heroic status among black Charlestonians who took a great deal of pride in finally seeing African Americans in Citadel uniforms. Seabrooks remembers fondly that the "black community in Charleston took me under its wing because they wanted to make sure the first black Citadel football player, who was also a good player, did not leave town because he was homesick."[57]

While family and friends tried to prepare black cadets for whatever difficulties they might face, once inside The Citadel's gates, their small number and the institution's insular nature forced them to rely on one another. Both Foster and Shine introduced themselves to Seabrooks early in his freshman year and offered advice on surviving the fourth class system. Foster made sure that Legare, Ferguson, and Graham knew his room number, while Shine would stop them periodically on the way to class. Black cadets from the classes of 1973, 1974, and 1975 continued such practices as they tried "to make The Citadel a place that [black freshmen] can come and feel like they have an upperclassmen looking out for them." In doing so, these men took care not to violate the rules governing fraternization between upperclassmen and freshmen. John McDowell's introduction to Larry Ferguson came when Ferguson "pulled me to the side, read me the riot act," and then offered encouragement. When McDowell first met Reginald Sealey, he remembers that "I was impressed seeing a black upperclassman on the cadre, and I guess I looked at him a little too long. And he let me know it." As McDowell's classmate Keith Jones suffered through the cadre's yelling and screaming, Sealey stepped in front of him and Jones thought, "Thank God, a black guy." Jones retracted this expression of relief when Sealey continued the abuse.[58]

Knowing that the entire school monitored their actions, black cadets pushed each other to excel. George Graham realized that "the black cadets were going to have to be twice as good" as white cadets, and they repeatedly met the higher standards. In addition to earning South Carolina Football Player of the Year honors, Norman Seabrooks served as captain of the football team and attained the rank of cadet officer. Reginald Sealey helped train incoming freshmen, and as a senior, he commanded a platoon. As a cadet sergeant, his squad won The Citadel's drill competition. George Graham was third battalion adjutant, and twice made the Commandant's Distinguished Service List. Two of Graham's more impressive and revealing accomplishments were his election to The Citadel's Honor Committee and his selection as a Summerall Guard; both are peer-elected groups steeped in Citadel tradition.[59]

In 1971, a controversy erupted that tested the strength of African American cadets collectively and individually. At an institution that prided itself on firing the first shots of the Civil War, "Dixie" and the Confederate battle flag played large roles in everyday life. "Dixie" served as The Citadel's unofficial fight song, and the waving of the Confederate flag and the playing of "Dixie" figured prominently in sporting events. As freshmen, many African Americans sang the song out of fear. As upperclassmen, they often refused to sing the song at all. Members of the Afro-American Society alerted the rest of the corps and school administrators to the "discomfort black cadets felt every time the school band struck up 'Dixie.'" Seabrooks tried to explain to his white classmates that "There is never going to be a place where I am going to be comfortable hearing it, or singing it, or feeling good about it." He would often sit down or walk away when he heard the tune. As captain of the football team, he would leave the locker room early and step on the field before the band started playing.[60]

Each cadet encountered resistance for his decision not to sing or play the song, but Larry Ferguson's refusal attracted the most attention and drew the most severe backlash. As a freshman in the Regimental Band, Ferguson played "Dixie" for fear of upper-class retribution. As a sophomore, he shared his discomfort over the song with some of his black classmates, and resolved to quit playing the tune regardless of the consequences. The group agreed that "once [Ferguson] made his personal decision not to play, all of us supported him in that."[61]

Ferguson's protest infuriated white cadets and school officials. White students asked their black classmates, "What's Ferguson's problem?" The band director threatened to kick him out of the company. Some school officials warned him that he could lose his scholarship. Ferguson's duties as president of the Afro-American Society solidified his image as a "troublemaker."

Ferguson received a company transfer, but his reputation followed him. Facing constant criticism and harassment, he contemplated leaving, but family and friends convinced him to stay.[62]

Continually frustrated in their efforts to have their voices heard on campus, Ferguson and the other black cadets opted for a more aggressive method of getting their point across. On numerous occasions, the Afro-American Society had requested that school officials ban the waving of the Confederate battle flag at Citadel football games. When these pleas went unheeded, they took matters into their own hands. Prior to the Illinois State football game, the black cadets constructed their own banner featuring a black fist crushing a Confederate flag. When The Citadel scored and the white cadets began waving the battle flag, the black cadets hoisted their banner. Displaying a remarkable flair for understatement, Graham admitted that their flag "excited some problems." Ferguson describes their action "as something that was totally reactionary to the situation that we felt we were involved in."[63]

Few white cadets saw it this way. In an article for *The Brigadier*, one white student expressed his initial outrage "at the obvious abuse of our heritage." After giving the matter more thought, the author confessed that the flag did not remind him of the Civil War, but of the fact that the Citadel football team had finally scored and that the corps' curfew might be extended until two a.m. Characterizing the flag as a symbol of his pride in The Citadel, he hoped that future shows of protest would not "visibly abuse the South, but . . . show the spirit which binds our institution and strengthens our future."[64]

Other students reacted more vindictively, singling Larry Ferguson out due to his already established notoriety. Ferguson and his roommate returned to the barracks one night to find their room trashed, racial threats painted on the walls, their books shredded, and a doll hung from the ceiling by a noose. An inquiry failed to uncover the culprits, and the incident drew the black cadets closer. They believed that "if they could do Ferguson the way they did him, then we weren't far behind."[65]

Soon after the Illinois State game, school officials upset many white cadets by banning the waving of all flags at Citadel athletic events. The responses to this decision reveal that although the makeup of the corps had changed, many cadets' image of the ideal Citadel man had not. One white cadet cried, "The Confederate flag must return to being the symbol of the spirit of The Citadel Man and the Corps of Cadets." Calling the flag a symbol of the "American way" and channeling Richard Nixon, he urged the "great silent majority of cadets" to refuse to allow "a proud tradition to be suppressed by the wishes of a few." The author cited the Citadel graduates who died "for a cause in which they dearly believed; states' rights and the Southern way of life, not slavery as so many are led to believe." Other white students expressed similar opinions, with one announcing "our history lies in the South and in the Confederacy, and we should be proud of that for the simple reason that Citadel cadets fought for what they felt was right and were not ashamed of it." Several cadets coupled this vision of the Confederacy with a lily-white assessment of the flag's meaning and impact. Ignoring the opinions of Seabrooks and other black students, one claimed the banner "instills a great deal of pride in the Corps of Cadets," while another argued that "the Confederate Flag has become a symbol of the spirit of the Corps, not a symbol of prejudice or oppression as some people would tend to believe." Certainly, not all white cadets felt this way, as evidenced by a letter two seniors wrote to *The Brigadier* following a home football game in which they blasted the corps and members of the band for antagonizing the opposing team's African American players and cheerleaders by repeatedly playing and singing "Dixie."[66]

Letters from those outside The Citadel convey just how adamantly some people refused to consider the black cadets' viewpoint. Calling the ban "nonsense," a 1937 alumnus declared that black cadets "should accept the traditions of The Citadel as they have developed over the years." The General Micah Jenkins Camp of the Sons of Confederate Veterans called the waving of the flag at football games "a long standing corps' tradition," adding The Citadel has "much to be proud of and thankful for — and nothing to be ashamed of or to hide."[67]

Such tensions went unresolved as black cadets took issue with many aspects of Citadel life beyond a preoccupation with the "Confederate Legend." They aired their grievances to a select committee of Citadel faculty and administrators who were conducting a comprehensive examination of the school's practices and policies. Their lists of concerns included the college's reluctance to recruit black students, the barbers' inability to cut black cadets' hair properly, the absence of black speakers at Citadel functions, the belief that many racial incidents went unpunished, and the faculty's tendency to overlook African American contributions to American history. These problems contributed to a sense of neglect and a lack of belonging among black cadets.[68]

The committee proved less than responsive to these matters. Regarding the complaint about the "Confederate Legend," the panel claimed that society's "current preoccupation with the influence of slavery is responsible for the extreme unpopularity of anything associated with the Confederacy." Although they questioned the Confederate flag's use as a "football standard," they decided "neither the black nor white cadet can presume to sit in judgment upon the past, nor can he expect the school to repudiate its heritage." The study dismissed the indictment of the school's recruiting policies, saying "there is no evidence that blacks are neglected in the recruiting program," but at the same time acknowledged that "blacks show some reluctance to come to The Citadel as cadets." It attributed criticism of Citadel barbers to a corps-wide disgruntlement with short hair. The reviewers conceded the need for more African American guest lecturers, but advised that the speaker's expertise should not be limited to the "narrow, however important, field" of civil rights. They recommended that professors emphasize the social and cultural contributions of African Americans but urged them to do so without "distorting their subject."[69]

The portion of the study dealing with campus race relations concluded, "It is currently fashionable among blacks — young blacks in particular — to become dissenters. While this circumstance may be perfectly understandable, it is not necessarily a positive influence." With this in mind, the committee treated most of the black students' requests as pleas for special treatment, particularly their proposal that an African American serve on The Citadel's Presidential Advisory Committee. The panel rejected this idea with the argument that "absolute equality [should] prevail with regard to race; special favors should be granted neither to blacks nor whites." Black cadets might have responded that placing an African American on the committee would have provided the school with a new and much-needed perspective on their feelings and ideas and that they did not ask for special treatment, merely a voice.[70]

A close examination of The Citadel's integration reveals how white apathy, resentment, and stubbornness thwarted the promise of desegregation. With the 1954 *Brown v. Board of Education* decision, the Supreme Court hoped to do more than integrate public schools. As J. Harvie Wilkinson points out in *From Brown to Bakke*, the Justices' larger purpose was to break down the Jim Crow mind-set, establishing a foundation whereby a new generation of white and black Americans might come to know one another "as classmates, as peers, and as friends." Reed Sarratt acknowledges that the Court's decision "changed the law, but it did not change the thoughts and feelings of vast numbers of white Southerners." Integration did not mean acceptance, and it certainly did not guarantee equality. At The Citadel, school officials regarded integration simply as the enrollment and retention of a handful of African American students. By taking no responsibility for ushering blacks into the institutional life of the college, they allowed racism and discrimination to fester within the student body.[71]

Still, The Citadel provided a unique testing ground for the theory that school desegregation could bring blacks and whites physically, socially, and ideologically closer. The military environment and physical rigors of the fourth class system certainly loom large in this regard. While those familiar with The Citadel may dismiss some of the hazing that black cadets suffered as "part of the system," many of the attacks betray a decidedly racist edge. The men who ran at Foster dressed in sheets, the burning cross on Shine's door, and the mock lynching of Patrick Gilliard were not merely byproducts of an impartial fourth class system designed to test the limits of these new plebes. They were historically specific acts of racial terror rooted in the region's not-too-distant past.

On the other hand, certain tribulations helped erode racial barriers and prompted the reevaluation of racist attitudes founded on stereotypes and unfamiliarity. While the first African American students at Clemson, the University of South Carolina, the University of Georgia, and the service academies faced nearly complete ostracism from their white classmates, The Citadel thrust blacks and whites into a hostile environment that forced them to work together to survive. The endless number of shirt tucks, inspections, "sweat parties," and training runs provided cadets with common experiences upon which relationships based on trust and ability, not skin color, could be built.[72]

Benefiting from this interaction and facing an obstinate and indifferent administration, certain members of the corps displayed the leadership lacking among Citadel officials by challenging outdated and unfair policies. While other state schools developed elaborate plans to ensure that they desegregated peacefully, responsibility for the integration of The Citadel fell largely upon the young college students themselves. Bill Riggs understood that "there are a lot of arguments some people have about giving young men and women at that age such responsibility over the lives of others. But to me, that is what

The [Citadel] system is about, to give that opportunity." In certain cases, then, a system that subsumed superficial socioeconomic differences between individuals worked to the advantage of both black and white cadets.[73]

The same cannot be said when it came to black students' dealings with Citadel administrators. Although African American cadets formed meaningful relationships with several of their white peers, Citadel authorities fostered a sense of isolation among black students by taking a reactive rather than proactive approach to integration. Some Citadel graduates commend school officials for not making a big production out of the college's integration, with one alumnus claiming that "it was so uneventful and so unremarkable that it almost doesn't make a very interesting story." Another remarked that the "school was still so white, nobody noticed." Both statements reveal the source of much of the black cadets' frustration and angst. For them, the integration of The Citadel was interesting, remarkable, and, in many cases, disconcerting. By failing to impress upon white cadets the social and cultural significance of integration, Citadel administrators made the black cadets' journey that much harder. A classmate of Joseph Shine rated school officials' performance as "damn poor," noting the student body "was not sensitized to what desegregation would bring." Keith Jones agreed, adding, "You need to know you don't say certain things to certain people."[74]

Since its inception, The Citadel had been geared to uphold the racial status quo, but as society changed the school needed to reevaluate its procedures and adapt to such changes, for its own sake as well as that of its students. From the outset, though, college officials neglected the fundamental needs of black men, made few allowances for cultural differences between black and white students, and let the minimum expectations of the federal government determine their commitment to integration. In doing so, they subverted not only the promise of *Brown*, but betrayed their stated institutional purpose. Chief Justice Earl Warren framed the Court's opinion in language that should have resonated at The Citadel. Citing education as "the very foundation of good citizenship," he declared academic opportunity a "right which must be available to all on equal terms." By perpetuating policies that alienated African American members of the corps, school officials denied black cadets this right and relegated them to the status of second-class citizen-soldiers.[75]

It could be argued that the pervasive institutional emphasis on manliness as the key to first-class citizenship compounded the frustration felt by black cadets. Many civil rights activists claimed segregation emasculated African American males. Echoing the sentiments from his famous eulogy for Malcolm X, Ossie Davis attributed the slain civil rights leader's popularity to the fact that "*Malcolm was a man!*" who inspired other black males to assert their own bold, aggressive masculinity. Attending The Citadel offered black cadets an opportunity to do just this, since, according to college brochures, officials, and students, graduating from the school affirmed one's manhood. Such a promise must have made it especially grating for the men who faced constant reminders that while they could now attend The Citadel, their acceptance as "whole men" remained qualified at best.[76]

Eric J. Sundquist has interpreted the *Brown* decision as an effort to make "equal education . . . the key to valued and meaningful membership in the nation." Historian James Cobb takes this a step further, viewing school integration as a means by which southern blacks could affirm their place as both full fledged Americans and Southerners. It was exactly this sense of belonging that many black cadets at The Citadel found missing from their college experience. George Graham commented that "Whites were part of this big community, and blacks were standing at the door knocking, saying please let me in, please let me in." Larry Ferguson remembered that at the end of his graduation ceremony, when other exuberant cadets threw their hats in the air, he placed his on his chair and quietly walked away.[77]

CHAPTER FOUR

"An Oasis of Order"

Citadel Cadets and the Vietnam Antiwar Movement

 A few hours before dawn in the spring of 1970, a car passed through Lesesne Gate and entered The Citadel's campus. The driver was a former cadet who had resigned earlier in the school year for undisclosed reasons. Beside him sat a stack of papers with *The Vigil* emblazoned across the top of each sheet. For several months, the former cadet and two of his friends from the senior class had collaborated and produced *The Vigil*, an underground publication exposing the alleged injustices, inequities, and censorship that plagued The Citadel's campus. When the corps awoke for the 6:30 breakfast formation, they would take copies of the unauthorized publication and read about the regular student newspaper's reluctance to defend students' interests and the administration's one-sided evaluations of events occurring outside The Citadel's gates. They would see complaints about the poor quality of mess hall food and the double standard separating cadet officers and cadet privates. The intrigue, rebelliousness, and mystery surrounding *The Vigil* fascinated many cadets, and they welcomed each edition. These same qualities appalled the more militarily inclined members of the corps, who saw the publication as seditious, tendentious, and inappropriate for the structured, orderly environment of a military college. School officials agreed, and pledged to uncover and expel *The Vigil*'s irresponsible publishers.[1]

It is not all that shocking that student unrest and underground newspapers came late to The Citadel. As a military college, The Citadel placed students, the dynamic bulk of the antiwar movement, in a disciplined, structured, and hierarchical environment that seemed to personify what many of their dissenting peers opposed.[2] Even the layout of the campus itself seemed designed to keep the antiwar protests of the 1960s at bay. To deliver *The Vigil*, for example, the driver of the vehicle passed a guardhouse and then turned right onto the Avenue of Remembrance, so named in honor of American soldiers who had died while serving their country. Then, as now, first-year cadets had to walk in the gutters along the avenue, a tradition that not only reminded freshmen of their lowly position among the cadet corps but reminded all cadets of the sacrifices made by U.S. servicemen and women.

After rolling by the library and Summerall Chapel, the car then had to stop at the intersection of Jenkins Avenue and the Avenue of Remembrance. On the right stood Mark Clark Hall, the relatively new student activities building that stood as a looming and literally concrete reminder of the general's ideas on citizenship and proper manly behavior. Across the street from Mark Clark Hall stood Jenkins Hall. This building contained the commandant's office and the offices of the more than two dozen active-duty military personnel who taught ROTC courses and oversaw the operations of the eighteen cadet companies. Only after reaching the end of Jenkins Avenue could the driver turn left and begin unloading his cargo in front of the four barracks that housed the corps of cadets.

The ideological barriers to dissent at The Citadel proved just as intimidating. For years cadets had learned that qualifying as a Citadel man meant following orders, conforming to societal standards, and exhibiting an uncompromising patriotism. While some members of the corps accepted this, others worried that a decade shaped by youthful protest might pass without their participating in some way. As David Farber explains, "Race issues, and then even more the war in Vietnam, gave many white students pressing reasons to become further involved in challenging the world they were to inherit." The tensions aroused by these challenges proved especially pronounced at The Citadel as they bore directly on the corps' assessment of themselves as men and citizens. Many cadets continued to rate the civic worth of an individual on a gendered scale that privileged obedience and conformity. Others, meanwhile, embraced a definition of masculine citizenship that allowed for and even encouraged dissent. The extent to which these cadets overcame considerable institutional constraints to formulate alternative assessments of what qualities good Citadel men and thus good citizens possessed offers valuable insight into the momentum and nature of the antiwar movement.[3]

Throughout his presidency, General Clark afforded students little opportunity to formulate or express dissenting viewpoints. He made certain that through "constant and respectful display of the Stars and Stripes on campus, through patriotic music, through the chaplain's sermons, through my talks to the Corps, through our Greater Issues Speeches and through military instruction," the "atmosphere on The Citadel campus is calculated to renew constantly a feeling of patriotism among cadets." As mentioned earlier, Clark invited speakers to address the corps who merged patriotism and anticommunism and never questioned the U.S. commitment to combating all forms of Soviet encroachment. Warning cadets that "Red China has the third-largest Air Force and more men in arms than the United States and Great Britain combined," Hawaii Congressman Daniel K. Inouye announced that "the time has come to put the welfare of the nation above the welfare of the individual." Secretary of the Army Elvis J. Stahr outlined the Soviet Union's plans for world conquest, receiving thunderous applause when he assured his audience that the U.S. Army would oppose the communist threat wherever it arose.[4]

Thrilled that their college president had "seen the ugly face of communism at close range," many cadets echoed the general's almost fanatical anticommunist stance. Editorials in the student newspaper implored U.S. officials to take a stronger stand against Soviet aggression. When politicians failed to meet the standards set by Citadel men, *The Brigadier* blasted them for their "poor leadership" and "timid foreign policy." After the Bay of Pigs fiasco, one cadet criticized John F. Kennedy's "half hearted" efforts in Cuba, but praised the president for sending more military advisors to South Vietnam. Under the headline "Practice Can Make Perfect," he argued that increased military intervention in not only Vietnam but also Laos, Cambodia, and Berlin might prevent the United States from "losing the Free World yard by yard, village by village, country by country."[5]

A sizable and lucrative military presence in the surrounding community fueled such views. In 1940, Charleston voters had elected Mendel Rivers to Congress for the first of sixteen consecutive terms. Beginning in the 1950s, Rivers used his position on the House Armed Services Committee to bring money, jobs, and military bases to the South Carolina Lowcountry. Between 1960 and 1966 alone, the number of military personnel living in or near Charleston jumped from 13,500 to 21,500. During that same span, the number of area civilians employed by the armed services leaped from 6,500 to 11,500.[6]

Government expenditures in Charleston rose in proportion to Rivers's seniority and to the U.S. involvement in Vietnam. Historian Walter J. Fraser argues "that by the late 1960s, the Charleston area was a microcosm of what President Eisenhower called the military-industrial complex." Commenting on the number of bases in the Lowcountry, one congressman joked, "If Rivers puts anything else [down there] the whole place will sink." By 1970, the military and related industries constituted 40 percent of the city's payroll and pumped about $200 million annually into the local economy.[7]

Immersed in the teachings, terminology, and business of the Cold War, cadets found protest rallies and student antiwar demonstrations difficult to fathom. In November 1960, well over half the corps watched an FBI film on the "Communist-inspired riots" outside a meeting of the House Un-American Activities Committee in San Francisco. Outraged over student opposition to ROTC on some other campuses, a Citadel undergraduate listed the military's declining popularity as "one of the most alarming signs of the decay of the spirit and character of the youth of America today." General Clark and other school officials echoed these sentiments, casting the corps as a bulwark against the "deterioration of American youth" and reminding cadets that a military education instilled students with the "moral fiber" needed to keep America strong.[8]

Assured of their own importance, many cadets commended their seemingly misguided colleagues for at least taking an interest in national affairs. In other cases, they accused the media of exaggerating the extent of the protest and of focusing too heavily on liberal student organizations. Cadet pundits argued correctly that conservative ideals reigned on most college campuses, pointing to a rally in New York where four thousand youths turned out in support of Barry Goldwater as evidence of the "rebirth of conservatism."[9]

This feeling of consensus began to fade following the 1962 Cuban missile crisis. Reporters for *The Brigadier* welcomed the showdown. One writer encouraged the student body to prepare for war. With the events that distressed students from Columbia to Berkeley invigorating cadets, many members of the corps began to distance themselves even further from their civilian peers. Casting The Citadel as a bastion of patriotism and morality, they condemned their rebellious colleagues as "weak willed and more than willing to go along for a joy ride." One student rebutted critics of the U.S. military by claiming that without "men like MacArthur . . . the left will have a free hand to hack away at our republic." Enthusiastic alumni praised the cadets' rejection of the "filth of the big coed colleges [and] the immature element of questioning and doubting and non-conforming." In late 1963, an article in *The Brigadier* published the results of a survey conducted by the decidedly conservative *National Review* asking college students nationwide, "If the United States should find itself in such a position that all other alternatives were closed save world war with the Soviet Union, would you favor a) war, or b) surrender?" Taking some liberties with the question's wording, the reporter announced that at one school 46 percent chose "unconditional surrender," while on another campus, 49 percent "preferred slavery to liberty, if a struggle was involved." Faced with these statistics, the author deplored the sad state of his generation and declared that the United States must continue fighting these internal as well as external enemies.[10]

By mid-decade, the cadets' disdain for dissent and protest collided with the increased militancy and exposure of the antiwar movement. Angered at LBJ's escalation of the air and ground war in Vietnam, teachers and students across the country held teach-ins on over one hundred campuses. In the spring, summer, and fall of 1965, public rallies in Washington, D.C., Berkeley, and New York drew crowds totaling in the tens of thousands. Citadel students wanted no part of these demonstrations. When the organizers of the International Days of Protest sent The Citadel a letter asking how they planned to contribute to the nationwide antiwar rally, *The Brigadier* staff responded to this "not-too-flattering request" with a massive rebuttal entitled "Vietnam Survey: Why the Protests Are Wrong." Describing Southeast Asia as "a current scene of communist aggression and the free world's struggle to stop it," the reporters equated U.S. withdrawal with appeasement, repeating Johnson's claim that "our honor and word are at stake in Vietnam."[11]

Numerous other factors drove the wedge between the corps and the antiwar demonstrators deeper. The rising antimilitarism of the 1960s contributed to a sharp drop in applicants, and Mark Clark's successor, General Harris, warned the Board of Visitors that "the roof is coming down faster than many realize." Many South Carolinians had begun to question the necessity of a half-filled, state-supported military college, and Harris looked for ways to enhance the college's reputation and enrollment. During his presidency, The Citadel launched a graduate program, began accepting transfer students, readmitted veteran students, and allowed women to attend evening classes. These initiatives troubled many alumni who responded in typically southern fashion, warning that "too much change" would cost the school its distinct place in society. Others scolded Harris for catering to the demands of "outside forces," setting the school on the road to "decadence." One accused him of transforming The Citadel from a "man's college" into a "boy's school." Charlestonian Alice Beckett argued that the enrollment of noncadets devalued a Citadel education since the corps could start "cheating and rubbing elbows with Communists like at the University." These concerns fueled rumors that the school planned to abandon its military traditions, admit females into the cadet corps, and discard the plebe system.[12]

While he never planned to abolish the fourth class system, General Harris worried that hazing at The Citadel had gotten out of hand, a development that he found especially troubling because it hurt enrollment, damaged public relations, and weakened the college's chances of receiving federal grants. In meetings with the commandant of cadets, Harris suggested numerous modifications to the corps' training methods with one plan dividing the plebes into three groups: the "normal" or "strongest" ones who seemed to adjust well, those who have potential but required extra guidance, and those "who are simply misfits." In his annual address to the training cadre on August 31, 1966, the commandant reminded upperclassmen that The Citadel's goal was to build men, not "wreck them," making it a point to add that each freshman should get "a well balanced meal three times a day, that he is given the opportunity to get a full nights rest from Taps to Reveille and that he is not harassed just for the sake of harassment."[13]

In *The Lords of Discipline*, Pat Conroy, a 1967 Citadel graduate, recounts the horrors of his freshman year in gruesome detail. In a later work, *My Losing Season*, Conroy describes the plebe system he endured as "mind-numbing, savage, unrelenting, and base." Many people associated with The Citadel dismiss the novelist's accounts as literary hyperbole, a skepticism Conroy himself accepts from older graduates who see no similarities between their freshman year and the one he describes. He explains, though, that by the early 1960s "the system had evolved into the extreme form of mob violence my classmates and I experienced."[14]

Although it cannot be determined with precise accuracy when and why this evolution took place, the increased violence of the fourth class system could be seen as a unique reaction by Citadel personnel to the social and political demands of the era. The ideological climate of the Cold War had already elevated toughness into the pantheon of manly values instilled at The Citadel, but increased American involvement in Southeast Asia intensified this aspect of the college's mission. With Vietnam looming over the heads of most Citadel graduates, the fourth class system might have taken on a greater sense of urgency among cadets who viewed the trials of freshman year as a way of not just building men, but of preparing them for the gruesome realities of a strange and discouraging war. The 1963 Citadel *Catalogue* lauded the school's method of producing "young men with alert minds and sound bodies, who have been taught high ideals, honor, integrity, loyalty, and patriotism." This assessment carried the rather ominous message that "these personal qualities must be deeply ingrained in order that neither time nor trouble will erase them from his personality."[15]

Domestic turmoil also influenced the citizen-soldiers who had committed themselves to combating anyone who "threatens the American way of life." Many members of the corps hoped that "every Citadel man can put aside foolish and selfish ideas concerning his personal well being and show the ungrateful collegiate Americans that in this country still live men who believe it is a privilege to defend their nation." Lauded by Harris as the "cream of American manhood," members of the corps seemed to believe that pushing freshmen to their physical and emotional limits would ensure that Citadel cadets would "continue to stand proudly apart from the permissiveness and decadence that surround us." A particularly overt method of distancing cadets from other college students involved haircuts. In the mid-1960s, as more and more young men challenged traditional mores by wearing their hair longer and shaggier, Citadel freshmen began sporting "baldy" or "knob" looks. While previous classes had received a "buzz" cut during their first week on campus, this new "tradition" required freshmen to have their scalps shaved practically bare. Due to the fourthclassmen's shorn appearance, upperclassmen began referring to plebes as "knobs," and alumni from earlier eras remember their shock upon seeing the new haircuts for the first time.[16]

Of course, the building of Citadel men involved more than shaved heads, and by 1968, General Harris had uncovered "impressive evidence" that hazing at The Citadel had spiraled out of control. In a meeting with the Board of Visitors he cited numerous letters he had received from parents who were "quite bitter" at the treatment their sons had endured. While labeling these problems an area of "severe concern," Harris waffled as to who to blame for the system's deficiencies. Speaking before a class of incoming freshmen, the general announced "the only harm to The Citadel that I know is being done is by about 5 percent who came here, cannot cope, and then go home and start rationalizing their weaknesses to mama." At least privately, however, Harris realized much of the trouble stemmed from abusive practices that had become accepted aspects of plebe year. In May, he informed the Board of Visitors "we must consider refinement or elimination of features which normal, intelligent, open-minded parents cannot accept." Failure to do so, he added, meant that The Citadel "cannot attract the outstanding students we want."[17]

With this in mind, school officials convened a panel to review and revise the fourth class system. James Whitmire, a U.S. Air Force colonel, Citadel graduate, and member of the college's ROTC department, chaired the committee, and the so-called Whitmire Report mixed specific and general analyses of the fourth class system's strengths, weaknesses, and overall purpose. The makeup of the committee left no room for critics to denounce their findings as the work of "outsiders" who did not appreciate The Citadel's traditions. The group consisted of two Citadel alumni, three faculty members, two members of the commandant's office and ten cadets. This combination met the approval of General Harris, who had demanded that cadets play a major role in this evaluation since they had "frequently, enthusiastically, and unanimously reaffirmed their complete support and insistence that the System be continued as the very best way and means of 'bringing up' the incomparable 'Citadel Man.'" As part of their research, committee members spoke with alumni of "all vintages," interviewed parents of "past, present, and future cadets," and solicited the opinions of "cadets with specialized and intelligent interests in the future of The Citadel and the type of 'Citadel Man' to be produced."[18]

As the above statements indicate, the Whitmire Report not only laid out in no uncertain terms how deeply rooted concepts of masculinity factored into most cadets' sense of their own and their college's worth, but it also underscored the fourth class system's central importance to the school's overarching goal: the building of men. Calling the plebe system the "fundamental cornerstone of the Military College's Operation," the authors announced that it should be "designed, tailored and geared to serve the unique purposes and traditions of The Citadel." They decided that among these purposes and traditions, "the development of the unique and highly valuable 'Citadel Man' is a matter of first importance."[19]

While confident of the fourth class system's importance to The Citadel, the panelists agreed that accusations of hazing had marred the college's image "in the eyes of the public, the taxpayer, the academicians, the military, the alumni, and, most importantly, the high school student." Without going into detail, the committee reported that "present abuses of the system generate unproductive physical demands and mental anxieties clearly not conducive to a Plebe's proper academic achievement." They found that due largely to upperclassmen harassment, few freshmen received enough to eat, got an adequate amount of sleep, or found time to study without interruption. Concerned that such abuses had almost overwhelmed "many of the admirable and positive advantages which can be expected to accrue to a consistent, mature, and well defined System for Plebe Training," the authors pushed for "a reorientation away from having the toughest plebe system in the country" to one in which knobs would face "a difficult, arduous, challenging and meaningful first year," not an "impossible one."[20]

The bulk of the Whitmire Report dealt with abstract theories about better educating the corps as to the purpose and meaning of plebe training. Encouraging cadets to take a "positive approach to a training situation," the committee suggested that by remaining "meticulous in appearance," avoiding vulgar language, and minding their manners, upperclassmen could train fourthclassmen "without using harsh or tyrannical treatment." Convinced that the "capabilities of the young men who comprise the Corps of Cadets are boundless," they expected the student body to "respond magnificently if they are made to understand the belief, the faith, the great trust being placed in their hands as a group responsible for the proper training of the newcomers to the school." The authors placed even "greater trust and authority" in the rising senior class, challenging all firstclassmen to keep a close watch over plebe training and suggesting that seniors form cadet boards of review that would investigate allegations of hazing.[21]

General Harris did not evince this same reverence for the corps' abilities, and he offered an interesting take on cadets' attitudes toward the plebe system. Some people advocated replacing knob training with more traditional forms of military instruction, but when pressed on this issue, Harris responded, "I find in my discussions with the cadets, they do not yet fully understand what the correct relationship is between an officer and an enlisted man, and consequently it is nebulous to them for me to try to substitute at this time a firm, courteous, correct, strict military relationship as a substitute for the fourth class system." Combined with the opinions expressed in the Whitmire Report, this assessment cast plebe year as a time to evaluate potential Citadel men, and not a period of formalized military training. With cadets more concerned with determining which men belonged at The Citadel than with who could lead a company into battle, the fourth class system had devolved into the ritualistic abuse that tormented students, parents, and school officials.[22]

The Whitmire Report quit theorizing on the building of whole men and the "boundless capabilities" of the corps when it came to reevaluating the practice of "dropping" freshmen for push-ups and regulating student behavior in the mess hall. By singling these two areas out for closer scrutiny, the reviewers exposed the most common methods cadets used for weeding out the "weak." The use of "on-the-spot push-ups" as a form of punishment had emerged during Mark Clark's tenure, and by 1968, it represented not only the "one feature which is most severely criticized by those whom [the committee] solicited reviews" but also the privilege cadets guarded most jealously. The 1966 *Fourth Class System Manual* restricted the number of push-ups upperclassmen could demand of freshmen at certain times, but these guidelines set no limits on how many times a freshman could be dropped in succession nor how long it should take to complete the exercise. Many upperclassmen drove freshmen to physical exhaustion by having them pound out repeated sets of push-ups, while others achieved similar results by exaggerating the cadence so that it might take fifteen minutes to complete fifteen repetitions. To remedy this, the Whitmire Report specified that the punishment be performed on "the *open* galleries and quadrangles of the barracks," and the repetitions follow a "normal cadence" with "no extended periods in the leaning rest position." In addition, upperclassmen could not assign freshmen more than fifteen push-ups every fifteen minutes. It fell upon fourthclassmen to "promptly inform any Upperclassmen of the point when he is in fact not eligible for additional push-up repetitions during a given period."[23]

At least one member of the panel demanded more drastic changes. Major C. A. Medberry, a chemistry professor and 1944 graduate of Texas A&M, wanted the use of punitive push-ups banned, declaring their only purpose was to achieve "discipline through fear." He pointed out the relative newness of the "tradition," concluding, "from what I have seen and heard, that this practice is not one designed to help with the overall objectives of training a fourth classman so much as it is to gratify a need to feel important and powerful in upperclassmen."[24]

The incessant harassment of freshmen at mealtimes posed another major problem for the reviewers. They learned that many knobs "find it *impossible* to eat at all during the lunch period" and noted that "every adult who testified before our committee, including cadets' parents, coaches of the athletic department and the school's public relations officer, *all of these* expressed the need for eating times to be pleasant periods, instead of times of horror for the freshmen." As part of their training, freshmen were expected to memorize and recite, verbatim, facts about the college's history, the names of all cadet officers, and wordy, scripted responses to inane questions. By constantly ordering freshmen to recount this "knob knowledge," many upperclassmen prevented plebes from eating. As a result, the Whitmire Report recommended not only limiting such information "to specific source documents i.e. *The Guidon* and the front page of the newspapers" but also eliminating any type of recitations in the mess hall. Two members found these measures inadequate. Donald Bunch, a 1948 Citadel graduate, recognized that because upperclassmen could still keep freshmen at attention or bracing during meals, a knob might *"legally have his time infringed upon in such a way as to leave no room for him to eat"* his food. Bunch suggested instead leaving the plebe system *"at the doors of the mess hall"* because *"all cadets, well-rounded as well as poorly adjusted, are entitled to three uninterrupted meals a day in a relaxed atmosphere."* Major Medberry agreed and pushed for specific provisions prohibiting "any possibility of a fourth-classmen being required to 'brace' or sit up without eating at any time after the blessing." He added that "the harassment of an individual is certainly without military value," and that school administrators must rein in not only "overzealous and unscrupulous" upperclassmen but any freshman who wants "to make it appear that he 'really has it tough but he is *man* enough to take it.'"[25]

In May 1968, General Harris delivered copies of the Whitmire Report to the Board of Visitors for their review. After deliberating and meeting with various cadets and members of the commandant's department, Harris and the board accepted most of the committee's recommendations. They commissioned a "complete rewrite" of the college's *Fourth Class System Manual*, and almost every passage from the Whitmire Report pertaining to the importance, purpose, and uniqueness of the fourth class system found its way into the new manual. The publication preached the necessity of positive leadership and demanded that every freshman receive adequate sleep, nourishment, and study time. Harris reinforced these provisions by threatening to expel any cadet who denied a freshman "any right, privilege or advantage to which he is legally entitled."[26]

The manual placed responsibility for the system squarely on the shoulders of the senior class. A firstclassman was assigned to each mess table to ensure that everyone ate "complete meals." Sophomores' interaction with freshmen was limited both to "reduce greatly major abuses to the intent and spirit of the System" and to allow thirdclassmen the opportunity to "observe the manner in which mature and experience[d] Seniors effectively supervise the plebes." To give senior cadets a vested interest in a plebe's well-being and to provide knobs with a "friend in the corps" who could help them adjust academically, militarily, and socially to Citadel life, Harris reinstated the detail system whereby freshmen were assigned to a senior "sponsor" for whom they would run errands and perform other duties. Worried that others might view this arrangement as a form of servitude, Harris stipulated that seniors assign their charges no tasks "distasteful to normal human relationships."[27]

For all their efforts, the authors of the Whitmire Report succeeded only in temporarily curbing hazing at The Citadel. Ignoring a recommendation of the Whitmire Committee, school officials made no effort to monitor how well or how poorly the revised fourth class system functioned. Had they done so, Citadel administrators would have discovered that the new push-up and mess hall polices were largely ineffectual in protecting freshmen. Without proper supervision, the use of excessive push-ups as a form of punishment continued unabated. In addition, the wording of the 1969 *Fourth Class System Manual* left out the Whitmire Committee's suggestion that push-ups be performed at a "normal cadence"; thus, the custom of drawing the repetitions out for extended lengths of time also endured.[28]

As for the mess hall, the concerns expressed by Bunch and Medberry proved prescient. Dismissing the proposal that cadets "not be required to recite on *any* item during the meal," school officials decided "fourthclassmen may be required to discuss current events in a mature and serious matter" as long as these discussions do not "interfere with the meals of the fourthclassmen." As school officials discovered later, by taking a broad definition of "current events," upperclassmen devised new ways to prevent plebes from eating at meal times.[29]

While struggling to corral rowdy upperclassmen, Harris and the Board of Visitors looked for ways to bolster the college's standing. The antiwar movement tarnished The Citadel's luster, but the war itself offered school officials ample opportunity to polish the institution's image as local, state, and national publications praised the battlefield heroics of Citadel alumni in Vietnam. The college held frequent ceremonies honoring graduates killed or wounded in the war, and these commemorations are vividly remembered by cadets from that era. One former student recalled, "The most haunting thing for me at The Citadel was when a Citadel cadet died in Vietnam. That night, when it was announced, they did echo taps. I'll never forget that as long as I live."[30]

Between 1963 and 1976, sixty-seven Citadel alumni died in Vietnam; forty-three of these deaths came between 1966 and 1969. During this time, the dedications of campus memorials, the unveiling of portraits, and the playing of echo taps strengthened the ties between the corps and U.S. military personnel. Hearing frequent reports of their friends dying overseas, most cadets despised antidraft demonstrations. Referring to protestors who burned their draft notices, one cadet asserted, "This is not our generation! These 'people' do not represent us." He called them traitors and regretted that "the American fighting man is dying so that these bearded, draft dodging, dope addicted, Communist-inspired, pseudo-intellectual coward[s] have the liberty and sanctuary" to disparage America.[31]

Although the corps' empathy for American soldiers heightened their disgust for antiwar demonstrators, it also opened the door for a wider critique of the war. In *The Shako*, a literary magazine containing poems, short stories, and essays written by cadets, a student poet lamented that "10,000 men may die before the sunrise / and leave a million children wondering." This discontent eventually spilled over into cadets' assessments of their college as the corps began to criticize Citadel administrators and challenge school policies. Some students began complaining publicly about old furniture in the barracks and stringent uniform regulations. Others questioned the administration's tendency to stress military duties over academic ones. To protest what they saw as nitpicky regulations, one group of cadets painted an image of Mickey Mouse on the water tower overlooking the campus. This admittedly limited rebelliousness fostered a certain degree of ideological tolerance within the corps. A few students defended Americans' right to protest and warned that outlawing dissent because it might damage the U.S. position in Vietnam "is one of the most dangerous courses that we could take."[32]

However, with some state lawmakers calling The Citadel "a luxury our state cannot afford," legislative threats to cut the school's funding quelled the corps' burgeoning unrest. Taking their cue from members of the Board of Visitors who continued blaming the school's woes on "outside forces," the besieged cadets saw the antiwar movement as an assault on themselves and their institution. When an antiwar organization mailed *The Brigadier* a letter arguing that the U.S. government had deliberately misinformed the public about Vietnam, the paper called the charges insulting to those serving overseas and wondered, "if honor is the most cherished principle of the cadet's life," what motivated those who opposed the war? In *The Shako*, a poet heard "democracy dying" over "the protests of cowards," while an essayist ridiculed those who protested while "soldiers died for their right to shirk." In November 1967, under the caption "No Hippies," an exasperated cadet cried that "the recent round of anti-war, anti-draft, anti-military, in fact, just about anti-everything demonstrations puts into a glaring light not only the growing disenchantment with the Vietnam War, but also sheds a most unfavorable light on the younger generation." Denouncing the protestors as "neither intellectual nor American," he urged the government to crack down on these members of society.[33]

The rage of "No Hippies" startled many members of the corps. One student pleaded for some form of compromise between "the fanatical stance of the true hippie" and the close-minded "nationalist who sets Victorian imperialistic sanctions above all else." Cadet Allen Beiner conceded Americans' right to dissent, but argued that legal protest fell short of destroying draft cards and burning the flag. Foreshadowing a shift in cadet opinion, Beiner affirmed his support of the war, but questioned the U.S. government's commitment to winning it.[34]

The Tet Offensive in January 1968 seemed to validate Beiner's concerns, and that year marked a turning point in the corps' attitude toward the war as well as the antiwar protestors. Many cadets accused politicians of hamstringing the military, and the 1968 yearbook honored alumni killed overseas while denouncing both "the protests of dissenters and promises of politicians." Later that May, Tom Brown, an assistant editor for *The Brigadier*, contributed a column on "The Right of Dissenting Opinions." Quoting Voltaire and drawing analogies to Socrates and Jesus, he defended the right to debate "antiquated, university regulations, oppressive governments, students' rights and civil rights." In that same issue, the newspaper's editor established the framework for dissent at The Citadel, acknowledging the benefits of constructive criticism, but reminding cadets "do not go too far. And never let those College Joes knock [The Citadel]."[35]

With this in mind, several members of the corps adopted certain aspects of the student movement compatible with their situation at a military college. Reminiscent of the Berkeley slogan "I am a student. Do not spindle, tear, or mutilate," an editorial in *The Brigadier* reminded school officials of students' individuality as well as their importance to the institution. Some argued for a reduced focus on the military and an increase in liberal arts courses. Tom Brown rendered a lighthearted, humorous evaluation of the Yippies without mocking or dismissing their views.[36]

Even moderate dissent worried school officials, though, especially since they spent much of 1968 cultivating the institution's image as an island of patriotic stability amid a sea of chaos. Throughout that tumultuous year, General Harris received numerous letters praising him for maintaining campus order. One correspondent claimed the "college stands out like a bright beacon" in troubled times. In Florida, a Rotary club member bragged that "one of those fine cadets can take care of five hippies." Parents congratulated Harris for pursuing true educational goals that counteracted the "hippie, Drop-out, Campus Riot, city riot–torn America we have today." When colleagues at other schools sought advice on how to avoid campus unrest, Harris replied smugly that "a disciplined environment" kept The Citadel unmarred by protest.[37]

Maintaining this "disciplined environment" proved more troublesome than Harris seemed willing to admit. When the administration refused to allow Brown to publish a cartoon picture of the biblical figure Samson being taunted by calls of "Fag" and "Long-Hair Freak," censorship of *The Brigadier* became an issue. While the earlier editorial staff described the newspaper as "the epitome of a free and uncensored press," this was not the case in late 1968. Each edition had to meet the approval of General Harris's assistant, Colonel Dennis Nicholson, who admitted removing passages he deemed "extremely detrimental" to the institution. In contrast, senior cadet Arthur von Keller complained to General Harris that "no criticism of any sort is allowed in any *student* publication." Eventually, the administration allowed the newspaper to run the cartoon, but not before Brown resigned his post as assistant editor due to Nicholson's excessive censorship.[38]

General Harris's self-proclaimed "oasis of order" proved to be a mirage during the 1969–1970 school year. Wishing to "radically change the ultra-conservative *Brigadier* of the past," the paper's new editor in chief, Jim Lockridge, encouraged students and faculty to submit articles reevaluating school policies. He broadened the paper's coverage of outside events, hoping to strike a balance within a school "military in its structure," but "primarily academic in its nature." Inspired by the "rising social revolution" that had already begun to ebb, he urged the corps to think critically of the government, society, and especially The Citadel.[39]

Many cadets heeded Lockridge's call. Several complained bitterly about the school's haircut policy. Others lobbied for new uniform requirements, longer furloughs, and televisions in the barracks. The cadets' lingering siege mentality tempered their protests, though, as they sought to improve their college without damaging its reputation. They regarded changes in the uniform policy, requests for appliances in the barracks, and decreased administrative intervention as positive goals, but treated "gripes" about mandatory chapel attendance, drill, and Friday afternoon parades as threats to The Citadel's uniqueness and therefore its value. The cadets realized that "None of us wants our school to become another Clemson," urging one another to keep this in mind the next time they muttered, "I hate this place."[40]

In an effort to stem cadet unruliness, General Harris mixed tough talk with minor concessions. He reduced the number of Saturday inspections, increased the number of furloughs, shortened drill periods, and looked to attract a more diverse group of Greater Issues speakers. At the same time, Harris emphasized the cadets' obligation to preserve the school's image, warning them of the threats posed by liberal legislators and societal antimilitarism. He promised to listen to complaints made through the proper channels, but indicating his disapproval of *The Brigadier*'s newest staff, he told cadets that proposals printed in the student newspaper would get a slow response.[41]

Harris's response failed to satisfy all cadets, and early in his senior year, Tom Brown and two friends began publishing *The Vigil*. Claiming to bring "to the surface the suppressed bitterness of a liberal minority," it blasted the administration's control of *The Brigadier* and bemoaned the poor quality of mess hall food. Not all students appreciated this subterranean critique of their institution, and they answered *The Vigil* with a conservative underground paper called *Common Sense*. Although most cadets dismissed the latter publication as a right-wing "propaganda rag," one that was possibly sponsored by school officials, the use of an underground newspaper to defend the establishment against another underground newspaper underscores the corps' somewhat schizophrenic reaction to the tumult of the 1960s. In the end, despite its popularity, *The Vigil* disappeared after only three installments when school officials threatened to uncover and expel the "small minority activist group in the cadet corps."[42]

By this time, many cadets had softened their position on the war and the protestors. A handful accepted that the conflict in Southeast Asia was not the result of a "plot for world-wide communist expansion." Some even considered the war futile. *The Brigadier* printed several cartoons ridiculing the U.S. government's heavy-handedness in stifling dissent. In November 1969, the *Charleston Evening Post* asked students from The Citadel, the College of Charleston, and nearby Baptist College for their opinions on an upcoming antiwar rally in Washington, D.C. All three condemned the protestors' actions, but only The Citadel spokesman conceded the activists' right to dissent. Another cadet opposed the goals of the fall "moratoriums," antiwar events that one observer has described as a "cascade of local demonstrations, vigils, church services [and] local petition drives," but respected this effort at legal, responsible protest. Reportedly, one Citadel student even participated in this nationwide event by wearing a black armband on the designated day.[43]

In the midst of this growing unrest at The Citadel, the May 1970 shootings at Kent State shocked the nation. Students at forty-four colleges engaged in some sort of demonstration. Several schools shut down for days, some for semesters. In an attempt to commiserate with those at other schools, Jim Lockridge printed an unauthorized copy of *The Brigadier* devoted entirely to Kent State. The front page featured a giant fist slamming down on the body of a bleeding student.[44]

The paper recorded a wide spectrum of reactions among the corps. In contrast to calls for sober reflection and open-minded tolerance, Doug Nelson compared student protests to Nazi book burnings and declared "To hell with tradition and down with sedition." Several cadets cheered the deaths of "four long hairs," while others reminded their classmates that cadets and "long hairs" shared common bonds as students. Most cadets sympathized with the National Guardsmen, but events closer to home muted the cadets' indictment of the protestors. Students at the University of South Carolina clashed with police and the National Guard on May 11, and some state legislators demanded harsh punishments for the demonstrators. One politician wanted to "annihilate" the offenders. Students at The Citadel undoubtedly had friends at USC, and proposals to "annihilate" them bothered many. For the most part, cadets wanted a break from the turmoil and called for a stable medium between violent protest and forceful repression.[45]

While cadet activism declined after May 1970, the corps did not return to its staunchly conservative ways. With increasing regularity, cadets grew their hair longer, refused to salute officers, and resisted most aspects of the military. Certainly, there remained a fair number of cadets who questioned what they saw as the benefits of "change for the sake of change," and who worried that relaxing the college's regulations would cost the school its unique military rigor. At the same time, numerous others pleaded with their colleagues to abandon the belief that "no matter what one does — The Citadel isn't going to change." These students clamored for more diverse Greater Issues speakers and an end to annoying "Mickey Mouse" regulations such as mandatory chapel attendance. One suggested that cadets be allowed to hang "posters, rugs, curtains, and lamps" in their rooms, while another revolted against a "dictatorship" that played only classical music in the mess hall, demanding, "Give us Funk, Crosby, Stills and Nash, The Who."[46]

Several of these students linked their appeals for change to the longstanding goals and claims of the college. One lamented that because the school "stifles the overall development of the student by placing in effect ridiculous regulations which serve no purpose beyond needlessly harassing cadets," The Citadel produced fewer citizen-soldiers who could "take command and lead men effectively in the defense of our nation." Another noted with regret, rather than pride, that the "already wide gap between the school and other institutions has grown wider." To remedy this, he and others urged school officials to abandon "archaic rules and practices" in order to attract more students and "save our school from the decay of sitting still in a fast-changing world." As part of this push to rid the college of "obsolescent traditionalism," several cadets lobbied school officials to amend the off-campus uniform requirement and allow upperclassmen to wear civilian clothes while in Charleston and the surrounding area. In 1970, the Board of Visitors reached a compromise with the corps, authorizing the wearing of a "blazer uniform" during specified leave times. The ensemble consisted of a blue coat bearing The Citadel's crest, gray slacks, and a specially designed tie. One cadet downplayed the significance of this change, maintaining "The Citadel man has been noted for being different for what he is, not how he looks or because his hair is shorter."[47]

Drug use also became a problem on campus during this time, and in November 1970, three cadets were arrested and expelled for selling amphetamines. Rather than condemn this illegal activity, students argued that because school rules banned coffee makers in the barracks, students used speed to study for exams or prepare for inspections. In the same issue that reported the bust, *The Brigadier* staff ran an article describing a "Marijuana High."[48]

Uneasy with these developments, Citadel alumni flooded the office of the president with complaints that their alma mater had grown "soft." General Harris had left by this time, replaced by Major General James W. Duckett, a 1932 graduate of The Citadel who had served the school as a chemistry professor, an administrative dean, and vice president. Compelled to reassert his authority on campus, General Duckett assembled all cadets in The Citadel's field house for an impromptu presidential address. Looking out at his audience, the general quipped, "Some of you have more hair on your mind than I have on my head," adding, "I have always thought that a Citadel man wanted to be identified as a Citadel man, and not, heaven forbid, to be mistaken for an ordinary college or university student." To those who disagreed, he snapped, "The solution is simple — transfer." Nevertheless, to discredit accounts that the president and the commandant ignored cadets' viewpoints, Duckett outlined a new, less stringent haircut policy both for freshmen and upperclassmen.[49]

He then chastised the students for their overall "sloppy" appearance, reminding them that their behavior and attitude had a direct bearing on the college's future. He announced that the administration needed their support to help "us keep up the flow of good men into the corps." Should the corps abdicate this responsibility, Duckett continued, The Citadel could well follow the lead of other military colleges that admitted civilian students only to "have either lost the corps or found it pushed in a corner as a kind of third cousin with bad breath." If cadets rose to the challenge, however, the college could continue "to foster patriotism and love of God and country and make no apology to anyone for it."[50]

Duckett's speech did little to alleviate the corps' morale problem. Torn between cadet calls for "relaxed disciplinary standards" and alumni's "strong demands" to "reduce cadet privileges, further restrict free time, and in general restore rigidity of discipline," the general leaned toward the latter. When the Board of Visitors ordered an end to the "laxness and permissiveness started by the previous administration," Duckett clamped down on the corps. School officials strengthened "the hand of both the President and the Board of Visitors" by increasing the number of offenses punishable by expulsion. As further proof of the administration's growing concern with student disdain for authority, two of the new regulations covered "disobedience" to school officials and "calling another cadet to personal account for having corrected or reported him while in the discharge of duty." Armed with these new directives, Duckett reported back to the board that the punishments for the 1971–1972 school year were "excessive both in numbers and severity." When such measures failed to bring the corps into line, the president and the Board of Visitors turned on one another, each questioning the ability of the other to recognize and fix the problems faced by the school.[51]

None of this sat well with the student body. The senior class president blamed Duckett's inconsistent behavior for the corps-wide malaise. The editor of *The Brigadier* found it impossible to reconcile "a presidential promise to eliminate the 'Mickey Mouse' side of The Citadel" with "a visible crackdown on enforcement of antiquated rules and regulations." He wondered what would happen if "The Citadel is ever taken to a Federal Court on civil liberties violations (mandatory chapel, weekend leave policy, etc.) and the judge was not a Citadel graduate?" He noted that "contrary to local popular belief, Federal laws and statutes supercede all state laws, rules, regulations, policies, and attitudes" and implored those who "hold Citadel tradition heavier in the balance than individual liberty, minority rights and protection of dissent" to replace their mantra of "love it or leave it" with "let's fix it."[52]

By the end of the school year, frustrated cadets began blatantly defying school authorities. In March 1972, cadet officers refused to attend a scheduled meeting with the commandant. That same month, the cadet regimental commander stood before the Board of Visitors and voiced the student body's dissatisfaction with what they considered an ineffectual president, overly detailed duties, and excessive administrative control over the corps. A few weeks before graduation, the current and rising members of The Citadel's Honor Court threatened to resign after General Duckett reversed one of the former group's decisions. After meeting with the president, the cadets withdrew their resignation lest the honor system "become another facet of school life not sufficiently controlled by the cadets." Their reasoning reflected many cadets' growing apprehension that due to the increasing involvement of the commandant's office in student affairs, "Every day the Corps loses a little piece of identity and a little bit more of 'esprit de corps' goes with it."[53]

Such cynicism colored the attitudes many cadets held toward the outside world as well. When the national antiwar movement of the 1960s gave way to the "popular antiwar mood" of the 1970s, The Citadel followed suit. By 1971, even General Harris hoped for an "honorable end to this undeclared, half-executed, and now unwanted war." For the first time, cadets acknowledged the existence of a credibility gap, and they issued sustained critiques of the U.S. government and its role in Vietnam. One embittered young man pointed out that, despite all the protests, politicians ignored the rallies, schools repaired damaged buildings, and friends of his died in a far-off land. Faced with these results, the cadet concluded that American society was "going to hell."[54]

The fact that students attending a military college with deep roots in a region often noted for its patriotism found aspects of the antiwar movement compatible with their ideals of citizenship and duty attests to the ideological malleability and broad appeal of the protestors' message. Intrigued by the energy of the protestors, certain members of the corps opened themselves up to new ideas and tried to promote cadet activism. Youthful rebelliousness and exuberance appealed to these cadets, but so did the military ideals of duty, honor, and country. As the corps vacillated between defending students' right to dissent and defending their school against outside dissenters, many cadets eventually came to realize that questioning the war, challenging school officials, and criticizing school policies did not necessarily constitute a treasonous attack on America or American GIs. In the end, many Citadel students decided to end their presumed isolation and start marching in step with their collegiate peers.

An emphasis on and a redefinition of manliness and manly behavior linked many Citadel cadets to their leftist contemporaries. In keeping with the early Cold War's emphasis on conformity and conservatism, good Citadel men, and by extension good Americans, of the 1940s and 1950s were expected to fit in, acquiesce, obey. During the 1960s, as the Cold War consensus crumbled, men rebelled, agitated, and questioned authority. Many cadets followed suit, and in doing so, they regarded themselves as no less manly than earlier alumni. The chauvinism of the cadets as well as their rebelliousness corresponded with many members of the New Left's views on proper gender roles. Many in both groups seemed convinced that waging war and protesting war were practices best left to men.[55]

The extent and volatility of student activism at The Citadel and other southern schools may have paled in comparison to that of their peers in other parts of the country, but it was not inconsequential. Except for mention of the civil rights movement, southern colleges and universities are often left out of general discussions about 1960s' campus unrest, with Merle Haggard's "Fightin' Side of Me" and "Okie from Muskogee" framing many people's perceptions of the region. Numerous authors have demonstrated the important impact that young black southerners had on the antiwar movement and the student movement, but many young white southerners were also swept up in the political ferment of the period, and not just as opponents of "peaceniks" and "integrationists."[56]

Such behavior corresponds with Rod Andrew's identification of a distinct "southern military tradition" that "combined elements of militarism" with "a heritage of individualism, personal autonomy, and rebellion *against* authority." This tradition encouraged Citadel students to embrace antiauthoritarian and nonconformist attitudes, but reject calls for revolution. Ideologically opposed to the most extreme and visible elements of the antiwar movement, many Citadel students nonetheless challenged authority and worked to reform their campus, more so than their country.[57]

In their efforts to deromanticize popular perceptions of the 1960s, many scholars make it a point to note that during this era, "*most* students moved through the standard labyrinth of courses, examinations and graduate requirements." In *Campus Wars*, Kenneth Heineman reminds readers that "it is vital to study institutions where the majority of students and faculty were either prowar or apathetic—a more perfect mirror of American society in the 1960s." Although these points are well taken, they tend to present student activism as an either/or proposition when, in actuality, it was more personal and more complex than these assessments imply. The resulting somewhat Manichean view of the era diminishes the activities of less "radical" students by failing to take into account less dramatic variations of what might qualify as "radicalism."[58]

In his study of Vanderbilt University, historian Paul Conkin acknowledges the importance of location and community in shaping and evaluating campus unrest, arguing that viewed within a regional context, the actions of many southern students in the late 1960s "seemed almost revolutionary." Clarence Mohr makes the same observation in his history of Tulane University, noting that the behavior of young southerners was "measured . . . by a different and less permissive social yardstick." While Citadel cadets, like most students of the era, refrained from seizing buildings, calling for revolution, or rioting in the streets, they did break from tradition and begin protesting college regulations, questioning authority, and adopting countercultural modes of dress and behavior. In doing so, they confronted an institutional and regional culture that leaned heavily toward a defense of the status quo. The relative conservatism of The Citadel's "radicals" exposes the artificiality of pitting "revolutionaries" against "the silent majority," suggesting that the era's social and political battle lines were neither as polarized nor as rigid as many believe. Taking this into account when evaluating student activism at The Citadel and other southern campuses might serve the dual purpose of continuing to demystify the 1960s, while at the same time, acknowledging the prominence rather than the absence of youthful rebelliousness.[59]

CHAPTER FIVE

"A *Disciplined College* in an *Undisciplined Age*"

The Citadel and Southern Distinctiveness

 In December 1970, the Citadel Board of Visitors issued a "Statement of Role and Scope" for the upcoming decade. Surveying the list of challenges that the school faced in the previous decade, they boasted that by resisting pressures for "rapid expansion, for lowered admission standards, for response to militant demands for special treatment and unique curricula, and for the modification of time honored rules of behavior," The Citadel had emerged from the 1960s "as a strong, mature institution with roots deep in a distinguished past, with an unshaken set of standards." The 1971 Citadel *Catalogue* provided a more revealing indication of the school's present condition, however, for unlike in the past, that year's edition contained no "good signs for the future."[1]

Such an assessment mirrored the broader temper of the times with political scandals, military defeat, rising inflation, and oil crises marking the early 1970s as a time of "confusion, frustration and a widespread feeling that America had lost its direction." An already pessimistic and frustrated populace grew increasingly jaded and self-involved as proof of the nation's declining global stature mounted and accounts of governmental wrongdoing surfaced with alarming regularity. Such traumas punctured, as C. Vann Woodward put it, the "national legend of success and invincibility," and, in the process, blurred the decades-old distinction many had drawn between an "enlightened" North (read America) and a "benighted" South. In his 1974 work, *The Americanization of Dixie*, John Egerton concluded that "having failed for the first time to win at war, having found poverty and racism alive and menacing in its own house, the North has lately shown itself to be more and more like the South in the political, racial, social and religious inclinations of its collective majority."[2]

This realization that the North was, in the words of James Cobb, "no longer, and perhaps never had been, quite the picture of health it had always seemed," came as a blow to northerners and southerners alike. Having lost their long-standing counterpoint in terms of assessing their own cultural, social, political, and economic distinctiveness, "the white South's uncontrollable urge to self-obituarize" continued unabated as "the last rites were still being said in profusion for a South that had actually never looked better." Indeed, money, jobs, and people flowed southward, toward a region that "held out the prospect of relaxed life-styles and lower living costs to an increasing number of Americans willing to forgive the Sunbelt South for its past transgressions and overlook its enduring deficiencies." This did not sit well with writers like Egerton who found the "Americanization of Dixie" just as troubling as the "Southernization of America." He lamented that in its rush "to rejoin the Union," the South had become "indistinguishable from the North and East and West." He cringed as an "on-the-make South, its views nationalized, its virtues evaporating if not already dissipated, is coming back to the Mother Country." John Shelton Reed noted that even *Esquire* magazine got into the act, declaring "the South is over" and explaining to readers how "the Cracker crumbled."[3]

While some mourned what they saw as the end of regional distinctiveness, others conjured up an image of the South and its people that promised guidance, stability, and proof that the nation would indeed rise again. The mainstream media celebrated its version of southern culture through television shows such as *The Waltons* and *Hee Haw*. With images of rural serenity and hillbilly high jinks warming viewers' hearts and picture tubes, Tennessee lawman Buford Pusser sated a craving for law and order. Ignoring the genre's edgier themes of alcoholism, infidelity, and murder, Richard Nixon applauded country music for strengthening America by renewing family and religious values. The exposure of Nixon's own less-than-admirable values also bolstered the South's reputation as North Carolina Senator Sam Ervin, a past opponent of the civil rights movement, presided over the Watergate hearings, charming viewers with his wit, piety, and folksy demeanor.[4]

As these scenes suggest, many of those who hoped that the South could, as Walker Percy put it, "save" the Union, described southerners in primarily masculine terms. Writer Albert Murray welcomed what he saw as a "workable coalition of poor whites, liberal whites and minorities" that understood that "Jimmy Carter's manhood is entwined with Andrew Young's, just like Huck

Finn's was with Jim's." Historian Paul Gaston remarked on a growing faith that this newest South might show the rest of the nation "how men may live harmoniously in a complex, interracial, urban society."[5]

Men at The Citadel tapped into these themes, linking the health of their school and their nation to the corps of cadets' ability to produce manly citizens. With the ranks of Citadel men having expanded to include, to some degree, African Americans and, to a greater degree, those who felt free to question tradition and authority, Citadel cadets and alumni elevated their exceptional manliness, above all else, as the key component of their distinctive purpose and value as citizen-soldiers. Convinced that the leadership of strong, tough, honest, disciplined men — Citadel men — was essential to the restoration of American greatness, many cadets and alumni made preservation of the system and environment that produced such men their paramount duty. Such efforts were intensified by the same regional identity crisis that was driving many white southerners "to search frantically for some tangible and demonstrative reaffirmation of their cultural distinctiveness." In both cases, but especially at The Citadel, a rarefied masculinity served as the cornerstone of an identity that many believed was uniquely southern as well as uniquely American. Thus, a desire to protect the manly composition of the corps permeated campus discussions, influencing decisions regarding the fourth class system, the readmission of civilian students, and even the design of class rings. Many argued that any dilution of the corps' masculine qualities and ideals would cost the nation and college dearly, denying the former scores of quality citizens and paving the way for coeducation and ultimate destruction of the latter.[6]

As schools across America struggled "in an era of energy shortages, runaway inflation, of recurrent recessions, of diminished federal support for higher education, of a declining college-age population," low enrollments hit The Citadel especially hard, raising serious questions about the institution's overall purpose, value, and obligations. In 1969, the Board of Visitors recognized that "The Citadel finds its traditional functions seriously endangered by steadily falling undergraduate applications," and they scrambled to attract more students. Mindful of the concerns of a disillusioned public, college publications promoted The Citadel as "one of the few schools in our country that pays attention to the development of a sense of honor and duty as part of the education of a young man." Such appeals gained greater traction in the wake of the Watergate scandal as writers for *The Guidon* informed incoming freshmen, "In our society today, honor has become an even more treasured asset as we witness politicians and other respected leaders participating in less than honorable activities." One student appreciated that "here we are teaching honor while we watch the rest of the world entangle itself in a host of dishonorable events." He warned that without institutions such as The Citadel, "We must be prepared to see the world crumble beneath our feet, for certainly man cannot exist without trustful relationships and communication." A series of widely publicized cheating scandals at the national service academies inflated the corps' ego, prompting the authors of the 1977 *Guidon* to remark that although "honor systems have not worked" at other schools, "honor is here at The Citadel."[7]

Another common theme ran through much of the literature sent to new and prospective cadets, one that had played a large role in the past and would play an even larger one in the years to come. High school students across America opened letters from The Citadel demanding to know "Are you man enough to accept a challenge" and "red blooded enough to venture into a system of education that is unique?" The reader learned that The Citadel offered "men of all races . . . a keen sense of 'belonging' in the unique fellowship of the Corps," where "each man stands on his own merit." Correspondence to accepted applicants bore much the same message, assuring teenagers that "becoming a member of The Citadel's *corps d'elite* will make you the man you've always desired to be." Each letter emphasized the importance of the college's "*male environment*" in preserving The Citadel's reputation as a "*disciplined college in an undisciplined age.*"[8]

This emphasis on honor and masculinity would eventually pay off, but in the meantime an emerging local threat upped the pressure on Citadel administrators to fill the barracks and classrooms. In 1968, the South Carolina General Assembly debated whether or not to add the College of Charleston to its list of state-supported colleges and universities. This proposal alarmed Citadel personnel for two reasons: they resented new competition for already limited state funds, and they construed the institution's conversion to public status as the first step toward consolidating all Charleston area colleges into one university. The Citadel's enrollment difficulties exacerbated both these concerns since state legislators were not likely to maintain their financial and political support of a college that consistently operated at well below its peak capacity.[9]

The findings of an internal "long range Academic Planning Committee" designed to study the situation drew a mixed response. The committee had little trouble convincing the Board of Visitors that the college could boost its overall image by expanding its graduate program, but their second proposal touched off a debate that raged for the next five years. In it, they presented the board with a choice: "to have a good corps of cadets by getting rid of the dead wood — in the hope that the community will give its support; or to utilize the faculty and facilities to the fullest to attract students and reduce the corps." Given the "present feeling against the military" and "the immediate need for educational opportunity in the local area," committee members favored opening the school up to civilian, nonveteran "day students," warning, "If we do not assume these responsibilities, somebody else certainly will do so."[10]

Acknowledging the economic and political benefits of increasing The Citadel's service to "the citizens of this state," the board authorized the enrollment of a limited number of "special students" for the 1970–1971 school year. These students consisted of fifth-year Citadel seniors who chose not to remain in the corps of cadets, juniors and seniors from other colleges who wanted to take classes that The Citadel offered but their schools did not, third-year attendees of The Citadel's evening program who wanted to attend day classes, and junior college transfers. While most of these specifications came straight from the academic committee's report, the board tweaked the original proposals a bit in order to protect what they saw as the school's most important attribute, citizen-soldiers trained and educated in an all-male environment. The first modification stipulated that other than fifth-year seniors, no other Citadel cadets could transfer into the civilian program. The second set of changes is more revealing, for while extolling their commitment to the citizens of South Carolina, the board limited such obligations by stressing that only "evening *male* students" and "junior and senior *male* students" could take classes with the corps.[11]

At least one board member viewed these reservations as potentially "disastrous." A month before the South Carolina legislature shifted the College of Charleston from private to public status, James Timmerman briefed his colleagues on the primary issues vexing Citadel administrators, highlighting the "apparent decline in interest by young men in all-male military colleges" and "the specter of a permanent, aggressive, growing competitor within the same city." Faced with such threats, Timmerman deemed it foolish to bar women from Citadel classrooms, warning that "an unreasonable insistence on maintaining absolutely the *status quo* might well jeopardize the essentials of military education that The Citadel is now trying to protect." Urging the board and other school officials to "separate carefully the important *essentials* of military education from the trivia," Timmerman placed mandatory drill and ROTC training for an all-male uniformed corps of cadets in his "essential" column while ascribing trivial status to all-male classes taught by uniformed faculty.[12]

The tensions generated by low enrollment and shifting societal expectations were not peculiar to The Citadel. National publications such as *Time* and *U.S. News and World Report* featured articles on the changes taking place at the service academies and all-male military boarding schools as a result of "the recession, the permissiveness of modern parents and public irascibility over the Vietnam War." They reported that these developments had forced many schools to close, while others sought a "more relaxed atmosphere inside the classroom and out" by cracking down on hazing, broadening their curricula, and courting student opinions on certain policy issues. *Time* revealed that one college had "even gone so far as to turn co-ed." Institutional spokespeople defended these "more lenient regimes" as necessary adaptations to changing cultural and societal demands and pointed to the positive results of lower attrition rates, larger student bodies, and rising grade point averages. On the other hand, skeptics of such changes wondered, "How much can a military academy relax and still remain military?"[13]

While most Citadel officials fought any attempt to "de-militarize" the college, practicality forced them to make some concessions. When a motion to allow civilians to take engineering and physics courses at The Citadel came before the board, proponents of the plan defended it as a sure-fire way to increase the school's revenue and popularity since the College of Charleston offered no majors in either subject. To bolster their case, they pointed out that admitting these students would cause no distractions owing to the fact that "because of the severe demands of these academic fields, the student majors are likely to be conservative and fully occupied in their courses." When opponents of the measure deemed it an "opening wedge, a foot in the door to 'civilianize' the college," their counterparts shot back, "If our educational activities are limited to cadets only, decreasing enrollments are almost certain to involve decreasing financial reports and the eventual phasing out of the corps of cadets." Eventually the two sides compromised, allowing only juniors and seniors to take engineering and science courses during the day.[14]

This halting acceptance of certain changes put the board in a precarious position as outside pressures to attract more students intensified. In January 1972, a "blue ribbon" panel appointed by the governor completed its review of South Carolina's public colleges and universities. The report, published and endorsed by the South Carolina Budget and Control Board, sent shockwaves across The Citadel's campus. The committee decided that by accepting one thousand to fifteen hundred more students per year, The Citadel could better "utilize existing facilities and administrative staff" and save $750,000 annually. Essentially, these figures would require The Citadel to expand its civilian programs since even if the corps' numbers rebounded, total student enrollment would still fall well shy of the suggested optimum capacity. Pulled between conflicting internal and external demands, one board member observed that the institution stood at "another crossroads in its long history and development."[15]

To help them choose which path to take, the board asked Citadel faculty, staff, and students to help them decide whether or not to allow more civilian students, especially female civilian students, to enter the day program. Civilians already taking classes at The Citadel advocated admitting "all qualified male students," while the school's American Association of University Professors (AAUP) chapter requested that "The Citadel accept qualified day students, both men and women, for full participation in the college's academic program and related activities."[16]

Others condemned both these measures, calling the existing day program corrosive and unnecessary. A history professor mocked those who considered civilian students "a panacea to cover all the ills of sliding enrollment" and urged Citadel administrators to focus exclusively on meeting and expanding the corps' capacity. Tying the institution's value and appeal to its all-male barracks and classrooms, he predicted that admitting women would destroy The Citadel, not save it. In his opinion, if the college abandoned its single-sex system, applications would dry up and the corps would wither away.[17]

Several cadets expressed similar views, although they saw the situation as much more dire. Aware that the school risked losing a great deal of financial and political support should it ignore the Budget and Control Board's directives, cadet Harry Rivers evaluated two of the most widely considered options: increase the size of the corps by lowering admission standards or accept more day students. He opposed both measures, viewing the latter as the "ultimate defeat" of The Citadel. Instead, Rivers pushed for a vigorous public relations drive, insisting that few people would consider cutting the school's funding upon learning that it "shall produce the bulk of intelligent leadership for the state of South Carolina."[18]

Others were not so optimistic, and their protests expose the extent to which many defenses of the college's traditions and purpose depended upon gendered assessments of men's and women's proper social spheres. Casting the school's rigorous military environment as an absolutely masculine realm, completely incompatible with perceived female capabilities and sensibilities, several Citadel men advanced the somewhat circular argument that efforts to "civilianize" the college would lead to the admission of women and that the admission of women would "demilitarize" and ultimately destroy the school. When the college's Faculty Council and AAUP chapter signed a petition supporting the acceptance of female students into the day program, the chairman of the Board of Visitors dismissed it, responding simply, "This is a military college and it will remain so." Upon learning of a push to make faculty uniform requirements optional, a request the board refused on the grounds that "teachers would probably start wearing turtle necks, beads, etc.," a reporter for *The Brigadier* wondered if such a change foreshadowed the hiring of female teachers. Another student connected such initiatives to a larger attempt by "liberal forces in education, in the guise of progress and enrollment growth, [who] are trying to do away with the old traditions and today's unique educational institutions i.e. Winthrop and The Citadel." It is worth noting that the author referred to the former as a "girl's school" and the latter as a "military college."[19]

With the college in its "death throes," cadet Gordon Bell announced that should The Citadel accept one thousand more students, including "co-eds, then they better find 1001 new students, because the day they bring girls into my once military college is the day before I leave." He argued that allowing more women to attend The Citadel's evening program posed no problem so long as they remained separate "from the strictly military life and background of cadets and veterans." Believing that The Citadel's "military reputation" set it apart from other schools, Bell predicted that if college officials chose to "de-emphasize our military status," presumably by admitting women, the institution would soon become just "another small liberal arts school with an ROTC program." A cartoon accompanied Bell's article showing the Grim Reaper preparing to shove a shackled, kneeling cadet into an open grave. The doomed man's headstone read, "South Carolina Corps of Cadets, 1842–197? . . . A proud body pierced through the heart while yet in its infancy. An honorable future denied."[20]

Citing "the preservation of the Military College is the primary consideration," the board voted against any significant expansion of the college's civilian programs. They agreed that the general admission of day students would serve as the "opening gambit in this blue print for disaster" since "the courts could not and would not accept any arbitrary limitations such as the sex, home residence, or educational major of the applicants." Still needing to address the concerns raised by the Budget and Control Board, the board conceded that "a limited number of day students of an appropriate type should be admitted," and they authorized the evening college to begin granting undergraduate degrees.[21]

Even these relatively minor concessions raised the hackles of Citadel traditionalists. Two recent graduates argued that "bringing in larger numbers of civilian students — even at night — is contributing to the further decline of the corps" and would inevitably lead to the "*demise of the South Carolina Military Academy.*" Upset that their alma mater had become a "half-assed military college" by permitting "civilians, women, etc. to become Citadel graduates," they regretted that "In trying to 'serve the community,' we are rapidly destroying our ability to serve the community and nation in a way that few other schools have done — to turn out Citadel men who have an unequaled record of service and leadership." In the eyes of these two men, at least, the admission of lesser citizens, namely women and those men who had not had their manliness tested by the fourth class system, would diminish the reputation of the true citizen-soldiers produced by the corps.[22]

Many of the complaints about undeserving "outsiders" masquerading as Citadel men echoed earlier complaints about veteran students, and sure enough, the changes occurring at The Citadel revived tensions between the two groups. With most cadets aware that the money generated by the school's "peripheral programs" kept the school afloat during this time, the rivalry centered not around the veterans' presence on campus, but with their right to bear the mark of true Citadel men: The Citadel ring. Many Citadel alumni treat their class rings with a reverence bordering on idolatry. Pat Conroy opens *The Lords of Discipline* with "I wear the ring," a phrase he later called "the best line I have ever written and the best English sentence I am capable of writing." Seniors count the days until they receive their rings in a formal ceremony held in Summerall Chapel, and some graduates wear them on the ring finger of their left hands, often over their wedding bands, as a symbol of their loyalty to and affection for their alma mater. Each edition of *The Guidon* listed the ring's many exceptional qualities, emphasizing that it is the "heaviest all-gold college ring in the United States." Most importantly, the ring "denotes not a member of a certain class, but the true Citadel man."[23]

On Valentine's Day 1970, cadet Jim Herritage fired the first shot in the war of the ring when he wrote an editorial for *The Brigadier* entitled "A Matter of Pride." In it, Herritage alerted readers to the "introduction of a new program which will allow civilian day students to infiltrate our campus and eventually pass themselves off as 'Citadel Men' with their unearned Citadel ring." He called into question the manliness of noncadets, arguing that "To those who graduate from The Citadel without tasting of a year long 'Plebe System,' cold morning formations, inspections, parades, and confinements, their Citadel rings are unearned symbols of achievement to which they have absolutely no right." He claimed that allowing "pseudo-Citadel men" to wear the ring devalued the accomplishment of cadets, and he insisted that the privilege belong only to the "corps d'elite."[24]

Herritage's comments unleashed a torrent of responses. One cadet deemed the ring "inappropriate for 'outsiders,'" adding, "We cadets are uniquely proud of the corps, and our pride is embodied in *our* class ring." Two Citadel graduates assumed that "allowing veterans and civilian students to qualify as 'Citadel Men' via the 'backdoor route' without having gone through a 'plebe system' and military training must surely gall any alumnus who has earned his ring the hard way." They maintained that such a practice "violates the ideals and code of ethics The Citadel has always stood for AND BECOME MOST FAMOUS FOR."[25]

On the other side, a Citadel professor connected such protests to the "provincialism that is rapidly strangling this institution as an effective entity in higher education in South Carolina." One veteran resented "being told that I reduce anyone's reputation by my presence." Reminding cadets of both their military service and their vital financial contribution to the college, most veterans believed themselves "just as capable of upholding the values of the Corps of Cadets as anyone." Some veterans did not find the corps' values worth defending, as they criticized the cadets' lack of "leadership qualities" and their tendency to "rule by punishment."[26]

On April 23, 1971, *The Brigadier* printed one editorial and fifteen letters to the editor from well over one hundred members of the corps arguing that only cadets should receive a Citadel ring. While some emphasized the veterans' "outsider" status by opposing "the devaluation of the ring through wear by increased numbers of non-cadets," the arguments of numerous other cadets demonstrate how much of their own identity depended upon The Citadel's ability to build, not just men, but a special breed of men, one far superior to those who had not gone through the fourth class system. The highest-ranking junior on campus explained that "for a four year period cadets are trained, disciplined, and educated in the tradition of Citadel Men," and only those who had "withstood the demands of both cadet military and academic systems deserve the ring." Almost all the letters stressed that "any man that has not been faced with the challenges of the fourth class system and met it, any man who has not been confined only to the life of a Citadel cadet, cannot call themselves whole 'Citadel Men.'" Another cadet commended the veterans for their past service, but concluded "the Corps wishes to be branded with a ring of gold" that indicated to others that "through a regimented four year system [they were] molded, as if by a blacksmith's hands, into Citadel Men."[27]

Despite such impassioned pleas, it was only when women qualified to wear the ring that Citadel officials acted. Four years after Herritage's article first appeared, the Association of Citadel Men authorized a separate ring to be worn by graduates of the college's civilian programs. This resolution came as more and more women earned Citadel diplomas from the school's evening college, a link *The Brigadier* confirmed when it reported that the new "ring was first considered after the Corps expressed dissatisfaction with sharing their ring with non-cadets and especially female night students."[28]

Given its central role in the building of manly citizens, debates over the fourth class system took on added importance during this time. Some alumni believed it had become too easy and thus diminished their alma mater's "product." Others feared it had grown too harsh and damaged the college's reputation. High-ranking administrators worried that rumored and confirmed abuses of the system contributed to the school's enrollment woes. Most cadets regarded any tampering with "their" system as further evidence of how heavy-handed school officials would eventually destroy The Citadel.

Soon after assuming office, as part of his pledge to "eliminate rules that cannot be proven to add measurably to the making of a Citadel Man," General

Duckett ended the practice of dropping freshmen for push-ups, a move that sparked a fierce and somewhat unusual reaction from the corps. In an emergency meeting of the cadet Presidential Advisory Committee, the committee members decided that the general's order raised two crucial questions: who runs the corps and is "The Citadel primarily an academic institution or primarily a military school"? The impetus for the first question seems obvious, but the second one implied that regardless of whether students wore uniforms, drilled, or stood inspections, The Citadel's military status depended upon an upperclassmen's ability to punish a plebe physically. In regard to the second question, Duckett replied that "academics come before military always." As for who ran the corps, he maintained that all Citadel personnel had a hand in student affairs. As proof of this, he met with the cadets, listened to their objections, and reinstated the push-up policy, albeit on a limited basis with an eye toward "long range gradual reduction."[29]

This time frame turned out to be more immediate than Duckett planned. By February 1971, the general had again outlawed push-ups because "upperclassmen abused the rules." In an interview with *The Brigadier*, Duckett explained his decision, citing his firm belief "that you don't train someone through harassment." While utilization of proper training techniques had some impact on Duckett's action, the school's declining enrollment figures entered into the equation as well. In his annual report to the Board of Visitors in June 1972, Duckett characterized the past school year as "one of contrasts, of substantial gains in many areas, and of disconcerting setbacks in others." That previous August, he had welcomed a large incoming freshman class and hoped that "we had successfully reversed the anti-military and anti-discipline sentiments" of the previous era. These hopes faded as Duckett watched the increase in students dwindle due to "our excessive losses of fourth year men." The process repeated itself the next year, leading Duckett to suspect "that the bitterness we detected among fourthclassmen who withdrew last year may have discouraged some applicants from enrolling this fall." With this in mind, he noted that ending push-ups as well as "no longer requiring the 'knob cut' after the initial in-processing unit" had been a "great morale boost" for freshmen.[30]

Many upperclassmen could not have cared less about plebe morale. Barred from punishing freshmen physically, they heaped demerits and tours upon them. This proved less than rewarding, however. Upperclassmen dismissed the present fourth class system as "worthless," grumbling that first-year cadets "do not endure enough to be proud of their plebe year." The editor of *The Brigadier* observed that Duckett's initiatives had bred a freshman class that failed to meet Citadel standards, who "neither act nor look like freshmen in the past."[31]

An editorial writer for *The Brigadier* agreed, attributing every problem at The Citadel to changes in the fourth class system. While easing up on freshmen might keep them from quitting, he argued, "It doesn't instill as much class pride, or even school pride for that matter." Editor Ralph Towell agreed that the "morale and discipline of the entire corps has suffered" from the dilution of the fourth class system. Calling the system the "backbone of the corps," he lashed out at those administrators and faculty members who he believed wished to eliminate plebe year altogether. He absolved the corps of any fault, recognizing "there have been some abuses," but very few "have actually been damaging to the freshmen." He concluded that "if anything, the system should be made tougher and at the same time more meaningful" so that all cadets might learn to deal with adversity while improving their physical fitness. A handful of cadets took their objections a step further, adding the abolition of push-ups to the long list of terminal diseases afflicting The Citadel. One cadet called it hypocritical for Duckett to venerate "the whole Citadel Man," but then abolish "an integral part of the training of the whole man." One senior alleged The Citadel "is dying before me" due in large part to the "relaxing of the plebe system."[32]

While cadets complained that the fourth class system no longer posed a challenge for freshmen, school officials worried that they had not done enough to curtail hazing. In November 1971, the Faculty Council sent a memo to General Duckett alerting him to the "serious and potentially dangerous" problem of "physical hazing at The Citadel." In February 1972, the Board of Visitors cited abuses of the fourth class system as one of four "problem areas." A corresponding study of the college found that almost all professors believed "the fourth class system seems to be practiced at The Citadel chiefly to determine how much physical and mental abuse an incoming student can take." Even South Carolina Governor and Citadel graduate John West received a letter from an outraged parent describing the physical and mental harassment occurring at The Citadel. With the school losing about 20 percent of the freshman class every year, General Duckett conceded that "in concept, the fourth class system is a superb vehicle for providing leadership training for young men, but in practice, the abuses appear to have grown to the point" where they cost The Citadel much-needed students. As Duckett grew "weary of mailing apologies to the parents of the victims of the abuses," he and the board authorized another formal evaluation of the fourth class system and its purpose at The Citadel.[33]

This new Fourth Class System Review Committee consisted of six cadets from the upper three classes, the school's chaplain, the athletic director, three members of the commandant's office, an associate dean, and the director of admissions. From the start, the panelists made it clear that they recognized and appreciated the purported goals of the fourth class system. They considered it "essential to the moulding of character," "intimately related to the existence of The Citadel as a *Military College*," and "the very indispensable basis of The Citadel Man concept." With 72 percent of the corps convinced that plebe year would "make me a better individual," the committee members described the fourth class system as the "mortar holding the Corps together and distinguishing it from other" student bodies, predicting that without it, the corps of cadets "would wither to death in short order."[34]

At the same time, the committee recognized that abuses of the fourth class system threatened the livelihood of the very institution it supposedly enhanced. As proof that plebe training was "*not* working as programmed or desired," they submitted survey results showing that many of the students who left The Citadel were not malcontents who resented or disliked military discipline. On the contrary, interviews with former cadets and their parents indicated that initially these young men were drawn to The Citadel's reputation for academic, martial, and physical rigor. They quit only after being denied adequate food and rest and "because they were physically hazed . . . all three of which are direct violations of the regulations governing the fourth class system." Turning the standard defense of the fourth class system on its head, the reviewers warned that allowing The Citadel "to drift along as we do now" could also lead to the "death of the Corps" and "destroy the mystique, utility and validity of The Citadel Man concept." To prevent this from occurring, the committee hoped to convince cadets that an effective fourth class system should "promote comradeship, builds confidence and realistic optimism, leads to a feeling of inner fullness within the individual, and a sense of his purpose in life." These qualities, they added, "are the basis of the 'whole man,' which, ideally, is in turn the basis of The Citadel Man."[35]

Like the 1969 Whitmire Report, the 1972 study uncovered "substantial areas of abuses," including lack of food, sleep, and study time as well as physical haz-ing and "degradation of the individual." The committee found that the earlier reforms had done little to curb hazing due to a combination of lax enforce-ment and faulty reasoning. For example, only six of the Whitmire Report's twenty-two major recommendations were still in effect three years later. Very few cadets had copies of the *Fourth Class System Manual*, while those who did viewed the publication with "disdain." Despite rules prohibiting such behavior, upperclassmen still harassed plebes during the three-hour block set aside as Evening Study Period (ESP). Directly refuting a crucial pillar of the Whitmire Report, the 1972 committee revealed "that the idea that the First Class is re-sponsible for, and controls the fourth class system, is a myth."[36]

The committee confirmed that almost all cadets despised the ban on push-ups and physical punishment, noting that the practice had not ceased, it had simply moved "underground" or, more accurately, behind closed doors. Many upperclassmen "used the abolishment as good reason to fashion more cruel 'correctives'" such as "breast plate beatings."[37] Rather than cracking down on such behavior, the committee decided that it would be best to appease cadets by reinstating the push-up policy on a "limited trial basis." Under their plan, freshmen could not be dropped after the middle of October, and only junior and senior students on the training cadre could administer the punishment. Furthermore, a plebe could only perform fifteen repetitions every fifteen min-utes, "without deviations such as extended 'holds.'" Upperclassmen could re-quire "*no more than* sixty push-ups per day per man in any case," with plebes being "honor bound" to stop once they reached the sixty push-up limit.[38]

Mealtimes remained "the major source of routine abuse," and although the 1972 Committee found the Whitmire Report's minority opinions on the issue particularly enlightening, they did not consider enacting them. Instead they advocated regulating mess hall behavior in stages, lifting restrictions and granting privileges with an eye toward "gradually 'easing off' on freshmen as the year progressed." They were adamant that all cadets should receive ade-quate nourishment, and suggested warning the corps "that continuation of the 'family style' mess is contingent upon proving the value of that option."[39]

With the only real change being the restoration of push-ups, the new fourth class system did not differ significantly from the old one. Convinced that "only the cadets can resolve some of the more serious problems which have devel-oped over a period of many years," the commandant, Colonel William Crabbe

Jr., gave the corps more responsibility for policing their ranks, instructing tactical officers "to spend as much time as possible away from the companies and to act only in an advisory capacity." *The Brigadier* celebrated the upcoming "year of change" as upperclassmen welcomed the chance to "let the corps run the corps." Even the Board of Visitors expected the 1972–1973 school term "to be a watershed in the overall revitalization of the corps."[40]

Such accolades proved premature as the hazing of freshmen continued to drive away students. With the corps "once again turned over to cadets," almost 19 percent of the freshman class quit during the 1973–1974 school year. Most had left by October, just over a month into the first semester. Charged with monitoring plebe training for that year as well as the next, the chairman of the Fourth Class System Review Committee, Citadel Athletic Director Eddie Teague, noted a great deal of improvement, but admitted that several issues addressed in both the 1969 and 1972 reviews remained unresolved. In a memo to General Duckett, Teague reiterated that the "fourth class system is and should be a major factor in the development of the character of Citadel Men," but urged school leaders to discredit the "faulty concept that a tough system must be a harsh demeaning one."[41]

Other committee members regretted that the "tradition of a cadet not reporting the improper behavior of another of the same or higher class is still a serious problem," with freshmen accepting hazing as "part of the game" and looking forward to when "their turn would come." In private interviews and anonymous surveys, several cadets broke their code of silence and rattled off a litany of violations, ranging from vandalism — scratching brass belt buckles, scuffing shoes, trashing rooms — to physical assaults — "kicks in the shins," "beatings with broom, sword, fists (on chest)," hanging from exposed pipes in cadet rooms, "shaving cream up noses, stuck with swords, knives thrown at feet, jabbed in ribs with towel hook, kicking." Older torments endured as well, including sweat parties and "holding push-up position for fifteen minutes."[42]

Most cadets continued to ignore the rules governing Evening Study Period, as almost every freshman admitted that they spent most evenings preparing for inspections, working on company projects, or being harassed by upperclassmen. After Citadel faculty member Judson Spence toured Band Company one night, he reported that "on four or five occasions during a three and a half hour visit," upperclassmen burst into plebes' rooms, then withdrew upon seeing him. Teague also collected letters from several parents who threatened to withdraw their sons from The Citadel if the violations continued.[43]

Almost all knobs claimed they were not getting enough to eat, with one calling mealtimes "the worst thing a freshman has to go through." This disturbed many members of the committee and outraged one who "hoped that upperclassmen will be made fully aware of the fact that the use of rank to hog food is diametrically opposed to armed forces policy and tradition that has existed since colonial days." Although the Whitmire Report banned "knob knowledge" as a means of denying freshmen food, upperclassmen relied upon "mess facts" to keep plebes from eating. Mess facts drew their "quasi-official status" from the *Fourth Class System Manual*'s requirement that freshmen be able to "discuss current events in a mature and serious manner." Stretching the definition of current events, upperclassmen ordered freshmen to tell jokes and ask or answer obscure questions that may or may not have pertained to The Citadel. The amount of food a knob ate depended upon his ability to amuse, stump, or otherwise satisfy the upperclassmen at his table. One parent wrote to Teague complaining that her son spent more time researching trivia than studying. Despite their recent invention, mess facts had become a "deeply ingrained part of cadet life." Most upperclassmen denied that the interrogations had become "excessive," retorting that there were "no plebes in the Corps who are starving."[44]

Several officials discovered other disturbing events not mentioned in either the Whitmire Report or the 1972 review. Sometime between final exams and commencement came "Recognition Day," a twenty-four-hour frenzy of abuse that constituted plebes' final hurdle in their quest to become upperclassmen. On this day, cadets hung blankets over the entrances to each barracks so that outsiders could not see freshmen being beaten with belts and brooms, doused with water, and passing out due to overexertion. When the ordeal ended, upperclassmen lined up, shook hands with each knob in their company, and welcomed them into the corps.[45]

Numerous administrators and faculty members questioned the wisdom, benefits, and legality of Recognition Day, insisting that the "the relatively new 'tradition' of beating the hell out of plebes should be brought within the limits of the law, fair play, respectable conduct becoming of future officers, and much older and more admirable Citadel 'traditions.'" Since few school officials had actually witnessed the year-end ritual, they relied on the experiences and advice of cadets when deciding what course of action to take. A junior reported that "no one in any companies I observed was harmed in any way beyond what was expected." He went on to defend Recognition Day as "something that a freshman will never forget and on the whole is something of an accomplishment and not a barbaric act." Besides, he continued, company and battalion commanders let knobs decide whether or not they wanted to participate so "no one has any reason to gripe."[46]

A cadet from third battalion told a different story after witnessing freshmen being "beaten much too severely." The cadet commander of fourth battalion limited Recognition Day activities to fifteen minutes and allowed upperclassmen to wield only brooms and black canvas belts since these weapons "do not cause any cuts, only a bruise." The second battalion commander also imposed a fifteen-minute time limit, but as a possible alternative to the existing practice, he singled out E Company's ceremony of yelling at freshmen and dropping them for push-ups, followed by a "very inspiring speech" from the cadet company commander explaining that "a leader and a man is not molded by defenseless beating." Several cadets hoped this presaged "the beginning of a meaningful and humane tradition and the destruction of a senseless brutal one."[47]

For his part, General Duckett pleaded with upperclassmen to change their attitudes toward plebe training, admonishing them to "*start* bragging about your college, your Corps, your class, your company" and "*stop* bragging about how tough it is — you know you do this only to show how tough you are." He instructed the cadre to deal with freshmen in a "humane and dignified manner," adding "regardless of any injustices or absurdities that may have been inflicted on you, I insist that you do not pass these same errors on to the new class." He condemned the "immature" practice of deciding "I don't like the way [a knob] parts his hair, the way he stands, the blubbery look he has or what have you, so I hereby dedicate myself to ridding the corps of him." According to the general, such an attitude indicated that The Citadel's system "can work only with those who come to us fully qualified to graduate" and ran counter to the school's mission of turning a "weakling" into a hardy Citadel cadet. Duckett tried to boost the confidence of incoming plebes by challenging traditional conceptions of Citadel exceptionalism, alerting freshmen "that of the tens of thousands of young men who have preceded you, most have succeeded and few have failed."[48]

A few students embraced Duckett's message. In a long editorial for *The Brigadier*, cadet John Chase alerted readers that although "hazing does not seem as bad a problem as in the past," violations of the fourth class system remained "widespread." Reluctant to discuss publicly what many of his peers considered a taboo subject, he nonetheless called the hazing of freshmen sadistic, unethical, immoral, and contrary "to every glorified belief on the subject of rights of the individual that we Americans have developed in the past two hundred years." He hated that most freshmen refused to report hazing violations because they either accepted the "propaganda that it is to his 'honor' to take the abuse to truly have 'been through' a plebe year" or because they knew of other knobs who had been run out of school for the "cowardly" act of turning in their assailant. Questioning the unspoken beliefs of many, Chase asked, "Is it the purpose of our plebe system to force freshmen to endure these physical and mental punishments in order to make them better men?" If so, he concluded, then this philosophy should appear in all Citadel publications, brochures, and pamphlets.[49]

A few other students joined in, railing against the "brutality and, yes, sadism, in general by significant members of the Corps." Leery of the claim that hazing constituted "an old traditional part of the Corps," the editor of *The Brigadier* informed readers that if they talked to Citadel alumni from the 1950s, they would learn that back then, "things were strict and that the college turned out dozens of fine classes without the physical abuse that has been so popular in recent years." The editor and others demanded to know "when are cadets going to stop these STUPID hazing traditions." Rather than treating a harsh plebe system as the source of the institution's strength, they did not want to see the college "ruined by people with sadistic ideas" and argued that the "elimination of brutality at The Citadel may well determine the survival of the school as an elite military college."[50]

Of course, not all cadets saw eye to eye on this issue. One cadet chastised Chase and the others for "hanging our dirty laundry out to the world," accusing them of "magnifying" the severity and frequency of hazing at The Citadel, thus giving the "fake impression that things here are badly wrong." Cadet Ralph Towell criticized administrators for violating the "purposes and ideals of The Citadel" by catering to "apathetic and unmotivated individuals" who diminished the "quality of the Corps." Towell believed that The Citadel's military aspects, in particular the fourth class system, gave the school its unique value.

As a result, he suggested Citadel officials not lower, but "raise our standards to create even more of a challenge to those who are willing to accept it and recognize its worth."[51]

The protests of students, however, paled in comparison to the furor raised by Citadel alumni. In March 1974, two recent graduates working in The Citadel's procurement office addressed the Board of Visitors at length about the "critical enrollment situation" at the college. In their report, they linked the decline of the school to what they saw as the post-1960s decline of the nation. According to them, "The Corps' decay of integrity began" under the tenure of General Harris, when, in an effort to attract more students, "irresolute" Citadel administrators catered to the whims of "outsiders" and started "adulterating, changing and weakening the demands of our system" in the name of "progress." They regretted that in succumbing to the "loss of values of society at large" by allowing cadets to follow an ideology where "'do your own thing' is the watchword . . . our military discipline, our standard of conduct, and integrity all have become a sorry façade." Over the past few years, the two men had witnessed "a rush to give away and demilitarize the Corps" through, among other things, "the complete elimination of the rigor and ordeal of the Plebe System with a consequent loss of class solidarity and pride in accomplishment."[52]

Despite such efforts to "civilianize The Citadel and corrupt an educational institution that has been successful as the Corps in producing leaders and successful men in every field," the two men resolved that "there remains a market for a tough demanding and rewarding military college." Concluding that "The Citadel can only justify its existence by being a very special world within itself," they saw "more leadership and less concessions" as the way to rescue an institution and a society where "*integrity, excellence, and discipline have lost their meaning.*" As part of this plan, they demanded Citadel leaders return to "the values, policies and traditions of Generals Summerall and Clark which are among the most important assets a young man could be associated with."[53]

The chairman of the Board of Visitors contributed his own views on "how to attract sufficient young men who will accept our way of life." Convinced that "the strength of The Citadel lies in its history and tradition" and that "in today's free wheeling times, the standards, the rules and regulations, and the very system of academic-military education seem to be anachronisms," he declared, "If these are anachronisms so are the American flag, the American democratic process, and the American system in which each individual is free to strive for what he considers success." He indicated that the rest of the country had strayed from these values when he presented The Citadel's regional identity as a liability, predicting that "as a deep-South institution" beholden "to principles that have limited appeal to liberal news media, we are not likely to gain national attention." Others saw the school's geographic location as a strength, expressing thanks that The Citadel was located in South Carolina, "a state with respect for the traditional values."[54]

Such arguments indicate that, for many, The Citadel's as well as the South's distinctiveness rested not on the belief that the institution and region were unique to America, but that they were uniquely American. In characterizing challenges to the status quo and efforts to expand the school's constituency as an assault on "traditional values," many Citadel men fought to protect the corps from a supposedly decadent society that had abandoned these values. By glossing over the prejudices, injustices, and inequities of the Summerall and Clark eras, they grounded the strength of their institution in a clouded, nostalgic longing for a supposedly less complicated pre-1960s America when old social and political hierarchies held firm, before African Americans, women, and students questioned the relevancy of and reasoning behind such values. In doing so, they continued to project a heavily gendered, implicitly racialized assessment of the traits "good" Citadel men possessed, an assessment that still resonated with a large segment of the U.S. population.

CHAPTER SIX

The Spirit of '76

The South, The Citadel,
and the "New America"

 As The Citadel limped into the second half of the 1970s, General
Duckett resigned as the college's president. He did so partly because he had already served longer than he had intended, but also
because the presidential candidate school officials had coveted since the end
of General Harris's term had finally become available. Lieutenant General
George M. Seignious graduated from The Citadel in 1942 and embarked on
an illustrious military and diplomatic career. He served as the military advisor
to the Paris Peace Talks in 1968, and since 1972, had held a position with the
Joint Chiefs of Staff. State and school officials celebrated General Seignious's
homecoming, expressing great confidence in his ability to revive the college.
South Carolina Governor James Edwards spoke at the inauguration of the new
president, lauding the general as one of "those who refuse to be swayed by
the shouting of those who would destroy America" and as one of the "leaders
who follow the ideals of the country more closely." When Seignious stepped to
the podium, he introduced what was to be a major theme of his presidency,
making it clear what type of people he thought America needed by pledging
to "enlighten, guide and inspire for the state and the nation, worthy leaders
of tomorrow — Men of learning/Men of integrity/Men of patriotism/Men of
self-reliance."[1]

Under its new president, The Citadel did enjoy a resurgence, and while the
general deserves some credit for this, larger social and political trends played
a key role as well. For example, Seignious turned the patriotic fervor accompanying the American bicentennial to the school's advantage, launching a very
successful "Spirit of '76" fund-raising campaign that established scholarships

for "patriotic, worthy young men." An even bigger boon came when the 1977 Miss USA pageant was held in Charleston and Citadel cadets appeared on the program as escorts for the contestants. When over 70 million viewers tuned in, the Board of Visitors called the event more valuable than a "million dollars worth of publicity."[2]

The corps' participation in the Miss USA pageant accentuated the three pillars upon which much of their identity rested: conspicuous patriotism, unassailable masculinity, and quaint southernness. By the latter half of the 1970s, these three traits led to the crowning of the "South as the New America"—a land of conservative, hard-working, patriotic, God-fearing, good ol' boys. According to a writer from *Time* magazine, such men possessed an "innate wisdom, an instinct about people and an unwavering loyalty that makes him the one friend you would turn to."[3]

In 1976, Jimmy Carter would capitalize on this "discovery of the admirable, adorable South," riding his image as an honest, clean-living, Georgia peanut farmer to the White House. Peter Applebome casts Carter's election as evidence of a "still quirky, but no longer menacing, domesticated South of hot cornbread, fried catfish, Jack Daniels, and racial peace." Jack Temple Kirby hits closer to the mark by recognizing that Carter "personified the resurgence of the *white* South." Kirby ought to have added a gender distinction as well, since the numerous tributes to southern culture conveyed a decidedly masculine as well as a decidedly pale version of the region's supposedly glorious present and the nation's promising future. A few weeks before Carter's inauguration, columnist Roy Reed wrote in an article for the *New York Times* that "for all the American encroachments, the southern countryside and small towns and even the suburbs and good-ole-boys preserves that sit in the very shadows of the southern skyscrapers are inhabited and given their dominant tone by men—and women who acquiesce in this matter."[4]

While Citadel personnel welcomed such perceptions, they portrayed themselves and their region not so much as a new America, but as the supposedly idyllic old America of Summerall and Clark. To their way of thinking, the good ol' boys at The Citadel were not going to lead the nation forward in the direction of change, but pull it back to a time when young people minded their elders and before women, African Americans, and other minority groups upset the status quo. This mind-set mirrored a national backlash toward the cultural and social reforms of the 1960s, a trend that sparked what historian

Gary Gerstle records as an effort "to restore national pride and power through," among other things, a "celebration of strong men in charge of their families, communities and nation."[5]

Such hopes found their embodiment at The Citadel, where a 1975 graduate asserted, "In these days of doubt, these days when the very foundations of civilization are being torn asunder, The Citadel clearly stands as a last stalwart, one of the last legions defending what we hold to be precious." Cadet Frederick Whittle mused that while students at other colleges "probably have meager interest in such long suppressed ideals as discipline, honor, humility, courtesy, morality, and pursuit of excellence," The Citadel's cultivation of these traits "separates us from the rest as we rise above the empty halls of deteriorating and mediocre standards." After boasting of his humility, Whittle exulted that because "The Citadel requires of her cadets discipline, and honor," the college stood as "the symbol of moral strength and character that it is today." In order to preserve this reputation, he encouraged all cadets and alumni to remain "ever watchful to ensure that this institution does not compromise one fiber of her character in the name of false progress or even equality."[6]

Promises to transform each knob into "a man of learning, a man of integrity, a man of patriotism, a man of self-reliance" grew in appeal as the number of applicants to The Citadel boomed between 1976 and 1979. Drawing on this momentum as well as his diplomatic background, General Seignious labored to turn his alma mater into "a focal point for international affairs in this area." He invited foreign dignitaries to campus and hosted symposiums on international relations. He also championed a preexisting program in which The Citadel accepted members of the Iranian Royal Navy into the corps of cadets. After four years of academic and military instruction, these students were expected to return home and train their soldiers utilizing the methods they learned in Charleston.[7]

While the number of Iranian cadets never exceeded one hundred, their presence generated a great deal of commotion on campus, drawing The Citadel into larger debates over U.S. foreign policy and international relations. If Vietnam punctured the nation's aura of invincibility, the OPEC oil embargo and, later, the Iran hostage crisis deflated it almost entirely. In his history of the 1970s, Peter Carroll called the embargo arguably "the most revolutionary shift of world power in the twentieth century." American cadets at The Citadel acknowledged this shift in numerous ways, including a half-joking cartoon in

The Brigadier that depicted a sheik standing in the middle of second battalion whispering to an Iranian cadet, "Some day, my son, this will all be yours."[8]

Given his particular interest in international relations, Seignious defended the program, contending that students from "nations that our country has explicit interests in trade and international affairs and security matters" would benefit from a Citadel education. He argued that accepting students from Saudi Arabia, Kuwait, Brazil, and Venezuela would strengthen U.S. global standing and broaden the educational experience of both foreign and American cadets. Several cadets pointed out that Seignious listed "primarily oil-producing countries for his source of international students," and although they acknowledged the "awesome economic power of the oil cartel," they accused their president of "playing politics" with their alma mater.[9]

As American troubles in the Middle East intensified, the controversy over Iranian students spilled beyond The Citadel's gates. Until 1977, the Iranian government paid each of their cadets a monthly allowance of eleven hundred dollars. According to one Citadel professor, it did not take long for the students to discover "what money can do in America." With memories of long gas lines still fresh in people's minds, local Charlestonians were outraged that Iranian cadets were "buying expensive cars and renting off campus apartments with their living stipends." General Seignious raised a few eyebrows when he suggested that "removed from the constraints of their own culture and environment and immersed in our society, there were bound to be some excesses." The head of Naval ROTC agreed that the students demonstrated "a great attraction for the American way of life and particularly its leisure time activities," concluding "maybe we Americanized the Iranians too much."[10]

Such explanations did not sit well with irate South Carolinians who demanded to know "why should one penny of my tax money be used for the education of a student from an oil-rich country which participated in an oil boycott against the United States just a few years ago." State Representative and Citadel graduate John Bradley latched onto this issue as he railed against using The Citadel as a "base for training a large number" of Iranian soldiers. When Seignious tried to impress upon legislators the diplomatic importance of the program, arguing "our oil interests in the Persian Gulf are paramount," Bradley shot back, "I don't understand about the Persian Gulf and I don't want to." Most Citadel graduates in the General Assembly backed Seignious, calling Bradley's crusade "potentially very dangerous to the school, the nation, and the world." A legislator who attended The Citadel with some Iranian cadets spoke positively of his experience, pleading to his colleagues, "Don't put up a roadblock to that kind of brotherhood."[11]

Tired of the scrutiny, the Board of Visitors set out to reduce the number of Iranian students on campus. In November 1979, after Iranian militants in Tehran took sixty Americans hostage, President Jimmy Carter took the matter out of the board's hands by ordering the deportation of all Iranian diplomats. Since they held diplomatic visas, this decision applied to the Iranian cadets, and with "deep reluctance" D. D. Nicholson broke the news to them. Thanking the students for their "constructive" contribution to Citadel life, he hoped that their experiences had been "rewarding."[12]

School administrators expressed less concern about the experiences of other students on campus as black cadets continued to suffer indignities at the hands of their white colleagues. On what remained an overwhelmingly white campus, Citadel personnel had made little headway in addressing the attitudes of white cadets who mocked past injustices and promoted derogatory racial stereotypes. In the 1977 yearbook, the white seniors of T Company posed as Ku Klux Klan members surrounding a black classmate. Smiling for the camera, one held a noose around the "victim's" neck, another aimed a toy pistol at his head, and yet another brandished a knife. In February 1978, an African American cadet won the honor of serving as the "rear guide" for the Summerall Guards. As the title indicates, the rear guide anchored the platoon, a fact that prompted an artist for *The Brigadier* to quip, "It may be a breakthrough . . . But he's still riding in *the back*."[13]

Calling the cartoon "unforgivable," cadet Eddie Lee Bracey Jr. denounced other "disturbing" caricatures from past *Brigadier*s, including depictions of black laundry workers as gorillas, black mess hall employees as "tribeswomen with bones in their hair," and a black tactical officer gleefully discovering a watermelon under a bed. To those who wondered, he pointed out that offenses such as these were "why blacks sit together at ball games." Bracey added that "when the school that is supposed to be developing men for leadership demeans its own," perhaps the members of that institution should reevaluate its priorities and attitudes. Upon receiving Bracey's letter, the editorial staff of *The Brigadier* apologized only for the original cartoon's ambiguity, claiming they printed it with "the intent to applaud him."[14]

Students and administrators left no room for ambiguity when it came to defending the all-male corps of cadets. As mentioned earlier, the number of applicants rebounded in the latter half of the 1970s, a development some attributed to a recruiting campaign that advertised the college as a place where "Manhood Meets Mastery." From his earliest days as president, Seignious harped on the notion that a "loyalty to the fundamental characteristics of manhood" made The Citadel distinctive from and superior to other colleges and universities.[15]

While certainly effective when it came to attracting students, such demonstrative assertions of the corps' masculinity arose, in part, as a response to the questions and challenges raised by modern feminists. This idea that fundamental characteristics of manhood actually existed was precisely what the women's liberation movement of the late 1960s and 1970s refuted. Struggles over the "radical reexamination of what it meant to be male and female in America" animated the cultural and traditional politics of the 1970s, threatening existing hierarchies in both public and private life. At the same time, the "assault on the efforts of modern feminists to redefine gender roles" served, according to Alan Brinkley, as "the most powerful single strain within fundamental conservatism through much of the 1970s and 1980s." Although one might expect the administrators, students, and alumni of an institution obsessed with masculinity to express a particularly virulent disdain for feminism, the opinions coming out of The Citadel echoed many of those held by society at large.[16]

The battle over the passage and ratification of the Equal Rights Amendment (ERA) captured the intensity with which many Americans defended "traditionalist views of womanhood." As Donald Mathews and Jane Sherron DeHart explain in *Sex, Gender and the Politics of ERA*, the amendment provoked an "apocalyptic" response from those who believed that "the supreme law of the land was about to be changed by women who had transcended gender definitions." Guided in part by this as well as misgivings about federally sanctioned equality, North Carolina Senator Sam Ervin led the congressional charge against the amendment. According to Matthews and DeHart, Ervin and other opponents of the amendment distorted its purpose and scope when they claimed that the ERA would "destroy all the laws that make distinctions between men and women." Ignoring clear indications that the bill "would not affect legislation in which the biological sex of the parties was relevant," Ervin warned that ratification would leave women at the mercy of sexual predators, convince men to abandon their families, and require males and females to share restrooms.[17]

Cadet Sidney Wise ran down a similar list of outrages when he defined the ERA as "the straw that would break America's back." Wise predicted that by "weakening family ties," the amendment would not only promote "social disruption, unhappiness, and increasing rates of divorce and desertion," it "may also lead to increased rates of alcoholism, suicide and possibly sexual deviation." Wise joined millions of others who supported the "admirable" goal of equal employment opportunities for women, but worried that the amendment would become a "tool of the Supreme Court," a court that "has been known to find meanings and powers in Constitutional amendments undreamt of by the Congresses that proposed them and the states that ratified them."[18]

National opponents of the ERA and especially the media focused on female opposition to the women's movement to the extent that the debate appeared to be a "catfight" between "the simpering, sheltered wife and mother on the one side and the ambitious independent outspoken bitch on the other." Pundits narrowed the field further by privileging sound bites from women activists who equated female support for the ERA with a desire to "become a man." Wise employed similar tactics when he argued, "The worth of the ERA is placed in doubt by the fact that most women do not want it. They ask if they should be denied their right to be a woman just to satisfy a small number of disillusioned women who proclaim their rights in a 'Bitch Manifesto' (that's what *they* call it)." That same edition of *The Brigadier* contained a cartoon of an overweight, frumpy, cigarette-smoking woman holding a placard declaring "We Want Freedom N.O.W." In the corner of the frame, a man looked on, mumbling "and they call us pigs."[19]

Corps-wide interest in the women's movement intensified in 1975 when President Gerald Ford signed a bill requiring the service academies to admit women. Soon after Ford's order, General Seignious assured cadets and alumni alike that although "we could have a problem" should women want to enter The Citadel's veteran program, federal law protected the all-male admissions policy regarding the corps of cadets. As the ERA wound its way through the ratification process, he noted that should the amendment pass, "our chances in denying entry by females would be much less."[20]

While the ERA represented a potential menace, the Charleston chapter of the National Organization of Women (NOW) drew immediate attention to The Citadel's single-sex policies. In January 1976, NOW members convinced the Charleston City Council to withhold its annual ten-thousand-dollar contribution to The Citadel's athletic scholarship fund as proof that sexual discrimination had "no place in 1976." These efforts unleashed the fury of Citadel cadets and administrators. General Seignious dug in his heels, vowing to preserve the all-male corps of cadets and informing the council, "If the city of Charleston doesn't feel it's a worthy institution, then you shouldn't support it."[21]

One Citadel student cast NOW as a "highly organized group" of "irate" and "clamorous ladies" led by "zealous and self-righteous individuals who believe with something approaching religious fervor that their's [sic] is a mission to eradicate sexual discrimination wherever in their opinion it's to be found." In his estimation, these activists tended to run "roughshod over the rights of others" as evidenced by their attack on "the favorite liberal whipping boy," a "military college run by a conservative military administration." The cadet thanked NOW and its spokeswoman Conni Ackerman for offering a "sober reminder" to all who supported the "time-honored concept of an all-male Corps of Cadets that there exists beyond the walls of our college an organization which is willing to patiently snipe away at us until it achieves its goal of destroying our system." Repeatedly referring to NOW as a group of misguided "outsiders" who "couldn't care less about our proud heritage," he dismissed claims that The Citadel could admit women "while continuing to function in the same admirable way it has for so many years without losing a step in the process," since "what kind of girl would result from a system designed to build tough men?"[22]

In addition to depicting NOW as a vindictive cabal intent on trampling cadets' rights, *The Brigadier* included a staged photo of a young, attractive woman saluting while dressed in a Citadel uniform. The line "Here's one woman on campus no one objects to" appeared underneath the picture. The contrasting of ill-tempered feminist "outsiders" with a pretty, nonthreatening female "cadet" exemplified not only American society's proclivity for viewing the women's movement in Manichean terms, but it also typified men's assumed role as arbiters of acceptable and unacceptable behavior.[23]

Citadel backers raised enough of a row to convince the city council to reverse its decision and restore the ten-thousand-dollar contribution. This did not quell the controversy, though. In February 1976, Conni Ackerman visited

The Citadel's campus to debate history professor John Coussons on the merits of the school's learning environment. Before a packed house of cadets, Ackerman went first, praising The Citadel as a "very, very unique institution" whose system of "training and discipline" would benefit "some women." She believed males and females needed lessons in "respecting authority and learning assertiveness, and learning how to express yourself, and learning how to get ahead, and learning how to take it rough." She recognized the college's long line of distinguished graduates and contended that "the same kind of experience" that produced these men "should be available to women if they want to come here."[24]

In his rebuttal, Coussons summarized the arguments made by Dr. S. I. Hayakawa, a linguist and former president of San Francisco State University, who argued that "throughout history boys have had to pass a test to prove their masculinity." This tradition had waned, in his estimation, as responsibility for raising and educating young males fell mainly to mothers and female teachers. With fathers exerting less of a "required masculine influence on the growing boy," The Citadel filled the void by "stretching a boy to his limit of endurance in order for him to reach his potential." Coussons conceded that some women could also benefit from such a challenge, but since "the test would have to be vastly different," he could not fathom "how girls could come to The Citadel, don the uniform of a cadet, and function in the Cadet Corps without basically altering the nature of the Cadet Corps." Furthermore, he denied that "by not being allowed to do so it is a denial of their constitutional rights."[25]

Ackerman acknowledged the physiological differences between men and women, but argued that by establishing "comparable" standards for females they would be "essentially exerting themselves as much as the men." Not surprisingly, this drew a heated response from the crowd. A reporter covering the debate for *The Brigadier* remarked wryly, "The cadets in the audience did not seem to agree with her." Indeed, Ackerman failed to win many converts at The Citadel. A month after her appearance, a cadet referred to her as "Ms. Ackerperson" since "the suffix man is sexist and as Conni is presently on an emasculating sexist rampage."[26]

With more attention being paid to the sexual composition of the corps of cadets, *The Brigadier* staff surveyed the student body to find out "How does The Citadel's isolated environment affect cadets' attitudes towards sex and girls in general?" Two respondents claimed The Citadel had helped them "accept and appreciate women," but the vast majority echoed the sentiments of one student who smirked, "Citadel guys may sometimes treat women like sex objects, but they love it." Some cadets appeared especially defensive about their all-male surroundings, with one denying that Citadel people "hate women," and another proclaiming, "I believe the question of cadets being gay because of this is ridiculous."[27]

Despite all the turmoil, The Citadel had yet to face a concerted challenge to its admissions policies. NOW's protest merely delayed the city council's final decision, and Conni Ackerman never again spoke on campus. In his study of women in the U.S. Armed Forces, Brian Mitchell notes that "the very year that saw the first perfumed plebe enter West Point also saw the ERA sitting dead in the water." Confident that the college had weathered the storm, D. D. Nicholson exulted, "During a period when other colleges were espousing permissiveness in the ways of drugs and coeds, The Citadel stuck to its principles. Now the national psychology has turned and everybody has come to The Citadel point of view."[28]

The next few years still proved tense for The Citadel as the thought of a coeducational corps haunted school officials and cadets. During this time, Citadel personnel honed a series of arguments they would present whenever they felt the need to defend the school's admissions requirements. Some Citadel students and alumni stressed the "drastic effect" coeducation would have on the college financially. According to one cadet, the college could resist the "ruinous progress" of admitting women since "we have neither the facilities for females nor the money to acquire them." Others, like General Seignious, questioned whether or not the few "women who would attend The Citadel would warrant the conversion of various facilities and programs which would be required to cater to the women's needs." Another line of reasoning cast coeducation as a violation of the rights of young men to attend an all-male military college. Not only that, Seignious and others condemned the ERA as a threat to all single-sex institutions, one that could cost all female colleges the "many special rights they have now."[29]

In 1977, *Brigadier* editor Peter J. Campbell raised a dissenting voice to the chorus denouncing coeducation. He reminded readers that the ERA would not abolish all single-gender colleges since the amendment did not apply to all public and private institutions. As for complaints that women would "weaken the corps," he argued just the opposite, claiming coeducation would allow cadets to "prove their worth" under the inevitable public scrutiny. To those who believed women could not "handle the physical aspects of Citadel life," he replied that no one would know that for sure until a female attempted it, concluding, "If the time does come, however, when women are admitted, it should be looked on as a challenge, instead of something to be feared."[30]

The most emotional rebuttals to such claims hinged upon the assumption that The Citadel simply could not function as a coeducational institution. Seignious spoke for most alumni and students when he explained, "The life and role of the cadet and the military college cannot be altered fundamentally without fundamentally altering The Citadel and what it's been since it was created in 1842." Although he never clarified what these fundamental aspects were, the only Citadel tradition that had remained unaltered since 1842 was its all-male corps of cadets. One student broached the issue directly, declaring the "admission of women to the South Carolina Corps of Cadets would in the least severely alter the proud tradition of The Citadel and rush the disintegration of the college." Another hoped the man-building process itself might stave off what he saw as the increasing threat of coeducation, warning, "We must avoid making the fourth class system too easy, for the ever present threat of women at The Citadel looms not far beyond our gates." This last argument marked an important shift in how many cadets and alumni were beginning to view the plebe system. While the corps continued to promote the fourth class system as the best way of forging men, many began stoking the fires of knob year with the added hope of keeping women at bay.[31]

This way of thinking proved problematic for some school officials, especially General Seignious, who had vowed that "The Citadel will remain a military college — emphasizing integrity and character and that American form of leadership that seeks the willing response of subordinates — not relying on the crutch of brutal or demeaning authoritarianism." Like his predecessor, Seignious worried that the fourth class system hindered the college's recruiting, especially since "word has gotten to the high school students of South Carolina that the discipline [at The Citadel] was on the severe side." While he questioned the accuracy of such rumors, he admitted that "the image persists that there is hazing, brutality, and that there's not an opportunity to eat, not an opportunity to sleep, and not many young Americans want to face that." Seignious resolved to "make sure there are no excesses" within the plebe system, and in the first two years of his presidency, the freshmen attrition rate dropped from 11.4 percent to 5.7 percent. By 1976, though, hazing was again on the rise. In February, the school's chaplain delivered a sermon before Seignious and the corps, condemning the indignities upperclassmen inflicted on knobs. Less than a month into the 1976–1977 school year, over 10 percent of the freshmen class had quit, and while Seignious promised to "remedy the situation," events in a small New Jersey suburb intensified the demand for such a cure.[32]

At 4:00 a.m. on November 28, 1976, in Montvale, New Jersey, Harry De La Roche Jr., a Citadel freshman home for Thanksgiving break, flagged down a police car screaming, "They're all dead!" The officer followed De La Roche the few blocks to his parents' house, where they found the murdered remains of the young man's mother, father, and youngest brother. Harry De La Roche Sr. and his wife Mary Jane had been shot twice in the head. Their son Eric died after "much struggle," having been shot three times and then bludgeoned to death. Hours later, investigators would discover the body of fifteen-year-old Ronnie De La Roche stuffed in a trunk in the attic. Soon thereafter, Harry De La Roche Jr. was charged with killing his family.[33]

News of the slayings garnered national attention, with most of the coverage connecting De La Roche to The Citadel. Initial coverage in the South Carolina *State* newspaper noted that although no motive had been offered, "Friends of the suspect reportedly said he was unhappy with the military school he was attending." It took two years for De La Roche to stand trial, and when the case finally made it to court, the *New York Times* printed daily synopses of the proceedings. Readers in Charleston remained especially attentive as they realized that The Citadel and its fourth class system would become "an alleged conspirator as the New Jersey tragedy unfolded."[34]

Less than two weeks after the murder, a writer for *The Brigadier* informed the corps, "De La Roche to blame Citadel." He reported that the former cadet planned to "plead temporary insanity caused by his treatment at The Citadel" and cited New Jersey area newspapers claiming that De La Roche ate only "grits, water, and one-half of a lima bean for thirty days." An alumni living in Charlotte, North Carolina, called D. D. Nicholson to relay details of a newscast he had just seen on the case. Nicholson's notes from the conversation read, "the physical and mental torture was horrendous; hazing far exceeding that of any of the U.S. military academies. Northern boys going down there are still expected to fight the Civil War."[35]

Although two detectives investigating the murder visited campus and uncovered no evidence that De La Roche had been "unjustly treated at The Citadel," the young man told a different story. He recalled doing push-ups until his "arms would give out" and claimed to have passed out one time after being kicked in the groin. According to the defendant, "Meal times were the toughest," and he rarely got enough to eat. In addition to upperclassmen throwing him "around for kicks," he alleged that one night, an unknown assailant burst into his room, threw a blanket over his head, sliced his leg open with a knife, and poured nail polish remover in the wound.[36]

By all accounts, De La Roche was a less than ideal cadet who made low grades and had few friends. He had even lied to Citadel officials about his mother having terminal cancer in order to leave early for Thanksgiving break. He had decided soon into the first semester not to return to The Citadel, but was reluctant to tell his father, who he said "loathed quitters" and would never forgive him for resigning. A series of letters De La Roche Sr. wrote to his son during that one semester seemed to come right out of *The Guidon* and helps explain, in part, a source of the young man's apprehension. The elder De La Roche drove his son to "prove the guys wrong who said that you wouldn't make it at The Citadel" and advised him, "Don't let the upperclassmen get to you. They are supposed to weed out the weak ones." He reminded him "Citadel grads are looked up to," and upon finishing, "Your career and entire life would be made." Conversely, should he become one of "the boys who didn't have the guts to stick it out . . . you would end up being nothing."[37]

In a signed confession made to the police and later read into evidence, Harry De La Roche Jr. described the events of November 28, 1976. After a night of drinking and smoking pot, De La Roche returned home around 3:00 a.m. and began pacing his bedroom floor, clutching his father's .22 pistol. Deciding "it was the only way I could get out of going to The Citadel," he entered his parents' bedroom, stood next to his sleeping father, murmured "'I can't go back' closed my eyes and pulled the trigger." He shot his mother "right then and there," and before his brothers fully realized what had happened, he walked in their room and shot Ron once and Eric twice. Eric continued breathing, so De La Roche shot him again and then hit him twice over the head with the pistol butt.[38]

De La Roche later recanted his confession, entering not guilty pleas to three of the murders and pleading guilty by reason of temporary insanity to the remaining charge. He testified that his brother Ron had committed the murders and that he had killed Ron in an act of rage and self-defense. This scenario seemed doubtful anyway, but on the last day of the trial, the defense shocked the courtroom by pleading guilty to all four murders. In doing so, they joined the prosecution in indicting The Citadel as an accomplice in the slayings. Prosecuting attorney Richard Salkin dismissed De La Roche's story about Ron as part of a "game," reminding jurors that he had argued from the start that the defendant had committed the murders in part because he "despised the hazing and harassment" he endured at The Citadel. The defense took the argument much further, contending that "the pressure of returning to the 'private hell' De La Roche lived at The Citadel, forced him over the edge of sanity." A psychiatrist testified that the young man "could not bring himself to return to the school because of the physical abuse he suffered in hazing rituals," but he also "felt his father would devalue him and make him feel worthless" should he quit. In his closing argument, De La Roche's attorney described, the "clock ticks and it's almost time to return to his hell. The pressure cooker builds" until "he finally screams out 'I can't go back' and then Harry starts firing the weapon and his family is gone."[39]

De La Roche received four concurrent life sentences, but as his trial ended, The Citadel's continued. D. D. Nicholson again took center stage, announcing that, "We were on trial simply because the defense — in the absence of a better case — decided to place the blame on his environment." Calling the strategy of blaming "the environment and society for whatever problems an individual may have" a "weird manifestation of American psychology," he announced that school officials would not modify the Citadel system just because "one person fails." As if unaware of the changes that had occurred in American society in the past 130 years, he offered the rather jarring defense that "the system was deliberately contrived in 1842, by some very profound thinkers as the best environment for a young man to learn." Nicholson even sought to turn the murder trial into a point of pride for The Citadel, boasting, "If this had been a University of South Carolina student, no one would have thought anything about the school," but since "we hold ourselves up as the paragon of many things . . . we would expect to get more blame."[40]

In contrast to Nicholson's cockiness, many others realized that the publicity had "tarnished The Citadel in the eyes of the nation." A few weeks after the trial had ended, Citadel representatives encountered a great deal of hostility on a recruiting trip through the New York and New Jersey area. In New

Jersey, a young man spit at them, while in New York an elderly women took her umbrella and swept all the brochures off their table. Whereas previously, New Jersey represented the fifth-largest recruiting base for The Citadel, in the first six months of 1978, the number of applicants from the state dropped by 50 percent.[41]

The high drama of the trial and its focus on The Citadel, while expected, detracted from a larger lesson that can be gleaned from the De La Roche tragedy. Although certainly an extreme case, the murders offer a glimpse into the personal toll exacted on those expected to conform to highly subjective, if not altogether artificial, standards of behavior. The Citadel and society at large placed a high value on certain "manly" attributes such as toughness and discipline. For many, including Harry De La Roche's father, graduating from The Citadel proved one's manhood, thus paving the way for future success. Conversely, quitting meant one was somehow inferior and doomed to failure. As the history of The Citadel and the fourth class system reveal, what it means to "be a man" is both historically and contextually contingent. With the stakes this high and the standards this malleable, the pressures and frustrations that come with meeting socially determined gender stereotypes can breed desperation among men like Harry De La Roche and others.

As part of their response to the De La Roche murders, school officials increased the number of "leadership classes" cadets had to attend and emphasized "positive" motivational techniques, discouraging upperclassmen from screaming at knobs or relying on push-ups as an immediate form of punishment. Viewing hazing as the byproduct of a general corps-wide disdain for military discipline, General Seignious, Commandant of Cadets Colonel John Gibler, and Assistant Commandant Lieutenant Colonel Harvey Dick cracked down on cadet behavior, monitoring the corps closely at football games, chastising cadets for meeting dates in the school library during Evening Study Period, banning the selling of food in the barracks, and ensuring that the punishments they doled out were administered correctly.[42]

Many Citadel students blasted "King George" and his "foolish" lackeys for coddling freshmen and persecuting upperclassmen. Despite such protests, more changes followed, some of which the corps approved and some they abhorred. The ones they deemed compatible with The Citadel's traditions involved relaxing the military requirements on upperclassmen, such as allowing them to skip morning breakfast formations and permitting seniors to wear civilian coats and ties, not just Citadel blazers, while off campus. At the same time, the commandant's department reduced the number of overnight passes allotted to each class, limited juniors' and seniors' opportunities to wear the blazer uniform, and cut three hours from upperclassmen's Sunday leave time. While the new breakfast and uniform policies raised no stir, cadets bristled at the "rapidity" of the other changes. One cadet turned the most common argument for preserving the fourth class system on its head when he criticized the commandant's office for being "in touch with the Corps of 1842" and "trying to revert us back to the 'Old Corps' of the fifties." It seems that when it came to inconveniencing upperclassmen, "old corps" traditions were archaic and unreasonable, but when it came to abusing freshmen, "old corps" traditions were sacrosanct.[43]

Such attitudes stemmed, in part, from the all-too-real anxieties generated by national debates over the ERA in particular and societal gender roles in general. While coeducation lay well in the distance, the idea that women might one day join men in the ranks of citizen-soldiers prompted a vigorous response from Citadel men. Determined, along with countless other Americans, to preserve traditional views of gender that exalted manly citizens, cadets and school administrators grew even more sensitive to any developments that may have undermined their privileged status. Many of them decided that the best way to ensure that their gendered notions of citizenship held firm was to bar women from an institution that offered male citizens the chance to prove their civic worth. For decades, such tactics had cost women access to the benefits, training, and experience provided by the U.S. Armed Forces. In Charleston, this practice was employed to shore up the barriers around The Citadel and its fourth class system.

Aerial view of the Citadel campus. (Courtesy of The Citadel Archives and Museum)

General Mark W. Clark reviewing the corps of cadets during parade. (Courtesy of The Citadel Archives and Museum)

The components of the "whole man," circa 1970. (Courtesy of The Citadel Archives and Museum)

This photo from the 1964 Citadel yearbook shows an upperclassmen "dropping" a knob for push-ups. (Courtesy of The Citadel Archives and Museum)

The harassment freshmen endured at meal times often kept them from getting enough to eat. (Courtesy of The Citadel Archives and Museum)

Charles Foster, the first African American cadet at The Citadel. (Courtesy of The Citadel Archives and Museum)

Yearbook photo of Joseph Shine, The Citadel's second African American cadet. (Courtesy of The Citadel Archives and Museum)

Afro-American Student Association, 1972. (Courtesy of The Citadel Archives and Museum)

Admiral and Mrs. Stockdale talking with General Clark. (Courtesy of The Citadel Archives and Museum)

Citadel cadets escorted contestants at the 1977 and 1978 Miss USA pageants. (Courtesy of The Citadel Archives and Museum)

Cadets in the stands at a Citadel football game, 1986. (Courtesy of The Citadel Archives and Museum)

Nancy Mace, the first female to graduate from the corps of cadets. (Courtesy of The Citadel Archives and Museum)

Petra Lovetinska, seen here marching off to a Friday parade, entered The Citadel with Nancy Mace, but graduated a year after her. (Courtesy of The Citadel Archives and Museum)

The first African American female cadets, class of 2002, showing off their Citadel rings. (Courtesy of The Citadel. Reproduced by permission of Russ Pace.)

CHAPTER SEVEN

"Tampering with America"

Masculinity, Feminism, and the Fourth Class System

 On March 1, 1979, at the behest of President Carter, General Seignious left The Citadel to assume the directorship of the U.S. Arms Control and Disarmament Agency. Following "the most comprehensive search for the ideal president for The Citadel that has ever been conducted," the Board of Visitors named U.S. Naval Academy graduate and Vietnam War hero Vice Admiral James B. Stockdale as the college's fifteenth president.[1]

When he accepted the post as president of The Citadel, Vice Admiral Stockdale was the most highly decorated officer in the U.S. Navy, having earned the Congressional Medal of Honor for organizing resistance efforts during his torturous seven-and-a-half years in a Vietnamese prisoner-of-war camp. At the same time, the admiral seemed to take greater pride in his intellectual achievements than his military accolades. He had published numerous scholarly articles, and as president of the Naval War College, he drew upon his wartime experience, teaching a class on the importance of maintaining one's morality under harsh conditions. He planned to teach a similar course at The Citadel.[2]

The corps welcomed their new president as a "man of outstanding credentials" who would bring to The Citadel a "wealth of fine guidance and leadership through years of distinguished experience." A reporter for *The Brigadier* considered him "the answer to our call," echoing the post-1960s mantra that as The Citadel "steams headlong into the worldly waves of permissiveness and decaying morality," the admiral would provide the school with the necessary "leadership, strength of character and moral fortitude."[3]

For his part, Stockdale called his new job the "culmination of a dream as I become a professional educator for the rest of my life." Considering The Citadel "a good old school [that] had gone through the wringer during the 1960s and had come out with a shattered academic profile," he assumed that the board had hired him to rebuild the school's educational reputation. In his introduction to the 1979 *Guidon*, he emphasized a cadet's intellectual growth more than his military and physical development. When speaking before the corps, Stockdale "stressed the goal of academic excellence," pointing out that great leaders exhibited compassion and understood that "all men are not products of the same mold."[4]

Although he measured manliness and leadership by different standards than his predecessors, Stockdale passed the crucial litmus test of many Citadel men when he publicly affirmed that "the school should resist trends and pressure to open its doors to women." It was what went on behind those doors, however, that brought the admiral into direct conflict with the Board of Visitors, the corps of cadets, and a very vocal segment of Citadel alumni. During his initial interview with the board before becoming president, Stockdale grew uneasy with the members' preoccupation with the fourth class system. After several confided in him, "We like to think of plebe year at The Citadel as being the toughest of any school in the country," an astonished Stockdale finally came to realize that the fourth class system had been "blown up in the minds of mature men to be *the* prime status symbol" of the school. Concerned initially with bridging the "gap between the academic and military elements within the college," his exposure to the harshness of the fourth class system fueled a desire to stamp out hazing that would consume his presidency.[5]

It did not take Admiral Stockdale long to figure out "that there was something mean and out of control about the regime I had just inherited." While rummaging through some of the correspondence General Seignious had left behind, Stockdale unearthed several memos from Dr. George Mood, The Citadel's surgeon, alerting the former president and the former commandant of cadets to several "inhumane" and "discourteous" aspects of plebe year, including denying freshmen food and exerting new cadets to the point of exhaustion. Stockdale also found letters from angry parents confirming such charges. One father, a Naval Academy graduate, called the torments his son endured a "disgrace," adding that harassment and sleep deprivation had transformed the young man "from a level headed optimistic, aggressive individual to a fatigued, irrational, confused and bitter one." Demanding that someone answer for this, the parent snarled, "Don't blame it on the 'system,' for if you do, then the system be damned."[6]

Stockdale's concerns about freshmen increased when over fifty fourthclassmen had quit by September. Making it clear that "too many freshmen are subjected to excessive physical punishment," Stockdale stepped up the enforcement of existing regulations and issued some new directives of his own. He ended the practice of requiring knobs to walk in the gutter on the Avenue of Remembrance, and he suspended all plebe training on especially hot days.[7]

Initially, much of the corps lauded this "admirable" attempt to reduce hazing. *The Brigadier* printed a cartoon mocking alumni who strutted around blustering, "Back when I was a knob . . ." The editor of the newspaper defended certain reforms as necessary to "prepare today's cadet for a constantly changing society" but also warned that "drastic unfounded changes should always be prevented." Another cadet encouraged classmates to humor alumni who prattled on about the "old corps" because "when you graduate, you will share with that alumnus something only a Citadel graduate can understand and that is being a Citadel Man." According to this student, at least, The Citadel could withstand any changes as long as they did not affect the manly purpose and product of the college.[8]

Whatever support Stockdale had enjoyed in September had faded by the end of the first semester. A chorus arose on campus accusing the admiral of making a mockery of The Citadel, turning it into an institution where freshmen "laugh" and "upperclassmen cry." In December, every cadet officer marched to Jenkins Hall and presented the commandant with a list of grievances, demanding the restoration of full leave privileges, more lenient uniform policies, and more control over the fourth class system. By coupling their concern over "drastic changes in the fourth class system" with demands for fewer military restrictions on upperclassmen, these requests suggest that many cadets still defined the value of their military education in gendered rather than martial terms. With feminism and the women's movement making headway against societal assumptions concerning men's and women's abilities and "proper" place in society, more and more Citadel students latched onto the institution's explicitly manly purpose, and more specifically, the fourth class system's ability to fulfill this purpose, as crucial not only to the college's preservation but also to the students' value as citizen-soldiers. Protecting the all-male environment and method that produced Citadel men trumped all other issues, and as Stockdale tinkered with the machinery of producing whole men, many saw him as paving the way for women.[9]

Conversations outside The Citadel's gates most likely intensified the cadets' objections to Stockdale's measures. In an interview with the *Charleston News and Courier*, D. D. Nicholson sought to clear up what he saw as several misconceptions about the college. While his claim that "we'll take anyone who wants to develop the ability to be a leader in any field" spoke volumes as to his views on women's ability to lead, it was Nicholson's evaluation of the fourth class system that angered many readers. Nicholson regretted the negative publicity The Citadel received when a plebe quit, since, according to his calculations, the school lost ten applicants every time someone resigned because "What does he tell the people at home? That he's not tough? If he washes out, he's going to go home and tell war stories about how bad the knob system is." Confident that "any average young man can, with considerable ease, get through the first year at The Citadel," he estimated that "those who drop out really aren't giving it a fight."[10]

Several people took offense at Nicholson's explanation of why certain cadets "washed out." Charlestonian Mary Ann Restivo wrote a letter to the *News and Courier* refuting Nicholson's assessment, claiming it was common knowledge that freshmen were nearly "starved to death." Restivo said she learned of the torments knobs suffered from her husband and two nephews who had quit The Citadel during their plebe years. Evoking unpleasant memories, she ordered Nicholson and the Board of Visitors to "wake up" and do something before another De La Roche tragedy occurred. The aunt of a former cadet who had just resigned seconded Restivo's remarks. She described her nephew as eminently qualified to attend The Citadel, having received numerous JROTC and academic awards. He viewed his enrollment as "a lifetime dream come true" but returned home a month later "twenty pounds lighter and very depressed." She never blamed her nephew's withdrawal on excessive hazing, but she hinted as much by proclaiming he "was equal to any honorable challenge given."[11]

Citadel supporters swarmed to the institution's defense, praising the school and attacking its critics. Almost every rebuttal maligned the women's accounts as the grousing of ignorant outsiders or malcontented failures. One response stated flatly, "The letters appear to be attempts to justify the failure of husbands, sons and nephews not being able to take the system." Another decided that those who wanted to change it "either do not understand The Citadel or could not successfully complete the fourth class system." One "knew of no graduate who condemns the system," while several others made the true but hardly praiseworthy assertion that "no cadet has ever starved to death because of upper-class harassment." Another author noted that the complaints came from "females and females naturally tend to be compassionate."[12]

Other defenders of the school echoed Nicholson by equating leadership with masculinity and affirming Citadel men's place atop the gender hierarchy. One Citadel proponent explained, "I feel that a 'man' that has got the 'whatever' to get through The Citadel will be a leader of men and a leader of the community." Conversely, "a 'boy' that does not have that 'whatever' and drops out and goes on to the College of Charleston or Baptist College will turn out to be a good music director, a good high school teacher, or a good bookkeeper." Another reminded Charlestonians, "The Citadel is not a Sunday school picnic. Its function is to build men and to mold leaders by teaching them to react, think and function under pressure." A woman from nearby Summerville repeated, "Let's face it, it separates the men from the boys."[13]

Not ones to let others fight their battles for them, members of the corps penned their own massive rebuttals to the accusations. Two seniors ridiculed Restivo's "ignorance of the system" and scoffed that her evidence came from family members "who are perfect examples of the many weak minded Americans of today's society." Chalking up such "attacks" to "jealousy on the part of many individuals who did not attend The Citadel or could not make it," they asked how a supposedly "unbearable" institution could "boast such a long line of distinguished graduates?" Under the headline "Ignorant Public Rallies Unjust Cause," the editor of *The Brigadier*, Frederick J. Whittle, implored his peers, "Do not let the unfounded, totally irresponsible letters of 'bleeding heart' women cause you to question the true purpose of 'Knob Year,'" developing "those qualities essential to a good leader."[14]

It was in this atmosphere that Stockdale decided to overhaul the fourth class system. Although the admiral favored an immediate restructuring of plebe year, cadets and members of his staff convinced him "not to go in like a white knight on a horse, but to get some expert advice." As a result, he and the Board of Visitors commissioned yet another major review of The Citadel's plebe system, the third in ten years. Unlike previous studies, the panel they

assembled consisted entirely of current and future Citadel alumni. They selected one graduate from each decade stretching back to the 1920s and added a
senior cadet set to graduate with the class of 1980. Years later, Stockdale traced
his undoing back to his and the committee's efforts to reform The Citadel's
"test of manhood that the bulk of the voting public, to say nothing of the radical elements of the alumni, swore was a key to state pride."[15]

Frank P. Mood, Citadel class of 1960, chaired the group, and page 1 of the
Mood Report confirmed that "over the period of the past several years, it has
become increasingly apparent to those sensitive to the traditions of The Citadel
that the nature of the fourth class system was undergoing a gradual and undesirable change." The committee found that while "real abuses, viciousness,
were relatively unusual," other "milder, but unacceptable excesses were fairly
widespread." They defined many of the corps' practices as "instant traditions,"
which, according to Mood, "were not in the system until five or ten years ago."
A list of these "time-honored" traditions included "sweat parties, excessive
push-ups, devious ways to get around excessive exercise rules, constant demand for recitation of mess facts with resultant interference of eating, racking
(mass punishment, etc.)."[16]

The report highlighted the 30 percent attrition rate among Citadel freshmen and contained a letter from the commandant of cadets describing plebe
year as "less a training program than a hazing session." The commandant
added that "the physical abuse seems to be the most dangerous," an assertion
supported by Dr. George Mood, who informed the committee that "over the
past twelve years I have been recurrently shocked by the abuses of what is
called the fourth class system." Dr. Mood admitted to cringing "every year
when August rolls around, knowing we'll have numerous freshmen leaving
The Citadel with nothing good to say about the school." He relayed stories of
freshmen being carried into the infirmary on stretchers due to "overdoses of
pushups or sweat parties." Singling out the corps' behavior in the mess hall as
"the most ridiculous and most difficult part of the system for me to accept,"
he found it unconscionable that after denying freshmen food, upperclassmen
expected them "to function as fully fueled machines." He found it infuriating
that the system's "so-called tradition is extracted from the experiences of the
preceding one or two years" and concluded that although "I sincerely believe
that The Citadel is an outstanding college and that we do graduate outstanding

patriots and leaders," when parents learned what their sons had gone through, "I feel ashamed for our school and its so called system."[17]

Like the other reports, the 1979 review recognized the fourth class system as "a critical part of the 'whole man' concept and is much of what makes The Citadel a unique institution." At the same time, the Mood Committee labored to recast cadets' definition of manly behavior by making compassion and gentility, not toughness, the measure of a Citadel man. In interviews with Citadel students and graduates, the reviewers sensed a fear that the fourth class system "would be emasculated by some of the changes which the committee is contemplating." Their subjects intimated that toughness was "the objective of the system in and of itself, that there is no higher purpose. They conclude in solemn terms that any planned reduction of this *severity for its own sake* would spell the death knell of this college as we know it."[18]

The Mood Report declared in no uncertain terms that "*this Committee does not accept this analysis or prediction.*" They championed a fourth class system "conducted by gentlemen for gentlemen," determining that "to accept arrogance, crudeness, demeaning conduct and language in the name of tradition is shortsighted." Believing the corps had "strayed from the line of gentlemanly toughness into a series of immature sophomoric routines which miss the mark by any measure of leadership development," they endeavored to create a fourth class system that would instill "integrity, honesty, compassion — in short, all the qualities of a gentleman." Certain that "any good educational system" required "respect for the essential worth and dignity of the individual," they agreed that the fourth class system should be "demanding and rigorous but should be predicated on individual interest, respect and goodwill."[19]

As for their specific recommendations, the alumni found it "noteworthy that many of our Committee's findings *have been found before.*" Indeed, they restated earlier suggestions that Citadel alumni and cadets quit disseminating "misleading and overglamorized" depictions of cadet life, that tactical officers assume a larger role in the "everyday operations of the corps," that sophomores undergo a "cooling off" period before receiving rank, and that all "prescribed study periods and sleep periods" remain "absolutely free from fourth class system activities." In addition to these common pleas, they suggested ending the fourth class system in March in order to allow freshmen to better concentrate on final exams and discontinuing such "indignities" as "baldy haircuts."[20]

The review committee's most important recommendations addressed the recurring problems of excessive physical harassment and malnourishment of knobs. The Mood Report came down hard on "racking," which it defined as "the resort to physical means by upperclassmen to punish fourthclassmen for indiscretions, inadequacies, or fourth class system violations." These punishments ranged from push-ups to "running in place, running up and down stairways, etc." The panel discovered that the line between "racking and hazing can be very fuzzy indeed," and they advocated replacing this "unwanted and unmonitored aberration" of the fourth class system with a formalized, mandatory physical fitness program geared toward each individual's strengths and weaknesses. Their solution for mealtime misconduct was simple and direct: "eliminate the fourth class system activities in the mess hall with the exception of instruction in good manners."[21]

While the earlier fourth class system reviews had languished in obscurity both on and off the Citadel campus, the Mood Report suffered from overexposure. With controversy already brewing around Stockdale's brief tenure in Charleston, state newspapers began leaking news of the study and "the resulting commotion echoed across the state." While the admiral played almost no role in the Mood Committee's investigation, opponents of the measures derided them as part of the "Stockdale Plan." In one of its initial reports, *The State* indicted "lax" school officials for allowing the fourth class system to spin out of control, forewarning "Vice Admiral James B. Stockdale has made it clear changes are coming to The Citadel."[22]

As the news spread, impressions of The Citadel's president shifted from that of a "provisionally okay outsider" to a "meddler into what was Citadel insider business." One state senator suggested the General Assembly cut the institution's funding as long as Stockdale sought "to change the school from the toughest military college in America to just another Annapolis." Former commandant of cadets and Citadel graduate Walt Clark "wholeheartedly and deeply" applauded many of the reforms, but he spoke for many alumni who worried that certain initiatives "smack far too much of being akin to the U.S. Service Academies." The corps of cadets took the bait as well, accusing Stockdale and his staff of "outsiders" of trying to ruin their school. Despite the backgrounds of the Mood Report's authors, the editor of *The Brigadier*, apparently unaware that the Board of Visitors was still solvent, complained that "only Citadel men, none of whom presently hold high positions within the administration . . . can comprehend and appreciate the benefits that exist in the present fourth class system." A cartoon in that same edition showed Stockdale sitting behind his desk, furiously copying rules from the "USNA Catalogue" into the Citadel guidebook.[23]

Media reports fanned the flames by highlighting some of the more controversial measures, exaggerating the extent of others, and presenting all the recommendations as accepted policies rather than proposals. An article in the *Charleston News and Courier* mentioned the plan's overall goal of "eliminating hazing" but focused on two suggestions the board later rejected, ending the plebe system early and no longer requiring knob haircuts. The *Columbia Record* reported that not only were Citadel barbers going to quit shaving plebes' heads but that school officials had outlawed any "punishment of freshmen by upperclassmen."[24]

A muddled interpretation of "racking" compounded many people's anxieties. Apparently, a large number of Citadel men believed the term applied not just to physical punishment but to even the most mundane aspects of Citadel life. For example, one student eulogized aspects of Citadel life not even mentioned in the Mood Report. He preached, "All the shoe shining, brass polishing, hat delinting, and shirt tucking that we were forced to perform has made us conscious of our personal appearance; all the corner squaring, running in the barracks, the popping off that we were compelled to do has made us realize that everyone else is watching our conduct." Many Citadel cadets and alumni howled that the "changes would soften the military college," until "only the shell will remain and like a corpse which houses no soul, [The Citadel] will cease living it will merely exist." With the college having cheated death earlier in the decade, the Grim Reaper returned to campus as yet another drawing of The Citadel's headstone appeared in *The Brigadier*, this time bearing the epitaph, "crippled and consumed by those who would destroy her."[25]

Many believed that even if the Mood Report did not kill The Citadel, it would still leave the institution susceptible to the deadly toxin of coeducation. Cries that when "you take away the fourth class system, you take away The Citadel" went hand in hand with the complaint that "they might as well make it a girl's school now." Laying bare their belief that a tough plebe year served as the school's best defense against a sexually integrated corps, many alumni were convinced that the proposed reforms "open the door for the admission of women students." State Representative John Bradley went so far as to introduce legislation requiring the college to drop its single-sex policies, arguing "if the fourth class system is going to be abolished at The Citadel, it would be economically impractical to prevent women from attending."[26]

Stockdale fought back, refuting that the suggested modifications "will eliminate the unique challenges of a military college." He explained that the "traditions" many people defended were foreign to older Citadel graduates and that "the only thing being tampered with is the modern innovations on the basic theme." He found the violence of the current fourth class system "debilitating toward the intellectual side of life." With over half of all freshmen posting below-average GPAs, he refused "to sponsor a system that makes it impossible for an ambitious boy to put his best foot forward when planning his life." Evoking his Vietnam record, he reminded his critics that he understood "as well as anybody what the plebe year can do for you" but clarified, "What I'm dealing with is cruelty and I've got to act."[27]

While Stockdale appeared to lead the fight, he resented having "to take the gas for what somebody else wants me to do." He informed *The State* that while he endorsed the Mood Report's findings, the final decision rested with the Board of Visitors. Speaking before that body, the admiral predicted, "If you saw how our current Regulations Book had to be changed to incorporate these recommendations, you would laugh." With the exception of ending racking and taming mess hall antics, he noted, "There were almost *no changes*" — the "key will be enforcement."[28]

A few board members worried that Stockdale was "attempting to change too many traditions at The Citadel too quickly," and when the group dragged its feet on approving the Mood Report, Stockdale threatened to resign. Whether or not this ultimatum factored into their decision, the board eventually accepted nineteen of the report's twenty-one proposals, refusing to shorten plebe year or abolish knob haircuts. In a public statement, they insisted that the "direction of these recommendations is consistent with the traditions of the college and in no way abolishes the fourth class system as a rigorous and demanding training program." Addressing the "apparent misunderstanding among cadets, alumni, and the public at large about the nature and scope" of the findings, they assured "all concerned that the recommendations do not substantially modify or change the fourth class system, but serve to eliminate inequities, real and potential." They outlined a new mess hall policy whereby freshmen would "eat in a relaxed atmosphere" and noted that the "elimination of unmonitored 'racking' in no way affects the traditional concept of 'bracing' familiar to generations of cadets." After announcing the ruling, the board's chairman, William "Buddy" Prioleau, confirmed, "It will still be the toughest system in the country."[29]

Admiral Stockdale never got to see how well or how poorly the new fourth class system functioned. On the same day they voted on the Mood Report, the board delayed action on the findings of an administrative reorganization plan conducted at the president's behest and with their approval. Stockdale hoped the report, filed by Price-Waterhouse, would convince the Board of Visitors to restructure The Citadel's admissions department with an eye toward attracting more qualified students to campus. Specifically, Stockdale suspected that the "incessantly featured parade ground motif was seen as a little bit corny by some of the real bright and vigorous kids out there," and he wanted an admissions office "run by an educator who knows how modern colleges fill their classrooms with bright people." At that time, the ubiquitous D. D. Nicholson served as The Citadel's vice president for development, which included public relations and "recruiting." A beloved figure among Citadel alumni and cadets, Nicholson had earned the moniker "Mr. Citadel" for his tireless boosterism and unwavering loyalty to the college. When the Price-Waterhouse package suggested assigning student procurement duties to the dean of academics, Nicholson rallied Citadel graduates to his side in an effort to, in Stockdale's estimation, "save his turf." The Association of Citadel Men "made very clear its concern over how at least one member of Admiral Stockdale's staff would fare in the reorganization," and when the board declined to accept the plan immediately, Stockdale scribbled on a notepad, "I hereby resign my office as President of The Citadel." His resignation came a week before his formal inauguration.[30]

Although the suddenness of Stockdale's actions shocked the Board of Visitors, they recovered quickly. Prioleau called it a "terrific loss," adding, "but we respect his decision." To reporters, an embittered Stockdale announced, "I've resigned and the reason is very simple. I'm just tired of hassling with the Board of Visitors over every change in the status quo I've tried to make." He fumed that the board considered every one of his efforts to improve the school a "threat to the traditions of The Citadel." In the end, Stockdale grumbled, "The forces of the status quo were marshaled and they won." In a parting shot, he sneered, "The place is locked in pre–Civil War concrete."[31]

The Board of Visitors named Major General James A. Grimsley, a 1942 Citadel graduate and the college's former vice president for admissions and finance, the interim president. Grimsley promised to restore "calm and stability" by getting "the focus of the college out of the headlines and into the classroom and parade grounds." Given the tumult of the previous eleven months, however, the new fourth class system regulations occupied the minds of most Citadel personnel. School officials placed renewed emphasis on "enforcing cadet regulations and ensuring timely disciplinary action against the cadets guilty of violations." As a result, plebe attrition remained about "average" that year, with most Citadel officials, tactical officers, and even Dr. Mood agreeing that the "treatment of freshmen is improved over last year and the year before." Grimsley spoke with several of the freshmen who quit and concluded, "Not a one was physically or psychologically maltreated, and I could not have said that last year." Exuding an air of confidence as the school year opened, the Board of Visitors welcomed the ABC television show 20/20 to campus to see for themselves if The Citadel is "as tough, and more importantly, as effective as we claim it to be."[32]

Despite such reports, alumni flooded the campus with letters denouncing the changes to the fourth class system. Many of the letters perpetuated key misconceptions surrounding the Mood Report. One alumnus proclaimed, "I am not ashamed of anything that happened within the barracks concerning the fourth class system and have nothing to hide." Possibly unaware of who authored the report, he mused that no one could "really comprehend the institution and the fourth class system unless he has been through it or associated with it." In his opinion, The Citadel was under siege from an "ignorant, ill informed public" that had naively accepted "exaggerated propaganda." In the end, he hoped "the recent changes brought about by Vice Admiral Stockdale" would keep Citadel officials cognizant of "our own vulnerability to outsiders and to public opinion."[33]

A 1978 graduate took Stockdale's "pre–civil war concrete" jab as a compliment, boasting that because of these moorings, The Citadel "has stood the test of time and held the mark of excellence for over 138 years." He promoted Citadel men as the "finest on the market" due to the "arduous training of the fourth class system." He not only regarded racking as the "best reinforcer for teaching self-discipline," he labeled it the "life's blood" of The Citadel. Operating under the assumption that the system "has almost been eliminated," he beseeched school officials, "Do not be influenced by the non-ring wearers" supposedly ruining the school.[34]

While some Citadel students appreciated that the modified plebe system tested the "leadership ability of the cadet chain of command as well as the freshmen's ability to follow," others scoffed that plebe year had become a "joke," since without fear of retribution, knobs "strive for nothing, they learn nothing, and they will be nothing." Viewing a harsh first year as the source of The Citadel's and Citadel men's uniqueness and value, they lamented that "what in the past has been a school for only the strong of mind and body has now become an institution for anyone who will shear his locks and wear pants with stripes." A drawing in *The Brigadier* showed the ghost of Confederate General and Citadel alumni Elison Capers rising from his grave, moaning, "Bring Back the Rack." The artist overlooked the fact that Capers would have been absolutely unfamiliar with the concept of racking.[35]

In contrast, a sizable percentage of the corps took a measured view of the Mood Report and even Admiral Stockdale. A freshman was grateful that "they toned it down some but didn't totally get rid of it." A group of seniors remarked "actually we've just gotten rid of the Mickey Mouse aspect of the school." The editor of *The Brigadier* understood that "a responsible alumni committee with much more hindsight than the class of 1981 made the recommendations which parented the present fourth class system, and we must respect their decisions." Recognizing that "all of the physical changes that have taken place were made with the school's best interest in mind," he thanked school officials for helping "us place our priorities in proper order" by stressing The Citadel's academic duties over its military ones. He even extended this sentiment toward Admiral Stockdale, who "if for nothing else, he should be remembered for re-emphasizing the mission of a military college — providing a disciplined education."[36]

Several cadets reserved some venom for the newly minted graduates who continued to wail about the "death of The Citadel." One student advised his colleagues, "The next time you're afraid The Citadel is about to crumble to the ground because of too many changes, go talk to an 'old timer' . . . you will probably learn that making changes to Citadel 'traditions' is not only inevitable, it is usually for the best." Two weeks prior to the 1981 commencement ceremonies, a junior informed members of the outgoing class that they could soon begin huffing "'Back when I was in the Corps'. . . or 'The Corps has gone to _____!!' and will start writing 'Letters to the Editor' about how proud [they were] to wear dress grays in the ninety degree Charleston weather."[37]

By the winter of 1980, school officials breathed a sigh of relief that The Citadel had weathered the storm and emerged seemingly as strong as ever. Applications increased almost 50 percent for the upcoming school year, and with General Grimsley at the helm, Prioleau rejoiced, "We are unified now in a way we haven't been for more than a year." The Board of Visitors and cadets alike praised Grimsley for bringing "optimism to a chaotic corps." The president seemed to draw much of his appeal from the fact that he was a Citadel man who would protect the college's traditions. As interim president, he cemented his relationship with the board by scrapping the Price-Waterhouse reorganization plan, replacing it with a new one that proposed "no major changes." At the same meeting where Grimsley introduced his administrative blueprint, the board surprised no one by removing his interim status and appointing him the sixteenth president of The Citadel. Soon thereafter, he began dismantling several of the Mood Committee's initiatives, reinstating push-ups as "an immediate form" of disciplining freshmen.[38]

Commenting on the resistance he faced when he tried to rein in the abuses of plebe year, Admiral Stockdale exclaimed, "You would have thought I was tampering with America," and in the minds of many cadets and the Board of Visitors, he was. For decades, Citadel backers had staked the institution's reputation on its ability to produce the type of leaders and superior citizens the country needed. Such claims rested in large part on a belief that such leadership and citizenship were synonymous with manliness. The Citadel's 1979 "mission statement" listed the school's objectives in gender-neutral terms, declaring that the "environment and philosophy of the college stress, along with academic proficiency, the qualities of duty, honor, patriotism, and integrity." In adding that "as one of the last two state supported military colleges with these objectives, The Citadel has a national reputation," the authors lumped The Citadel in with another all-male military college, the Virginia Military Institute, thus implying that the successful inculcation of civic virtues depended upon preserving an all-male corps of cadets.[39]

By the late 1970s, with debates over women's rights flaring up in legislative halls and private homes nationwide and with more and more people questioning rigid gender distinctions, plebe year at The Citadel became not just a method of building men but also a justification for excluding women. With the college's worth yoked to its single-sex environment, a palatable fear of coeducation explains, in part, why Citadel men reacted so fiercely to the Mood Report. A few months after Admiral Stockdale resigned, the 1980 *Guidon* stated explicitly that "although there will be changes and modifications, the overall goal of The Citadel will continue to be that of producing men of learning, integrity and patriotism." Since nothing inherently prevented women from being as intelligent, forthright, and patriotic as men, the physicality of the fourth class system served as both a prime tool for manufacturing men and barring women.[40]

When it came to protecting the all-male environment that produced exceptional American citizens, Citadel men relied on a traditionally "southern" method of disparaging challenges to the status quo as the work of ignorant, hostile "outsiders." Despite their dubious authenticity when it came to the origins and authorship of the Mood Report, shrieks of outsider interference effectively demonized the report in the eyes of most Citadel cadets, alumni, and administrators. Such charges echoed those from the past that were leveled at southern civil rights workers and union organizers with similar vitriol and varying degrees of success. The lingering power and parallels of these accusations make it important to remember that just as Citadel men supported and instigated several of the reforms attributed solely to Stockdale, many homegrown activists spurred and championed the broader protest movements aimed at eliminating the region's social, political, and economic disparities.[41]

In his description of the college for the *Encyclopedia of Southern Culture*, Walter Fraser, a former professor at The Citadel, provided a succinct summation of the school's standing and attitude at the dawning of the 1980s. He intimated that Stockdale's failure "to minimize hazing, to change the school's 'macho' image, to attract scholarly students and to reorganize the command structure" stemmed largely from his inability to overcome the fact that he was "neither a graduate of the institution nor a southerner." Fraser's entry concluded that when General Grimsley, "a native South Carolinian and Citadel graduate" stepped in promising "no changes," he fulfilled "the wish of the board of visitors, the students and most of the faculty."[42]

CHAPTER EIGHT

Marching Backward

Race and The Citadel in Reagan's America

Enrollment at The Citadel soared during the 1980s. In 1983, the school received over two thousand applications, the highest number ever until the record was broken the next year. Such success prompted the chairman of the Board of Visitors, "Buddy" Prioleau, to boast that "in light of the college's experiences, The Citadel enrollment picture is quite unusual — we are oversubscribed while others are begging for students." Increased competition for a limited number of slots meant that the college registrar could be more selective, and sure enough, the average SAT and academic credentials of each incoming class either matched or surpassed those of the previous ones. By mid-decade, the college had regained its national reputation, repeatedly receiving high marks in *U.S. News and World Report*'s annual ranking of the nation's best colleges and universities.[1]

While a few observers attributed this boom to "the well known unique character of the college," the trend actually revealed that The Citadel was marching in step with the American mainstream. With conservative pundits hailing the "return of old-fashioned patriotism," Citadel spokesman D. D. Nicholson crowed that "the national philosophy is turning back to The Citadel's philosophy," a shift that boded well for some and ill for others. Various media outlets reported on the rising prestige and popularity of military schools across the country. Some of the most flattering articles focused on southern institutions in particular, emphasizing and lauding their subjects' manliness as well as their whiteness. A June 1985 article in *Esquire* offered a Dunning-esque analysis of Reconstruction that celebrated white southerners' fascination with and affinity for martial values, asserting that generations of southern males willingly endured hardships and deprivations out of respect for their Civil War ancestors who spent Reconstruction "under the fist of the conqueror." The author of the piece theorized that a fear of having lost "power so completely once" drove these southerners to become especially "brutal politicians and good soldiers" lest they lose power again. Certainly, women and African Americans played no part in this national or regional reading of the past or present, an omission that merely reinforced what many already believed were "attributes associated with The Citadel."[2]

Voicing an ideology that, according to Haynes Johnson, "perfectly matched the temper of his times," Ronald Reagan entered the White House vowing to "redeem America" from what he saw as the excesses and weaknesses of earlier administrations. Using military spending and patriotic rhetoric to sell his "anti-tax; anti-communism; anti-government" panacea for the nation's woes, the new president lavished billions of dollars on defense, gutted welfare programs, crippled the Civil Rights Commission, and demonized affirmative action. Johnson adds that even as Reagan's policies weakened the economy, produced legions of unemployed workers, and created armies of homeless people, his greatest impact was on political attitudes "characterized by its small-mindedness and even at times by its meanness." Nowhere was this more evident than in Reagan's racial politics, where he reaped tremendous political rewards by "pitting white male Americans against the 'special interests' and pleadings of African-Americans." With national leaders now defending states' rights, rolling back the accomplishments of the civil rights movement, and espousing thinly veiled racist arguments against welfare, busing, and affirmative action, Hodding Carter noted, "It's a new America, Ronald Reagan's America, and at times it smells a lot like the old Mississippi."[3]

The consequences of Reagan's subtle and not-so-subtle appeals to white racism played out on college campuses across America. In February 1989, historian Jon Weiner penned an article for *The Nation* entitled "Reagan's Children." In it, he documented the "upsurge in campus racism," declaring this trend "the most disturbing development in university life across the nation during the past decade." Citing glaring examples of racial violence and abuse from Ann Arbor, Michigan; Madison, Wisconsin; Purdue, Dartmouth, and UCLA, Weiner offered the "outbreak of student hatred" as proof of "how white attitudes towards minorities have changed on campus during the Reagan years."[4]

Campus race relations deteriorated at The Citadel as well, bottoming out in October 1986 when the hazing of a black cadet brought to the fore racial problems that had been festering for decades. Responses to what came to be known as "the Nesmith incident" sparked heated debates over The Citadel's past as well as its present. Many of these debates took on a particularly "southern" tone as confrontations erupted over the corps' prominent display of Confederate symbols. Unwilling to face up to the racial problems plaguing the corps, most whites at The Citadel clung tenaciously to a one-sided image of the South's past, refusing to accept a less noble, but more inclusive, depiction of their southern heritage.[5]

Just as Reagan's patriotic platitudes and appeals to family values carried with them an implicit condemnation of the cultural, social, and sexual reform movements of the 1960s, key Citadel officials used the post-*Brown*, preintegration "golden years" of Mark Clark's tenure as their template for reviving school spirit and prestige. In doing so, they revived the same racialized notions of manliness that dominated the earlier era. General Grimsley in particular emulated the "American Eagle's" approach to instilling cadets with the proper Citadel attributes, harping on many of the same themes as his predecessor and aping many of the former president's practices. Most notably, he renewed focus on the "whole man" concept, expounding regularly on the "hallmark of a successful man," the "development of the 'physical man,'" and The Citadel's proficiency at developing "'whole men' with all that term connotes." He identified these paragons of masculinity as those who had been "educated academically, physically, militarily, spiritually, patriotically, and honorably." He often concluded that "no other education could be as rewarding" as the one offered by his alma mater since "the exceptional demands placed on a Citadel cadet are more than compensated for by the ultimate result — a Citadel Man."[6]

The Board of Visitors joined in the chorus when they set cultivating "awareness of the essential role that the military environment of The Citadel plays in educating the 'whole man'" as one of their goals for the next ten years. Apparently they succeeded, as student publications offered numerous tributes to The Citadel and its reputation for building men. The 1981 edition of the *Guidon* defined the "The Citadel system" as one that "matures, refines, trains and schools the totality of a young man's being" and wished new cadets luck as they "begin the infinitely rewarding task of aspiring to attain that coveted title of *Citadel Man*." Alumni got into the act as well, with a Citadel graduate from Union, South Carolina, paying for billboards advertising his alma mater as a place where parents "Send Us a Boy — We'll Send You a Man."[7]

Despite these repeated glorifications of manliness, Citadel boosters frequently listed their presumably masculine attributes in gender-neutral terms. Most echoed Grimsley's assertion that "the teaching of The Citadel for love of country, patriotism, honor, courage, loyalty, and devotion to duty have been hallmarks for its graduates." With nothing inherently rendering females incapable of patriotic, honorable, or courageous behavior, the 1980s witnessed an acceleration of the trend whereby Citadel personnel linked the college's ability to produce men primarily to their success at excluding women. In 1982, the Advisory Committee to the Board of Visitors warned of the "possibility that competent authority might at some time direct the admission of females into the corps" and urged the board to develop an "effective plan to counter any movement toward requiring admission of females into the corps." The chairman of the Board of Visitors heeded this advice, noting that "the federal academies have gone downhill" since accepting women. The corps generally evinced similar attitudes, albeit with more vehemence than their elders, as one student demanded that The Citadel remain a "fortress of *Masculinity*."[8]

With this in mind, most cadets disapproved of women who either challenged male authority or violated what they considered proper gender norms. When a lampoon edition of *The Brigadier* announced "Corps to go co-ed," the fictional female enrollees were depicted as unhygienic and unfeminine, bearing a strong resemblance to "early Cro-Magnon Man." In 1982, a student vilified a recently hired female professor for imposing "her views on feminist domination on those she 'teaches.'" A year later, the same faculty member outraged several members of the corps when she ordered a cadet to remove a poster she deemed offensive from the walls of an academic building. One young man boasted that the pictures hanging in the barracks made the poster she saw seem tame, adding if she "cannot stand the heat of the all-male Military Monastery, she should find employment in another kitchen."[9]

Such attitudes left cadets ill-equipped to handle some of the changes occurring outside school walls. One student despaired for the future of America when he saw a photo of a twelve-year-old girl playing middle school football. Disappointed to find out that the picture was not of an "extremely effeminate boy" and that instead of being "crunched by the clotheslining right arm of some twelve year old male linebacker," the female quarterback had thrown for two touchdowns and run for another, the author viewed her success as "an end to all that I had believed in for the past twenty-one years." Begging for someone to "save us," he longed for the "good old days when a woman knew her place in the sporting world." Nostalgic for "sweaty little cheerleaders" who gleefully congratulated their male heroes and clueless mothers who cheered for the wrong team until their husbands corrected them, he grumbled, "now you have your Chris Everts, your Dorothy Hamills, and those women body builders." Uncomfortable with the popularity and prowess of female athletes, he feared that they would soon dominate the sports world, pleading, "Oh don't let it happen! It was so perfect."[10]

At an institution populated predominantly by males of similar cultural, social, and ideological bents, no one stepped forward to challenge this man's view of a "perfect" society. Although some cadets still complained that off-campus uniform requirements left Citadel graduates unprepared for civilian life, the perpetuation of gender stereotypes and narrow parameters of proper societal behavior proved a greater hindrance to the students' ability to adjust to and interact in a diverse society. For example, although several women who attended the College of Charleston found most cadets "honest and considerate," they had also met others who were unable to "control themselves in the presence of other women" and who tended to treat females "as sex objects or as something on which to release their frustrations." Unconcerned with the opinions of "outsiders," most cadets responded to this information with "I don't really care what they think."[11]

While Citadel personnel's macho worldview went largely unchallenged throughout the 1980s, the same cannot be said for many of their highly selective, unquestionably white interpretations of the school's and the South's past and present. With applications rolling in, Citadel officials exercised greater control over whom they admitted, but fostering campus diversity ranked low on their list of priorities. From 1980 to 1985, African American students never made up more than 5 percent of a cadet corps that was 93 percent white. Furthermore, at the beginning of the decade, the college had no black professors, no black administrators, and no black professional staff members.[12]

While many white cadets seemed oblivious to the startling homogeneity of their surroundings, black cadets did not. One student remarked, "You're a black spot in a white crowd, and you can't hide." Another agreed, adding, "With the ratio of whites to blacks there, some people show you clearly they don't like you because you're black." Seeing the college as a microcosm of America, one cadet asserted, "You have to live and die in a white society," and "If you can make it at The Citadel, you've proven you can make it in white society."[13]

When college officials made it a point to attract more African American students to The Citadel's campus, they often did so only at the prodding of state and federal authorities. Even then, they tried to do so with minimal effort on their part. In 1981, as proof of their "commitment" to affirmative action, the Board of Visitors hired one black air force officer to help recruit minority students. In later years, school officials asked African American alumni, preachers at black churches, and black cadets to step up their recruiting efforts. Meanwhile, their contribution to the campaign consisted largely of distributing brochures "illustrated to appeal to blacks." At the same time, the attitudes of certain administrators indicated a superficial commitment at best to promoting racial diversity. One in particular demanded that the school not lower its standards to fill "quotas," while D. D. Nicholson admitted, "We haven't made much of an effort to go out and fill this place with black students because that would be inequitable."[14]

Given the intransigence of school leaders, the lack of racial diversity on the Board of Visitors drew more attention than the absence of minorities in the corps of cadets. In 1979, the Department of Health, Education and Welfare (HEW) conducted an examination of South Carolina's colleges and universities to check the state's overall progress in dismantling its "dual system of education." The Palmetto State fared poorly in this as the HEW agents discovered that none of the eleven colleges they visited met federal desegregation requirements. Concluding that the educational and social climates at South Carolina's public universities "encourage students to enroll at institutions on the basis of their racial identity," department officials threatened to withhold over $75 million in federal funding should South Carolina not take steps to eradicate "the vestiges of unconstitutional segregation," giving state officials sixty days to devise a viable desegregation plan.[15]

While Citadel administrators voiced no opposition to the use of "incentive scholarships" and other initiatives designed to entice black students and faculty to traditionally white colleges, a major battle ensued over the HEW's contention that "the low representation of blacks on governing boards of the institutions has precipitated the racial identities of the schools." Part of the hastily assembled "South Carolina Plan for Equity and Equal Opportunity in the Public Colleges and Universities" included a proviso reconfiguring the method by which all school trustees were chosen, with each member either elected by the General Assembly or appointed by the governor. At the time, state law mandated that all members of The Citadel's Board of Visitors be graduates of the college. Since this new proposal carried no such stipulation, the current members of the board opposed it on the grounds that it might require them to share power with someone who did not appreciate the "traditions and uniqueness" of the college.[16]

In April 1981, the Board unanimously rejected the entire $19.5 million desegregation package based solely on their objection to the trustee measure. Chairman Prioleau tried to explain that "we are not opposing this from any racial standpoint," but to endorse "a major policy change in the composition of our board which we do not approve of, this would violate our honor and integrity." To counter those who might accuse them of racially discriminatory behavior, the chairman laid out a telling definition of racial integration in which "color doesn't have a thing to do with it." Prioleau and other school personnel claimed that The Citadel, a college with a 2 percent African American student population, was the "most integrated school in the state" because "we are the only school where everyone wears the same clothes, eats the same food, lives in the same rooms."[17]

Not everyone agreed that The Citadel was leading South Carolina down the path of racial progress. When the Office of Civil Rights announced that it would not approve the state's desegregation plan unless every school signed it, an editorial in *The State* newspaper announced, "Only Citadel Stands in Schoolhouse Door." Several high-ranking state officials warned that the Board of Visitors' stubbornness could cost South Carolina millions of dollars and lead to numerous federal lawsuits. Should this happen, many politicians decided that The Citadel ought to "face federal wrath — and the loss of federal money — alone." State Senator Harry Chapman favored adding a rider to the 1982 budget stipulating that if South Carolina lost federal funds because of any school's refusal to sign the desegregation plan, then those responsible must reimburse the state.[18]

In late June, the Board of Visitors signed an amended plan, one that committed the college "to a good faith effort to effectuate the goal of increasing black representation on its governing board," but did not require them to make any changes in their trustee requirements. Still, with this last signature in place, Governor Riley and the South Carolina attorney general quickly approved the entire report, and two weeks later HEW officials did the same.[19]

The fight continued, though, with many South Carolinians resenting the fact that The Citadel's special alumni stipulation "disfranchises 99.9 percent of the population." After meeting with officials from the federal Department of Education, members of South Carolina's Commission on Higher Education (CHE) drafted a plan to enact legislation that would quickly and effectively desegregate every college's governing board. The CHE singled out Citadel supporters as the primary opponents to their goal, and sure enough, Citadel graduates proved extremely effective at beating back challenges to their way of doing things. School alumni serving on both the Senate Education Committee and the CHE kept proposals bottled up in committees, but when one of the bills eventually made it to a vote, one observer noted, "It looked like a Citadel pep rally in the state Senate chamber with about one hundred alumni cheering speakers opposing a change in the structure of the school's trustees."[20]

In an effort to reach some sort of compromise, the CHE devised a milder desegregation method that allowed the governor to add one member to the governing body of every South Carolina college. When Citadel officials again demanded that their appointee be a graduate of the college, a member of the commission suggested that since no other public institution asked permission to "exclude two and half million citizens of this state," perhaps The Citadel "should become a private college and start paying its own bills." Legislators and CHE members eventually gave in, passing a version of the bill upholding The Citadel's alumni restriction. This bothered many, and the U.S. Department of Education (DOE) informed the CHE that "since blacks were barred from admission for many years and few blacks have enrolled since the era of (court ordered) desegregation, the requirement that all members of the board who are not *ex officio* be alumni screens out many otherwise eligible blacks and perpetuates the racial identity of the board." George James, the new chairman of the Board of Visitors, called such objections "garbage."[21]

While the debate over opening up membership on the Board of Visitors was framed in the context of racial diversification, Citadel officials saw themselves fighting what they considered a much more important, although not unrelated, battle: preserving the college's single-sex environment. When they argued, "The very nature of this institution requires that it be governed by persons familiar with its background, its traditions, its mission," the foremost mission in their minds was the production of Citadel men. D. D. Nicholson spoke for many Citadel cadets and alumni when he predicted that "the first vote a board with non-alumni would take would probably be to accept women," a move Prioleau warned "would pull down what The Citadel stands for." A cadet described the thought of allowing anyone to serve on the Board of Visitors as "comical and perhaps absurd," finding it "incredible" that a female might actually qualify for membership on The Citadel's controlling body. The president of the Association of Citadel Men called any such change "the beginning of the end of The Citadel as we know it," for "we could have a Board of Visitors with no Citadel Men on it, but with all probability some female members." This desire to preserve the most precious and long-lasting of the school's traditions helps explain the intensity with which most Citadel personnel fought the desegregation plan, but it also shows how one form of discrimination fed into another since the school's policy denied all women and the vast majority of African American men a role in developing institutional policies.[22]

Nonetheless, with the legislation finally in place, Governor Riley wasted no time appointing Alonzo Nesmith, a twenty-six-year-old 1979 graduate of The Citadel, to the Board of Visitors. That same year, the board reported that representatives from the Office of Civil Rights had visited campus and left "with a favorable opinion of Citadel actions in the Civil Rights area." Later evaluations were not near as positive, as South Carolina colleges in general and The Citadel in particular made "little measurable progress" in meeting their desegregation goals. By 1985, ten out of the state's twelve public colleges had fallen well short of the minority recruitment standards they set for themselves. At The Citadel, the number of nonwhite students had actually decreased over the previous four years. Fred Sheheen, the chairman of the CHE, expressed his dissatisfaction with these figures, taking a jab at The Citadel by citing "change-resistant organizational structure alumni, which too often defend the status quo" as a major "force which may counter any affirmative action plan, desegregation plan, or equal opportunity plan in the country." The next year, Citadel officials and cadets would suffer the consequences of their dogged efforts to prevent or at least impede any meaningful diversification of the college's cultural, social, or intellectual environment.[23]

When Alonzo Nesmith took his seat on the Board of Visitors, it appeared as though The Citadel had emerged from the turmoil surrounding South Carolina's desegregation plan stronger than ever. In his annual recap of the 1985–1986 school year, General Grimsley predicted that "this year will be recorded in the annals of The Citadel as one in which the future of the college has been assured." To back up this claim, he cited the "continued revitalization of the Corps of Cadets and the unprecedented number of quality applicants for admission; the surge in alumni enthusiasm and support world wide; and the solid national media recognition." This last boon pleased Grimsley the most as he saw fit to repeat that "there were no negative aspects to publicity connected with The Citadel." This public relations coup would prove short lived when, early in the upcoming school year, the hazing of a black Citadel cadet drew the critical eyes of the nation to Charleston.[24]

At around 12:45 a.m. on October 23, 1986, five white cadets, Maurice Bostic, Paul Koss, Jimmy Biggerstaff, Jeffrey Plumley, and Steve Webb, took a break from studying and began discussing the behavior and attitude of Kevin Nesmith, a freshman in their company and the younger brother of the newest member of the Board of Visitors. The five juniors decided that Nesmith was not "pulling his weight," and in order to motivate the "notoriously slack knob," Webb suggested that they dress up as Ku Klux Klansmen and pay Nesmith an early morning visit. They all went to their rooms to get into costume, and unbeknownst to the rest of the group, Plumley returned with a small, slightly singed, paper cross. About 1:00 a.m., the cadets, clad in white sheets and wearing towels over their heads so as to "give the appearance of Klansmen," assembled outside Nesmith's room and then entered chanting "Nesmith get your shit together." This awoke Nesmith's roommate, Michael Mendoza, who leaped out of bed, threatening to "beat every one of your asses." Mendoza swung at one of the intruders, and his roommate woke up just as the five men scampered out the door. As he escaped, Plumley dropped his paper cross on a piece of furniture, and Mendoza knocked the hat and towel off Koss's head. The whole encounter lasted approximately ninety seconds, but when the two freshmen saw the singed cross, they considered it a "serious incident." Mendoza decided they should notify school officials, including his roommate's brother, and they took what evidence they had to a couple of upperclassmen for safekeeping. The towel had Koss's name and Social Security number sewed on it, and with him clearly implicated, cadet and college officials began tracking down his accomplices. By 11:44 p.m. the next day, the other four cadets had confessed.[25]

News of the hazing spread quickly, and recognizing the gravity of the situation, General Grimsley held a series of meetings with cadets, faculty, and members of the press "to present all the facts in the case; to tamp down rumors; and to relieve tension." On October 24, he spoke with all African American cadets, assuring them that he would investigate the matter thoroughly. A few days later, he addressed the entire corps, exhorting them to "work toward relieving any pressures that may rest" within the student body. Three days later, he held a news conference in which he called the hazing an "aberration and is not an indication of the status of our relations between black and white cadets." He corrected earlier reports that the five upperclassmen had shouted racial slurs at Nesmith, adding, "I would like to write it off as a prank that got out of hand, but the college has too much at stake to write this off." Announcing that he would not "tolerate any action that is divisive to the corps of cadets," he assembled a panel to "review the alleged problem of racial discrimination at The Citadel" and vowed to take "appropriate action" based on their findings.[26]

While the Federal Bureau of Investigation, the U.S. Justice Department, the South Carolina Law Enforcement Division (SLED), the air force, and the army sent representatives to investigate the assault, many school officials and most white cadets responded to the uproar by denying that The Citadel had any racial problems whatsoever. Grimsley countered what he called "scare headlines" by proclaiming, "In my judgment, after my detailed review of all facts, this was not a racially motivated incident." One white student described the hazing as simply a manifestation of the corps' "sarcastic humor," akin to "jokes about people's girlfriends, about their families, about their cars."[27]

Several white cadets cast the pre–"Nesmith incident" Citadel as a social utopia, a place where bonds of brotherhood overwhelmed any other divisions or differences. One such student found it amazing that "a system of patternized behavior can group together individuals stemming from such different sociocultural backgrounds, with both mingling and clashing values, and produce a body of men, a corps, that functions as true brothers in search of a common goal: to become Citadel Men." Another regretted that the controversy had caused some of his colleagues to begin focusing on "the distinction of color," driving a wedge between "brothers who until the past month had forgotten there were differences between people." Yet another claimed that "The Citadel ring does not represent one race or nationality, but what it does represent is that we are all part of one *fraternity*, that of Citadel men."[28]

Implicit in such arguments is that only lesser men, not "whole men," would be aware of or even bothered by racism within the corps of cadets. The fact that five white students choose to masquerade as the South's foremost practitioners of racial terrorism in an attempt to "motivate" an African American cadet flies in the face of claims that the corps had no "memories of prejudices, of racial injustices, of times that have long passed." Rather than confront the callousness, bigotry, and cruelty of some of their peers, many white cadets fell back on claims that Citadel men shared universal goals and values that, in their minds, rendered offensive comments and actions harmless.[29]

Such attitudes pushed black cadets even further to the margins of the Citadel family. This is not to say that black cadets did not try to alert whites to the racial implications of certain remarks, behavior, or "jokes." For decades, African American students expressed their opinions in a variety of ways, from letters to *The Brigadier* to waving homemade banners at football games. Having already alerted the regimental commander to white cadets' brazen use of racial slurs, most black cadets refused to characterize the Nesmith incident as a benign prank or an innocuous aspect of the fourth class system. A senior believed the hazing "was somewhat racially motivated. There was a bit too much symbolism to be anything else." Numerous other African American cadets denied that the events represented an "aberration." One student recalled returning to his room and finding a burnt cross made out of popsicle sticks laying on his bed. A few others remembered upperclassmen telling them, "I hate black people. I don't want you in my school, and I'll do anything I can to run you out." A member of the Afro-American Society viewed the five whites' act as the product of an "adamantly depraved insensitivity," while the president of the organization stated that racism "is a disease in the corps and all we have to do is face it."[30]

Despite hopes that punishing the five cadets would resolve the controversy, the sentence handed down by Grimsley and the Board of Visitors magnified negative perceptions of the college. On November 1, General Grimsley announced that the five cadets would walk 195 tours[31] and had been placed on probation, facing expulsion should they commit another offense in their remaining two years at The Citadel. The chairman of the Board of Visitors confirmed that "the punishment accorded these cadets is very severe," finding it necessary to reiterate that The Citadel "does not have a racial problem." Nesmith's assailants apologized to him privately and issued a public apology to "The Citadel community," regretting that "our thoughtlessness has generated opinions of our school that are simply unjustified by the reality of the relations between the races on our campus." They described their act as "arrogant and improper," adding, "We turned an inappropriate practice into a condemnable one by thoughtlessly choosing theatrics that are offensive to all persons of good will." For his part, Grimsley declared the matter closed, reaffirming yet again that The Citadel had no "major racial problems."[32]

Soon after Grimsley issued this proclamation, voices from inside and outside The Citadel began disputing claims that the matter had been resolved to everyone's satisfaction. Cadet Calvin Robinson wrote a letter to *The Brigadier* on behalf of the Afro-American Society, expressing their "heartfelt outrage and disgust with the outcome of this sordid, despicable affair." He argued that by making it possible for "the five racists" to eventually graduate, school officials had rendered the "intolerable tolerable and the immoral moral." Robinson predicted that "just as these types of incidences have occurred in the past (however major or minor) they will now continue in the future." Alonzo Nesmith called the hazing an "act of terrorism" and demanded that the young men be expelled for their "hideous" and "arrogant" behavior. Kevin Nesmith asked the general to reconsider the punishment, calling the "dishonorable, premeditated, and racially motivated" assault the "epitome of arrogant ignorance, racism, and offensiveness." Grimsley declined the request, and in mid-November, the younger Nesmith left The Citadel, alleging that other cadets "terrorized" him, calling him a "troublemaker," and blaming him for the negative publicity the school was receiving.[33]

The South Carolina NAACP and a group of eight ministers from local African American churches joined the fray, deeming the punishment "tantamount to executive endorsement of this heinous act" and an insult to the black community's "dignity as human beings." When the clergymen informed General Grimsley of black Charlestonians' concerns with the negative racial climate at The Citadel, the school's president responded that most people he spoke with supported his action, an assertion that prompted one minister to note, "Evidently he hadn't talked to the black community." Jesse Jackson came to the Lowcountry and spoke at a Charleston church, imploring every "decent South Carolinian" to denounce the five students' behavior. Flanked by seven black cadets, Jackson challenged "The Citadel to do justice [and] get your house in order," telling his audience to "pray for Kevin, but have pity on the five," for "if they can't respect people of color, they can't make it in the world."[34]

This intense public glare brought to light examples of past cadet transgressions, which stoked the protestors' anger. In December 1986, the NAACP filed an $880,000 lawsuit against General Grimsley and the Board of Visitors, accusing them of condoning "racially discriminatory conduct" and fostering "a pervasive atmosphere of overt racial bigotry and harassment." In making the plaintiff's case, William Gibson, the head of the South Carolina NAACP, pointed to the "repeated displays of racist symbols and stereotypes" in cadet publications, such as photos from the 1977, 1981, and 1982 *Sphinxes* depicting cadets posing with swastikas, dressed in Klan garb, or staging mock lynchings. Gibson condemned these pictures as examples of "insensitivity at its worst," offering them as evidence that the "administration's feelings and thoughts permeated that campus. And they are the ones that allow this type of racism to continue." Citadel officials answered these charges, saying that while "we are not proud of the photographs . . . we do not practice censorship here."[35]

Many of the school's most vocal critics looked to the past, present, and future for sources of and solutions to The Citadel's troubles. Benjamin Hooks, the executive director of the national NAACP, attributed the hazing of Nesmith to either "sheer ignorance or racism," noting that "one is about as bad as the other." Both Hooks and Gibson referenced the lingering aura of the Confederacy, with the former urging South Carolinians to "correct the injustices that exist behind the walls of this last bastion of the Old South." They and others suggested several ways to dissipate "the atmosphere of insensitivity and negativism" hanging over the corps, including hiring black professors, prohibiting the playing of "Dixie" and the waving of the Confederate flag at school-sponsored events, increased recruiting of African American students, and the admission of women into the corps of cadets. One native Charlestonian endorsed each of these measures, maintaining that unless school officials addressed the lack of diversity among the corps and the faculty, "Racism will haunt The Citadel," and its graduates would find themselves unprepared for life in a multicultural society.[36]

While Citadel administrators had been hearing these same suggestions for years, one of the protestors' demands indicate some recognition on their part that The Citadel's problems stemmed from more than just an underrepresented minority presence on campus. Rather than bifurcate the struggle for racial and sexual equality, the NAACP and the Charlestonian clergymen merged the two, with one group threatening to challenge the legality of The Citadel's all-male admissions polices and another suggesting that accepting women might help mitigate some of the damage done to the college's reputation. Despite their method of persuasion, members of both groups appreciated that discriminatory behavior against one group of people contributed to the marginalization of others by perpetuating a stagnant intellectual and cultural environment that allowed the majority to ignore or discredit the voices and opinions of those on the fringes. In The Citadel's case in particular, they understood that the exclusion of women eliminated a potentially dramatic challenge to many white cadets' worldview, thus making it easier for these students to dismiss ideas or interpretations that may differ from their own. Frank Portee, the spokesperson for Charleston's black community during this period, listed The Citadel's policies on "Dixie," the Confederate flag, and women as "things that would contribute to an incident" like the hazing of Kevin Nesmith. A white cadet exposed the link between The Citadel's lack of diversity and the corps' narrow-minded views on race and gender when he denounced the NAACP's questioning of the school's single-sex traditions as an attempt to undermine "The Citadel and its high ideals." Whether one associated these "high ideals" with the Confederacy, as many white cadets, alumni, and administrators did, or with the building of manly citizens, as almost all cadets, alumni, and administrators did, the inescapable impression was that a Citadel education served primarily to exalt the presumably unassailable virtues of white manhood.[37]

While Citadel officials never considered allowing women into the corps of cadets, General Grimsley did meet with ministers to discuss several of their requests, and by late November, the two had reached an "accord." As part of the agreement, the clergymen conceded that the students' punishment "adequately addressed the offense" and that "total expulsion would remove these five cadets from experiences which their own development and maturity require in a multi-racial society." In response, the general agreed to set up a racial advisory committee comprising Citadel alumni, school administrators, and black leaders from across South Carolina to monitor race relations at the college. The chances of this panel bridging racial divides seemed slim, however, for when Portee and others told reporters that they planned to put discussions of "Dixie," the Confederate flag, and the admission of women at the top of their agenda, Grimsley replied curtly, "I'm not making any changes."[38]

The general's comment echoed the sentiments of many Citadel supporters who countered any criticism of the school with attacks on the protestors, the media, and Kevin Nesmith himself. To be sure, Grimsley, the five cadets, and The Citadel endured their share of criticism. Several South Carolinians condemned school officials' "gutless" and "tepid" response to the incident. Others blasted the actions of the five "back-water reactionaries" and informed those who wished to characterize the hazing as a prank that "from the perspective of oppressed blacks, the Klan and its trappings were and are consummate terror and evil incarnate." Yet another letter claimed the scandal marred the school's reputation for developing "men of honor."[39]

Still, most of the public responses to the Nesmith incident, especially those from Citadel alumni, praised General Grimsley and the Board of Visitors for their handling of the matter. An editorial writer for *The State* asserted that The Citadel had "nothing to apologize for" and pointed to cadets' 1861 role in firing the initial shots of the Civil War as a prime example of the college's success "as the molder of good soldiers and good citizens." One particularly exuberant correspondent claimed that "The Citadel has been revealed as representing the best of Southern traditions and not the worst." By turning a mock-up of the Ku Klux Klan's brand of racial terror from a negative into a positive, several white South Carolinians made it clear that they had no intention of reevaluating the racial implications of any of their "southern traditions."[40]

Although they disavowed the "infantile judgment" and "ignorance" of Nesmith's tormentors, a large number of South Carolinians refused to take the "imaginary" racial problems at The Citadel seriously. An editorial in the *Charleston News and Courier* suggested that the "five misguided youths" might have accidentally dressed as Klansmen, and in their "unwitting use of the symbols of racial hatred, revealed that their minds have been tainted by prejudices which have no place in today's South." Not willing to confront the uncomfortable reality that "today's South" faced many of the same problems as "yesterday's South," this writer and others viewed the actions of the five white cadets as a "practical joke" that the media and protestors had "blown out of proportion."[41]

Many editorial writers deflected attention away from The Citadel and its traditions by blaming the media and the "professional racists of the NAACP" for "causing more trouble for everyone than all the incidents that have ever happened on the campus." Dismissing any notion that the "'little' racial incident" brought already existing tensions to the surface, they argued that "the hype raised by those events has polarized and segregated the cadets on The Citadel campus." A local woman believed that "we as Charlestonians and Americans had long passed those anxious days of black versus white, protest marches and labor disputes," but rather than acknowledging that racial divisions still existed or even blaming the white cadets for evoking the nasty images of those "anxious days," she directed her angst at the NAACP. School officials welcomed this view, with General Grimsley vowing to return Citadel life to "normal" following the "cessation of inflammatory actions and rhetoric by certain of those on the outside."[42]

Just as the method of discrediting the views of outsiders proved effective in undermining the 1979 Mood Report's conclusions regarding the fourth class system, repudiating a "bunch of outside racist fanatics" went a long way not only toward preserving the normal campus environment that gave rise to the five cadets' "prank" but also to ensure that The Citadel remained predominantly white as well as absolutely masculine. An editorial in the *Greenville News* hoped that the controversy surrounding The Citadel would not lead college administrators to adopt "quotas, softened admission standards for blacks and preferential treatment." At the same time, an absolute faith in the college's unique ability to produce Citadel men factored heavily into arguments that "The Citadel is a closed society which is fully capable of handling problems such as this." A 1959 graduate of the school demanded that the media "get off The Citadel's back unless they really know what The Citadel is all about — making men out of boys." Another alumnus contextualized the events of October 23 as part of "a system of discipline, instruction and training to turn boys into men — 'Citadel Men.'" The sister of a cadet boasted that her brother and his classmates "were hosed down, lined up and beaten about the buttocks until he was black and blue and literally could not sit down," yet "he was strong enough and determined enough to take whatever was dished out to him by upperclassmen."[43]

Implicit in this woman's argument and in the arguments advanced by several other people was that Kevin Nesmith had not been "man enough" to make it at The Citadel. One Charlestonian declared that the "clear message was the boy is a quitter, that he could not withstand the discipline and training necessary to earn the right to be a Citadel Man." Possibly aware that many white South Carolinians, to say nothing of the majority of white Citadel alumni, were willing to overlook their culpability in the whole affair, cadets Steve Webb and Jeffrey Plumley struck a decidedly less contrite tone than they had months earlier, as they told a reporter for *The State* that Nesmith entered The Citadel "knowing full well the practices and procedures" of the corps and thus "did assume the risk of being subjected to a certain amount of harassment that might help him to become a man."[44]

These challenges to Kevin Nesmith's masculinity illuminate the unique as well as important role race and gender played in shaping the identity of many Citadel men. For one, claims that the attack on Nesmith served as an opportunity for him to prove his manliness turn on its head the argument put forth by numerous scholars that white vigilantes used violence as a means of emasculating African American males. In addition, the pervasive institutional emphasis on manliness enabled many white cadets and administrators to ignore the obvious tensions that existed among Citadel cadets and alumni. In denying that their alma mater had any racial problems, whites convinced themselves that the masculine bonds of the Citadel brotherhood subsumed any divisions arising from the college's overwhelmingly white environment and traditions. Since the school's initial integration, however, African American cadets realized that their acceptance into The Citadel's fraternity was incomplete so long as many on campus failed to appreciate and, in some cases, exhibited a hostility toward the cultural differences between black and white cadets. Not surprisingly then, African American students at The Citadel in 1986 grew increasingly frustrated when others refused to acknowledge not only the validity of their views and grievances but also the racial connotations of their peers' behavior. A month after the news of the Nesmith incident broke, Kenneth Gordon, the president of The Citadel's Afro-American Society, sent a letter to the *News and Courier* informing them that he was "fed up with the speculations, opinions, and views" of those filling a "desperate need to justify this abhorrent act," asking, "If there is no problem, as many people seem to believe, why do black cadets feel that there is?"[45]

School officials' response to the findings of two investigations of the Nesmith incident in particular and campus race relations in general further exposed the shallowness of their commitment to promoting ethnic diversity and indicate that their attitudes toward integration had changed little since the 1960s. For the most part, they continued to believe that the mere presence of nonwhites in the student body fulfilled their obligation to achieving racial equality, refusing to alter certain customs and attitudes that tended to alienate and discourage the relatively few minority students who did attend the college.

The first evaluation, conducted by the South Carolina Human Affairs Commission at the behest of the governor, attributed much of the controversy to a "failure in communication" between Citadel officials and the black community when it came to the severity of the sentence handed down by General

Grimsley and the Board of Visitors. The report placed much of the blame for this on Citadel officials' "marked insensitivity to (or ignorance of) community concerns," but confirmed that the awarding of 195 tours and the accompanying "months of grueling public penance" was "the most severe punishment ever handed out by the school to any cadet(s)" short of expulsion.[46]

Through interviews with almost every African American cadet at The Citadel, the commission discovered that while racially motivated hazing was "not a widespread problem," the use of racial slurs and the telling of offensive ethnic jokes "were not uncommon," adding that many "white cadets feel that saying bad things to blacks is funny." Connecting this trend to the events of October 23, the commissioners pointed out that "when white people get so bold as to do something like that, joking or not, something is wrong." The cadet regimental commander from that year tried to offer some excuse for white cadets' callousness, explaining that most cadets had "grown up at the end of the civil rights movement and were ignorant of it," adding "Martin Luther King Jr. is to me something I've seen on a videotape." This explanation not only highlighted where The Citadel had fallen short as an institution of higher education, but at a college whose students and administrators consistently evoked the glory of their forebears, it also demonstrated whose ancestors and whose accomplishments they deemed worthy of preserving and commemorating.[47]

The Human Affairs Commission suggested that school officials compensate for the fact that "The Citadel is an overwhelmingly white environment" lacking both "ethnic diversity and cultural sensitivity" by offering mandatory "human relations" courses designed to broaden cadets' views and "make students sensitive to the backgrounds and beliefs of other races." The authors of the report realized that Citadel leaders ought to reevaluate their attitudes as well, pointing out that the school ranked last among South Carolina colleges in a "recent comparison of affirmative action progress." Again, calls for increasing the number of African American students on campus, hiring black professors and administrators, and finding ways to overcome African American cadets' "feeling of exclusion" were not new, but they remained necessary so long as Citadel officials refused to listen. For example, as a justification for their belief that whites at The Citadel "seem culturally insensitive" to their needs, black students referred interviewers to the school's barbers' inability to cut their hair properly, a complaint made almost fifteen years ago by the first African Americans who enrolled at the institution.[48]

An internal investigation conducted by Citadel faculty and staff members took a much more sanguine view of corps-wide race relations, but reached many of the same conclusions as the Human Affairs Commission. Reinforcing the role of gender identifications in obscuring ethnic divisions, the investigators determined that "The Citadel has established a record of positive racial and religious openness of which it can be proud," reaching this conclusion based on the widely expressed cadet opinion that "the fourth class system established bonds among classmates that ignored racial or religious differences." Therefore, with a deep appreciation for "the college's commitment to excellence, its emphasis on the 'whole man,' its insistence that integrity, responsibility, and self-discipline are goals intertwined with the pursuit of intellectual competence," they devised several ways "to make what is good better."[49]

Paying due notice to the lack of African American students, faculty, and administrators at The Citadel, the examiners decided that "the most pervasive concern is best summarized under the heading of 'insensitivity,'" most notably white cadets' propensity for making offensive racial comments. According to the report, some students even went so far as to require freshmen to tell racist jokes as mess facts. The panelists agreed with those students who believed that The Citadel was "too white," and as a result, "Inappropriate stereotypes were often the extent of a cadet's knowledge about persons of other races or cultures." As part of their solution, the committee members seconded the Human Affairs Commission's call for "awareness training which focuses on helping cadets be cognizant of the multi-cultural society in which we live."[50]

Upon reviewing and distributing copies of each report, General Grimsley held a press conference reminding reporters that "at the time of the incident, I stated unequivocally that The Citadel has no major racial problems." In his opinion, both studies confirmed that belief. Grimsley accepted many of the inquiries' suggestions such as mandatory sensitivity training, greater "vigilance" regarding the fourth class system, continued efforts to meet the "college's goals in its Affirmative Action Plan," and increased attention to public perceptions of the college.[51]

School officials enjoyed mixed results in these endeavors, improving their standing in the black community by increasing the amount of money and number of contracts they awarded to minority-owned businesses and by staging a series of public ceremonies honoring African American citizens from all walks of life.[52] They fared poorly, however, when it came to the more substantive and more difficult goal of diversifying the college's faculty and student body. While the negative publicity did not hurt The Citadel's overall enrollment, the number of minority applicants for the 1987–1988 school year dropped sharply. Some tried to downplay the significance of this dip, but The Citadel's dean of undergraduate studies admitted, "There's no way to deny that the incident, and the fact that it continues to surface, is going to hamper our capacity to recruit." Other factors hindered them as well, since the addition of one African American admissions officer failed to make up for the loss of the school's most valuable public relations resources: black cadets, black parents, and black preachers. While the president of the Afro-American Society wrote letters encouraging potential black applicants to visit the school, other African American students declined to help, with one explaining, "The Citadel has offered me great returns, but it's the small differences that may make me refuse to endorse" the institution. Evidence of these "small differences" are reflected in the somewhat arrogant refusal of Citadel officials to accept any responsibility for the problems on campus. Absolving anyone connected with The Citadel for the school's negative public image, the chairman of the Board of Visitors remarked that "black leaders have recognized that the rancor and exaggerated charges stemming from this incident have caused a serious drop in black applicants and they must now counter this trend." According to the President of the Association of Citadel Men, alumni were more concerned that "as a result of recent events, academic and military standards would be lowered to enhance recruiting" than with the school's dismal record of hiring black faculty and attracting black students.[53]

In 1988, the school hired two African American faculty members, bringing the total number of black professors to three, but despite "considerable effort to employ blacks and other minorities," The Citadel's director of personnel complained that qualified African American candidates either found better-paying jobs elsewhere or considered the South Carolina Lowcountry a less than "attractive location." The views expressed by an anonymous faculty member in an article for *The Brigadier* suggested another reason for the low number of black professors at The Citadel. The source resented requests that he "be aggressive in recruiting a black," contending "the best qualified should be chosen otherwise that would be discrimination."[54]

As part of Grimsley's pledge to foster a "greater sensitivity to black cadets," school officials assembled a fourteen-member Race Relations Advisory Committee, made human-relations training a regular aspect of all ROTC courses, and enrolled the college in a statewide Role Model Project designed to help black and white students "assess their perceptions about minorities on a predominantly white campus." Despite these efforts, most whites at The Citadel remained indifferent or hostile to African Americans' concerns as evidenced by the most enduring legacy of the Nesmith incident: the intense battle over white cadets' waving of the Confederate battle flag and the continued playing of "Dixie." The public debate over these practices showed not only the limits of tolerance at The Citadel, but testified to how deeply many white southerners allowed their sterilized version of the past to shape their image of the present. White Citadel cadets and administrators venerated the college's traditions and heritage, but only so long as they could interpret these things in ways that made them feel comfortable, secure, and important. Casting themselves and their institution as the caretakers and beneficiaries of a southern culture built upon the memory of heroic Confederate soldiers, bucolic plantations, and glorious lost causes, they rejected those who pointed out that their inheritance included Klansmen, slavery, and Jim Crow.[55]

The debate over these issues offers further proof of the ideological and cultural rift separating not just black and white cadets but South Carolinians in general as they grappled with the legacy of slavery and segregation. Disagreements within the corps over "Dixie" and the Confederate battle flag paralleled ongoing arguments concerning the banner's place atop the State House in Columbia. These controversies were as much about the present as they were about the past, since to many black South Carolinians the flag symbolized, in the words of author K. Michael Prince, "a lack of respect, a feeling of second-class status." This was certainly the case at The Citadel where African American cadets continued to feel marginalized over twenty years after the college initially integrated.[56]

In interviews conducted by the State Human Affairs Commission, almost every black cadet they spoke to expressed uneasiness with the college's "'Old South' traditions," traditions that to them "summoned a history and heritage of pain and abuse." One African American student exclaimed, "No black person I know wishes they were in 'the land of cotton,'" while others wished white cadets would "get rid of the Confederate flags and put the Civil War to rest."

Black members of the corps waged nonverbal protests as well, sitting down when the band played "Dixie" at football games and waving large American flags whenever whites brandished their Confederate ones.[57]

Although a fair number of white cadets commiserated with them, deciding that "if these symbols are offensive to part of the corps, then their use should be discontinued in the interest of corps unity," black cadets found more support from the "many blacks in the community [who] see that flag as The Citadel's senseless reluctance to change." James Clyburn, the chairman of the state's Human Affairs Commission, hoped that once South Carolinians "recognize white and black people have some basic cultural differences," they might "take a serious look at the symbolism behind displaying the flag at the college and atop the State House." In the meantime, he asked Citadel leaders to "establish less offensive ways of showing school spirit."[58]

Even this fairly mild suggestion drew a heated response from state and school officials who called it a "repudiation of our heritage" and "abhorrent to the vast majority of South Carolinians." Continuing with their selective use of the pronoun "our," they presented the Confederate flag and "Dixie" as a symbol of "our regional pride, our heritage, and also our hospitality," defending its display as the "embodiment of the southern spirit" and "recognition of the effort and sacrifice that was made by many in this state in an earlier time." Despite these objections, The Citadel's race relations committee asserted that the college's "tradition of moral leadership does not permit the ignoring of the negative feelings of the black cadets," and they offered a variety of steps college officials might take, such as "create greater awareness of the symbolic connotations of 'Dixie' and the Confederate flag to blacks," substitute the official and more "appropriate" Citadel flag at school events, and "reduce the prominence of 'Dixie'" by replacing it with another fight song and by not playing it after every weekly parade.[59]

While Grimsley hoped that cadets would "gain a greater perception of the sensitivity involved in race relations," he did not seem that concerned about modifying his own views or those of other vocal white alumni. A couple of outraged Citadel graduates called the African American students' protests at football games "a personal affront to The Citadel and to its heritage," deciding "cadets who cannot accept this are the racists." When an alumni group in Washington, D.C., asked General Grimsley if all the negative publicity would affect "Citadel traditions," the school's president assured them, "I have no intention of doing away with the fourth class system. . . . There will be no women admitted to The Citadel . . . and we will still play 'Dixie.'" While several students and alumni found the battle flag and "Dixie" "demeaning" and "insulting," Grimsley described them as "symbols that reflect characteristics in which Citadel men of all generations take pride — honor, gallantry, sacrifice, duty, and dedication to cause." When asked to curtail the waving of the flag at athletic events, the school's president and the Board of Visitors pointed out that "The Citadel does not fly the Confederate flag," and while Grimsley could and did ban crowd surfing at football games, the general said he was unable to stop individual cadets from waving banners. The chairman of the Board of Visitors agreed, and both men expressed confidence in the corps' ability to "consider it, understand it, and decide what they want to do about it."[60]

When cadets responded in ways that did not meet certain people's approval, however, school officials again reasserted their authority on campus. In November 1987, a white cadet was reprimanded for violating a "verbal policy" issued by cadet regimental commander Keller Kissam allowing members of the corps to wave the Confederate flag only when the band played "Dixie." When a couple of state senators wrote Grimsley protesting this "contemptuous act," the general intervened, rescinded the punishment, and assured legislators "the policy on the Confederate flag will be in consonance with the applicable state statutes."[61]

With school and state officials leaping to defend cadets' right to fly the flag and standing by silently while those who refused to sing "Dixie" were vilified, it is no wonder most white cadets flunked their lessons on accepting "varying possible perceptions of symbolic materials." Indeed, many white students clung to a past and a present that simply did not exist, covering their eyes and ears to anything that might lead them to question their opinions of their region and their school. Rather than face their own racialized view of the past, most fell back on the assertion that "the [corps] is grey" and those who saw otherwise should leave "before the cancer spreads." When a white cadet asked a black cadet, "What's it with 'Dixie'?" the latter responded, "I don't want the old times. They weren't good times for my people, picking cotton." When the white student demanded, "What do you mean 'my people'?" his opponent informed him, "My people were slaves, brought here against their will, whipped, chained. . . . I don't want to go back." The chronicler of this exchange remarked that the white cadet "seemed unmoved." While admitting that "Dixie," "like any other song, means what an individual wants it to mean," an editorial writer for *The Brigadier* dismissed any interpretation that clashed with his own, asserting "we can all sing 'Dixie' together with a sense of pride in the South of today." Pleading "we should not turn our backs on the past," he proposed to do just that, deciding "we must focus on the good things." Again deeming himself and those who thought like him the final arbiters of southern culture, he proclaimed "no one should be offended by 'Dixie' being played in today's society, especially at The Citadel in 1987, where cadets are brothers regardless of their backgrounds or their likes and dislikes."[62]

With white cadets boasting that they had weathered the attacks on the "values and traditions of our school" to emerge as a "model of class and corps unity," black students thought otherwise, saying as long as their colleagues flew Confederate flags and sang "Dixie," "there will be a feeling of division among the Corps, whether or not it is outwardly displayed." Cadet Jon Thomas, for one, observed that while some treat the banner and the song as symbols of "southern pride and heritage . . . we cannot escape the reality that the flag and the singing of Dixie does carry racial overtones in our society, regardless if it is done out of pride and school spirit." Hoping that appeals to the bond among Citadel men might serve to bridge rather than mask racial divides, Thomas asserted that as long as "we belong to an illustrious fraternity which prides itself on a strong brotherhood regardless of race, religion or creed, then we should try to eliminate the things which may offend and isolate a fellow brother." In conclusion, he predicted that "the settlement and the opening of dialogue on this issue will not only make the racial atmosphere more comfortable for all, but will also enable black cadets and athletes to feel respected, accepted and truly a part of this strong bond which makes us Citadel men."[63]

When General Grimsley retired in May 1989, his successor, Air Force Lieutenant General Claudius E. Watts III, a 1958 graduate of The Citadel, inherited an outwardly thriving institution, but one wracked by internal divisions. Under Watts, The Citadel continued to earn high marks in *U.S. News and World Report*'s yearly evaluations, and the number of African American applicants to the school rose slightly over the next four years. Watts kept a close watch on minority recruitment, announcing publicly in 1990 that black enrollment had reached its highest level ever, but stressing privately the need to improve these numbers and strengthen ties with the black community.[64]

Despite Watts's best efforts to downplay the issue, tensions over "Dixie" and the Confederate flag dominated the first few years of his presidency. Before the 1989–1990 school year, Charleston County Councilman Robert Ford asked Watts to prohibit the playing of "Dixie" and the waving of the flag when The Citadel played South Carolina State in football later that year. Ford understood "that this practice is a long-time tradition at all Citadel football games, but I fear many will interpret it as a personal attack on and a blatant disrespect to the black community." With Watts responding simply, "The Citadel will continue to do what we've always done," Charleston Senator Glenn McConnell assailed Ford's request, claiming, "'Dixie' has nothing to do with race. . . . It is a song that invokes good feelings."[65]

On September 9, tourists attending the first parade of the school year witnessed history when, for the first time in about ten years, the Citadel band did not end the ceremony by playing "Dixie." The next day, the front page of the *News and Courier* blared "No Dixie," and when asked about his decision not to play the song, Watts responded simply, "We didn't play it. That's it." People across the state refused to accept this answer, with many taking time out of their weekend schedules to not only monitor when the Citadel band played "Dixie," but how often they played it. Following that Saturday's Wofford-Citadel football game, confusion reigned as to whether or not the band played "Dixie" every time the Bulldogs scored. Some reported that they only heard the song once, when it could have been played "at least seven times." Watts again tried to defuse the situation, telling reporters he had "no comment. I'm not refusing to answer, I'm just telling you I have no comment." Not satisfied with this response, Senator McConnell demanded to know if the military college is "silently acquiescing or silently retreating from using the flag and 'Dixie' at any time."[66]

McConnell must have breathed a sigh of relief the next weekend when "Dixie" rang out from The Citadel's parade ground and echoed through the football stadium. A reporter for the *News and Courier* polled fans about their attitudes toward the song, with most calling it a part of "our tradition" and adding, "I don't think they should take that from us." Continuing with the "us versus them" dichotomy, one observer, apparently unaware of the decades of protests surrounding the symbols, thought, "If they had any real anger about it or resentment, they would have said something about it before now."[67]

A few days later, Hurricane Hugo ripped through Charleston, and while the storm toppled buildings and trees, it did not disperse the ill winds swirling

around the Citadel campus. Not two months into Watts's tenure, a reporter for
The Brigadier detected a corps-wide mix of "melancholy and anger" over the
administration's "indecision" concerning "Dixie." Most white cadets repeated
arguments that the song and the flag "should forever be held dear as reminders
of our proud history as men of honor and duty," and although a handful of cadets and school administrators tried to offer the flag Citadel cadets fought under during the Civil War as an alternative to the Confederate battle flag, almost
no one took to the new banner. Describing the waving of the Confederate flag
as the "most identifiable tradition" of this "commemorative institution of the
South," one student asserted correctly that The Citadel "was originally established for the protection of Charleston." He neglected to point out more specifically that The Citadel was built to protect white Charlestonians from rebellious slaves.[68]

Race relations at The Citadel worsened over the next few years, and in 1991,
faced with mounting charges of racial discrimination by cadets and faculty
alike, Watts asked the school's Race Relations Advisory Committee to come
up with ways of "generating an awareness and sensitivity" to racial matters.
Not surprisingly, the committee found that "Dixie" and the Confederate flag
loomed as the largest "unresolved issues" on campus. Admitting that "there is
no legitimate tie between the Confederate Flag and the Corps of Cadets," the
panelists suggested that school officials bar any cadet not acting in an official
capacity from carrying a flag into the football stadium. As for "Dixie," they
decided it should be played only on special occasions such as Homecoming or
Corps Day and that Citadel administrators needed to come up with a "non-
controversial" fight song. While some of his advisors pushed Watts to "bite the
bullet" and accept the committee's proposals, others worried about the backlash to such a decision and suggested he "not make precipitous changes." This
same range of opinions could be found within the corps as members of the
Presidential Advisory Council endorsed the panel's conclusions, while other
cadets called such moves a violation of free speech. In the end, the board rejected both the committee's proposals, although Watts pledged that "Dixie"
would not be played in a "taunting" manner.[69]

Soon after this decision had been made, an incident in the barracks gave
pause to those who maintained that "Dixie" represented "simply a symbol of
reverence for the courage of our forefathers." In August 1992, after refusing to

obey an upperclassman's order that he sing the song, a black freshman returned to his room and found a miniature noose hanging from his bunk. Citadel authorities immediately called state officials in to investigate, but the culprit was never apprehended. Fear of a mounting public backlash to the racial and other controversies surrounding the college finally convinced the board of the need for a new fight song. They also banned all unofficial flags from The Citadel's football stadium.[70]

A few years later two more racist confrontations caused an even greater stir on campus, coming at a time when the college was facing intense scrutiny due to its all-male admissions policies. In February 1995, one black cadet found "die niger [*sic*]" scrawled on the wall of his room, while another turned in an intracampus letter addressed to him, filled with racial slurs and threats. General Watts, the commandant of cadets, and other school officials launched an investigation, asking the South Carolina Law Enforcement Division (SLED) and the FBI to assist them in their search. Watts mailed letters to Citadel students, faculty, staff, parents of cadets, and "friends of The Citadel family" asking for help in uncovering the offenders. This forceful response to the racial incidents of the early 1990s reflect not only General Watts's stated commitment to improving The Citadel's racial image but also a fear of losing supporters that they desperately needed to prevail in the fight against admitting women. In a speech before the entire corps, Watts denounced "intoleration and racism" and again confirmed the link between the internal and external struggles enveloping the school by informing cadets that "displays of racial intolerance play into the hands of those who" currently sought "to destroy the Corps of Cadets as it has existed for 152 years."[71]

Such admonitions eventually began to have an effect on the school, but even when confronted with the fairly obvious consequences of their limited commitment to promoting racial diversity, Citadel officials throughout the 1980s avoided making the hard decisions, paying lip service to the "needs of black cadets," but doing very little to meet or even acknowledge these needs. More concerned with preserving the college "traditions" than with fixing the deep-seated problems caused by these traditions, Citadel officials begged off the stickier issues of increasing minorities' presence on campus or considering the multiple meanings of certain "time-honored" customs. Unwilling to acknowledge the legacy, or at times even the occurrence, of racial injustice,

General Grimsley and others took few steps toward making The Citadel more appealing to minority students, thus fostering a campus environment ripe for antisocial outbursts.

Certainly, The Citadel's military structure and regional identification heightened tensions on campus. As discussed in earlier chapters, the fourth class system offered numerous opportunities for, as one man put it, "little bigots to become big bigots — bigots with power."[72] In addition, debates over "Dixie" and the Confederate battle flag tend to grow especially heated south of the Mason-Dixon line. Still, it was not so much The Citadel's military or southern environment that led to the harassment of Kevin Nesmith as it was the lack of any cultural or intellectual awareness that might have caused the five white cadets to think twice before bursting into a black man's room dressed as Klansmen. Little seemed to have changed at the school in the twenty years since a group of similarly clad white upperclassmen charged at the only African American cadet; most cadets were still white and most apparently knew or cared little about racial injustice. Indicating that times had changed a bit, however, a vocal segment of the southern population now publicly condemned such acts as unacceptable or at least distasteful. By the end of the 1980s, a number of black cadets, many of them southerners, were loudly condemning the subtle and not-so-subtle indignities they regularly suffered. One wonders if Nesmith would have slept without interruption on October 23, 1986, if, over the years, there had been more such voices on campus offering white cadets another lens through which to view the past as well as the present.

While many whites at The Citadel, students as well as administrators, conceded, albeit grudgingly, that a group of cadets dressed as Klansmen "might" have racial overtones, they refused to believe that a symbol adopted by actual members of the Klan and other hate groups could also evoke negative feelings and imagery. The corps' overall ethnic homogeneity allowed whites to talk of "our" traditions and heritage without having to take a hard look at the historical meaning behind the images they evoked. The overwhelming whiteness of the entire campus made it easier for whites to determine whose pasts they privileged, which memories they venerated. With few people around to challenge their views and assumptions, most whites at The Citadel continued to cast the idyllic Citadel man in their own image, drowning out those who struggled to advance more inclusive, but less admirable interpretations of their southern heritage.

The Citadel's all-male environment added another element to the school's racial controversies. Some saw a link between college personnel's exclusion of women and their apparent disregard for African Americans, realizing that by insulating themselves from divergent viewpoints, many whites at The Citadel found it easier to disparage or ignore the opinions and viewpoints of "outsiders." Certainly, Grimsley and others employed just such tactics in order to avoid altering certain traditions. In his initial response to suggestions that the school deemphasize "Dixie" and the Confederate flag, the general had asserted, "We must not take any action that will arbitrarily diminish our heritage, but we will be conscious at the same time of the bonds which hold all Citadel men together — white and black." In the first part of this statement, the "our" to which Grimsley refers consisted primarily of white cadets and alumni. In the second half of the sentence, though, he touched on an attitude shared by most Citadel graduates. Amid the controversy over "Dixie" and the flag, cadets on both sides of the issue hoped that the fraternal bond among Citadel men trumped any racially contrived allegiances or commitments. In the year following the Nesmith incident, a cadet reminded his colleagues, "The most important concept of the ring is the fact that those who wear it are Citadel Men." Several years later, with campus racial tensions at their peak, a survey conducted by *The Brigadier* found whites and blacks split on a variety of subjects, but when asked if "the Corps should be a unified brotherhood," 98 percent of white cadets and 95 percent of black cadets answered yes, making this "the only response that both groups overwhelmingly agreed upon."[73]

CHAPTER NINE

Save the Males

The Fight over Coeducation

 The Citadel entered the final fight to keep women out of the corps of cadets already reeling from a swarm of negative publicity concerning tales of cadet brutality and racism.[1] These reports probably factored into the slumping enrollment figures that worried Citadel officials, but the greater damage seemed to fall on The Citadel's standing among South Carolinians. Although the college enjoyed a great deal of public support following the "Nesmith incident" a few years earlier, by the early 1990s, with the school fending off "allegations of hazing, allegations of racism, allegations of improper Honor Committee functioning, and the perception of problems between the athletes and the rest of the corps," many people seemed to have lost faith in The Citadel's method of building men, a development that did not bode well for school officials in their efforts to exclude women.[2]

As usual, when the school's president attempted to rein in the upperclassmen, students eulogized the "whole man," with one remarking, "I wouldn't be too surprised if our tradition of an all male school is soon lost." Early in the 1991–1992 school year, the highly publicized hazing and subsequent withdrawal of four Citadel athletes undermined the institution's all-male tradition more than any so-called weakening of the fourth class system. One of the knobs, Brian Alewine, suffered a bruised lung and a bruised kidney after being beaten by an unknown assailant or assailants in the barracks. A football player, Karl Brozowski, resigned and then filed criminal charges against his upper-class antagonist.[3]

When news of these stories broke, media from across the country descended on Charleston. Reporters for the *New Yorker* and *Sports Illustrated* wrote full-length articles on The Citadel's "record of violence and cruelty." *Sports Illustrated*'s Rick Reilly described an institution where the "night is cleaved by mysterious screams" and nightmarish sophomores roamed the barracks with "hell in [their] eyes." Editorials in the *Charleston News and Courier* and the *Post and Courier*, usually two stalwart defenders of The Citadel and its cadets, declared "there is obviously something wrong" at the school and reminded readers that "abuse of power, earned or unearned, is the act of a coward." A writer for *The State* took a jab at the Board of Visitors, saying the group now "probably wishes it had deferred to Admiral Stockdale's prudent ideas for reform." Alumni joined in as well, with a graduate from the 1950s hoping his "quiet, but courageous" brethren "who helped win the last four wars," would let the school know it has a duty to bring about discipline without cruelty."[4]

General Watts and the board responded to these criticisms by adopting a series of reforms put forth by yet another fourth class system review committee. The changes included no push-ups in the barracks, replacing freshmen "Hell Night" with a "dignified, challenging, introduction to the fourth class system," stricter enforcement of the rules governing Evening Study Period, and no unsupervised sophomore interaction with knobs. Most alumni accepted these reforms silently, but vocal members of the corps accused the administration of pandering to "irresponsible media attention" brought about by those "not willing to make the sacrifices and do what it takes" to become Citadel men. They believed the new plebe regulations would "ruin our school" because the "life of the Corps has been sucked completely out." One student groaned, "The Citadel amazingly survived through the 1960s and 1970s, but the products of those misguided generations are finally getting to us."[5]

These developments set the stage for the struggle that dominated the 1990s. In the spring of 1989, Citadel officials learned that the U.S. Justice Department had threatened a lawsuit against the Virginia Military Institute (VMI) on the grounds that the college's all-male admissions policy violated the Fourteenth Amendment and the 1964 Civil Rights Act. William Risher, the chairman of the Board of Visitors, admitted that The Citadel was "very interested" in the case, but added, "We're staying as far away from it as possible." This distance closed rapidly in February 1990 when The Citadel's admissions office rejected an application from a female student. Less than a month later, the Justice Department sent a letter to The Citadel informing school officials that they had received written complaints from women "who are interested in attending The Citadel but believe they are ineligible to do so because The Citadel allegedly admits only males to its daytime undergraduate programs." Should this be the case, the letter concluded, the policy "may constitute unlawful discrimination on the basis of sex."[6]

Initial reactions to this news indicated that public support for The Citadel had waned somewhat over the years. An editorial in *The State* announced, "Citadel tradition guards gutless all male policy." Other pundits urged the "grand old bastion of male chauvinism" to accept the inevitable. One cartoonist compared The Citadel's stance to "another Lost Cause" of 130 years ago. One Citadel graduate informed South Carolinians that a large number of his peers opposed "the immoral exclusion of women" and feared that their alma mater would "remain stagnant in an ever-changing world to become a resented bastion."[7]

A bill floating around the South Carolina General Assembly hinted that the college had lost some of its allure among that body as well. Sarah Manly, a representative from Greenville, sponsored legislation decreeing "no persons shall be excluded from any public school in the state on account of race, creed, color, gender or national origin." Manly's bill never made it out of committee, but only by a narrow 6-5 vote. When she tried to attach the resolution as a rider to the state budget, she lost by a significantly wider 68-29 margin, indicating that although some legislators and many citizens agreed that the "outdated regime of white male dominance" ought to "discard old ways that have evolved beyond tradition into prejudice and discrimination," the college and its backers still commanded a great deal of support from the state's traditional power structure.[8]

Another public relations disaster ensued when Citadel officials abruptly discontinued its veterans program rather than admit three women who had sued for permission to take day classes with cadets. This decision came on the heels of the first Gulf War in which female American soldiers earned national recognition for their service and heroism. Patricia Johnson, Elizabeth Lacy, and Angela Chapman all sought engineering degrees, and, at the time, The Citadel's day program was the only one in the Charleston vicinity offering accredited courses in their area of interest. The lawyer for the three women found it incredible that his clients "are eligible to go to war . . . and yet they are not able to get into The Citadel." Patricia Johnson resented the fact that she "served my country for twelve years and get out and this is the kind of thanks I get from something that calls itself a military school."[9]

The Board of Visitors justified their decision, explaining that they had a "fiduciary duty to protect the primary mission of The Citadel," a mission they defined as educating "male undergraduate students as members of the South Carolina Corps of Cadets." The "cadet lifestyle, including the single-sex admissions policy," they added, "is an essential aspect of the educational program." Addressing the legal issues that led to the demise of the veterans program, The Citadel's attorney explained that under the current arrangement, the college's all-male admissions polices were legal due to a special exemption granted single-sex colleges under the 1972 Education Amendment to the 1964 Civil Rights Act. Since the amendment "does not recognize a separation between policies of class participation in the admission polices of the specific college," school officials worried that should they admit females into the day program, The Citadel would then be considered a coeducational institution and have to either accept women into the cadet corps or lose federal funding.[10]

On a more esoteric level, the board believed that allowing women to attend classes with cadets would result in an "inevitable relaxation of the requirements now imposed on male cadets" and in the process "destroy the value and uniqueness of the institution." In their estimation, exposing cadets to coeducation of any sort would undermine corps discipline and derail the training of whole men. The problem, in their minds, lay not so much with having to alter school rules to accommodate female students, but with the seeming inability of male students to control themselves and stay focused on the building of men in the presence of women. They believed wholeheartedly that the "distracting and disruptive" presence of women "would become a major factor in the daily life of cadets, both in the barracks and in the classroom, displacing to a considerable degree the present concentration of the cadets on their military, physical, and academic performance." The board offered yet another and even more telling glimpse into the manufacturing of Citadel men when they distinguished between male and female veteran students, noting that only the former posed no threat to either the "single gender character or the military character of the Day Program." Having served their country honorably in the Armed Forces, the military character of the women veterans matched that of the school. The same could not be said when it came to the "single gender character" of The Citadel. Having singled out martial values and masculinity for special recognition, the board confirmed that although both characteristics were important, when it came to building citizen-soldiers, manliness remained the essential component of the finished product.[11]

Still, the abrupt termination of the veterans program drew virulent criticism from those within and without the walls of The Citadel as many sympathized with the seventy-eight male veterans who found themselves expelled from school. Two of the former students sued The Citadel in an effort to force school officials to readmit them. A newspaper editorial offered the board's decision as proof that Citadel officials reacted irrationally to "even modest reforms," while one South Carolinian compared the move to that of a "wild animal who will eat its young to avoid starvation." Citadel faculty members issued a statement demanding that the school reinstate those already enrolled in day classes and "honor the moral contract a college assumes when it admits a student." A handful of cadets even chastised administrators for their "shameless abandonment" of the veterans.[12]

While the names of the three female veterans who first demanded entry into The Citadel's classrooms remain unknown to most people, Shannon Faulkner became famous, or infamous, for her attempts to enter the long gray line of the corps of cadets. Late in 1992, Faulkner sent an application and copies of her high school transcript to The Citadel's admissions office, carefully omitting or deleting any reference to her sex. She was accepted for the upcoming school year, but when school officials found out she was a woman, they quickly reversed their decision. Citadel spokesman Rick Mill admitted "were it not for The Citadel's male only policy, Ms. Faulkner might very well be suitable for admission." He added, though, that by submitting "masterfully altered" documentation, she had violated the school's honor code, and "there is no place in our day program or evening college for anyone cloaked in subterfuge." Undeterred, in early 1993, Faulkner filed a lawsuit against The Citadel, claiming that its male-only policy violated her civil rights and telling reporters that in years to come, "Every girl that walks through those gates will know they can because of me."[13]

In most respects, the public debate over The Citadel versus Shannon Faulkner mirrored the legal arguments made by attorneys in both the Virginia and South Carolina cases. The largest difference seemed to be one of emphasis, for while the American Civil Liberties Union, which had intervened on Faulkner's behalf, and the Justice Department, which tried the VMI case, questioned the legality of a publicly funded institution denying women access to its facilities, this argument played only a relatively minor role in their overall strategy. On the other hand, many South Carolinians seized upon this seemingly cut-and-dried issue of state and "federally funded discrimination." Representative Manly noted, "There are many people, male and female, who don't think their tax money ought to go to support an all-male institution." Others found it "unconscionable" that "The Citadel has declared war on women who only wish to utilize the taxes paid by their parents and themselves to receive an education at the college of their choice." A couple of influential Citadel alumni agreed, as Pat Conroy argued that "women should not be taxed for an education they are denied," and U.S. Senator Ernest "Fritz" Hollings maintained, "You cannot have government supported programs, with tax support, without the right of every race, color, creed, and sex to utilize the program."[14]

For some, including one of Shannon Faulkner's attorneys, the solution to this problem seemed straightforward: The Citadel could either admit women or become a private institution. One commentator explained the constitutional viability of single-sex private colleges, pointing out that while the Fourteenth Amendment "does not now, and never has, dictated or governed admission policies of privately supported colleges not operated by the public sector," courts have ruled that "public institutions have a constitutional obligation to provide equal educational opportunity to men and women, absent an 'exceedingly persuasive justification.'" In support of this argument, the author cited a ruling from the Fourth U.S. Circuit Court of Appeals that VMI could avoid coeducation by becoming a private institution. One South Carolinian spelled it out bluntly when she challenged "those of you who want to keep The Citadel a males-only school to get your hands out my pocket. Buy the place and support it yourselves."[15]

Aware that The Citadel could not afford to convert to private status, the school's proponents cast the fight as one over the benefits and legality of any brand of single-sex education, public or private. One man argued that "implementing the remorseless argument of denying public funds for single-gender education will not only destroy" The Citadel but private, all-female colleges such as South Carolina's Columbia College and Converse College that also received "some form of federal or state funding in order to survive." When someone pointed out that The Citadel received five times as much state money as the other two schools, The Citadel's backers accused them of quibbling over the price, asking, "How many public dollars does it take to render single-sex education unacceptable?"[16]

Convinced that "as The Citadel and VMI admission policies go, so must all single-gender 'private' educational institutions follow," the military college's boosters positioned themselves as the defenders of every American's right to receive a single-sex education. In this scenario, Citadel cadets became only the most immediate victims of Shannon Faulkner's callous disregard for all students' freedom to choose what kind of school they attended. With several cadets threatening, "I won't go back if we have to admit females. I didn't choose a coed education," many in South Carolina assumed that Faulkner was the only female who would ever want to attend The Citadel and wondered, "Is the right of one woman more important than the rights of 1,960 young men who choose to attend a military style college without women?" One Citadel student reasoned, "I do want a single gender education and The Citadel is my only choice in the state to get it. As an individual and taxpayer of the state and federal government, I demand the same thing [Shannon Faulkner] does: equal access."[17]

In addition to co-opting the rhetoric of freedom and individual rights for their side, Citadel supporters cast their stance as a principled defense of "diversity in education." While some found that "being a military college is diversity enough," cadets, alumni, and school officials countered, "If you make all colleges co-ed, there's no diversity." While in the past, Citadel men had demanded their peers conform to certain institutional and societal standards, they demonized the "Justice Department's senseless rush to conformity" and sighed, "Why has society got to homogenize everything?" In 1991, a U.S. District Court in Virginia validated this line of reasoning, finding that while VMI discriminated against women, "The discrimination is not invidious but rather to promote a legitimate state interest — diversity in education."[18]

Again, arguments about freedom of choice, diversity in education, and "legitimate" discrimination supplemented the primary focus of The Citadel's defenders. According to them, the battle "is not The Citadel versus Shannon Faulkner. It is The Citadel versus an educational concept," specifically one questioning "the value of a single-gender education." They argued that on the most basic level, single-sex environments "freed [students] from playing the 'mating game'" and other distractions. They quoted an expert witness from the VMI case who explained that by limiting "opportunity for routine association with members of the opposite sex," schools such as VMI, The Citadel, Wellesley, and Randolph Macon "narrow the range of developmental tasks a student confronts in the interest of enhancing development of selected characteristics." The result, supposedly bore out by the success rate of the aforementioned school's alumni, was a more confident, civic minded, and prosperous member of society.[19]

Several of The Citadel and VMI's critics conceded the benefits of single-sex education. When asked by a federal judge whether or not she thought "that single-gender education per se, violates the Fourteenth Amendment," an attorney for the U.S. Justice Department answered flatly, "No your honor, we don't." For many of them, the issue boiled down to the fact that neither The Citadel nor VMI offered "persuasive justification" for barring women and that neither South Carolina nor Virginia offered women an equal opportunity to obtain a military education on par with those offered by VMI and The Citadel.[20]

Bearing this in mind, both sides assembled panels of experts arguing for and against the notion that men and women learn differently or "have different educational needs which validate the offering of different types of state-funded programs on the basis of sex." At the heart of this argument lay The Citadel and VMI's method of building exceptional citizens. VMI's attorneys called several witnesses who testified that males learn best in "an atmosphere of adversativeness or ritual combat in which the teacher is a disciplinarian and a worthy competitor," while "females tend to thrive in a cooperative atmosphere in which the teacher is emotionally connected with the students." In other words, "Men had to be challenged and cowed, while women required gentle encouragement." An editorial by Citadel graduate Kenneth McKenzie Jr. exposed the problematic nature of such blanket evaluations of individual abilities. While discussing the "well researched differences in male and female socialization," McKenzie pointed out that "many — not all — young males respond well to an adversative single gender environment," and "by the same token, a more supportive single-gender educational environment is beneficial for many — not all — young women." These qualified assessments of who might benefit from the adversative method are important because The Citadel and VMI were excluding not just some, but *all* women on the belief that their system of education was not suitable for females. Also, with his use of the term "socialization," McKenzie indicated that these presumed differences between men and women were not fixed, but instead that gender roles were taught and, in some measure, imposed on members of society.[21]

The attorneys prosecuting The Citadel and VMI raised precisely these same issues. One of Shannon Faulkner's lawyers, Val Vojdik, argued that the "underlying assumption that a military education is not appropriate for women is offensive and denigrating to all women." Lawyers representing the Justice Department presented their own expert witnesses who dismissed "fixed notions concerning the roles and abilities of males and females" in order to convince the judge that "the fact that many or even most women wouldn't be able to comply with the current requirements cannot be a justification for keeping out those women who can comply with them."[22]

The lower courts accepted VMI's and The Citadel's arguments that men and women learned differently and that the latter would not benefit from each school's adversative methods. According to a judge in the VMI case, "It all traces back to maleness, physical vigor, the ability to withstand adversity, the ability to withstand invasions of privacy." In October 1992, a panel of judges from the Fourth U.S. Circuit Court of Appeals ruled that the "question of a woman's ability to perform and endure the physical training in VMI's program," "the physiological differences between men and women," problems that may arise from "cross-sexual confrontations," and certain unstated "psychological" differences compelled them to uphold VMI's all-male admissions standards. They still found the school in violation of the Fourteenth Amendment since the "Commonwealth of Virginia offers the unique benefits of VMI's type of education and training to men and not to women." Accepting the argument that "VMI's male-only admissions policy is in furtherance of a state policy of 'diversity,'" the court found "the explanation of how the policy is furthered by affording a unique educational benefit only to males is lacking." With this in mind, the judges now gave VMI three options: admit women, become a private institution, or convince the state to fund "parallel institutions or parallel programs" for women.[23]

Citadel backers took up this challenge, urging the state to "expand choices for female citizens" by filling a "demand for women's single gender baccalaureate degree granting institutions — either adversative or supportive." As their guiding principle for meeting this need, they embraced the court's message that these parallel programs need not be identical but merely "substantially comparable," since, according to the appellate court, the Fourteenth Amendment allows states to "treat different classes of persons in a different way," and, in this case, a "gender classification is justified by acknowledged differences." As a result, Citadel and other state officials followed VMI's and Virginia's lead and looked to set up a "military leadership" program at an all-women's college that would meet the "educational needs of most women" by focusing on "cooperative confidence" rather than presumably character-building individual stress.[24]

As Citadel officials cast around for a school willing to implement such a program, the South Carolina legislature passed a resolution pledging "to begin the process of providing single-gender opportunities for women" and appropriating $3.4 million to fund the project. The Board of Visitors raised $5 million as seed money for the project and set aside another $1.6 million for "contingency funds." When Sandra Thomas, the president of Converse College in Spartanburg, South Carolina, offered the use of her campus and facilities, General Watts applauded her "bold move" that "will enable the young women of our state to have greater opportunity to experience the unique benefits of a single-gender education."[25]

Strong legislative backing of the fledgling South Carolina Women's Leadership Institute (WLI) proved that The Citadel still enjoyed a great deal of support from the state's political leaders, a realization that rubbed numerous people the wrong way. A few state officials called the legislature's decision "ludicrous" and "absurd." Several politicians and private citizens agreed with an editorial writer for *The State* who asked, "At a time when the General Assembly is cutting millions from higher education, is it rational to take on an expensive new leadership program at a private college?" Interestingly enough, The Citadel's critics used the college's lobbying success to bolster their claims that all citizens should be allowed access to the school's obviously powerful alumni network. One pundit pointed out that the benefits of attending The Citadel had "very little to do with education" and "instead have very much to do with wealth, power, and the ability of those who have it now to determine who will have it later." After watching in "amazement" as the state donated millions of dollars to Converse, a woman from Lexington, South Carolina, remarked, "No wonder Shannon Faulkner wants the opportunity to be a part of this power structure." On some level, at least, the Board of Visitors validated these claims as they stressed "the importance of our alumni groups interfacing with WLI graduates and eventual graduates so that they are made to feel a part of The Citadel network."[26]

After touring the Converse campus and reviewing the WLI curricula, which included eight semesters of specialized physical education, ROTC training, leadership seminars, and math courses, Val Vojdik called the program about as similar to The Citadel as the "Girl Scouts." Faulkner herself explained, "If I wanted to go to Converse, I would have applied there two and a half years ago." Her attorneys argued in court that providing women with a "half-baked Citadel" served only to "reinforce stereotypes that women aren't athletic and make them feel inferior." One man found it "unimaginable that a program patched together in a few months, a program that has not been reviewed in court, a program that so far has only fourteen students, could be considered a fair offering for our state's female college students." A junior attending Converse issued a provocative assessment of the WLI program, concluding, "Basically, what they've said is 'Ladies, you can get on the bus of education, but you've got to sit in the back.'"[27]

Comparisons of Shannon Faulkner's struggle to the fight against racial segregation sparked emotional and interesting responses from a wide variety of sources. One South Carolinian wondered, "Has the financial catastrophe of 'separate but equal' faded that far from the minds of our elected officials?" A state senator who voted against allocating millions to Converse did so because "I don't believe in funding segregation." Syndicated columnist James Kilpatrick regretted that the Citadel controversy evoked memories of "all the prejudice, all the passion, all the injustice of another age," while one Faulkner supporter could not "remember anyone rallying to defend the last school that segregated African Americans in the name of diversity." The executive director of the South Carolina ACLU pointed out that the idea that "men and women learn differently" echoed arguments employed thirty years earlier to keep South Carolina schools all-white. Vocal defenders of The Citadel fueled such comparisons by promising to fight for "some fundamental beliefs present in our society," including "the freedom of choice in associating with and not associating with, whomever one chooses."[28]

In a survey of "opinion shapers of the general African American community" conducted at Citadel officials' behest, the respondents repeated critiques made following the Nesmith incident in regard to the mutually reinforcing nature of racial and gender discrimination. Most based their negative perception of the school on the belief that it "resists diversification" and had a "long history of being an exclusive white male institution." In discussing the Board of Visitors' unanimous decision to continue the fight to exclude women, one person tried to imagine how much pressure the lone African American member of the board was under and "how many black people he had to explain himself to."[29]

Numerous references to the power of The Citadel's "brotherhood" might have provided an answer to why some black alumni denied any similarities between Shannon Faulkner and Charles Foster. Several of The Citadel's defenders cited biological and other "legitimate differences between the sexes" that would require Faulkner "to be housed in separate facilities, given less strenuous training and accept special treatment in just about all activities." With no "relevant differences between the races," some argued that "The Citadel lowered *not one* standard when blacks broke the color barrier." Such a contention left out the fact that while The Citadel did not have to lower any standards when African Americans entered the corps, many people opposed racial integration based on the assumption that standards would have to be lowered. As late as 1987, several vocal alumni and administrators opposed affirmative action on the grounds that the college would have to make special concessions to increase the number of black students in the corps.[30]

Some African American cadets and alumni empathized with Faulkner's efforts. Joe Shine for one found it hard not to feel some connection to "a person who is breaking new ground." Based on his cadet experience, he predicted that the fourth class system would facilitate "bonding among members" of any class, regardless of race or sex. Junior Von Mickle approached Shannon Faulkner on The Citadel's campus one day, shook her hand, and replied, "At one time, blacks were considered to be inferior to whites. That's no longer considered true. Women used to be considered inferior to men. That's no longer true. It's time for a woman at The Citadel." Several other African American cadets disagreed, however, and their objections not only revealed how deeply concepts of manliness factored into the individual and collective identity of most cadets but also how much they had invested in The Citadel as the proving ground for their masculine and civic self-worth. Some black students argued, "You can't compare the feminist movement, the gay movement to that of the African-American movement" because "our forefathers helped build this nation with their blood, sweat and tears." By devaluing and even denying the contributions and sacrifices made by those considered less manly, such an assessment testifies to how deeply certain students' sense of entitlement and accomplishment was tied to their masculine image.[31]

This emphasis on manly accomplishments and service relates directly to people's attitude to the crucible in which Citadel men were formed: the fourth class system. Many Citadel supporters believed wholeheartedly that allowing women into the corps of cadets would change or "soften" the plebe system, and as they had contended for decades, any such modification to this "tradition" would "destroy the foundation of the institution." The epitaphs from the 1970s resurfaced as cadets mourned the "Corpse of Cadets" and began looking around for a "horse drawn carriage" to cart away the college's remains. A woman implored school officials to keep females out lest they "water down that which makes you great."[32]

As before, such fears incorrectly depicted The Citadel's fourth class system as static and treated trivialities as absolutely vital components of Citadel graduates' success. In this case, these misconceptions fueled a heated and very public debate over whether Shannon Faulkner should have her head shaved during her freshmen year. Most people decided that she should, arguing that the ritual symbolized the traditional egalitarianism of the plebe experience. Such claims obscured the fact that although Citadel graduates from the 1940s and 1950s never had their heads shaved, no one had questioned their manly credentials.[33]

A large portion of those who opposed Shannon Faulkner's entry into The Citadel based their objections on societal mores concerning the proper "relationship between the sexes." Adhering to rigid absolutes about male and female behavior, supporters of both VMI and The Citadel believed some unalterable aspect of the female psyche or possibly their genetic makeup left them unable to muster the "male dominant attitude of fierceness" necessary not only to survive but also to administer the adversative learning method employed by both schools.[34]

As these evaluations indicate, preserving The Citadel and VMI's "much harsher ritual discipline and utterly . . . masculine environment" carried larger social implications. In defending "a system which has consistently produced *men* capable of enduring the harassment, bullying and humiliations the real world has to offer," many revived the theory that men and women ought to occupy separate social spheres, with men best suited for life in the "real world" of politics, business, and military service. The idea that The Citadel "is no place for a lady" fed off notions expressed by Sallie Baldwin, a Charlestonian who launched the "Save the Male" bumper sticker campaign, that men are "bred in society to be protectors." Indeed, etiquette classes at The Citadel taught cadets that women "must be sheltered and protected not only from the elements and physical harm, but also from embarrassment, crudity, or coarseness of any sort."[35]

With The Citadel's purpose yoked to rigid social definitions of what it meant to be a man or a woman, several people struggled with the idea of why Shannon Faulkner apparently wanted to become a man. One female commentator questioned Faulkner's motives, asserting that despite her own numerous academic and civic accomplishments, "Never once have I felt the need to be anything but a woman." Another asked how could Faulkner remain "a woman when she's doing push-ups with three hundred other men." Although both these letters were written in support of The Citadel's case, they ended up challenging it by accepting that "men" and "women," as they and many others used the terms, were not biological classifications, but socially constructed identities. This does not mean that intangible masculine and feminine qualities were not as real to some people as anatomical attributes. While gender categories appear fluid in theory, they remained absolutely rigid in the minds of some. The idea that Faulkner's desire to attend The Citadel marked her as wanting to become a man indicated that some saw no difference between a medical sex change and a breach of socially proscribed gender roles.[36]

Discerning what exclusively masculine qualities Citadel men possessed, however, proved much more difficult than simply asserting their manhood. Indeed, while alumni praised their alma mater for helping students "fully develop their masculine characteristics," the characteristics they listed remained gender neutral. Most Citadel men supported the views of a 1993 graduate who explained that "The Citadel cadet system is soaked in traditions such as honor, country, self-discipline, appreciation of freedom, fear of God, and desire for truth and honesty," adding, "All of the aforementioned are ideals to be sought after when shaping a man." No doubt, numerous people accepted his conclusion, with many finding these same qualities desirable in women as well. For several of The Citadel's male defenders, with their tendency to focus on men's accomplishments and potential while excluding those of women, perhaps the major reason females could not become Citadel men was that the school produced "leaders of men," and few of them could fathom taking orders from a female.[37]

While Citadel graduates exalted their own virtues, critics of the college argued that the institution's environment instilled its subjects with far less praiseworthy attributes. Many pointed to past incidents regarding the hazing of athletes and Kevin Nesmith as evidence that The Citadel's "climate of cruelty" bred sadism and racism. Sallie Baldwin and others praised The Citadel for teaching young men "how to treat women with respect," and cadet Norman Doucet claimed, "We appreciate [women] more because they are not here." Others believed that this exclusion fostered chauvinistic and misogynistic attitudes. When Faulkner's attorneys asked, "Approximately how many times over your four years did you hear the word 'woman' used as a way of tearing a cadet down," Ronald Vergnolle, a 1991 graduate of The Citadel, answered, "It was an everyday part, every moment, every hour part of life there." "If the term 'woman' was used," Vergnolle added, "then that would be a welcome relief," since "the majority of the language, in my experience, was gutter slang for women" and homosexuals. According to Vergnolle, upperclassmen consistently insulted freshmen and each other by accusing them of being "either a faggot, a queer or weak as a woman." Other cadets sustained these charges, with one warning his colleagues that unless they checked the "rather disturbing" degree of chauvinism within the corps, "The Citadel is going to continue to turn out men who are not fully capable of coexisting with women on a professional basis."[38]

Of course, most Citadel backers discounted such claims, believing instead that the mere presence of women in the classroom or the barracks would destroy the school. Besides the previously stated arguments calling females a distraction, many offered a far more intriguing analysis of how women would compromise their ability to build men. Contrary to the notion that the college's system spawned crude, loutish behavior and attitudes, several students claimed that The Citadel allowed them to establish intimate bonds with their cadet brothers. When referring to the barracks as "a place where a man can be a man," several cadets felt most free to express themselves in the communal showers. One cadet explained that, especially as freshmen, "We are in the showers, it's very intimate. We're one mass, naked together, and it makes us closer. . . . You're shaved, you're naked, you're afraid together. You can cry." Another continued, "I know it's all trivial but all of us in one shower, it's like we're all one, we're all the same, and — I don't know — you feel like you're exposed, but you feel safe. . . . I just can't explain it, but when they take that away it's over. This place will be ruined." One summed it up succinctly, "With no women, we can hug each other." The irony lies in the fact that these students believed that by shutting out the judgmental eyes of the outside world, their closed, all-male environment helped them become men by giving them the freedom and security to be more intimate and sensitive, traits some of them might have deemed feminine.[39]

Of course, despite all these arguments, The Citadel and VMI eventually lost their cases. While the extremely brief cadet career of Shannon Faulkner was well documented, the final act came a year after she quit, when the Supreme Court found VMI's all-male admissions policy unconstitutional. Ruth Bader Ginsburg wrote the final decision, and in it, she explained that "neither the goal of producing citizen soldiers, nor VMI's implementing methodology is inherently unsuitable for women." She noted that while "physical differences between men and women . . . are enduring," they "remain cause for celebration, but not for denigration of the members of either sex or for artificial constraints on an individual's opportunity." Finally, she concluded that stereotypical assumptions about "what is appropriate for most women, no longer justify denying opportunity to women whose talent and capacity place them outside the average description."[40]

Almost immediately following the Supreme Court's ruling, The Citadel's Board of Visitors, in what the group's chairman called the "biggest, hardest decision" the body had ever made during his tenure, voted unanimously to eliminate an applicant's sex as an admission requirement. Val Vojdik praised the "speed and graciousness" with which the board acted, and she appreciated that "from now on they will be committed to building the whole person." South Carolina Senator Strom Thurmond spoke for many when he hoped that the admission of women to The Citadel would "mark the beginning of a proud new tradition at this very fine military institution." A classmate of Charles Foster agreed, asserting that "The Citadel will not only survive the admission of female cadets, but will eventually be recognized as having become a better school for having admitted women."[41]

The fight to bring The Citadel, as one person put it, "into the twentieth century" by admitting women into the corps of cadets reflected the post–World War II struggles and anxieties that plagued not only a large portion of the college's students and alumni but a sizable number of Americans as well. The changes that swept the nation in the decades following 1945 invigorated some, frustrated others, and frightened even more. Despite appearances, the latter two concerns stem from more than an absolute fear of any and all change. As one commentator put it, "People are mad about the world changing" because "they feel like they don't have a lot of control about it changing."[42]

This lack or loss of control made many uneasy, and while some people regretted that The Citadel was out of touch with modern society, others were grateful. For them, The Citadel seemed to offer stability and order in an "ever-changing world." This attitude stemmed in large measure from a nostalgic longing for "better days," which the college embodied. For many, the coeducation of The Citadel marked not only the college's downfall but the imminent demise of American society, a society whose greatness, according to one cadet, rivaled that of all other "civilized societies" that had "been constructed and organized with an emphasis on male dominance." Another student described "Faulkner and her legal army" as committed to destroying "the values established by men who laid the cornerstone of our country." What these arguments amounted to was a fear among white males that they no longer enjoyed unassailable privileges in society. One cadet voiced the concerns of many when he grumbled, "I have the worst chance in society of getting a job because I'm a white male and that's the major difference between me and my father."[43]

For many, the presumably dismal prospects for white males were the legacy of the social upheavals of the 1960s. It was during this decade that the country's so-called decline in moral values and ethics had supposedly begun. Tellingly, it was also a time period in which more and more people questioned and challenged the beliefs and practices that many Americans and, most especially, the defenders of The Citadel's particular "traditions" held dear. From the veneration of the South's Confederate past to the rigid definitions of proper male and female behavior, The Citadel's decidedly white, exclusively male traditions were no longer viewed as sacred, and a large number of cadets, to say nothing of a substantial portion of the American populace, spent the ensuing decades trying to recover or at least retain certain aspects of the world and authority they had lost.

In this sense, The Citadel offered young white men an environment where they felt safe, comfortable, and appreciated — an ostensibly unchanging setting, insulated from those who would point out that what some cadets referred to as the "age-old, tried and true values which have been the cornerstone for this republic" and their college, grew, as a woman from South Carolina noted, from an era when "women could not vote and blacks were enslaved." Within The Citadel's walls, they could state without much fear of contradiction that *men* built their nation and *men* should lead it. Not only that, they could sing "Dixie," wave the Confederate flag, and pay tribute to a southern heritage that did not include slavery and Jim Crow, thus freeing them of any responsibility for the legacy of such past injustices. While some found this appealing, it left many Citadel students, alumni, and administrators ill equipped to deal with the changes occurring inside and outside the institution's gates.[44]

Certainly, a Citadel education in and of itself did not spawn these all-too-American interpretations of the nation and the South's past, but the lack of ethnic, cultural, racial, and gender diversity did allow certain ideals to flourish unchallenged. The homogeneity of The Citadel's campus fostered a consistently narrow view of the college's, the region's, and the country's history, one that nurtured hostility toward unpopular or unfamiliar views. Once they became entrenched, it proved difficult to disabuse cadets of their restrictive notions, not only of what it meant to be a good Citadel man, but also to be a good southerner and a good American. The struggles over "Dixie" and the Confederate flag indicated that many Citadel people saw a lily-white perception of the past as a key component in the first two categories, while the exclusively masculine emphasis on who built the country and who was best suited to lead and defend it marked manliness as an essential ingredient in the makeup of all three paragons.

As W. J. Cash put it when describing the pre–World War II South, by "exhibiting within itself a remarkable homogeneity," the corps of cadets often took a distinctly southern approach to propagating the image of an ideal Citadel graduate, and by extension an ideal citizen, as a white male. They seized upon a distorted "moonlight and magnolias" view of the past and parlayed this idyllic vision into a noble defense of the South's heritage and tradition. In this context, the battles over Confederate imagery and the ability of women to withstand the Citadel system took on a larger meaning as part of a struggle for inclusion in the past as well as the present. One Citadel backer called The Citadel and VMI "institutions unique to the South, remnants of Southern chivalry, and holdovers from a proud cultural heritage nearly disemboweled by the War Between the States." He argued that these schools "instill and cultivate in their cadets what were once commonly referred to as the virtues of

Southern manhood — honor, chivalry, and devotion to God, state and family." Unfortunately, he appeared to see no place for either black men or women in the "proud cultural heritage" of the antebellum South.[45]

Especially in The Citadel's case, such selective and highly emotional assessments of the South's past proved popular with those who wished to block certain changes in the present, feeding off notions that, to use John Shelton Reed's phrasing, "hundreds of thousands of 'meddlers' are conspiring to undermine the South's institutions and the 'Southern way of life.'" Indeed, many attributed both Shannon Faulkner's lawsuit and the drive to remove the Confederate flag from the top of the South Carolina State House to a "massive invasion of people from the North telling us what to do, telling us what flag to fly, how institutions will be run." What many people feared, in part, was that these assaults on southern "traditions" would eventually result in the loss of regional distinctiveness, a fear shared by many Citadel personnel as it applied to their institution.[46]

Throughout the school's history, Citadel boosters had cast the school's value in terms of its uniqueness and the peculiar value of its contribution to society. In the post–World War II period, many Citadel boosters latched onto the production of "whole men" or Citadel men as the key to the college's value and distinctiveness. Again, this fit nicely with the school's regional setting as several historians have pointed out the important role that gender has played in shaping southern identity, politics, and culture. Glenda Gilmore calls the South "hypergendered" in that "the difference between male and female roles was especially sharp and these accentuated roles functioned in a variety of ways to define not only gender relations, but class politics and racial controls as well." Gilmore's observation is clearly affirmed by the many Citadel graduates who invested a great deal of themselves in the "whole man" concept, enjoying the prestige, recognition, and sense of accomplishment that came with a Citadel ring and diploma. In a sense, the struggle to defend the school's exclusion of women was also a struggle to preserve a "defining feature" of not only The Citadel but of the region.[47]

Despite their constant emphasis on manly virtues, even The Citadel's most ardent supporters could never quite articulate what exclusively masculine qualities the school cultivated. In several cases, their attempts to explain how their single-sex college environment made them better men and citizens exposed the artificiality of gender constructions. Indeed, the experience of The Citadel reinforces the notion that what it means to "be a man" is both historically and contextually contingent, shaped primarily by current societal standards and developments. In the 1950s, for example, Citadel men were expected to conform to lawful authority, but during the 1960s, Citadel men were expected to and did question the supposed wisdom of the school's acknowledged leadership. Permutations in the fourth class system, many of them spearheaded by Citadel graduates, reflected changing societal definitions of manliness, attesting further to the fact that not all men, not even all Citadel men, fit into the same mold nor are they "made" the same way. While the final outcome of the fight over coeducation at The Citadel testifies to the untenability of arguments based on blanket assumptions about the differing physical and emotional capabilities of men and women, the sense of urgency that drove such battles reveals the primacy and power of gendered assumptions in shaping people's views of themselves and the world in which they live.

Epilogue

 In May 1999, Nancy Mace became the first woman to graduate from the corps of cadets. Two years later, Padgett-Thomas Barracks, a Citadel landmark, crumbled to the ground. The two events are not related, of course, with the latter actually proving that predictions about co-education destroying The Citadel had been greatly exaggerated. Indeed, after a rough start to this new era in school history, the college eventually regained its footing. Increased revenues helped fund construction of new barracks and the renovations of old ones. Applications from males and females rose steadily after 1996, part of a trend whereby total enrollment kept increasing, with the school repeatedly breaking new records for the number of applications received. The college consistently received high marks in *U.S. News and World Report*'s annual rankings of the best colleges and universities. In 2005, The Citadel ranked among *Newsweek*'s 25 hottest colleges in America.[1]

The Citadel did not get to that point by avoiding hard decisions and refusing to change. In 1997, the commandant of cadets, Brigadier General Emory Mace, endured heavy criticism for overhauling the entire fourth class system. In his own words, General Mace, a 1963 graduate and father of Nancy Mace, looked to reestablish the type of system he remembered, one that was demanding yet, in his experience, refrained from violent hazing. A year later, Citadel president Major General John S. Grinalds limited the playing of "Dixie" at school functions, explaining his decision as "a matter of public responsibility and personal honor. Public responsibility because I am responsible for the patriotic stance of our institution and the solidarity of the Corps of Cadets. Personal honor because many of my friends and comrades-in-arms sacrificed life and limb to preserve the freedom provided by the Constitution." In 1999, the Board of Visitors sent a resolution to the South Carolina General Assembly, the governor, and "all other interested parties" urging them to remove "the Confederate battle flag from the dome of the State House and according it appropriate display as part of the history of this State."[2]

School officials also placed a greater emphasis on diversity when it came to the building of "principled leaders." Lieutenant General John Rosa, a 1973 Citadel graduate and nineteenth president of the college, listed diversity alongside "honor, duty, discipline, morality" as the "core values" of the institution. In his view, "For The Citadel to go from good to great, we must all embrace diversity." In 2004, the school launched an African American Studies Program that not only stresses "the importance of diversity to the Corps of Cadets" but also invites members of the "black community to come on The Citadel's campus to be a part of what we are trying to do." In all, such efforts have helped make those at The Citadel "much more aware of things that impact folks other than your typical white, male cadet."[3]

As of 2002, women comprised 6 percent of the corps of cadets. In May of that same year, seven African American women broke new ground when they graduated from the corps of cadets. Taking this and other milestones as evidence that "The Citadel has eliminated to the extent practicable the discriminatory effects of the past," a federal district court ruled and the U.S. Justice Department agreed that the college would no longer have to submit quarterly progress reports concerning coeducation. School officials welcomed this confirmation of "our intention to offer young women the same opportunities for success and leadership that have made such a difference to generations of young men in the South Carolina Corps of Cadets." According to General Grinalds, "While our shaky beginnings with coeducation provide interesting material for enterprising writers, the real story is that we have been successful with coeducation."[4]

This is true to a certain extent, but resentment still lingers among male alumni and cadets over a variety of issues. One group calling itself The Citadel Men Foundation has posted a list of grievances including "admission of women to the Corps of Cadets," the "elimination of the official fight song, 'Dixie,'" and "reductions in the rigid fourth class system." The chairman of the organization, a 1993 graduate, estimates that "70 percent of current alumni and cadets have problems with the current policies of the administration." Attitudes like this have made life difficult for men and women on a campus one cadet described as a "testosterone breeding ground."[5]

The importance of changing this mind-set became evident in 2006 when

Citadel officials released the results of a self-initiated study showing that 20 percent of the women and 4 percent of the men attending the college had endured some form of sexual abuse. While knowing that sixteen women and fifteen men had been forced to engage in unwanted sexual acts including intercourse, anal sex, oral sex, and violation with an object is staggering, the fact that Citadel officials took it upon themselves to compile and publish such information offered some promise. Rather than hastily assembling a "review committee" at the same time TV cameras filmed Lesesne Gate and newscasters asked cadets crossing the parade field for their opinion on the latest controversy, school officials invited the press, and by extension the public, through the gates, informed them about problems on campus, and then promised action. To those who wondered why college officials would conduct and then publish a survey that cast the institution in an unflattering light, Rosa responded in a manner familiar to generations of Citadel graduates, asserting that "we do hold ourselves, and I think, this state . . . and this country holds us to a higher standard."[6]

In further discussion with the public and the press, Lieutenant General Rosa admitted that while inexcusable, the violence described in the survey is not unique to The Citadel. He made it clear as well that "this is not a female coed issue." Indeed, the study highlighted in graphic terms a problem that has vexed the college for decades, namely the physical abuse of others in a misguided attempt to prove or demonstrate toughness and authority. Rosa attributed these abuses to a broader lack of respect within the corps and society in general. Such behavior would decrease, he believed, "if we had young people that treated each other with respect and respected themselves." Thus, the general took measures to change "the climate of The Citadel, making it a place where cadets respect themselves and each other." As part of this process, the school launched an extensive and mandatory Values and Respect Program designed to educate cadets about the causes and consequences of discrimination, sexual harassment, and substance abuse.[7]

As for the cadet whose opinion about Citadel men and Shannon Faulkner opened this book, that was me. Born and raised in South Carolina, I graduated from The Citadel in 1994. My father and uncle are also graduates, members of the classes of 1963 and 1956, respectively. When I made that comment to the reporter years ago, I thought I was being cute and clever. I do not think that anymore.

I did not know until recently that this exchange had appeared in the *New York Times*, and it was jarring to read my twenty-one-year-old self espousing views that I no longer support. I never intended to hide what I said that day. As a matter of fact, I had planned to include the quote and identify its source somewhere in this work. It is one thing to remember saying something you now find distasteful; it is another thing to see your words immortalized in the national paper of record. The experience proved beneficial, though, as it pushed me to think harder about the power of history as well as the responsibility of those who study it.

For one, it made me more aware of how readers might react when confronted with their own past views and actions. The purpose of this work has not been to judge these men and women, but to question the reasoning behind and consequences of their words and deeds. The most important weapon wielded by historians and citizens is the question "Why?" We must interrogate choices, assumptions, traditions, and decisions that are all too often taken for granted or accepted as timeless. The reluctance to rethink the meaning, purpose, and legitimacy of certain practices marks The Citadel as one of many settings where the "willfully recalled and deliberately forgotten past" weighs heavy upon the present. Dissenting voices and narratives face an uphill struggle when challenging the "cultural authority of tradition and habit," since such challenges often threaten existing social hierarchies, sparking fierce, emotional battles over what it means to be a man, a woman, a citizen, and an American. The struggle is worthwhile, though, in order to create a more tolerant, just, and democratic nation.[8]

The words I spoke to the reporter in January 1994 remain permanent; the *New York Times* has seen to that. My worldview has changed considerably since then. This transformation began with a greater desire to question beliefs and ideals that I had long accepted as inarguable truths. In his inaugural address, Lieutenant General Rosa remarked that "change is inevitable . . . even at a place as steeped in tradition as The Citadel." He added that "change — even our battles with adapting to change — has made us stronger." The goal at The Citadel remains, as always, the building of principled leaders and citizens. Part of this process now involves disabusing people of the notion that fixed racial and gender categories determine the quality of one's leadership and citizenship.[9]

INTRODUCTION

1. *New York Times*, 13 January 1994.

2. Alice Kessler-Harris has argued that "Until late in the 1960s, and perhaps even after, most men and women tended to agree that the normal order of family life properly subsumed women within its boundaries, rendering their need and desires as well as rights and obligations secondary to those of husbands and children." Kessler-Harris, *In Pursuit of Equity*, 3–4.

3. Horwitz, *Confederates in the Attic*, 66; *Newsweek*, 1 September 1980, 83; Wilson and Ferris, eds., *Encyclopedia of Southern Culture*, 277; Tyson, "Dynamite and the 'Silent South,'" 279–280; Faludi, *Stiffed*, 138; Andrew, *Long Gray Lines*, 8.

4. Faludi, *Stiffed*, 16 (emphasis in original), 138; *Brigadier*, 18 May 1957. There seems to be no set standard when it comes to capitalizing "man" or "men" in reference to "Citadel men" or "the Citadel man." I have chosen not to capitalize "men" or "man" when I use them, but have left them capitalized when they appear that way in the primacy source.

5. Andrew, *Long Gray Lines*, 11; *Bulletin of The Citadel — Catalogue Issue 1940–1941*, 3, cited hereafter as Citadel *Catalogue*; 1943 Citadel *Catalogue*, 3; *Bulldog*, 4 June 1948.

6. Alexander, *Holding the Line*; Zinn, *People's History*, 421; Navasky, *Naming Names*, 7; Edgar, *South Carolina*, xx; Whitfield, *Culture of the Cold War*, 53.

7. Chafe, *Unfinished Journey*, x, 29, 125, 134. Charles Payne examines the successes and setbacks of the early generation of modern civil rights activists in *I've Got the Light of Freedom*. Beth Bailey tracks how emerging tensions and opportunities played out at the local level in *Sex in the Heartland*. Leisa D. Meyer examines the "absolute double-bind" that constrained female soldiers who both defied and reinforced traditional gender roles during the war in *Creating GI Jane*, 180. Susan Hartmann outlines the opportunities and challenges women faced during and after the war in *Homefront and Beyond*. Also see Douglas, *Where the Girls Are*, 49, 54; Whitfield, *Culture of the Cold War*, 72; Kessler-Harris, *In Pursuit of Equity*, 206–207.

8. For a broad, but fairly detailed analysis of the post–World War II South, see Bartley, *New South*. Cobb, *Selling of the South*, 194, 206, 227; Fraser, *Charleston!*, 419–421; Cobb, *Redefining Southern Culture*, 27, 28, 30, 31, 43, 48–49; Edgar, *South Carolina*, 511; Sosna, "More Important Than the Civil War?" 145, 147–150, 154; Sosna, "The GIs'

South," 322; Daniel, *Lost Revolutions*, 1, 7, 9, 16–19, 92; Mohr, "World War II and the Transformation of Southern Higher Education," 34.

9. Andrew, *Long Gray Lines*, 1, 3–4, 16, 17, 44; Bond, *Story of The Citadel*, 16, 24–25, 107, 110–113, 119, 125, 128, 140; Kantrowitz, *Ben Tillman*, 98–99, 118–119.

10. Cobb, *Away Down South*, 212–214, 333; *The Brigadier*, 11 December 1970.

11. Pat Conroy's brutal depiction of this system permeates his novel *The Lords of Discipline*. Catherine Manegold placed the escalating physical violence of plebe year at the center of her study of Shannon Faulkner and The Citadel entitled *In Glory's Shadow*.

12. Watts, ed., *White Masculinity in the Recent South*, 4; Cobb, *Redefining Southern Culture*, 89; Cobb, *Away Down South*, 4–5; Zinn, *Southern Mystique*, 218, 262. The popular image of the South as an island region operating outside the ebb and flow of the American mainstream has prompted authors such as John Egerton and Peter Applebome to attribute the national popularity of conservative ideals to the "Southernization of America." Egerton, *Americanization of Dixie*; Applebome, *Dixie Rising*.

13. Kimmel, *Manhood in America*, 280; Gerstle, *American Crucible*, 178–180; Scott, "Gender," 1069.

14. Foner, *Story of American Freedom*, xix–xx; Gerstle, *American Crucible*, 8, 9, 13, 161, 178–180, 246; Bailey, *Sex in the Heartland*, 14, 16–18, 38, 40–41. Although it covers an earlier era, Gail Bederman's *Manliness and Civilization* remains a landmark study of how Americans have defined citizenship and their place in the national body politic. Like most scholars, I have relied upon the groundbreaking essays of Joan Scott and Barbara Fields in forming my theoretical models regarding the construction, meaning, and authority of socially constructed gender and racial categories. Scott, "Gender," 1053–1075; Fields, "Ideology and Race in American History," 143–177.

15. Scott, "Gender," 1063, 1068–1069; Faludi, *Stiffed*, 136; Addelston and Stirratt, "Last Bastion of Masculinity," 205–220; Stockdale and Stockdale, *In Love and War*, 467; McEnaney, "Gender Analysis and Foreign Relations," 127.

CHAPTER ONE. *"The Best Chance of Becoming Men and Leaders"*

1. Sass, "The Citadel: American Epic," *Saturday Evening Post*, 20 March 1943, 12, 13, 100, 103.

2. Cash, *Mind of the South*, 429; Chafe, *Unfinished Journey*, x, 29, 125, 134.

3. Egerton, *He Shall Go Out Free*, 163–168, 204–205, 211–213; Baker, *Cadets in Gray*, 1.

4. Fraser, *Charleston!* 203; Bond, *Story of The Citadel*, 2–5; Egerton, *He Shall Go Out Free*, 213–214.

5. "A Self Study: The Citadel, 1972," documents in possession of author, 10, 11; Bond, *Story of The Citadel*, 10, 16, 17; Baker, *Cadets in Gray*, 1–2.

6. Bond, *Story of The Citadel*, 49–51; Baker, *Cadets in Gray*, 188–189; Andrew, *Long Gray Lines*, 36–37.

7. Bond, *Story of The Citadel*, 87; Fraser, *Charleston!* 269; Kathleen Clark, "Celebrating Freedom: Emancipation Day Celebrations and African American Memory in the Early Reconstruction South," in Brundage, *Where These Memories Grow*, 111, 117–120, 125.

8. Andrew, *Long Gray Lines*, 38; Donald, "Generation of Defeat," 17; Burton, "The Effects of the Civil War and Reconstruction," 204–224; Grantham, *Southern Progressivism*, xvii–xviii, 3, 271–274; Bauman, "Confronting the New South Creed," 100.

9. Andrew, *Long Gray Lines*, 2, 3, 12, 13, 18, 22; Foster, *Ghosts of the Confederacy*, 6–8, 79, 195.

10. Andrew, *Long Gray Lines*, 64, 72–73; Macaulay, "Discipline and Rebellion," 30–47.

11. "Self Study," 11; Fraser, *Charleston!* 269; Bond, *Story of The Citadel*, 87, 92, 94, 98, 100–102, 111; Andrew, *Long Gray Lines*, 34, 36–39.

12. Fraser, *Charleston!* 219, 313; "Self Study," 11–12, 1-5; Nichols, "General as President," 317, 319; Nicholson, *History of The Citadel*, 14.

13. Nicholson, *History of The Citadel*, 12, 23, 59, 61, 62, 70–74, 84, 85, 87, 93, 97–98, 119–121; Nichols, "General as President," 314, 315, 319, 320; *Time*, 22 June 1953.

14. Nicholson, *History of The Citadel*, 22–94, 168, 182, 196–97; Nichols, "General as President," 320.

15. Sass, "American Epic," 12; *The Bulldog*, 11 February 1949, 13 September 1945; Board of Visitors, "Minutes," 29 May 1942, document 600, The Citadel Archives and Museum, Charleston, S.C.; Board of Visitors, "Minutes," 11 June 1948, document 913; Board of Visitors, "Minutes," 1 July 1944, document 768; Board of Visitors, "Minutes," 9 June 1945, document 800; President's Annual Report to the Board of Visitors, 3 June 1944, The Citadel Archives and Museum, Charleston, S.C.

16. Board of Visitors, "Minutes," 16 January 1943, document 600; Nicholson, *History of The Citadel*, 206.

17. Nichols, "General as President," 321; Letter from J. S. Bragdon to Summerall, dated 2 December 1942, General Charles C. Summerall Papers, Box 1, Folder 7, "Army Specialized Training Program, 1942," The Citadel Archives and Museum, The Citadel, Charleston, S.C.; Nicholson, *History of The Citadel*, 173–175, 210; Letter from L. B. Clapham to Summerall, dated 16 July 1942, Box 1, Folder 7, Summerall Papers; Letter from Willis S. Fitch to Summerall, dated 27 January 1943, Box 1, Folder 8, "Army Specialized Training Program — January — March 1943," Summerall Papers; War

Department Memo No. w145-4-42, Box 1, Folder 7, Summerall Papers; Citadel SCU-3410-Schedule 4, Section A, Box 1, Folder 8, Summerall Papers; undated letter from C. F. Myers Jr. to Summerall, Box 1, Folder 6, "Army Specialized Training Program, undated," Summerall Papers.

18. 1940 Citadel *Catalogue*, 3.

19. Ibid.; Grimsley, *Citadel*, 2; 1942 *Guidon*, 66, Daniel Library, The Citadel, Charleston, S.C.; 1943 *Guidon*, 31.

20. Letter from Summerall to Edward Smith, dated 8 December 1942, Box 1, Folder 7, Summerall Papers; Board of Visitors, "Minutes," 16 January 1943, documents 659–661; 1943 Citadel *Catalogue*, 24.

21. Nicholson, *History of The Citadel*, 210–212, 215–220.

22. 1942 *Guidon*, 69–70.

23. 1946 *Guidon*, 54–55.

24. 1944 *Guidon*, 12; Nicholson, *History of The Citadel*, 211–212, 214–219.

25. "Memorandum RE Proposed Contract for Army Training," dated 25 February 1943, Box 1, Folder 8, Summerall Papers; "Resolutions Adopted at the meeting of Presidents of Military Colleges, Washington, D.C., 1/8/43," Box 1, Folder 8, Summerall Papers; Undated letter from C. F. Myers Jr. to Summerall, Box 1, Folder 6, Summerall Papers; "Salaries of Teaching Staff Employed For 1943/1944," dated 3 June 1943, Box 1, Folder 9, "Army Specialized Training Program, April — December 1943," Summerall Papers; Headquarters Fourth Service Command to Citadel, 25 August 1943, Box 1, Folder 9, Summerall Papers; "Memo to CPS," no date, Box 1, Folder 6, Summerall Papers; D. S. McAlister to Summerall, 3 and 4 March 1944, Box 1, Folder 8, Summerall Papers; Board of Visitors, "Minutes," 29 April 1944, document 751, 754; Board of Visitors, "Minutes," 15 April 1944, document 745; E. E. Uhl to Summerall, 13 May 1944, Box 1, Folder 10, "Army Specialized Training Program, 1944," Summerall Papers; Memo to Commandant from Summerall, 13 May 1944, Box 1, Folder 10, Summerall Papers; Board of Visitors, "Minutes," 1 July 1944, document 767; Board of Visitors, "Minutes," 15 July 1944, document 776; Summerall to J. M. Moorer, 21 June 1944 and to John P. Thomas, 30 October 1944, Box 1, Folder 10, Summerall Papers; Board of Visitors, "Minutes," 5 February 1944, document 732, and 15 April 1944, document 743; President's Annual Report for 1945; D. S. McAlister to Summerall, 23 August 1943, Box 1, Folder 9, Summerall Papers; Summerall to Commanding General Fourth Service Command, 26 April 1943, 5 June 1943 and 21 August 1943, Box 1, Folder 9, Summerall Papers; "Government Payments," undated, Box 1, Folder 6, Summerall Papers; William Bryden to Burnet Maybank, 6 November 1943, Box 1, Folder 9, Summerall Papers.

26. 1943 Citadel *Catalogue*, 46; 1951 *Guidon*, 22.

27. Board of Visitors, "Minutes," 15 April 1944, documents 733–736, 743; Board

of Visitors, "Minutes," Folder 19, document 800; Board of Visitors, "Minutes," 18 August 1945, document 810; *Bulldog*, 13 September 1945; Board of Visitors, "Minutes," 30 September 1944, document 779; Link, *William Friday*, xii, 64; Frank K. Hyatt to Summerall, 14 May 1945, Box 1, Folder 11, "Association of Military Colleges, 1941–1952," Summerall Papers; Summerall to Hyatt, 26 May 1945, Summerall Papers; *Bulldog*, 13 September 1945, 5 December 1947.

28. *Bulldog*, 13 September 1945; Nicholson, *History of The Citadel*, 221–222, 225, 226.

29. Board of Visitors, "Minutes," 11 June 1948, document 913; Board of Visitors, "Minutes," 9 June 1945, document 793; Board of Visitors, "Minutes," 28 February 1945, document 789; 1946 Annual Report.

30. Link, *William Friday*, 64; Board of Visitors, "Minutes," 20 June 1947, document 880; 1946 Annual Report; 1947 Annual Report; Nicholson, *History of The Citadel*, 226; Board of Visitors, "Minutes," 20 June 1947, documents 838, 839, 841.

31. Summerall to Frank Hyatt, dated 26 May 1945, Box 1, Folder 11, Summerall Papers; Board of Visitors, "Minutes," 14 June 1946, document 818–819; 1947 Annual Report; Board of Visitors, "Minutes," 3 June 1949, document 41; Board of Visitors, "Minutes," 12 October 1946, document 825; Board of Visitors, "Minutes," 28 December 1946.

32. *Bulldog*, 7 February 1947, 5 December 1947; Board of Visitors, "Minutes," 27 December 1947, document 880; Nicholson, *History of The Citadel*, 243; Board of Visitors, "Minutes," Folder 20, document 911; 1948 Annual Report; Board of Visitors, "Minutes," 16 October 1948, document 3; Board of Visitors, "Minutes," 17 September 1949, 50–51, 113.

33. Board of Visitors, "Minutes," 13 April 1946, document 815; Board of Visitors, "Minutes," 20 June 1947, document 843; Board of Visitors, "Minutes," 11 June 1948, document 909; Board of Visitors, "Minutes," 3 June 1949, document 43; Board of Visitors, "Minutes," 8 June 1951, document 148; *Bulldog*, 25 April 1947, 17 October 1947, 19 November 1948.

34. Similar transformations occurred at the service academies during this time. Lovell, *Neither Athens Nor Sparta?* 249, 269, 272, 274, 300, 301, 331; Ambrose, *Duty, Honor, Country*, 8, 50, 59, 191, 208. *Bulldog*, 7 March 1947, 21 November 1947, 5 December 1947, 17 December 1948, 28 January 1949, 20 November 1952; Board of Visitors, "Minutes," 12 October 1946, document 825; Board of Visitors, "Minutes," 2 November 1950, document 118; Board of Visitors, "Minutes," 17 November 1951, documents 205, 206, 208; Board of Visitors, "Minutes," 20 June 1947, document 843; 1948 Annual Report; Board of Visitors, "Minutes," 11 June 1948, documents 838, 903, 905–906, 910, 913; Board of Visitors, "Minutes," 20 June 1947, document 839; Board of Visitors, "Minutes," 3 June 1949, documents 37, 41, 45; Board of Visitors, "Minutes," 8 June 1951, documents 142–146, 147.

35. Nicholson, *History of The Citadel*, 225.

36. *Bulldog,* 7 March 1947, 25 April 1947, 30 May 1947, 20 June 1947, 28 January 1949, 11 February 1949, 22 April 1949, 3 December 1949, 27 October 1950.

37. Ibid., 28 January 1949.

38. Ibid., 11 February 1949, 25 February 1949.

39. Ibid., 13 June 1946, 4 June 1948, 3 December 1948, 7 May 1949, 16 December 1949.

40. Ibid., 17 October 1947; 1949 *Guidon,* 54.

41. *Bulldog,* 7 November 1947, 4 June 1948, 19 November 1948.

42. 1948 Annual Report; Board of Visitors, "Minutes," 11 June 1948, documents 903, 907; 1946 Annual Report; Board of Visitors, "Minutes," Folder 21, document 35; 1948 Citadel *Catalogue;* 1953 Annual Report; *Bulldog,* 19 November 1948, 28 January 1949; Board of Visitors, "Minutes," 3 June 1949, documents 35–36, 40; Board of Visitors, "Minutes," Folder 22, document 385.

43. Board of Visitors, "Minutes," Folder 21, documents 114, 146, 252; 1952 Annual Report; Nicholson, *History of The Citadel,* 227–228; Board of Visitors, "Minutes," 20 October 1956.

44. Nye, "Western Masculinities in War and Peace," 418; *Bulldog,* 11 February 1949.

45. *Bulldog,* 28 January 1949.

46. Dean, *Imperial Brotherhood,* 241–242; Whitfield, *Culture of the Cold War,* 10, 72.

47. Whitfield, *Culture of the Cold War,* vii, 7, 10, 22, 23, 53, 62–63, 69; Caute, *Great Fear;* Zinn, *People's History,* 416–421; Navasky, *Naming Names,* 7; Chafe, *Unfinished Journey,* 62, 65, 66–68, 82; Faludi, *Stiffed,* 19.

48. *Bulldog,* 13 September 1945, 20 June 1947, 17 October 1947, 29 October 1948, 25 February 1949.

49. Nicholson, *History of The Citadel,* 230; *Bulldog,* 21 November 1947, 20 June 1947, 17 October 1947, 29 October 1948.

50. 1942 Citadel *Catalogue,* 46; 1944 *Guidon,* 12; *Bulldog,* 4 June 1948.

51. *Bulldog,* 21 February 1947, 7 March 1947, 23 January 1948, 6 February 1948.

52. Ibid., 21 February 1947, 9 May 1947, 20 June 1947, 21 November 1947, 5 December 1947.

53. Ibid., 5 June 1950, 14 October 1950, 11 November 1950, 14 October 1950, 16 February 1951, 8 June 1951, 28 April 1951, 27 October 1951, 14 December 1951, 28 February 1953, 18 April 1953, 9 May 1953.

54. Frederickson, "'Slowest State,'" 177–202; *Bulldog,* 6 February 1948, 27 February 1948, 28 January 1949, 28 April 1951.

55. "Remarks of General Summerall at the Graduating Exercises, 12/20/52," Box 6, Folder 8, Summerall Papers; *Bulldog,* 16 March 1951, 14 December 1951, 1 March 1952,

21 March 1952, 9 May 1952, 8 November 1952, 19 December 1952, 10 October 1953, 19 October 1953.

56. *Bulldog*, 13 June 1946, 11 November 1949, 26 January 1952.

57. Ibid., 20 March 1953.

58. Ibid., 25 October 1952.

59. Ibid., 26 November 1952.

60. Nicholson, *History of The Citadel*, 23; *Bulldog*, 3 June 1949, 10 March 1951, 1 March 1952, 21 March 1952, 14 February 1953; *Brigadier*, 10 October 1953, 24 October 1953; "Address by General J. Lawton Collins, Chief of Staff U.S. Army," Box 6, Folder 8, "Summerall, General Speeches, 1952–1953," Summerall Papers; 1952 *Guidon*, 42; Board of Visitors, "Minutes," 10 October 1953, document 288.

61. Chafe, *Unfinished Journey*, 123.

62. Hartmann, *Homefront and Beyond*, 163–181; Douglas, *Where the Girls Are*, 22, 47; Cuordileone, "'Politics in an Age of Anxiety,'" 528. Other informative works on the Cold War's politicalization of private lives include Elaine Tyler May's *Homeward Bound* and Laura McEnaney's *Civil Defense Begins at Home*.

63. Chafe, *Unfinished Journey*, 124–128.

64. *Bulldog*, 11 February 1949, 25 February 1949, 5 June 1950; Letter from Summerall to John P. Thomas, Box 7, Folder 4, "Summer School, 1949," Summerall Papers; Board of Visitors, "Minutes," 8 June 1951, document 133; 1953 Annual Report.

65. *Bulldog*, 7 May 1949; *Brigadier*, 7 May 1955.

66. *Bulldog*, 7 February 1947, 21 February 1947, 7 March 1947, 25 April 1947, 9 May 1947, 30 May 1947, 17 October 1947, 7 November 1947, 21 November 1947, 27 February 1948, 4 June 1948, 27 January 1950, 24 February 1950; *Brigadier*, 17 April 1954.

67. *Bulldog*, 17 October 1947, 27 February 1948, 4 June 1948, 29 October 1948, 25 February 1949, 11 November 1949, 3 December 1949, 16 December 1949, 8 March 1949, 7 May 1949, 27 January 1950, 24 February 1950, 17 March 1950, 5 May 1950.

68. Ibid., 28 January 1949, 17 December 1948, 18 March 1949, 3 June 1949, 27 January 1950, 19 May 1950.

69. Emilio and Freedman, *Intimate Matters*, 292, 295; Whitfield, *Culture of the Cold War*, 10; Collins, "The Post War Boy Scout Handbooks," 15; Mzorek, "Cult and the Ritual of Toughness," in Browne, *Ritual and Ceremonies in Popular Culture*, 178–179, 183–184, 189–190.

70. Board of Visitors, "Minutes," 11 June 1948, document 912; *Bulldog*, 13 September 1945, 4 June 1948, 3 December 1948, 3 June 1949, 16 December 1949, 7 March 1950, 5 June 1950, 16 February 1951; Board of Visitors, "Minutes," 4 November 1953, document 297.

71. Nicholson, *History of The Citadel*, 140; Bill Marett, interview by author, 22 December 2001.

72. 1943 Citadel *Catalogue*, 50–51; 1951 *Guidon*, 38; 1950 *Guidon*, 55–56.

73. Board of Visitors, "Minutes," 17 November 1951, document 166; Board of Visitors, "Minutes," Folder 21, document 141, 247, 252.

74. *Bulldog*, 21 March 1952; 1953 *Guidon*, 90.

75. 1949 *Guidon*, 7; 1953 *Guidon*, 11; "Message of General Summerall to the New Fourth Class," Box 6, Folder 8, Summerall Papers.

76. Zinn, *People's History*, 421, 428; Kirby, *Media-Made Dixie*, 103, 106.

CHAPTER TWO. *Soaring with the American Eagle*

1. Nicholson, *History of The Citadel*, 252–253; Nichols, "General as President," 322; Board of Visitors, "Minutes," 13 June 1952, documents 182, 196, 198, 208, 229–230.

2. *Time*, 22 June 1953, 43; Board of Visitors, "Minutes," 12 June 1953, documents 235, 240–243; 13 June 1952, 229–230.

3. Board of Visitors, "Minutes," 13 June 1952, documents 182, 230; Nichols, "General as President," 322–323.

4. Nichols, "General as President," 323–324; *Brigadier*, 21 November 1953; Nicholson, *History of The Citadel*, 260–261.

5. Nicholson, *History of The Citadel*, 261, 268, 271–272; *Brigadier*, 3 December 1955.

6. *Time*, 2 November 1953; *Brigadier*, 21 November 1953; Board of Visitors, "Minutes," 3 March 1954, documents 328–336.

7. Zinn, *People's History*, 420–421, 428; Gerstle, *American Crucible*, 267; Whitfield, *Culture of the Cold War*, 24–25, 33; Chafe, *Unfinished Journey*, 108, 134. Broad surveys of these trends include Elaine Tyler May's *Homeward Bound*, David Caute's *The Great Fear*, and Mary L. Dudziak's *Cold War Civil Rights*.

8. Cuordileone, "'Politics in an Age of Anxiety,'" 516; Stearns, *Be a Man!* 89, 155; Whitfield, *Culture of the Cold War*, 43–44; Douglas, *Where the Girls Are*, 54; Emilio and Freedman, *Intimate Matters*, 289, 290, 292–294; Collins, "The Post War Boy Scout Handbooks," 15, 89.

9. *Brigadier*, 14 February 1959, 15 April 1961.

10. Board of Visitors, "Minutes," 13 June 1953, documents 246, 251–252; Board of Visitors, "Minutes," 12 November 1953, document 300; Board of Visitors, "Minutes," 27 February 1954, document 309; Board of Visitors, "Minutes," 12 January 1954, document 304; Nichols, "General as President," 321–326.

11. Board of Visitors, "Minutes," 3 December 1954, document 439; *Brigadier*, 20

January 1954, 9 October 1954, 8 October 1955, 3 December 1955, 26 November 1960; Board of Visitors, "Minutes," 11 June 1956, document 639; Board of Visitors, "Minutes," 3 June 1955, Annual Report, document 466; Board of Visitors, "Minutes," 3 May 1957, document 758; Board of Visitors, "Minutes," 5 June 1959, document 22; Board of Visitors, "Minutes," 3 June 1960, document 147.

12. Board of Visitors, "Minutes," 11 June 1954, document 414; Board of Visitors, "Minutes," Book 6, Folder 23, document 539.

13. Board of Visitors, "Minutes," Book 6, Folder 21, documents 215–217; Board of Visitors, "Minutes," 9 October 1954, documents 404, 414; Board of Visitors, "Minutes," 3 June 1955, documents 458, 466–468; Board of Visitors, "Minutes," Folder 24, document 801; *Brigadier*, 8 October 1955; Board of Visitors, "Minutes," 1956 Annual Report, document 642; Nichols, "General as President," 326–327.

14. Board of Visitors, "Minutes," 11 June 1954, documents 380–381; 1955 Annual Report; 1956 Annual Report; *Brigadier*, 27 October 1955, 16 December 1955, 22 October 1954, 3 December 1955; *Time*, 25 April 1955, 19–21; Board of Visitors, "Minutes," 3 December 1954, document 448.

15. *Life*, 28 November 1955, 113–117.

16. Board of Visitors, "Minutes," 11 June 1954, documents 378, 390, 434; Board of Visitors, "Minutes," 3 June 1955, documents 464–465, 471, 480; Board of Visitors, "Minutes," 13 October 1955, documents 539–540, 541; 1955 Annual Report; Board of Visitors, "Minutes," 2 June 1956, document 614; Board of Visitors, "Minutes," 11 June 1956, documents 636–637, 639, 648–649, 663, 664; Board of Visitors, "Minutes," 31 May 1957, documents 730–731, 745–746; Board of Visitors, "Minutes," 19 October 1957, documents 782, 784, 788; 1958 Annual Report; 1959 Annual Report; 1960 Annual Report; *Brigadier*, 7 May 1955, 8 October 1955, 6 December 1955, 14 April 1956, 22 November 1958, 6 December 1958; Nichols, "General as President," 326–327, 332.

17. Board of Visitors, "Minutes," Folder 24, Book 6, documents 1009–1011.

18. Board of Visitors, "Minutes," 27 February 1954, document 309; Board of Visitors, "Minutes," 30 May 1958, document 878; Board of Visitors, "Minutes," 13 February 1957, documents 722, 731; Nichols, "General as President," 333.

19. Board of Visitors, "Minutes," Folder 24, Book 6, 1958 Annual Report, documents 947, 1006–1007; Nichols, "General as President," 333, 334.

20. Willingham, *End as a Man*; *Brigadier*, 25 February 1956.

21. Board of Visitors, "Minutes," 25 May 1956, documents 620–622.

22. Ibid., 11 June 1954, document 379; *Brigadier*, 18 December 1953, 27 February 1954, 17 April 1954, 1 May 1954, 11 June 1954, 26 February 1955, 8 October 1955, 22 October 1955, 2 November 1955, 20 March 1981, 14 January 1956, 25 February 1956, 8 December 1956, 15 October 1960, 15 April 1961; 1956 *Catalogue*.

23. In his novel *The Lords of Discipline*, Pat Conroy, a 1967 graduate of The Citadel, exclaims that "if [The Citadel], indeed, is something special, then the code is the central fact of that specialness." He adds that when someone graduates from the school "the code goes with you and the code lives as long as you live." Conroy, *Lords of Discipline*, 75.

24. "The Proposed Honor System of the Corps of Cadets," Folder AF Citadel/Honor System, The Citadel Archives; Memo to Clark from Leonard B. Smith dated 25 February 1953, RC-6, "Records of President's Office — Publications," Box 11, File "Honor Code (Miscellaneous 1956, 1958)," Citadel Archives.

25. 1949 *Guidon*; Nicholson, *History of The Citadel*, 256–257; *Brigadier*, 13 February 1960; Smith memo; Board of Visitors, "Minutes," 12 June 1953, document 238.

26. Board of Visitors, "Minutes," 11 June 1954, document 359; "Proposed Honor System."

27. "Proposed Honor System"; Honor Code in RC-6, Box 11, File "Honor Code," Citadel Archives.

28. Board of Visitors, "Minutes," 11 June 1954, document 359; Board of Visitors, "Minutes," 9 October 1954, document 404; "Proposed Honor System"; *Brigadier*, 15 September 1954, 20 November 1954.

29. *Brigadier*, 5 January 1955.

30. Ibid., 23 April 1955, 4 June 1955; 1955 *Guidon*; 1956 Annual Report; Board of Visitors, "Minutes," 3 June 1955, document 469.

31. *Brigadier*, 21 May 1955, 4 June 1955, 8 October 1955; 1955 *Guidon*.

32. *Brigadier*, 14 February 1958, 13 February 1960.

33. Board of Visitors, "Minutes," Folder 23, documents 664, 670–671; Board of Visitors, "Minutes," 2 June 1956, documents 613–614, 615, 624; 1958 Annual Report; Board of Visitors, "Minutes," 30 May 1958, document 879.

34. *Brigadier*, 14 February 1959; 1959–1960 President's Report, Board of Visitors, "Minutes," 3 June 1960, documents 147, 153–154; 1959 President's Annual Report; Board of Visitors, "Minutes," 5 June 1959, document 8.

35. Chafe, *Unfinished Journey*, 76–77; Caute, *Great Fear*, 11, 21, 36; Foner, *American Freedom*, 252, 254; Fraser, *Charleston!* 405, 410; Whitfield, *Culture of the Cold War*, 94; *Brigadier*, 20 November 1954, 17 December 1954, 15 January 1955, 23 April 1955, 21 May 1955, 8 January 1958; Nichols, "General as President," 324, 327; Board of Visitors, "Minutes," Folder 22, document 471; Board of Visitors, "Minutes," Folder 23, document 648.

36. *Brigadier*, 20 November 1954, 17 December 1954, 19 March 1955, 21 May 1955, 27 October 1955, 12 November 1955, 16 December 1955, 25 February 1956, 17 March

1956, 28 April 1956, 8 December 1956, 21 December 1956, 1 April 1957, 30 May 1957, 18 December 1958.

37. Zinn, *People's History*, 417; Foner, *American Freedom*, 254–255; Navasky, *Naming Names*, 28, 29; Caute, *Great Fear*, 404–405; *Brigadier*, 22 May 1954, 11 June 1954, 3 December 1955, 22 October 1956, 17 November 1956, 30 May 1957.

38. *Brigadier*, 15 January 1955.

39. Board of Visitors, "Minutes," Folder 24, documents 1009, 1010–1011; Board of Visitors, "Minutes," 2 October 1959, document 112.

40. *Brigadier*, 22 February 1958, 6 December 1958, 14 February 1959, 15 April 1961; 1958 *Guidon*, 6.

41. *Brigadier*, 23 January 1954, 3 December 1955, 18 May 1957, 14 February 1959.

42. Ibid., 23 January 1954, 18 December 1958.

43. Ibid., 4 May 1957, 18 May 1957.

44. Ibid., 3 December 1955; Whitfield, *Culture of the Cold War*, 43; Mzorek, "Cult and the Ritual of Toughness," 178–179, 182, 183–184, 189–190; May, *Homeward Bound*, 10.

45. *New York Times*, 21 August 1950; *Brigadier*, 9 October 1954.

46. Conroy, *My Losing Season*, 100; *Brigadier*, 9 October 1954; 1956 *Catalogue*; 1959 *Guidon*; *Brigadier*, 18 May 1957.

47. *Brigadier*, 9 October 1954, 24 October 1959.

48. Ibid., 20 March 1981; Board of Visitors, "Minutes," 13 October 1955, document 515; Board of Visitors, "Minutes," 15 October 1955; 1956 *Catalogue*; 1959 *Catalogue*.

49. May, *Homeward Bound*, 16, 18, 19, 58, 90; Douglas, *Where the Girls Are*, 49; *Brigadier*, 23 January 1954, 27 February 1954, 11 February 1956, 17 March 1956.

50. *Brigadier*, 20 November 1954.

51. Daniel, *Lost Revolutions*, 152, 155, 156, 158–159; *Brigadier*, 24 October 1953, 23 January 1954, 27 February 1954, 11 February 1956, 17 March 1956.

52. Woodward, *Burden of Southern History*, 251; Bartley, *New South*, 163, 186; Bartley, *Massive Resistance*, 45, 340; Sarratt, *Ordeal of Desegregation*, 34; Sproat, "Firm Flexibility," 167.

53. Woodward, *Strange Career of Jim Crow*, 156–157; *Charleston News and Courier*, 15 February 1956; Synnott, "Desegregation in South Carolina," 58; Sarratt, *Ordeal of Desegregation*, 131, 140–141, 186; Bartley, *Rise of Massive Resistance*, 75–76, 228, 230–232; J. M. Moorer to Clark, 17 February 1956, Clark Papers.

54. Board of Visitors, "Minutes," 2 June 1956, documents 613–614; Nichols, "General as President," 331; Pratt, *We Shall Not Be Moved*, 17–18; Clark, *Calculated Risk*, 413–415; Clark to Dink R. Rigsby, 13 June 1956, Clark Papers; Clark to Eric F. Goldman, 24

April 1956, Clark Papers; *Brigadier*, 12 May 1956. The integration of the U.S. Armed Forces had occurred years before, but many "old guard" military officers clung to this distorted view of black troops. Since at least World War I, the debilitating effects of a racially segregated army hindered the effectiveness of American troops. Segregation fostered resentment and isolation among black soldiers and heightened racial tensions. White instructors offered African American soldiers little practical training, and their attitudes and performance suffered as a result. With Executive Order 9981, Harry Truman banned racial discrimination in the U.S. military, but it was the Korean War that forced the U.S. Army to integrate. The massive influx of black and white recruits rendered continued segregation impossible as field commanders could not afford to waste manpower. MacGregor, *Integration of the Armed Forces*; Dalfiume, *Desegregation of the U.S. Armed Forces*; Coffman, *War to End All Wars*, 69–73, 231–233, 314–320.

55. *Brigadier*, 21 May 1955; Board of Visitors, "Minutes," 12 April 1955, document 445; Board of Visitors, "Minutes," 5 June 1959, document 47.

56. Carter, *Politics of Rage*, 248–249; Edgar, *South Carolina*, 524–525; *Brigadier*, 28 April 1956, 9 February 1957.

57. Bartley, *Rise of Massive Resistance*, 116, 145–146; *Brigadier*, 25 February 1956.

58. *Brigadier*, 25 February 1956.

59. Weisbrot, *Freedom Bound*, 12; *Brigadier*, 25 February 1956.

60. *Brigadier*, 17 March 1956.

61. Ibid.

62. Ibid., 28 April 1956.

63. Ibid., 12 May 1956.

64. Ibid., 25 February 1956. John Walker Davis argues persuasively that the "flag change was a symbolic representation of 'massive resistance' in Georgia." Davis, "Air of Defiance," 308.

65. *Brigadier*, 6 October 1956.

66. Ibid.

67. 1958 *Sphinx*, 165, Citadel Archives.

68. *Brigadier*, 14 February 1959, 10 October 1959; Board of Visitors, "Minutes," 15 November 1958, document 117; Board of Visitors, "Minutes," 3 June 1960, 153–154; 1959 Annual Report.

69. W. L. O'Neill, *Coming Apart*, 8; Pach and Richardson, *Presidency of Dwight D. Eisenhower*, 208–209, 215; Ambrose, *Eisenhower*, 2:542–544; Whitfield, *Culture of the Cold War*, 205–208; *Brigadier*, 14 February 1959, 2 May 1959, 10 October 1959.

70. *Brigadier*, 17 January 1959, 14 February 1959, 3 March 1959, 14 March 1959, 18

April 1959, 24 October 1959, 21 November 1959, 5 December 1959, 29 October 1960, 26 November 1960; 1957 Honor Manual, Citadel Archives.

71. *Brigadier*, 15 April 1961.

CHAPTER THREE. *Black, White, and Gray*

1. O'Neill, "From the Shadow of Slavery," 151–152; Fraser, *Charleston!* 411–412; Drago, *Initiative, Paternalism, and Race Relations*, 240, 272.

2. For more detailed examinations of the integration of South Carolina's public schools, see Edgar, *South Carolina*, 538–540; Sproat, "Firm Flexibility," 164–184; Synnott, "Desegregation in South Carolina," 51–64; Cox, "1963 — The Year of Decision."

3. Edgar, *South Carolina in the Modern Age*, 105, 106, 151; Bartley, *Rise of Massive Resistance*, 146, 212, 335; Sarratt, *Ordeal of Desegregation*, 34, 173–174; Synnott, "Desegregation in South Carolina," 52, 53, 58–61; Edgar, *South Carolina*, 538–540; McMillan, "Integration with Dignity," 381, 382, 385; Black, *Southern Governors and Civil Rights*, 79–80, 83; McNeill, "School Desegregation," 23; Cox, "1963 — The Year of Decision," 469; Sproat, "Firm Flexibility," 173–174.

4. Cox, "1963 — The Year of Decision," 81–82, 84, 93–95; Lesesne, *History of the University of South Carolina*, 144–147.

5. Wofford College and Winthrop College integrated in 1964. Furman University desegregated in 1965, and the College of Charleston admitted African American students in 1966. Soon thereafter, Senator Marion Gressette dissolved the Segregation Strategy Committee. O'Neill, "From the Shadow of Slavery," 238; Cox, "1963 — The Year of Decision," 63, 130, 139; McNeill, "School Desegregation," 58; Sarratt, *Ordeal of Desegregation*, 218, 256–257; Black, *Southern Governors and Civil Rights*, 83, 84.

6. 1955 *Guidon*, 9; Nichols, "General as President," 331; Nicholson, *History of The Citadel*, 348; Board of Visitors "Minutes," 25 October 1963, John Kennedy to David E. McCuen Jr., letter dated 12 July 1963, documents 632 and 633; Board of Visitors, "Minutes," 25 October 1963, McCuen to Francis Keppel, 9 August 1963, documents 634 and 635; T. Nugent Courvoisie, interview by author, tape recording, 4 October 1997.

7. Board of Visitors, "Minutes," 1 April 1964, document 668; Board of Visitors, "Minutes," 13 November 1964, document 793; Board of Visitors, "Minutes," 19 March 1965, document 797.

8. Nicholson, *History of The Citadel*, 348–349; *Charleston News and Courier*, 6 September 1964.

9. *Brigadier*, 2 March 1963, 18 April 1964.

10. *Charleston News and Courier*, 13 July 1966, 1 December 1996; *Charleston Evening*

Post, 12 July 1966; Michael Barrett, interview by author, tape recording, 14 January 1998; Scott Madding, interview by author, tape recording, 10 October 1997; Philip Hoffmann, interview by author, tape recording, 29 October 1997; Adolphus Varner, interview by author, tape recording, 20 November 1997; William Jenkinson, interview by author, tape recording, 5 October 1997; Charles Funderburk, interview by author, tape recording, 15 January 1998; Paul Short, interview by author, tape recording, 6 October 1997; Philip Clarkson, interview by author, tape recording, 10 October 1997.

11. Charles Foster died in 1986, and his cadet career must be pieced together from interviews with his classmates and other people who knew him. The author spoke with many of Foster's friends and roommates, as well as cadet officers from his freshman year. *Charleston Evening Post*, 12 July 1966; *The Citadel Official Register For the Period September 1966–September 1967*, The Citadel Archives and Museum, Charleston, South Carolina; *State*, 6 September 1966; *New York Times*, 8 September 1966; *Charleston News and Courier*, 1 December 1996.

12. *Charleston Evening Post*, 12 March 1968; *Brigadier*, 28 November 1964; Board of Visitors, "Minutes," 1 January 1967, documents 468–476; Board of Visitors, "Minutes," 22 March 1968, documents 736–741; Board of Visitors, "Minutes," 25 November 1969, documents 213, 219, 220; "Self Study," 17, III-83, III-20, III-21, III-23, III-24; Board of Visitors, "Minutes," 1 January 1967, documents 468–476.

13. Courvoisie interview; J. Palmer Gaillard to Harris, 12 April 1968, Box 44, Folder 7, Harris Papers; Memo to Harris from Dennis D. Nicholson, no date, Box 50, Folder 1, Harris Papers; H. V. Manning to Harris, 18 April 1969, Box 42, File C, Harris Papers; Edwin C. Coleman to Harris, 3 March 1969, Box 42, Folder C, Harris Papers; Benjamin Payton to Harris, 11 August 1970, Box 41, File B, Harris Papers; Harris to Paul B. Robinson, 5 May 1966, Box 48, Folder 1, Harris Papers.

14. Alderman Duncan to Harris, 9 January 1967, Box 44, Folder 1, Harris Papers; Harris to Duncan, 16 January 1967, Box 44, Folder 1, Harris Papers.

15. Board of Visitors, "Minutes," 1 June 1967, documents 571–572.

16. Memo to Harris from Dennis Nicholson, 14 July 1966, Box 44, File F, Harris Papers; *Charleston News and Courier*, 14 July 1966.

17. Courvoisie interview; David Eubanks, interview by author, tape recording, 10 October 1997; Michael Bozeman, interview by author, tape recording, 19 October 1997; Hoffmann interview; Varner interview; Leon Yonce, interview by author, tape recording, 14 January 1998; David Banner, interview by author, tape recording, 22 January 1998; Madding interview; William Riggs, interview by author, tape recording, 7 December 1997; D. P. Conroy, *Boo*, vi, 13.

18. George Gray, interview by author, tape recording, 25 November 1997; Jenkinson interview, Varner interview, David Dawson, interview by author, tape recording, 27

January 1998; Henry Kennedy, interview by author, tape recording, 24 October 1997; Courvoisie interview.

19. Bozeman interview; Banner interview; Riggs interview; Gray interview; Yonce interview; Jenkinson interview; David Hooper, interview by author, tape recording, 14 October 1997; David McGinnis, interview by author, tape recording, 20 January 1998; Kennedy interview; Dawson interview.

20. Courvoisie interview; Bozeman interview; Yonce interview; Gray interview.

21. McGinnis interview; Dawson interview; Hooper interview; Courvoisie interview; Bozeman interview; Richard Bagnal, interview with author, tape recording, 13 January 1998; Kennedy interview. Apparently Foster had more than one roommate after Hooper, but it is unclear whether he lived with more than one classmate at a time during his freshman year. Several of the people I interviewed remember Richard Bagnal, a southerner and a member of the Citadel wrestling team living with Foster. According to a memo from cadet regimental commander James Probsdorfer, another cadet by the name of R. E. Watts requested to share a room with Foster. Box 44, File F, Memo from Probsdorfer to Harris, 13 December 1966, Harris Papers.

22. Riggs interview; Jenkinson interview; Dawson interview; Hoffman interview; Gray interview; Ira Stern, interview by author, tape recording, 30 January 1998; Varner interview; Short interview; Alan Hughes, interview by author, tape recording, 10 October 1997; Bagnal interview; Thomas Byrd, interview by author, 13 January 1998; Barrett interview; Madding interview; Kennedy interview.

23. Barrett interview; Hoffman interview; Hughes interview; Hooper interview; Dawson interview; Madding interview; Kennedy interview; Courvoisie interview; McGinnis interview; *Charleston News and Courier*, 1 December 1996; Yonce interview; Laurence Moreland, interview by author, 22 October 1997.

24. *Rockland County Journal-News*, 16 October 1967, Box 44, File G, Harris Papers; *Charleston Evening Post*, 8 June 1967; Letter to Riggs from Harris, 1 June 1967, Box 49, Folder 7, Harris Papers.

25. Short interview; Bagnal interview; Barrett interview; Kennedy interview; Dawson interview; Hughes interview; Hoffman interview.

26. Gray interview; Norman Seabrooks, interview by author, tape recording, 17 October 1997; Kennedy interview; Hoffmann interview.

27. Herbert Legare, interview by author, tape recording, 15 January 1998; Courvoisie interview.

28. Dawson interview; Legare interview; Riggs interview; *Charleston News and Courier*, 1 December 1996.

29. Joseph Shine, interview by author, tape recording, 20 December 1997; Hoffmann interview.

30. Shine interview.

31. *Brigadier*, 23 September 1967; Shine interview; Stern interview; James Cassidy, interview by author, tape recording, 23 January 1998; Funderburk interview; Robert Vogel, interview by author, tape recording, 17 November 1997; Barrett interview; John Reid, interview by author, tape recording, 30 October 1997; James Lockridge, interview by author, tape recording, 26 January 1998; Douglas Rich, interview by author, tape recording, 21 January 1998; Samuel Jones, interview by author, tape recording, 16 November 1997; Reid interview; Joseph Shine, interview for WCSC News, 16 June 1997, Charleston, tape of interview in Shine's possession, hereafter cited as Shine interview for WCSC; *Charleston News and Courier*, 13 March 1987.

32. Shine interview; Lockridge interview.

33. Shine interview for WCSC; Fitzgerald interview; Vogel interview; Cassidy interview; Hoffmann interview; Reid interview; Rich interview; Lockridge interview; Funderburk interview; Stern interview; Shine interview; Claude Moore Jr., interview by author, tape recording, 20 January 1998; Larry Gantt, interview by author, tape recording, 5 February 1998.

34. 1971 *Sphinx*, 134, 143; *Brigadier*, 2 October 1970; Martin interview; Fitzgerald interview; Lockridge interview; Shine interview.

35. *Brigadier*, 23 October 1970, 13 November 1970; Vogel interview.

36. Lockridge interview; Stern interview; Shine interview.

37. Lockridge interview; Shine interview; Larry Ferguson, interview by author, tape recording, 23 January 1998; *Brigadier*, 5 February 1971; Shine interview; Patrick Gilliard, interview by author, tape recording, 13 December 1997; Kenneth Feaster, interview by author, tape recording, 9 January 1998; Keith Jones, interview by author, tape recording, 9 January 1998; George Graham, interview by author, tape recording, 28 January 1998; Legare interview; Seabrooks interview; Reginald Sealey, interview by author, tape recording, 18 October 1997, hereafter cited as Sealey interview.

38. Board of Visitors, "Minutes," 27 September 1968, documents 14 and 15.

39. No African American students graduated in the class of 1972. An African American cadet named Nathaniel Addison entered with the class of 1972, but he resigned prior to graduating. The author was unable to contact these men.

40. Legare interview; Seabrooks interview; Graham interview; Ferguson interview.

41. Legare interview; Seabrooks interview; Ferguson interview; Kennedy interview.

42. Graham interview.

43. Legare interview; Seabrooks interview; Ferguson interview; Graham interview.

44. Barrett interview; *Brigadier*, 11 May 1968.

45. *Brigadier*, 7 March 1970.

46. Ibid., 1 May 1970, 8 May 1970.

47. *Charleston News and Courier*, 3 February 1969; *Brigadier*, 1 May 1970.

48. Board of Visitors, "Minutes," 26 September 1970; "Self Study," 1-7; Board of Visitors, "Minutes," 29 May 1970, letter from Dewey E. Dodds to Hugh Harris, 22 April 1970, documents 335–340.

49. Board of Visitors, "Minutes," 29 May 1970, Harris's "Comments For Board of Visitors on Civil Rights Report," 2 May 1970, documents 341–342.

50. Legare interview; Ferguson interview; Sealey interview; Seabrooks interview.

51. *Charleston News and Courier*, 22 November 1991; *State*, 22 November 1991; "Self Study," III-84; Feaster interview; John McDowell, interview by author, tape recording, 21 January 1998; Sealey interview; Keith Jones interview; Gilliard interview.

52. Feaster interview; McDowell interview.

53. Sealey interview; Keith Jones interview.

54. Keith Jones interview; Gilliard interview.

55. McDowell interview; Seabrooks interview; Graham interview; Legare interview; Keith Jones interview; Ferguson interview; Sealey interview; Feaster interview.

56. McDowell interview; Legare interview; Ferguson interview; Keith Jones interview; Gilliard interview; Graham interview; Feaster interview; Sealey interview.

57. Shine interview; Feaster interview; Graham interview; Legare interview; Keith Jones interview; Ferguson interview; Seabrooks interview; McDowell interview.

58. Graham interview; Keith Jones interview; Feaster interview; Legare interview; Shine interview; McDowell interview; Gilliard interview; Sealey interview; Seabrooks interview; Ferguson interview.

59. Seabrooks interview; Ferguson interview; Sealey interview; Graham interview; McDowell interview; Gilliard interview; Legare interview; Keith Jones interview; Feaster interview; 1973 *Sphinx*, 285, 300; 1974 *Sphinx*, 323.

60. Gilliard interview; Seabrooks interview; Graham interview.

61. Ferguson interview; Graham interview.

62. Ferguson interview; Graham interview; Seabrooks interview; Kennedy interview.

63. Graham interview; Ferguson interview; Feaster interview; Keith Jones interview; *Brigadier*, 19 November 1971.

64. *Brigadier*, 19 November 1971.

65. Graham interview; Legare interview; Ferguson interview.

66. *Brigadier*, 19 November 1971, 29 September 1972, 8 December 1972, 5 October 1973, 22 February 1974.

67. Ibid., 2 February 1973, 19 April 1974.

68. "Self Study," VII-29, VII-30, VII-31.

69. Ibid., VII-30, VII-31.

70. Ibid.

71. Bartley, *New South*, 159; Wilkinson, *From Brown to Bakke*, 42; Sarratt, *Ordeal of Desegregation*, viii.

72. Daniel, *Lost Revolutions*, 274; Henry Flipper, West Point's first African-American cadet, recorded his experiences in *Colored Cadet at West Point*. Briefer accounts may be found in Ambrose, *Duty, Honor, Country*, 231–34; Fleming, *West Point*, 213–27. Sweetman, *United States Naval Academy*, 104–105; Riggs interview; Pratt, *We Shall Not Be Moved*, 115; Lesesne, *History of the University of South Carolina*, 147–148; Cox, "1963 — The Year of Decision," 43–44.

73. Riggs interview.

74. Gray interview; Hoffmann interview; Barrett interview; Albert Fitzgerald, interview with author, tape recording, 21 December 1997; Lockridge interview; Gantt interview; Cassidy interview; Kennedy interview; Rich interview; Bagnal interview; Vogel interview; Keith Jones interview; Legare interview; Short interview; Banner interview; Jenkinson interview; Riggs interview; Bozeman interview.

75. *Brown v. Board of Education*, 347 U.S. 493 (1954).

76. Estes, *I Am a Man!*; Malcolm X, *Autobiography of Malcolm X*, 457–460 (emphasis in original).

77. Eric Sundquist, "Blues for Atticus Finch: Scottsboro, *Brown* and Harper Lee," in Griffin and Doyle, *South as an American Problem*, 189; Cobb, *Brown Decision*, 57–58; Seabrooks interview; Keith Jones interview; Legare interview; Feaster interview; Ferguson interview; Graham interview.

CHAPTER FOUR. *"An Oasis of Order"*

1. The author used information from the student newspaper and administrative proceedings to re-create this scenario. The information from these sources will be examined, presented, and cited more fully in the pages to follow.

2. Zaroulis and Sullivan, *Who Spoke Up?* xii; DeBenedetti and Catfield, *American Ordeal*; Heineman, *Campus Wars*. Although the timing of *The Vigil* coincided with what Abe Peck deems the "highwater mark of protest" and the underground press, the paper, like many aspects of student activism at The Citadel, lacked the scope and longevity of similar ventures at other colleges and universities. Peck, *Uncovering the Sixties*, xv.

3. Farber, *Age of Great Dreams*, 199.

4. Nichols, "General as President," 327, 329–330; *Brigadier*, 13 February 1960, 27 February 1960, 15 October 1960, 15 December 1961.

5. *Brigadier*, 16 January 1960, 4 November 1961, 18 November 1961, 16 April 1963.

6. Nichols, "The General as President," 324; Fraser, *Charleston!* 405, 410, 418.

7. Fraser, *Charleston!* 410, 418, 419.

8. *Brigadier*, 13 February 1960, 27 February 1960, 15 October 1960, 12 November 1960, 15 April 1961, 15 December 1961, 17 February 1962.

9. Ibid., 18 March 1961, 20 May 1961.

10. Gitlin, *Sixties*, 89–90, 117; O'Neill, *Coming Apart*, 65; *Brigadier*, 19 May 1962, 3 November 1962, 9 November 1963, 18 April 1964, 16 May 1964, 31 October 1964. The tendency to view complicated Cold War issues in stark, all-or-nothing terms was especially pronounced in debates over the nuclear arms race. Katz, *Ban the Bomb*.

11. Sale, *SDS*, 186; Zaroulis and Sullivan, *Who Spoke Up?* 38–42, 56,63–64; Matusow, *Unraveling of America*, 320, 318; DeBenedetti and Catfield, *American Ordeal*, 110–111, 123, 162; *Brigadier*, 6 November 1965, 4 December 1965.

12. *Brigadier*, 28 November 1964, 18 March 1967, 13 May 1967; *Charleston Evening Post*, 12 March 1968; Board of Visitors, "Minutes," 22 March 1968, documents 736–741; Board of Visitors, "Minutes," 25 November 1969, documents 213, 219, 220; "Self Study," 17, I-9, I-10, III-83, III-20, III-21, III-23, III-24; *Charleston News and Courier*, 12 March 1968, 12 November 1968; Board of Visitors, "Minutes," 17 March 1967, documents 541–544; Alice Beckett to Harris, 29 September 1965, Box 41, Folder 5, Harris Papers; 1972 Citadel *Catalogue*, 210; Board of Visitors, "Minutes," 21 March 1969, document 122; Board of Visitors, "Minutes," 20 March 1970, document 319.

13. Board of Visitors, "Minutes," 1 October 1965, documents 177–180; Harris to Reuben H. Tucker, 19 November 1965, Box 50, Folder 2, Harris Papers; Memo to Tucker from Harris, 27 September 1965, Box 50, File T, Harris Papers; Memo to Tucker from Harris, 11 November 1965, Box 50, File T, Harris Papers; Memo to Tucker from Harris, 27 September 1967, Box 50, Folder 2, Harris Papers; Board of Visitors, "Minutes," 6 January 1967, documents 464, 468–476; "Commandant's address to cadre," 31 August 1966, Box 50, Folder 2, Harris Papers.

14. Conroy, *Lords of Discipline*, 127–206; Conroy, *My Losing Season*, 98, 100; Marett interview.

15. 1963 Citadel *Catalogue*, 40–41.

16. Harris to Dr. Horace Greeley, 2 May 1969, Box 44, Folder 7, Harris Papers; Memo from Association of Military Colleges and Schools of the United States, Box 48, Folder 2, Harris Papers; L. H. Jennings to Harris, Box 46, Folder 3, Harris Papers; Manegold, *In Glory's Shadow*, 121; *Brigadier*, 15 October 1960; Frank Mood, interview by author, tape recording, 18 May 2002.

17. "Report to the President and Board of Visitors of The Citadel By the Special Advisory Committee on the Fourth Class System" (hereafter cited as Whitmire Report), The Citadel Archives and Museum, Charleston, South Carolina, 9; Board of Visitors,

"Minutes," 31 May 1968, document 8; Board of Visitors, "Minutes," 27 January 1968, document 728; Manegold, *In Glory's Shadow*, 83.

18. Whitmire Report, 1, 4, 10.

19. Ibid., 7, 9, 12, 42, 43, 51.

20. Ibid., 1, 2, 3, 9, 11, 12, 40, 41–44, 47.

21. Ibid., 12–13, 14–16, 20, 23–27, 46–47 (emphasis in original).

22. Board of Visitors, "Minutes," 31 May 1968, document 12.

23. 1966 *Fourth Class System Manual*, Whitmire Report, Tab A, 9–10; Whitmire Report, 19 (emphasis in original).

24. Whitmire Report, Tab B, 2–4.

25. Whitmire Report, 18, 45; Whitmire Report, Tab B (emphasis in original).

26. Whitmire Report, 17–18, 49, General Order, No. 1, 1 July 1968; 1969 *Fourth Class System Manual*, passim, RC 6 Records of President's Office, Box 5, The Citadel Archives and Museum, Charleston, South Carolina.

27. Whitmire Report, 28–31, 34, 35; 1969 *Manual*, 6–7, 8–9; Board of Visitors, "Minutes," 31 May 1968, documents 10, 12.

28. Whitmire Report, 49; 1969 *Manual*, 10.

29. Whitmire Report, Tab A, 3 (emphasis in original); 1969 *Manual*, 6–7.

30. *Brigadier*, 3 November 1962, 10 April 1965, 15 May 1965; *Charleston Evening Post*, 23 September 1967; Board of Visitors, "Minutes," 26 May 1966, document 308; *Time* 80, no. 17 (26 October 1962): 40; Barrett interview; Kennedy interview; Lockridge interview; Hoffmann interview; Riggs interview; Rich interview; Cassidy interview.

31. "The Citadel War Record — Vietnam Casualties," The Citadel Archives and Museum; Heineman, *Campus Wars*, 140; DeBenedetti and Catfield, *American Ordeal*, 195; Zaroulis and Sullivan, *Who Spoke Up?* 47, 54, 58, 112–114; *Brigadier*, 2 May 1964, 6 November 1965, 4 December 1965, 26 February 1966, 29 April 1967, 2 March 1968, 9 November 1968.

32. Harris to Reuben H. Tucker, 19 November 1965, Box 50, Folder 2, Harris Papers; *Brigadier*, 26 February 1966, 12 April 1966, 8 October 1966, 13 January 1967, 25 February 1967; *Shako*, The Citadel Archives and Museum, Fall 1966 edition, 14.

33. Board of Visitors, "Minutes," 6 January 1967, documents 468–476; Board of Visitors, "Minutes," 17 March 1967, documents 541–544; Robert Daniel to Alumni, dated 22 August 1968, Box 44, Folder 1, Harris Papers; *Brigadier*, 22 October 1966, 3 December 1966, 18 March 1967, 8 April 1967, 29 April 1967, 23 September 1967, 4 November 1967; *Shako*, 30 May 1967.

34. *Brigadier*, 18 November 1967, 9 December 1967.

35. Ibid., 13 January 1968, 2 March 1968, 6 April 1968, 11 May 1968; 1968 *Sphinx*, 330; *Shako*, Spring 1969.

36. *Brigadier*, 19 October 1968, 19 April 1969, 10 May 1969.

37. Heineman, *Campus Wars*, 186; Zaroulis and Sullivan, *Who Spoke Up?* 149, 153, 156, 200; Matusow, *Unraveling of America*, 390, 391; *Brigadier*, 13 January 1968, 2 March 1968, 6 April 1968; Robert Daniel to Citadel Alumni, 22 August 1968, Box 44, Folder 1, Harris Papers; L. H. Jennings to Harris, 9 January 1968, Box 46, Folder 3, Harris Papers; Walter Albrecht to Harris, 7 June 1968, Box 41, Folder 1, Harris Papers; Memo from Colonel McAlister to Harris, 24 April 1968, Box 50, Folder 7, Harris Papers; Harris to Kenneth E. Wacker, 29 April 1968, Box 50, Folder 7, Harris Papers; Martha Sweeney to Harris, 12 September 1968, Box 43, Folder 1, Harris Papers; Connie Hoffman to Harris, 21 May 1968, Box 44, Folder 7, Harris Papers; Harris to Gail Gideon, 1 May 1968, Box 4, Folder 7, Harris Papers; Peter Sammartino to Harris, 9 May 1968, Box 41, Folder 1, Harris Papers; Harris to Dr. V. R. Easterling, 6 August 1968, Box 44, Folder 3, Harris Papers; Thomas Davis to Harris, 3 September 1968, Box 44, Folder 1, Harris Papers; L. H. Jennings to John Holliday, 24 June 1968, Box 44, Folder 4, Harris Papers; "Faculty Coffee Klatch," 8 April 1968, Box 49, Folder 4, Harris Papers; Memo to James Duckett, 8 July 1968, Box 49, Folder 4, Harris Papers.

38. *Brigadier*, 13 January 1968, 8 March 1969; D. D. Nicholson to R. L. Bergmann, 9 November 1968, Box 41, Folder 9, Harris Papers; Arthur von Keller to Harris, no date, Box 46, Folder 4, Harris Papers (emphasis in original); interview with Thomas Brown, 5 February 1999.

39. Harris to Arthur von Keller, 2 June 1969, Box 46, Folder 3, Harris Papers; Board of Visitors, "Minutes," 20 March 1970, document 319; Board of Visitors, "Minutes," 21 March 1969, document 122; Board of Visitors, "Minutes," 25 November 1969, document 205; *Brigadier*, 13 September 1969, 11 October 1969, 14 February 1970, 7 March 1970, 17 April 1970, 24 April 1970, 11 December 1970; memo to James Duckett from James Whitmire, 15 August 1969, Box 41, Folder 14, Harris Papers; Lockridge interview.

40. *Brigadier*, 14 February 1970, 7 March 1970, 11 December 1970.

41. "Faculty Coffee Klatch," 8 April 1968, Box 49, Folder 4, Harris Papers; Harris to George Lott, 28 April 1969, Box 47, Folder 1, Harris Papers; Harris to Horace Greeley Jr., 2 May 1969, Box 44, Folder 7, Harris Papers; "Talking Papers for Discussion Topics on Monday Morning Program," Box 48, Folder 3, Harris Papers; "Speak to All Students," 12 September 1969, Box 36, Harris Papers.

42. *Brigadier*, 7 March 1970; Board of Visitors, "Minutes," 20 March 1970, document 311; Brown interview.

43. *Charleston Evening Post*, 8 November 1969; Anne Cote to Harris, no date, Box 47, Folder 1, Harris Papers; *Brigadier*, 21 March 1970, 11 April 1970, 24 April 1970, 8 May 1970, 15 May 1970; Brown interview; Moreland interview; Gitlin, *Sixties*, 379.

44. Heineman, *Campus Wars*, 256; DeBenedetti and Catfield, *American Ordeal*, 279–280; *Brigadier*, 15 May 1970; Lockridge interview.

45. *Brigadier*, 8 May 1970, 15 May 1970; *Charleston News and Courier*, 12 May 1970, 13 May 1970, 14 May 1970; James Cuttino to Harris, 25 May 1970, Box 42, Folder 2, Harris Papers; Harris to Cuttino, 27 May 1970, Box 42, Folder 2, Harris Papers.

46. *Brigadier*, 14 February 1970, 7 March 1970, 17 April 1970, 1 May 1970, 23 October 1970, 6 November 1970, 11 December 1970, 5 February 1971, 12 February 1971, 19 February 1971, 26 February 1971, 19 March 1971, 2 April 1971, 4 February 1972, 25 February 1972, 3 March 1972, 23 February 1973, 20 April 1973, 22 February 1974; "Self Study," 111-7; Board of Visitors, "Minutes," 31 January 1972, document 60; Board of Visitors, "Minutes," 11 February 1972, document 74; Board of Visitors, "Minutes," 17 March 1972, document 80; President's Report to the Board of Visitors 1973/74, 44.

47. *Brigadier*, 14 February 1970, 7 March 1970, 11 December 1970, 5 February 1971, 12 February 1971, 15 October 1971, 10 December 1971, 17 February 1972, 6 October 1972, 19 April 1974; Board of Visitors, "Minutes," 12 December 1970, document 608.

48. *Brigadier*, 25 September 1970, 13 November 1970, 2 April 1971, 4 February 1972; Board of Visitors, "Minutes," 20 December 1970, document 608; Board of Visitors, "Minutes," 18 April 1971, document 684; Board of Visitors, "Minutes," 11 September 1971, document 1; "Self Study," 11-7; Board of Visitors, "Minutes," 23 September 1972, document 254.

49. *Charleston News and Courier*, 22 November 1991; *State*, 22 November 1991; *Brigadier*, 14 February 1971, 26 February 1971, 5 March 1971; Board of Visitors, "Minutes," 12 February 1971, documents 673–675; Board of Visitors, "Minutes," 25 February 1971, document 681.

50. Board of Visitors, "Minutes," 12 February 1971, 675–680.

51. *Brigadier*, 26 February 1971, 17 September 1971; Board of Visitors, "Minutes," 12 February 1971, document 657; Board of Visitors, "Minutes," 11 September 1971, documents 1, 2, 5, 6; Board of Visitors, "Minutes," 31 January 1972, document 60; Board of Visitors, "Minutes," 11 February 1972, documents 74, 75; Board of Visitors, "Minutes," 17 March 1972, documents 80-82, 85, 88; Board of Visitors, "Minutes," 23 September 1972, document 316; Board of Visitors, "Minutes," 9 December 1972, document 400; Board of Visitors, "Minutes," 10 February 1973, document 746; 1972 President's Report, 316.

52. *Brigadier*, 2 April 1971, 30 April 1971, 17 September 1971.

53. Ibid., 19 November 1971, 10 December 1971, 17 March 1972, 24 March 1972, 5 May 1972, 8 September 1972; Board of Visitors, "Minutes," 17 March 1972, document 80.

54. DeBenedetti and Catfield, *American Ordeal*, 300, 317; Harris to Frank Pace, 29 April 1971, Box 49, Folder 1, Harris Papers; *Brigadier*, 1 October 1971, 29 October 1971, 13 October 1972, 17 March 1972, 24 March 1972, 28 April 1972; *Shako*, Winter 1971.

55. McAdam, *Freedom Summer*, 107–111; Gitlin, *Sixties*, 364–371.

56. McLaurin, "Country Music and the Vietnam War," 145, 146, 148–149, 153, 155–156, 158; Cobb, *Redefining Southern Culture*, 82. Sara Evans's *Personal Politics* offers a clear demonstration of how involvement in the civil rights movement and the New Left helped radicalize young southern whites. William Billingsley and Doug Rossinow have written in-depth studies of student activism at the University of North Carolina–Chapel Hill and the University of Texas–Austin respectively. Evans, *Personal Politics*; Billingsley, *Communists on Campus*; Rossinow, *Politics of Authenticity*.

57. Andrew, *Long Gray Lines*, 2, 3, 4 (emphasis in original), 7. Numerous historians have discussed the media's tendency to present militant, outrageous, antiwar radicals as representative of the peace movement, and Todd Gitlin offers one of best analyses of the media's role in the unraveling of the student movement. However, Gitlin also recognizes the students' contributions to their own negative image. The recklessness and idealism that spawns student movements leaves them vulnerable to exploitation and distortion. In many cases, when the media called for more radical stances and behavior, students obliged. Gitlin, *Whole World Is Watching*.

58. Farrell, *Spirit of the Sixties*, 169 (emphasis in original); Heineman, *Campus Wars*, 5, 80–81, 150–151.

59. Conkin, *Gone with the Ivy*, 613, 625–630; Mohr and Gordon, *Tulane*, 192, 269–270, 305.

CHAPTER FIVE. *"A Disciplined College in an Undisciplined Age"*

1. Board of Visitors, "Minutes," 13 December 1970, document 612; 1971 Citadel *Catalogue*.

2. Zinn, *People's History*, 529, 538, 545, 552–553; Chafe, *Unfinished Journey*, 430, 446–447, 454; Woodward, *Burden of Southern History*, 214; Egerton, *Americanization of Dixie*, xix; Cobb, *Redefining Southern Culture*, 70, 78, 82; Cobb, *Away Down South*, 215–217; Tindall, *Ethnic Southerners*, 4; Paul Gaston, "Sutpen's Door: The South since the *Brown* Decision," in Lander and Calhoun, *Two Decades of Change*, 99–102.

3. Cobb, *Away Down South*, 216–217, 222–223; Cobb, *Selling of the South*, 179–180; Fraser, *Charleston!* 425; Reed, *Enduring South*, 2–3; Egerton, *Americanization of Dixie*, 17, 19, 22, 24; Cobb, *Redefining Southern Culture*, 83–84; Tindall, *Ethnic Southerners*, 1, 3; Kirby, *Media-Made Dixie*, 159–160.

4. Gaston, "Sutpen's Door," 100–101; Cobb, *Selling of the South*, 183; Schulman, *Seventies*, 114; Cobb, *Redefining Southern Culture*, 70–71; Kirby, *Media-Made Dixie*, 138, 141–146, 150–151, 154–156.

5. Cobb, *Away Down South*, 237; *Time*, "Other Voices," 27 September 1976; Gaston, "Sutpen's Door," 102.

6. Cobb, *Away Down South*, 223.

7. Conkin, *Gone with the Ivy*, 582; 1970 Citadel *Catalogue*, 41–42; President's Annual Report to the Board of Visitors, 1971/72, 409, 418, The Citadel Archives and Museum; *Brigadier*, 25 September 1970, 19 March 1971, 31 January 1975, 14 March 1975, 12 September 1975, 17 September 1976, 25 March 1977; Board of Visitors, "Minutes," 7 October 1969, document 205; Board of Visitors, "Minutes," 17 September 1976, documents 255–260; 1975 Annual Report, 47; Atkinson, *Long Gray Line*, 397–400; Lovell, *Neither Athens Nor Sparta*, 229, 225–226, 266–267; 1975 *Guidon*, 28; 1977 *Guidon*, 28; 1978 *Guidon*, 28.

8. 1972 President's Report, 422, 444, 445 (emphasis in original).

9. Board of Visitors, "Minutes," 20 March 1970, document 325; Board of Visitors, "Minutes," 21 August 1970, document 354; Board of Visitors, "Minutes," 12 December 1970, document 648; Board of Visitors, "Minutes," 13 December 1970, document 614; Board of Visitors, "Minutes," 18 March 1971, document 694, 695; Board of Visitors, "Minutes," 17 February 1972; Board of Visitors, "Minutes," 18 January 1974, document 332; Board of Visitors, "Minutes," 2 March 1968, document 732; Board of Visitors, "Minutes," 15 March 1968, document 733.

10. Board of Visitors, "Minutes," 25 November 1969, documents 212, 213, 215–216; Board of Visitors, "Minutes," 13 December 1969, documents 223, 226; Board of Visitors, "Minutes," 13 December 1970, document 613; *Brigadier*, 7 March 1970.

11. *Brigadier*, 7 March 1970; Board of Visitors, "Minutes," 11 November 1969, documents 208, 210; Board of Visitors, "Minutes," 25 November 1969, documents 215–216; Board of Visitors, "Minutes," 13 December 1969, document 223; Board of Visitors, "Minutes," 13 December 1969, documents 223–226 (emphasis in original).

12. Board of Visitors, "Minutes," 20 March 1970, documents 320–321 (emphasis in original).

13. *U.S. News and World Report*, 9 November 1970, 47–48; *Time*, 6 September 1971, 35.

14. Board of Visitors, "Minutes," 29 May 1970.

15. Ibid., 31 January 1972, documents 66–67; Board of Visitors, "Minutes," 17 March 1972, documents 109, 131.

16. Board of Visitors, "Minutes," 31 January 1972, documents 54–59; Board of Visitors, "Minutes," 17 March 1972, documents 111, 115, 117.

17. Board of Visitors, "Minutes," 17 March 1972, documents 119–125.

18. *Brigadier*, 25 February 1972.

19. Ibid., 17 April 1970, 1 May 1970, 8 May 1970, 16 March 1973.

20. Ibid., 25 February 1972.

21. Board of Visitors, "Minutes," 17 March 1972, documents 95, 100.

22. Ibid., 15 March 1974, documents 352, 357 (emphasis in original).

23. Conroy, *Lords of Discipline*, 1; quote from Pat Conroy's Commencement address at The Citadel on May 12, 2001, http://citadel.edu/pao/addresses/conroy.htm; *Brigadier*, 16 February 1973; 1972 President's Report, 317; Board of Visitors, "Minutes," 17 February 1972, document 253; 1952 *Guidon*, 54–55.

24. *Brigadier*, 14 February 1970.

25. Ibid., 7 March 1970, 21 March 1970 (emphasis in original); Board of Visitors, "Minutes," 20 March 1970, document 313.

26. *Brigadier*, 7 March 1970, 20 November 1970, 12 May 1971.

27. Ibid., 23 April 1971.

28. Ibid., 15 February 1974.

29. Board of Visitors, "Minutes," 13 February 1971, documents 673–680; President's Annual Report to the Board of Visitors, 1970/1971, 47; *Brigadier*, 13 November 1970, 20 November 1970.

30. Board of Visitors, "Minutes," 13 March 1971, document 676; Board of Visitors, "Minutes," 17 February 1972, document 253; Board of Visitors, "Minutes," 17 March 1972, document 87; 1972 President's Report, 316, 361; *Brigadier*, 17 September 1971, 22 September 1972.

31. *Brigadier*, 1 May 1970, 29 October 1971, 10 December 1971.

32. Ibid., 12 February 1971, 26 February 1971, 19 November 1971, 3 March 1972, 5 May 1972.

33. Board of Visitors, "Minutes," 11 February, document 25; Board of Visitors, "Minutes," 17 March 1972, document 158; "Self Study," VII-6; "Fourth Class System Review Committee — Record of Events, 13 December 1971," in RC6, Box 5, Records of the Commandant's Office, Office of the President — Fourth Class System Review Folder, The Citadel Archives and Museum, The Citadel, Charleston, S.C.; Faculty Council Memo to Duckett, 23 November 1971 in RC6, Records of the Commandant's Office, Box 5, Fourth Class System Review Folder; Board of Visitors, "Minutes," 17 March 1972, documents 98, 121, 151–152

34. Board of Visitors, "Minutes," 17 March 1972, documents 159–162, 163, 164, 166 (emphasis in original).

35. Ibid., 17 March 1972, documents 168–169, 176, 177–179, 181–182, 188, 192, 206 (emphasis in original).

36. Fourth Class System Review Committee Record of Events for 25 October 1971 and 1 November 1971, RC6, Records of the Commandant's Office, Box 5, Fourth Class System Review Folder; Board of Visitors, "Minutes," 17 March 1972, documents 167, 170–171, 172, 195, 197.

37. Breast plates are convex pieces of brass about the size of an adult fist that cadets attached to their uniform when "under arms" during inspections or parade. Upperclassmen would often pound on the plates with their fist or rifle butt while freshmen were wearing them.

38. Board of Visitors, "Minutes," 17 March 1972, documents 168–169, 184–185 (emphasis in original).

39. Ibid., documents 168–169, 186, 195, 198.

40. *Charleston News and Courier*, 19 August 1972; *Brigadier*, 8 September 1972, 15 September 1972, 29 September 1972, 13 October 1972; President's Annual Report to the Board of Visitors 1972/73; Board of Visitors, "Minutes," 17 February 1972, documents 254–256.

41. Board of Visitors, "Minutes," 10 October 1975, document 787; *Brigadier*, 20 April 1973, 28 February 1975; RC6, Records of the President's Office, Box 5, Fourth Class Review Committee Report to the President For the Academic Year, 1972–73; Memo from Eddie Teague to Duckett, "Special Report in Fourth Class System, School Year, 1973–1974," RC6, Records of the President's Office, Box 5.

42. RC6, Records of the President's Office, Box 5, Fourth Class Review Committee Report to the President For the Academic Year, 1972–73; Memo from Judson Spence to Chairman, Fourth Class System Review Committee, 27 March 1973, RC6, Records of the Commandant's Office, Box 5, Fourth Class System Review Folder; Memo from Edward Teague to Cadet Lieutenant Colonel Malmquist, 12 September 1973, RC6, Records of the Commandant's Office, Box 5, Fourth Class System Review Folder; Memo to Members of Fourth Class System Review Committee from Teague, 9 May 1973, RC6, Records of the Commandant's Office, Box 5, Fourth Class System Review Folder.

43. Board of Visitors, "Minutes," 17 March 1972, documents 84, 86; RC6, Records of the President's Office, Box 5, Fourth Class Review Committee Report to the President For the Academic Year, 1972–73; Memo from Eddie Teague to Duckett, "Special Report in Fourth Class System, School Year, 1973–1974," RC6, Records of the President's Office, Box 5; Memo to Fourth Class System Review Committee, 5 November 1973, RC6, Records of the Commandant's Office, Box 5, Fourth Class System Review Folder; Memo to Teague from J. R. Wilkinson, 7 September 1972, RC6, Records of the Commandant's Office, Box 5, Fourth Class System Review Folder; Memo to Teague from Spence, 5 November 1973, RC6, Records of the Commandant's Office, Box 5, Fourth Class System Review Folder; Memo to Teague from Wilkinson, 24 October 1973, RC6, Records of the Commandant's Office, Box 5, Fourth Class System Review Folder; Memo to Duckett from Teague, 13 November 1973, RC6, Records of the Commandant's Office, Box 5, Fourth Class System Review Folder.

44. Fourth Class Review Committee Report to the President For the Academic Year, 1972–73, RC6, Records of the President's Office, Box 5; Memo to General Seignious from the Fourth Class System Review Committee, Subject — Mess Facts, RC6, Records of the Commandant's Office, Box 5, Fourth Class System Review Folder; Memo to Fourth Class System Review Committee from Teague, 5 March 1974, RC6, Records of the Commandant's Office, Box 5, Fourth Class System Review Folder; memo entitled "Subject Mess Facts" dated 2 December 1974, RC6, Records of the Commandant's Office, Box 5, Major H. B. Alexander Folder; 27 March 1973 Record of Events, RC6, Records of the Commandant's Office, Box 5, Fourth Class System Review Folder.

45. Fourth Class Review Committee Report to the President For the Academic Year, 1972–73, RC6, Records of the President's Office, Box 5.

46. Ibid.

47. Ibid.

48. Memo to Duckett from Fourth Class System Review Committee, 7 June 1973, RC6, Records of the President's Office, Box 5, Fourth Class Review Committee Report to the President For the Academic Year, 1972–73; *Brigadier*, 22 September 1972, 3 November 1972, 25 January 1974 (emphasis in original); 1973 *Guidon*, 34.

49. *Brigadier*, 27 April 1973.

50. Ibid., 16 February 1973, 27 April 1973, 4 May 1973, 17 May 1974.

51. Ibid., 8 December 1972, 17 May 1974.

52. Board of Visitors, "Minutes," 15 March 1974, documents 350–351, 352, 353, 361, 364.

53. Ibid., documents 349, 352, 353, 358, 365 (emphasis in original), 367.

54. Ibid., 18 January 1974, document 38; Board of Visitors, "Minutes," 15 March 1974, document 349.

CHAPTER SIX. *The Spirit of '76*

1. *State*, 26 January 1974; *Columbia Record*, 1 March 1975; *Brigadier*, 24 January 1974, 6 December 1974, 2 May 1975.

2. President's Annual Report to the Board of Visitors, 1975/76, 13, 52; President's Annual Report to the Board of Visitors, 1977/78, 67; President's Annual Report to the Board of Visitors, 1976/77, 68; *Brigadier*, 6 December 1974, 27 October 1974; Board of Visitors, "Minutes," 9 January 1976; Board of Visitors, "Minutes," 14 April 1977, document 382; Board of Visitors, "Minutes," 16 February 1979, document 247.

3. Cobb, *Redefining Southern Culture*, 83–84; Cobb, *Selling of the South*, 184–186; Tindall, *Ethnic Southerners*, xi; *Time*, "Those Good Ole Boys," 27 September 1976; *Saturday Review*, 4 September 1976.

4. Cobb, *Redefining Southern Culture*, 83–84; Cobb, *Selling of the South*, 179–180, 184–185; Cobb, "Epitaph for the North," 7; Applebome, *Dixie Rising*, 329; Kirby, *Media-Made Dixie*, 170–171 (emphasis added); *New York Times*, 5 December 1976.

5. Gerstle, *American Crucible*, 348; Brinkley, "Problem of American Conservatism," 415, 422; Carter, *Politics of Rage*, 11–12, 371, 375–381; McGirr, *Suburban Warriors*, 202–205, 240–241,

6. *Brigadier*, 19 November 1976, 14 September 1979.

7. 1976 *Guidon*, 18; 1977 *Guidon*, 17; Board of Visitors, "Minutes," 8 January 1974, documents 175–179; Board of Visitors, "Minutes," 16 May 1975, documents 673, 674; Board of Visitors, "Minutes," 31 July 1975, documents 686, 687, 694; Board of Visitors, "Minutes," 12 September 1975, documents 701, 703, 704, 732; Board of Visitors, "Minutes," 10 October 1975, documents 787–788, 793; Board of Visitors, "Minutes," 9 January 1976, documents 31, 33; Board of Visitors, "Minutes," 17 September 1977, document 437; Board of Visitors, "Minutes," 28 February 1975, documents 659, 668; 1977 Annual Report, 7, 13; 1978 Annual Report; 1979 Annual Report, 8; President's Annual Report to the Board of Visitors, 1980/81, 34–35; *Brigadier*, 13 September 1974, 12 September 1975, 23 April 1976, 10 September 1976; *Columbia Record*, 5 May 1975; 1976 Annual Report, 18; 1977 Annual Report, 23.

8. Carroll, *It Seemed Like Nothing Happened*, 117–118; Dumbrell, *Carter Presidency*, 168–169; *Charleston News and Courier*, 1 January 1978; *Brigadier*, 8 February 1974, 15 February 1974, 26 September 1975, 16 April 1976, 23 April 1976, 17 September 1976, 8 October 1976, 17 October 1976; Board of Visitors, "Minutes," 5 April 1975, document 668; 1976 Annual Report, 39.

9. *Brigadier*, 31 January 1975, 14 February 1975; *Charleston News and Courier*, 1 January 1978.

10. *Charleston News and Courier*, 1 January 1978; *State*, 4 January 1979.

11. Board of Visitors, "Minutes," 17 March 1978, documents 70–72; Board of Visitors, "Minutes," 31 March 1978, document 89; *State*, 23 February 1978, 1 March 1978, 2 March 1978, 13 April 1978, 14 April 1978; *Charleston News and Courier*, 1 January 1978.

12. Carroll, *It Seemed Like Nothing Happened*, 231–232, 340; *Columbia Record*, 8 April 1980, 9 April 1980; Board of Visitors, "Minutes," 17 March 1978, document 63; Board of Visitors, "Minutes," 14 April 1977, document 388; Board of Visitors, "Minutes," 31 March 1978, documents 86–87; Board of Visitors, "Minutes," 5 January 1979, document 223; Board of Visitors, "Minutes," 16 February 1979, document 247; 1979 Annual Report, 74.

13. *Brigadier*, 19 April 1974, 14 November 1975, 24 September 1976, 17 February 1978 (emphasis in original), 21 March 1980; 1977 *Sphinx*, 138.

14. *Brigadier*, 17 March 1978.

15. 1980 Annual Report; *Brigadier*, 6 December 1974.

16. Farber, *Age of Great Dreams*, 241; Chafe, *Unfinished Journey*, 432; Mathews and DeHart, *Sex, Gender and the Politics of ERA*, 211; Brinkley, "Problem of American Conservatism," 423; Douglas, *Where the Girls Are*, 164–179, 193–201, 202–219.

17. Mathews and DeHart, *Sex, Gender and the Politics of ERA*, 36–37, 45–47, 48, 49, 50–53, 218; Brinkley, "Problem of American Conservatism," 423.

18. *Brigadier*, 23 March 1973.

19. Douglas, *Where the Girls Are*, 232–233, 242–244; Farber, *Age of Great Dreams*, 257; Brinkley, "Problem of American Conservatism," 423–424; *Brigadier*, 23 March 1973, 13 April 1973 (emphasis in original).

20. Holm, *Women in the Military*, 305; *Brigadier*, 17 October 1975, 14 November 1975, 19 November 1976.

21. *Brigadier*, 30 January 1976; *Columbia Record*, 2 February 1976.

22. *Brigadier*, 13 February 1976.

23. Ibid.

24. Ibid., 13 February 1976, 27 February 1976.

25. Ibid., 27 February 1976.

26. Ibid., 27 February 1976, 19 March 1976.

27. Ibid., 20 February 1976, 23 April 1976; *State*, 7 May 1975.

28. Mitchell, *Women in the Military*, 33; *Columbia Record*, 21 January 1976.

29. *Brigadier*, 20 February 1976, 4 March 1977, 16 March 1979; *Columbia Record*, 21 January 1976.

30. *Brigadier*, 25 March 1977, 19 March 1976.

31. Mansbridge, *Why We Lost the ERA*, 86; Mathews and DeHart, *Sex, Gender and the Politics of ERA*, 71; *Brigadier*, 6 December 1974, 13 February 1976, 21 October 1977.

32. *Brigadier*, 6 September 1974, 6 December 1974, 20 February 1976, 17 September 1976, 8 October 1976; Board of Visitors, "Minutes," 10 October 1975, document 787; *Columbia Record*, 7 August 1974; Board of Visitors, "Minutes," 17 September 1976, document 80.

33. *State*, 29 November 1976, 6 January 1978; *New York Times*, 29 November 1976; *Columbia Record*, 29 November 1976, 6 December 1976, 16 January 1978, 27 November 1978; *Brigadier*, 18 November 1977.

34. *Columbia Record*, 25 October 1977, 24 November 1977, 3 January 1978, 5 January 1978; *New York Times*, 1 December 1976, 2 December 1976, 4 December 1976, 14 December 1976, 25 October 1977, 4 January 1978; *Charleston News and Courier*, 1 February 1978; *State*, 29 November 1976, 25 October 1977, 3 January 1978.

35. *State*, 30 November 1976, 2 December 1976, 1 January 1978; *New York Times*, 29 November 1976, 30 November 1976, 5 January 1978; *Brigadier*, 10 December 1976.

36. *Brigadier*, 10 December 1976; *State*, 15 January 1978; Roesch and De La Roche Jr., *Anyone's Son*, 75–76, 77–78.

37. *New York Times*, 30 November 1976; *State*, 1 January 1978, 3 January 1978, 4 January 1978, 5 January 1978, 18 January 1978; *Brigadier*, 18 November 1977; Roesch and De La Roche Jr., *Anyone's Son*, 80–81, 84–100; *Columbia Record*, 5 January 1978, 6 January 1978, 10 January 1978, 13 January 1978, 16 January 1978.

38. Roesch and De La Roche Jr., *Anyone's Son*, 142, 144, 239; *State*, 25 October 1977, 14 January 1978; *New York Times*, 7 January 1978, 27 January 1978; *Columbia Record*, 3 January 1978.

39. *New York Times*, 8 January 1977, 6 January 1978, 10 January 1978, 14 January 1978, 19 January 1978, 20 January 1978, 25 January 1978, 26 January 1978, 27 January 1978; *Columbia Record*, 6 January 1978, 10 January 1978, 16 January 1978, 27 January 1978; *State*, 24 January 1978, 26 January 1978, 27 January 1978; Roesch and De La Roche Jr., *Anyone's Son*, 259; *Brigadier*, 18 November 1977.

40. *New York Times*, 27 January 1978; *Charleston News and Courier*, 1 February 1978; *State*, 2 February 1978; 1979 Annual Report, 76.

41. Board of Visitors, "Minutes," 17 September 1977, documents 439, 442; Board of Visitors, "Minutes," 28 January 1977, document 327; Board of Visitors, "Minutes," 18 March 1977, document 353; *Brigadier*, 10 December 1976, 18 November 1977; *Charleston News and Courier*, 11 February 1978.

42. *Brigadier*, 8 October 1976, 6 May 1977, 9 September 1977, 16 September 1977, 23 September 1977, 7 October 1977, 20 January 1978, 8 September 1978; Board of Visitors, "Minutes," 14 April 1977, document 387; Board of Visitors, "Minutes," 9 December 1977, document 509; 1977 Annual Report, 44–45; 1978 Annual Report, 57; 1979 Annual Report, 65.

43. *Brigadier*, 9 September 1977, 16 September 1977, 23 September 1977, 7 October 1977, 21 October 1977, 3 February 1978, 10 February 1978, 28 April 1978, 8 September 1978, 15 September 1978, 22 September 1978, 10 November 1978, 11 September 1981; "Study of Cadet Time Management," Records of President's Office, RC6, Box 5.

CHAPTER SEVEN. *"Tampering with America"*

1. Board of Visitors, "Minutes," 20 October 1978, documents 184–185; *Brigadier*, 27 April 1979; Board of Visitors, "Minutes," 25 April 1979, document 269.

2. Board of Visitors, "Minutes," 10 May 1979, document 280; *Brigadier*, 27 April 1979.

3. *Brigadier*, 27 April 1979, 11 May 1979.

4. *Columbia Record*, 26 April 1979, 30 April 1979, 29 August 1979; 1979 *Guidon*, 17; Stockdale and Stockdale, *In Love and War*, 461, 466, 475.

5. *Charleston News and Courier*, 5 February 1980; *Columbia Record*, 31 May 1979; Board of Visitors, "Minutes," 5 October 1979, document 313; *Brigadier*, 1 February 1980; Stockdale and Stockdale, *In Love and War*, 462–464, 468.

6. Stockdale and Stockdale, *In Love and War*, 470–471; "The Mood Report — Enclosure 3" in the David S. McAlister Papers, Box 1, A1987.4, The Citadel Archives and Museum, The Citadel, Charleston, S.C. (hereafter cited as Mood Report).

7. *State*, 24 August 1980; Board of Visitors, "Minutes," 15 November 1979, document 320; *Brigadier*, 7 September 1979, 28 September 1979, 22 February 1980.

8. *Brigadier*, 2 November 1979, 16 November 1979, 8 February 1980.

9. Ibid., 12 October 1979, 16 November 1979, 7 December 1979, 22 February 1980, 21 March 1980, 28 March 1980.

10. *Charleston News and Courier*, 8 October 1979.

11. Ibid., 15 October 1979, 21 October 1979.

12. Ibid., 25 October 1979.

13. Ibid., 25 October 1979, 28 October 1979.

14. *Brigadier*, 26 October 1979.

15. *Charleston News and Courier*, 8 April 1980; Stockdale and Stockdale, *In Love and War*, 474, 484; Mood Report, Enclosure-7.

16. Mood Report, 1, 2; *State*, 13 April 1980.

17. Mood Report, 3, Enclosures 1 and 4; Mood Report, 6, Enclosure 3.

18. Mood Report, 1, 2, 3, 11 (emphasis in original).

19. Ibid., 1, 2, 7, 11 (emphasis in original).

20. Ibid., 2, 3, 4, 5, 7–9 (emphasis in original).

21. Ibid., 3, 5, 6, 8, 9.

22. Stockdale and Stockdale, *In Love and War*, 473–474, 477, 483, 484; *State*, 13 April 1980.

23. Stockdale and Stockdale, *In Love and War*, 467, 473; *State*, 13 April 1980; *Charleston News and Courier*, 17 May 1980; *Brigadier*, 11 April 1980.

24. *Charleston News and Courier*, 18 April 1980; *Columbia Record*, 2 April 1980; *Brigadier*, 11 April 1980; *State*, 2 April 1980.

25. *Brigadier*, 11 April 1980, 18 April 1980, 14 November 1980; *State*, 13 April 1980; *Charleston News and Courier*, 17 April 1980.

26. Stockdale and Stockdale, *In Love and War*, 467; *Columbia Record*, 2 April 1980; *State*, 11 April 1980; *Brigadier*, 18 April 1980.

27. *Charleston News and Courier*, 8 April 1980, 17 April 1980; *State*, 8 April 1980, 12

April 1980, 13 April 1980; Stockdale and Stockdale, *In Love and War*, 464; *Columbia Record*, 8 April 1980.

28. *State*, 8 April 1980, 13 April 1980, 17 April 1980; *Charleston News and Courier*, 19 August 1980; Board of Visitors, "Minutes," 15 May 1980, document 401 (emphasis in original).

29. Stockdale and Stockdale, *In Love and War*, 486; *Charleston News and Courier*, 17 April 1980, 19 August 1980; *New York Times*, 9 April 1980; *State*, 4 April 1980, 17 April 1980; Board of Visitors, "Minutes," 20 June 1980, documents 422–424; Board of Visitors, "Minutes," 16 April 1980, documents 383–385

30. Board of Visitors, "Minutes," 16 April 1980, document 385; Stockdale and Stockdale, *In Love and War*, 475–476, 486–488; *Charleston News and Courier*, 17 May 1980, 19 August 1980; Board of Visitors, "Minutes," 23 August 1980, documents 450–452.

31. *Charleston News and Courier*, 19 August 1980; *State*, 19 August 1980, 20 August 1980; *Columbia Record*, 19 August 1980; *Brigadier*, 15 September 1980.

32. *State*, 24 August 1980, 26 August 1980, 6 September 1980; Board of Visitors, "Minutes," 23 August 1980, documents 450–452; Board of Visitors, "Minutes," 15 May 1980, documents 392–393; Board of Visitors, "Minutes," 15 August 1980, documents 436, 437, 440; President's Annual Report to the Board of Visitors, 1980/81, 35, 73; Board of Visitors, "Minutes," 15 September 1980, document 462.

33. *Brigadier*, 5 September 1980, 14 November 1980.

34. Ibid., 21 November 1980.

35. Ibid., 5 September 1980, 12 September 1980, 14 November 1980, 21 November 1980, 5 December 1980, 30 January 1981.

36. Ibid., 5 December 1980; *State*, 24 August 1980.

37. Ibid., 14 November 1980, 1 May 1981.

38. Board of Visitors, "Minutes," 5 December 1980, documents 485, 487, 503–507; Board of Visitors, "Minutes," 15 September 1980, documents 460, 462; 1981 President's Report, 35; *Brigadier*, 11 April 1980, 5 September 1980, 30 January 1981, 20 February 1981; *Columbia Record*, 25 September 1980; *State*, 6 September 1980, 6 December 1980, 7 December 1980.

39. *Newsweek*, 1 September 1980, 83; Board of Visitors, "Minutes," 5 January 1979, document 231.

40. 1980 *Guidon*.

41. For accounts of locally led and locally inspired resistance in the South see Dittmer, *Local People*; Payne, *I've Got the Light of Freedom*; Tyson, *Radio Free Dixie*; Simon, *Fabric of Defeat*; Roscigno and Danaher, *Voice of Southern Labor*; Hall et al., *Like a Family*; Gilmore, *Defying Dixie*.

42. Wilson and Ferris, eds., *Encyclopedia of Southern Culture*, 277–278.

CHAPTER EIGHT. *Marching Backward*

1. *State*, 6 June 1981, 19 September 1981, 28 July 1982, 28 March 1987; *Columbia Record*, 1 April 1980; Board of Visitors, "Minutes," 30 October 1981, document 186; Board of Visitors, "Minutes," 11 December 1981, document 197; Board of Visitors, "Minutes," 10 September 1982, document 317; Board of Visitors, "Minutes," 18 March 1983, document 356; Board of Visitors, "Minutes," 25 March 1983, document 366; Board of Visitors, "Minutes," 13 May 1983, document 370; Board of Visitors, "Minutes," 30 March 1984, document 427; Board of Visitors, "Minutes," 10 February 1984, document 418; Board of Visitors, "Minutes," 14 September 1984, document 469; Board of Visitors, "Minutes," 28 June 1985, document 6; Board of Visitors, "Minutes," 29 March 1985, document 529; Board of Visitors, "Minutes," 27 May 1987, document 299; Board of Visitors, "Minutes," 7 February 1986, document 79; Board of Visitors, "Minutes," 18 March 1988, document 216; Board of Visitors, "Minutes," 17 March 1989, document 78; 1981 and 1982 Annual Reports, RC6, "Records of President's Office — Publications," Box 9, "Annual Reports of The Citadel"; *Brigadier*, 9 September 1983, 6 December 1985, 5 September 1986, 27 March 1987, 9 September 1988, 14 October 1988, 21 October 1988.

2. Board of Visitors, "Minutes," 18 March 1983, document 357; *State*, 6 February 1983, 3 November 1986; *U.S. News and World Report*, 12 September 1983, 59–62; *Esquire*, June 1985, 98–100; *Southern Living*, April 1981, 146, 149; *Brigadier*, 19 November 1982, 30 September 1983, 9 November 1984.

3. H. Johnson, *Sleepwalking through History*, 14, 32–33, 36, 67, 92, 139, 140, 157, 166, 181–184, 254, 375, 418, 425–426, 449, 455, 456, 454; Chafe, *Unfinished Journey*, 461–463, 471, 476–477; Cobb, *Redefining Southern Culture*, 71; Applebome, *Dixie Rising*, 7, 329, 339; O'Reilly, *Nixon's Piano*, 358–361, 366, 370, 373, 376.

4. Jon Weiner, "Reagan's Children: Racial Hatred on Campus," *The Nation*, February 27, 1989, 260–264.

5. *State*, 13 December 1986, 12 January 1987, 14 January 1987; *Atlanta Constitution*, 7 January 1987; *Jet*, 1 December 1986, 15 December 1986, 22 December 1986, 23 March 1987.

6. *Brigadier*, 19 April 1985, 27 September 1985, 18 October 1985, Commencement 1986, 20 March 1987, 23 September 1988; "President's Spot," 9 November 1982, 31 January 1984, 13 March 1984, 11 September 1984, 4 December 1984, 15 February 1985, 1 September 1986, 12 May 1988; James A. Grimsley, President, The Citadel, 1980–1989 Papers, 1981–2001, File, "President's Spot, 1982–1989, The Citadel Archives and Museum; 1982 *Guidon*, 17; 1983 *Guidon*, 17; 1986 *Guidon*, 19; 1987 *Guidon*, 19; *Charleston Evening Post*, 2 September 1980.

7. Board of Visitors, "Minutes," 18 September 1981, documents 168–177; *Brigadier*,

1985 Commencement, 22 November 1985, 21 February 1986; 1981 *Guidon*, 15, 16, 18 (emphasis in original); *State*, 5 July 1982.

8. Grimsley, *Citadel*, 12; Minutes of the Advisory Committee to the Board to Visitors, 15–16 October 1982, document 3; *State*, 19 March 1983; *Brigadier*, 22 November 1985 (emphasis in original).

9. *Brigadier*, 29 January 1982, 21 January 1983, 3 December 1982, 25 March 1983, 6 December 1985.

10. Ibid., 19 February 1982.

11. Ibid., 29 January 1982, 2 February 1982, 21 January 1983, 12 February 1988.

12. Ibid., 2 November 1984; Board of Visitors, "Minutes," 15 September 1980, document 461; Board of Visitors, "Minutes," 10 February 1984, document 418; Board of Visitors, "Minutes," 14 September 1984, document 469; Board of Visitors, "Minutes," 6 September 1985, documents 20–23; *State*, 31 May 1981.

13. *State*, 31 May 1981.

14. Board of Visitors, "Minutes," 5 June 1981; Board of Visitors, "Minutes," 19 March 1982, document 278; Board of Visitors, "Minutes," 14 May 1982, document 295; Board of Visitors, "Minutes," 10 June 1983, document 375; Board of Visitors, "Minutes," 18 February 1983, document 337; Board of Visitors, "Minutes," 9 November 1984, document 493; Board of Visitors, "Minutes," 8 February 1985, document 505; Board of Visitors, "Minutes," 15 March 1985, document 519; Board of Visitors, "Minutes," 10 May 1985, document 2; Board of Visitors, "Minutes," 6 September 1985, documents 17, 23; Advisory Committee Minutes, 15–16 October 1982, document 4; *State*, 31 May 1981.

15. *State*, 23 December 1978, 27 December 1978; *Columbia Record*, 3 January 1979, 5 January 1979, 6 August 1979, 7 January 1981, 8 January 1981, 16 January 1981, 26 January 1981.

16. *Columbia Record*, 30 April 1980, 7 January 1981, 3 March 1981, 1 July 1981, 3 July 1981, 25 July 1981; *State*, 8 January 1981, 6 March 1981.

17. Board of Visitors, "Minutes," 29 April 1981, documents 40–41; Board of Visitors, "Minutes," 14 May 1981, documents 44–45; *State*, 30 April 1980, 24 June 1981; *Columbia Record*, 15 May 1981, 11 June 1981.

18. *Columbia Record*, 15 May 1981, 9 June 1981, 11 June 1981; *State*, 18 June 1981, 26 June 1981, 8 May 1981, 10 May 1981, 12 May 1981, 7 May 1982, 19 June 1982.

19. *Columbia Record*, 29 June 1981; *State*, 29 June 1981, 30 June 1981, 18 July 1981.

20. *State*, 8 May 1981, 10 May 1981, 31 May 1982, 18 February 1982, 25 February 1982, 5 November 1982, 3 December 1982, 5 February 1983; *Columbia Record*, 26 July 1982, 7 February 1983, 30 August 1983.

21. *State*, 18 February 1982, 5 November 1982, 6 November 1982, 3 December 1982, 19 January 1983, 27 January 1983, 5 February 1983, 21 April 1983, 12 May 1983, 2 July 1983,

30 August 1983; *Columbia Record*, 7 February 1983, 20 April 1983, 30 August 1983, 7 October 1983, 26 January 1983, 20 April 1983.

22. Board of Visitors, "Minutes," 14 May 1981, documents 44–45; *State*, 16 May 1981, 31 May 1981, 6 November 1982; *Columbia Record*, 29 June 1981; *Brigadier*, 26 February 1982.

23. *State*, 8 July 1983, 2 March 1984, 2 July 1983, 25 July 1983, 16 August 1984, 27 September 1984, 2 July 1986; Board of Visitors, "Minutes," 9 September 1983, document 386; Board of Visitors, "Minutes," 4 November 1983, document 404; *Columbia Record*, 30 August 1983, 7 October 1983, 17 June 1985, 4 October 1985.

24. *State*, 10 September 1983; Board of Visitors, "Minutes," 14 March 1986, document 87; Board of Visitors, "Minutes," 27 June 1986, documents 130, 133, 134, 141; Advisory Committee Minutes, April 11–12, documents 1, 7; *Charleston Evening Post*, 14 January 1987; *Washington Post*, 29 November 1986.

25. *State*, 11 November 1986, 12 December 1986, 22 January 1987; "A Report on Hazing/Race Relations At The Citadel," 16 January 1987, documents in possession of author, hereafter cited as "Hazing Report," 3–4, 5.

26. "Through the Sallyport," December 1986 in AF Racial Incident 1986, The Citadel Archives and Museum, The Citadel, Charleston, S.C.; *Charleston News and Courier*, 28 October 1986, 29 October 1986; *State*, 25 October 1986, 28 October 1986, 29 October 1986; Hazing Report, 7.

27. *Washington Post*, 21 November 1986; *Jet*, 22 December 1986; *State*, 4 December 1986, 14 January 1987, 22 January 1987, 31 January 1987, 14 October 1987; *Columbia Record*, 13 March 1987; "Sallyport," 2; *New York Times*, 21 November 1986; *Brigadier*, 10 November 1986; *Charleston News and Courier*, 28 October 1986, 9 November 1986.

28. *New York Times*, 23 November 1986; *Brigadier*, 3 February 1984, 8 December 1986 (italics in original), 14 November 1986; *Charleston Post and Courier*, 9 November 1986.

29. *Brigadier*, 14 November 1986.

30. Ibid., 10 November 1986; *Washington Post*, 21 November 1986, 29 November 1986; *New York Times*, 23 November 1986; *West 57th*, "The Citadel: Marching in Place," executive producer, Andrew Lack, produced by Peter Michaelis, CBS News; CBS.

31. A tour consists of walking back and forth across the barracks' quadrangle for fifty minutes carrying a rifle. Cadets may not leave campus, except for furloughs, without finishing all their tours.

32. *State*, 1 November 1986; Board of Visitors, "Minutes," 8 November 1986, documents 249–250; undated newspaper clipping in author's possession; *Charleston News and Courier*, 1 November 1986; "President's Spot," 3 November 1986, 19 November 1987.

33. *Brigadier*, 10 November 1986; *Washington Post*, 21 November 1986; Hazing Report, 6, 11; *State*, 28 October 1986, 9 November 1986, 13 November 1986, 15 November 1986; *Charleston Post and Courier*, 9 November 1986; *Charleston News and Courier*, 14 November 1986; Board of Visitors, "Minutes," 8 November 1986, document 249; *Jet*, 1 December 1986; *Columbia Record*, 8 January 1987.

34. Hazing Report, 11–12; *State*, 11 November 1986, 12 November 1986, 13 November 1986, 15 November 1986, 16 November 1986, 18 November 1986, 24 November 1986; *Charleston News and Courier*, 28 October 1986, 11 November 1986, 12 November 1986, 18 November 1986, 24 November 1986.

35. *Columbia Record*, 12 January 1987, 1 April 1987, 7 March 1987; *State*, 18 November 1986, 30 November 1986, 19 December 1986, 6 January 1987, 24 February 1987, 6 March 1987; *Jet*, 15 December 1986, 12.

36. Hazing Report, 12–13, 15–16; *State*, 13 November 1986, 16 November 1986, 24 November 1986, 9 December 1986, 12 January 1987; *Charleston News and Courier*, 11 November 1986, 16 November 1986, 18 November 1986, 24 November 1986.

37. *State*, 18 November 1986, 23 November 1986, 24 November 1986, 1 December 1986; Hazing Report, 12–13, 15–16.

38. Hazing Report, 16; *State*, 21 November 1986; *Charleston News and Courier*, 21 November 1986; Board of Visitors, "Minutes," 20 March 1987, documents 295–297.

39. *State*, 28 October 1986, 31 October 1986, 1 November 1986, 17 November 1986, 20 November 1986, 6 December 1986, 7 December 1986, 12 December 1986, 24 December 1986; *Charleston News and Courier*, 13 November 1986, 15 November 1986, 18 November 1986; *Atlanta Constitution*, 7 January 1987; Hazing Report, 13.

40. *State*, 4 November 1986, 17 November 1986, 1 December 1986, 27 January 1987, *Charleston News and Courier*, 14 November 1986, 18 November 1986, 20 November 1986, 21 November 1986, 26 November 1986, *Greenville News*, 23 November 1986; *Florence Morning News*, 16 November 1986; *Columbia Record*, 13 March 1987.

41. *State*, 17 November 1986, 23 November 1986, 1 December 1986, 7 December 1986; 8 December 1986, 27 January 1987, 28 January 1987, 15 March 1987; *Charleston News and Courier*, 13 November 1986, 14 November 1986, 15 November 1986, 18 November 1986, 19 November 1986, 26 November 1986.

42. *State*, 31 October 1986, 21 November 1986, 30 November 1986, 12 December 1986, 27 January 1987, 15 March 1987; *Charleston News and Courier*, 14 November 1986, 15 November 1986, 19 November 1986, 20 November 1986, 21 November 1986, 26 November 1986; *Brigadier*, 8 December 1986; *Florence Morning News*, 16 November 1986; "Sallyport," 1, 2.

43. *Charleston News and Courier*, 13 November 1986, 15 November 1986, 18 November 1986, 20 November 1986, 24 November 1986, 26 November 1986; *State*, 17

November 1986, 20 November 1986, 23 November 1986, 26 December 1986, 28 January 1987; *Greenville News*, 23 November 1986; *Brigadier*, 8 December 1986.

44. *Brigadier*, 8 December 1986, 23 January 1987; *State*, 17 November 1986, 29 November 1986, 25 March 1987; *Charleston News and Courier*, 13 November 1986, 15 November 1986, 20 November 1986, 21 November 1986, 26 November 1986.

45. *Charleston News and Courier*, 26 November 1986.

46. Hazing Report, 9, 10, 14; *State*, 16 November 1986, 22 November 1986, 23 November 1986, 9 December 1986, 12 December 1986; *Charleston News and Courier*, 22 November 1986.

47. *Charleston News and Courier*, 23 November 1986; *State*, 12 December 1986; Hazing Report, 14, 20, 22; *Columbia Record*, 12 January 1987; *Washington Post*, 21 November 1986.

48. Hazing Report, 19, 20, 23, 26–30; *State*, 12 January 1987, 17 January 1987; *Columbia Record*, 12 January 1987; *Brigadier*, 14 November 1986.

49. "Report of the Special Board of Inquiry to Review Racial Climate at The Citadel," documents in possession of author, cited hereafter as Citadel Report, 2–3, 4, 5; *Columbia Record*, 19 February 1987

50. *Columbia Record*, 19 February 1987, 13 March 1987; Citadel Report, 5–6, 10, 12, 13.

51. "*Statement by*: MGen James A. Grimsley, Jr. USA Ret.," dated 18 February 1987 in "The Citadel AF Racial Incident 1986," Citadel Archives and Museum; *State*, 18 February 1987, 19 February 1987, 27 June 1987; Board of Visitors, "Minutes," 26 June 1987, documents 377, 378.

52. In the five months following October 23, Citadel administrators invited economist Walter Williams to campus as part of the Greater Issues Lecture Series, welcomed the chairman of the NAACP to address a meeting of the Afro-American Society, held a parade in recognition of a black cadet's winning of the Palmetto Award, and named Charleston Police Chief Reuben Greenberg an honorary graduate of The Citadel. *Brigadier*, 27 March 1987; Board of Visitors, "Minutes," 30 January 1987, document 274; Board of Visitors, "Minutes," 30 October 1987, document 23; *State*, 1 February 1987.

53. Board of Visitors, "Minutes," 22 April 1988, document 255; Board of Visitors, "Minutes," 9 September 1988, document 97; Annual Reports from 1988 to 1990; *State*, 5 February 1987, 21 March 1987; *Washington Post*, 21 November 1986; Hazing Report, 20, 21; Board of Visitors, "Minutes," 20 March 1987, document 275; Advisory Committee Minutes, 27–28 March 1987, document 2.

54. Board of Visitors, "Minutes," 29 January 1988, documents 143, 215; *Brigadier*, 8 December 1986.

55. *State*, 13 December 1986, 21 March 1987, 27 June 1987; *Brigadier*, 19 February 1987, 30 October 1987.

56. Prince, *Rally 'Round the Flag*, 5, 66, 104, 131; Goldfield, *Still Fighting the Civil War*, 312–314; Cobb, *Away Down South*, 294–295.

57. Hazing Report, 19; Citadel Report, 7; *Columbia Record*, 12 January 1987; *State*, 11 November 1986, 13 November 1986, 12 January 1987, 17 January 1987; *Charleston News and Courier*, 16 November 1986.

58. Citadel Report, 7; *Charleston Evening Post*, 12 January 1987; *State*, 17 January 1987, 6 February 1987; Hazing Report, 20; Board of Visitors, "Minutes," 20 March 1987, document 297; *Columbia Record*, 19 February 1987; *Jet*, 23 March 1987.

59. *Charleston News and Courier*, 21 January 1987; *Brigadier*, 20 April 1987; *State*, 16 November 1987; Citadel Report, 11.

60. *State*, 17 January 1987, 19 February 1987; *Brigadier*, 28 September 1984, 20 February 1987; Grimsley statement dated 18 February 1987 in "The Citadel AF Racial Incident 1986"; *Columbia Record*, 19 February 1987, 13 March 1987; "Sallyport," 2; *Charleston News and Courier*, 15 November 1986; Board of Visitors, "Minutes," 20 March 1987, document 297; *Washington Post*, 21 November 1986; *Charleston Post and Courier*, 9 November 1986.

61. *Brigadier*, 30 September 1988; *Columbia Record*, 5 November 1987; *State*, 5 November 1987.

62. Citadel Report, 10, 12; *Brigadier*, 30 January 1987, 30 September 1988, 21 October 1988; *Washington Post*, 21 November 1986; Advisory Committee Minutes, 27–28 March 1987, document 2.

63. *Brigadier*, 11 May 1989, 13 October 1989, 17 November 1989.

64. Board of Visitors, "Minutes," 27 January 1986, document 58; Board of Visitors, "Minutes," 24 June 1995, document 80; *Brigadier*, 11 May 1989, 21 September 1990, 2 October 1992; Board of Visitors, "Minutes," 19 April 1991, document 643; Board of Visitors, "Minutes," 21 November 1991, document 70; Board of Visitors, "Minutes," 20 August 1995, document 191; Board of Visitors, "Minutes," 19 March 1993, document 57; Board of Visitors, "Minutes," 13 May 1993, document 67; Board of Visitors, "Minutes," 13 May 1994, document 137.

65. *Charleston News and Courier*, 22 August 1989; *Brigadier*, 3 November 1989.

66. *Charleston News and Courier*, 9 September 1989, 12 September 1989.

67. Ibid., 16 September 1989, 17 September 1989.

68. *Brigadier*, 6 October 1989, 13 October 1989, 20 October 1989, 3 November 1989, 10 November 1989, 17 November 1989; *Charleston News and Courier*, 19 June 1990.

69. *Brigadier*, 1991 Issue Four, 13 March 1992; *State*, 6 October 1991, 20 October 1991, 12 September 1992; *Charleston News and Courier*, 8 October 1991, 9 October 1991, 5 March 1992; Board of Visitors, "Minutes," 4 October 1991, document 45; Board of Visitors, "Minutes," 17 August 1992, documents 287, 288, 295–298, 300, 303; Board of

Visitors, "Minutes," 11 September 1992, document 247; Board of Visitors, "Minutes," 25 June 1993, document 102; Board of Visitors, 'Minutes," 24 June 1994, documents 186, 288; Advisory Committee Minutes, 3-4 April 1992, documents 78, 79, 81-82.

70. Advisory Committee Minutes, 3–4 April 1992, 81–82; *Charleston News and Courier*, 25 August 1992, 30 October 1992; *Brigadier*, 16 October 1992; *State*, 25 August 1992; Board of Visitors, "Minutes," 16 October 1992, document 368.

71. *Brigadier*, 10 February 1995; Board of Visitors, "Minutes," 27 January 1995, documents 1, 2, 24, 30.

72. *West 57th*, "Marching in Place."

73. Grimsley statement dated 18 February 1987 in "The Citadel AF Racial Incident 1986"; *Columbia Record*, 19 February 1987; *Brigadier*, 1987 Commencement, 9 October 1987, 18 March 1988, 22 November 1991.

CHAPTER NINE. *Save the Males*

1. During this same period, the Virginia Military Institute (VMI) was waging an almost identical battle to preserve its all-male admissions policies. VMI waged a longer, more publicized court battle, and Citadel officials watched developments in the VMI case with great interest, since representatives from the two schools offered similar arguments in regard to the legality and benefits of their single-sex systems. It was the Supreme Court ruling in regard to VMI that convinced Citadel officials to accept female applicants, and so given the obvious parallels between the two trials, I quote here from decisions handed down by lower courts in the VMI case to articulate arguments made and endorsed by Citadel supporters.

2. Board of Visitors, "Minutes," 2 February 1990, document 84; Board of Visitors, "Minutes," 19 April 1991, documents 598, 645; Board of Visitors, "Minutes," 6 September 1991, documents 2, 4; Board of Visitors, "Minutes," 21 November 1991, document 69; Board of Visitors, "Minutes," 26 June 1992, document 181; Board of Visitors, "Minutes," 24 June 1994, documents 177, 213; Board of Visitors, "Minutes," 20 August 1995, documents 165–183; Advisory Committee to the Board of Visitors, "Minutes," 4 October 1991, document 52.

3. Board of Visitors, "Minutes," 3 November 1989, document 53; Board of Visitors, "Minutes," 27 April 1990, document 259; Board of Visitors, "Minutes," 21 June 1991, documents 734, 758; Board of Visitors, "Minutes," 2 October 1993, documents 193, 198; Board of Visitors, "Minutes," 6 September 1991, document 15; *Charleston Post and Courier*, 16 October 1991; *Brigadier*, 15 September 1989, 13 October 1989, 10 November 1989, Issue Three 1991; *State*, 6 October 1991, 26 October 1991; *Charleston News and Courier*, 18 October 1991.

4. *State*, 21 May 1991, 4 October 1991, 13 October 1991, 20 October 1991, 26 November 1992; Susan Faludi, "The Naked Citadel," *New Yorker*, September 1994, 69; Rick Reilly, "What Is The Citadel?" *Sports Illustrated*, Issue 11, September 14, 1992, 73–79; *Charleston News and Courier*, 3 October 1991; *Charleston Post and Courier*, 6 October 1991.

5. *State*, 9 December 1991, 5 October 1992, 17 August 1993; Board of Visitors, "Minutes," 4 October 1991, document 45; Board of Visitors, "Minutes," 4 January 1992, documents 3–5, 7; Board of Visitors, "Minutes," 31 January 1992, document 11; Board of Visitors, "Minutes," 1 September 1992, documents 283–286; Board of Visitors, "Minutes," 28 August 1992, document 243; Board of Visitors, "Minutes," 24 June 1994, document 181; 1993 Citadel "Self Study," viii-17–18, documents in author's possession; Advisory Committee to the Board of Visitors, "Minutes," 3–4 April 1992, document 79; Board of Visitors, "Minutes," 4 October 1992, document 52; *Brigadier*, 1 November 1991, 17 January 1992, 7 February 1992, 13 March 1992, 18 September 1992, 2 October 1992, 16 October 1992, 30 October 1992, 1 November 1992, 11 December 1992, 19 February 1993, 19 March 1993.

6. Board of Visitors, "Minutes," 21 April 1989, document 95, 96–97, 108; Board of Visitors, "Minutes," 11 May 1989, document 117; *Brigadier*, 8 September 1989, 16 March 1990; *State*, 12 May 1989, 13 July 1989, 21 July 1989, 2 February 1990; 1989 Annual Report.

7. *State*, 18 February 1990, 8 March 1990, 7 March 1991, 13 May 1991.

8. *Brigadier*, 10 April 1991, 14 February 1992; *State*, 15 March 1991, 16 March 1991, 23 March 1991, 24 March 1991, 18 June 1991, 19 June 1991; Board of Visitors, "Minutes," 1 February 1990, documents 541, 543; Board of Visitors, "Minutes," 15 March 1991, document 546; Board of Visitors, "Minutes," 21 June 1991, document 791.

9. *New York Times*, 27 June 1996; *Brigadier*, 28 August 1992, 16 October 1992; *State*, 20 June 1992, 5 October 1992, 14 December 1992, 20 September 1993.

10. *State*, 5 October 1992; *Brigadier*, 11 December 1992; Board of Visitors, "Minutes," 3 September 1992, documents 245–246.

11. *Brigadier*, 18 September 1992; Board of Visitors, "Minutes," 3 September 1992, documents 245–246; Advisory Committee to the Board of Visitors, "Minutes," 11–12 September 1992, document 365.

12. Manegold, *In Glory's Shadow*, 143; *State*, 5 September 1992, 6 September 1992, 10 September 1992, 26 November 1992, 16 December 1992; Board of Visitors, "Minutes," 7 November 1992, documents 414, 429; *Brigadier*, 18 September 1992.

13. *Brigadier*, 5 March 1993, 3 September 1993; *State*, 13 August 1993, 26 August 1993, 21 January 1994, 3 March 1994, 14 March 1994.

14. *State*, 8 March 1990, 23 March 1990, 18 June 1991, 19 June 1991, 7 July 1991, 7 August 1991, 26 August 1991, 13 September 1991, 14 September 1991, 26 October 1992, 26

November 1992, 1 June 1993, 4 August 1993, 26 November 1993, 24 January 1994, 23 July 1994, 13 August 1995; *Brigadier*, 5 September 1995.

15. *State*, 9 April 1989, 5 October 1992, 26 October 1992, 26 November 1992, 13 January 1994, 4 August 1994; *Brigadier*, 14 February 1994, 21 February 1994.

16. Board of Visitors, "Minutes," 13 May 1994, document 148; *Brigadier*, 18 March 1994, 21 October 1994, 14 March 1995; *State*, 13 November 1992, 21 August 1993, 24 August 1993, 28 September 1993, 15 May 1994; Advisory Committee to the Board of Visitors, "Minutes," 15–16 April 1994, document 83.

17. *Brigadier*, 3 September 1993, 8 October 1993, 15 October 1993, 18 March 1994, 2 May 1994, 21 October 1994, 18 November 1994, 10 February 1995, 14 March 1995, 5 September 1995; *State*, 8 November 1992, 22 August 1993, 26 August 1993, 10 February 1994, 28 May 1994, 13 August 1995, Advisory Committee to the Board of Visitors, "Minutes," 15–16 April 1994, document 69.

18. *Brigadier*, 18 March 1994, 2 May 1994, 14 March 1995; *State*, 18 February 1990, 18 June 1991, 5 July 1991, 7 July 1991, 5 October 1992, 14 October 1992, 30 October 1992, 27 May 1993, 28 May 1993, 24 August 1993, 5 December 1993, 29 January 1994, 3 March 1994; Advisory Committee to the Board of Visitors, "Minutes," 15–16 April 1994, document 97.

19. *State*, 3 March 1990, 8 June 1993, 13 January 1994, 13 March 1994, 17 May 1994, 18 June 1994, 12 August 1995, 13 August 1995; *Brigadier*, 4 February 1994, 27 January 1995, 14 March 1995; Advisory Committee to the Board of Visitors, "Minutes," 15–16 April 1994, documents 82, 100.

20. Strum, *Women in the Barracks*, 140, 193.

21. Advisory Committee to the Board of Visitors, "Minutes," 15–16 April 1994, documents 84, 96; *State*, 21 June 1994, 31 July 1994; Strum, *Women in the Barracks*, 211.

22. Strum, *Women in the Barracks*, 192, 223–224, 232, 235; *State*, 17 June 1994, 21 May 1995.

23. *State*, 6 October 1992; Strum, *Women in the Barracks*, 194–195, 196.

24. *State*, 21 September 1992, 30 October 1992, 16 November 1992, 25 May 1993, 28 September 1993, 19 November 1993, 6 December 1993, 10 February 1994, 14 February 1994, 2 April 1994, 20 May 1994, 24 May 1994, 11 June 1994, 21 June 1994, 24 July 1994, 3 August 1994, 20 September 1994, 19 November 1994, 13 May 1995; *Brigadier*, 22 November 1993, 28 January 1994, 10 February 1995; Strum, *Women in the Barracks*, 173; Advisory Committee to the Board of Visitors, "Minutes," 15–16 April 1994, documents 98–100.

25. Board of Visitors, "Minutes," 27 January 1995, document 40; Board of Visitors, "Minutes," 12 May 1995, document 67; Board of Visitors, "Minutes," 5 October 1994, document 370; Board of Visitors, "Minutes," 24 June 1995, documents 145, 147; *State*,

25 May 1993, 27 May 1993, 15 September 1993, 20 November 1993, 18 May 1994, 19 May 1994, 20 May 1994, 28 April 1995, 10 May 1995, 18 May 1995, 19 May 1995, 20 May 1995, 21 May 1995, 25 July 1995, 19 August 1995; *New York Times*, 27 June 1996.

26. *State*, 30 October 1992, 28 May 1993, 26 August 1993, 27 August 1993, 26 November 1993, 29 January 1994, 11 June 1994, 24 July 1994, 5 October 1994, 18 April 1995, 5 May 1995, 6 May 1995, 9 May 1995, 19 May 1995, 21 May 1995, 27 May 1994, 3 June 1995, 22 June 1995; Board of Visitors, "Minutes," 2 September 1995, document 227; Board of Visitors, "Minutes," 27 October 1995, documents 291–292.

27. *State*, 5 October 1992, 27 May 1993, 29 January 1994, 29 March 1994, 17 May 1994, 26 May 1994, 28 April 1995, 5 May 1995, 6 May 1995, 7 May 1995, 20 May 1995, 25 May 1995, 6 July 1995, 13 July 1995, 27 July 1995, 22 October 1995; *New York Times*, 27 June 1996.

28. *State*, 15 August 1993, 26 September 1993, 2 October 1993, 5 January 1994, 29 January 1994, 10 February 1994, 3 March 1994, 30 May 1994, 9 May 1995, 19 May 1995, 14 June 1995.

29. "A perception analysis of The Citadel from select traditional and nontraditional African-American community leaders of South Carolina," conducted by Sunrise Enterprise of Columbia, Inc., documents in author's possession.

30. *State*, 6 July 1995; *Brigadier*, 18 March 1994 (emphasis in original), 14 April 1995, 27 June 1995.

31. *State*, 18 February 1990, 13 June 1993, 5 December 1993, 13 January 1994; *Brigadier*, 2 May 1994.

32. *State*, 31 March 1990, 16 November 1992, 26 August 1993, 28 September 1993, 5 December 1993, 15 May 1994, 11 June 1994, 13 June 1994, 23 July 1994, 6 July 1995, 25 July 1995; *Brigadier*, 16 February 1990, 5 October 1990, 13 November 1992, 28 January 1993, 3 September 1993, 4 March 1994, 7 October 1994.

33. *Brigadier*, 1 November 1991, 23 April 1993; *State*, 27 June 1989, 8 February 1990, 25 March 1990, 1 April 1991, 11 August 1991, 28 September 1993, 6 December 1993, 13 January 1994, 4 February 1994, 28 June 1994, 29 June 1994, 1 July 1994, 16 July 1994, 2 August 1994, 3 August 1994, 4 August 1994, 5 August 1994, 6 August 1994, 8 August 1994, 11 August 1994, 18 August 1994, 11 May 1995, 2 June 1995, 8 June 1995; Board of Visitors, "Minutes," 22 November 1993, document 286.

34. Board of Visitors, "Minutes," 22 November 1993, document 286; Strum, *Women in the Barracks*, 148, 164, 168, 183, 193; *Brigadier*, 18 March 1994; *State*, 31 July 1994.

35. *State*, 8 June 1991 (emphasis in original), 19 November 1992, 21 November 1992, 26 November 1992, 8 August 1994, 18 May 1994; Strum, *Women in the Barracks*, 238; Faludi, "Naked," 71–72.

36. Faludi, "Naked," 73; *Brigadier*, 3 September 1993; *State*, 14 December 1993, 8 August 1994.

37. Faludi, "Naked," 70; *State*, 26 January 1994, 21 June 1994; *Newsday*, 27 June 1996; *Brigadier*, 9 March 1990, 15 October 1993, 10 October 1996; 1994 *Guidon*, 5.

38. *State*, 18 February 1990, 25 March 1990, 15 April 1990, 8 October 1991, 13 November 1992, 10 June 1993, 21 May 1994, 23 May 1994, 7 July 1994; Faludi, "Naked," 67–68, 70–72; *Brigadier*, 21 April 1989, 9 March 1990, 24 April 1992, 5 September 1995; Faludi, *Stiffed*, 114.

39. *State*, 5 October 1992, 19 November 1993, 5 December 1993, 15 May 1994, 17 May 1994, 13 June 1994, 8 August 1994; Board of Visitors, "Minutes," 12 April 1993, document 65; *Brigadier*, 28 January 1993, 4 February 1994, 18 March 1994; Strum, *Women in the Barracks*, 50, 147, 150, 160, 161; Faludi, "Naked," 65, 69, 79, 80; Faludi, *Stiffed*, 126.

40. Strum, *Women in the Barracks*, 269, 275, 286, 287, 289, 290, 293, 294; *State*, 17 June 1995, 6 August 1995, 9 August 1995, 13 August 1995, 15 August 1995, 16 August 1995, 17 August 1995, 18 August 1995, 19 August 1995, 20 August 1995.

41. *New York Times*, 27 June 1996, 29 June 1996; *Charleston Post and Courier*, 29 June 1996; *State*, 14 March 1994, 23 July 1994.

42. *State*, 14 September 1991, 8 August 1991, 20 January 1994, 12 August 1995.

43. Ibid., 17 March 1990, 19 July 1992, 13 November 1992; *Brigadier*, 13 March 1992, 18 March 1994; Faludi, "Naked," 75–76.

44. *Brigadier*, 21 October 1994; *State*, 18 February 1990, 23 March 1990, 30 April 1991, 7 July 1991, 28 May 1993.

45. Cash, *Mind of the South*, xlvii; *Brigadier*, 23 April 1993; *State*, 2 April 1991, 8 August 1994.

46. Reed, *Enduring South*, 88–89; Sheldon Hackney, "Southern Violence," 924–925; Goldfield, *Still Fighting the Civil War*, 313–314; *State*, 10 February 1994, 8 August 1994.

47. Gilmore, "Gender and *Origins of the New South*," 771; Kirby, *The Countercultural South*, 3; *State*, 21 June 1994.

EPILOGUE

1. *Charleston Post and Courier*, 2 May 1999, 25 May 2001, 6 November 2001; *State*, 26 June 2005; Kenneth Franklin West, "The Long Gray Line," *Charleston Magazine*, 7 May 2007; McCandless, "In a White Man's World," 17; *Newsweek*, 22 August 2005.

2. Emory Mace, interview by author, tape recording, 7 June 2002; "Enhancement Initiatives for the South Carolina Corps of Cadets (The Mace Plan)," memo from

Brigadier General Mace to Major General Grinalds, dated 19 May 1997, documents in possession of author; *Charleston News and Courier*, 6 December 1998, 16 April 2000; *State*, 10 December 1999; *New Orleans Times Picayune*, 6 November 2002; *Charleston Post and Courier*, 2 May 1999.

3. *New Orleans Times Picayune*, 6 November 2002; "Lieutenant General Rosa makes first address as president," 11 January 2006, Citadel News Service; email from General Rosa to Citadel Alumni dated 22 August 2006, email in possession of author; *Charleston Post and Courier*, 2 May 1999, 6 December 2004, 23 April 2006; McCandless, "In a White Man's World," 18–19. Some information on the Citadel African American Studies Program came from the program's Web site: http://citadel.edu/africanamerican/index.shtml.

4. *Greenville News*, 17 August 2002, 12 August 2006; *State*, 26 June 2005; *Charlotte Observer*, 9 May 2002; *Charleston Post and Courier*, 30 March 2002; *Washington Post*, 12 March 2000.

5. *Charleston Post and Courier*, 15 November 2005; http://www.citadelmen.com/; McCandless, "In a White Man's World," 17, 18, 20–21; West, "Long Gray Line"; *Charleston Post and Courier*, 23 August 2006.

6. *Charleston Post and Courier*, 23 August 2006; *State*, 24 August 2006; *Seattle Post-Intelligencer*, 24 August 2006.

7. *Charleston Post and Courier*, 23 August 2006, 24 August 2006, 25 August 2006; *State*, 24 August 2006.

8. David Blight, "Southerners Don't Lie; They Just Remember Big," in Brundage, *Where These Memories Grow*, 349. Although it deals with the South, Brundage's collection carries a message that could and should be applied to the nation. Brundage, *Where These Memories Grow*, 3, 5, 6, 9, 11, 12–14, 16–19, 20.

9. *Charleston Post and Courier*, 22 April 2006, 23 April 2006.

BIBLIOGRAPHY

PRIMARY SOURCES

Manuscript Collections

General Mark W. Clark Papers. The Citadel Archives and Museum, The Citadel, Charleston, S.C.

General Hugh P. Harris Papers. The Citadel Archives and Museum, The Citadel, Charleston, S.C.

David S. McAlister Papers, 1932–1972. The Citadel Archives and Museum, The Citadel, Charleston, S.C.

General Charles P. Summerall Papers. The Citadel Archives and Museum, The Citadel, Charleston, S.C.

Thomas R. Waring Papers. "Charles C. Martin Correspondence." South Carolina Historical Society, Charleston, S.C.

———. "Mark Clark Correspondence." South Carolina Historical Society, Charleston, S.C.

Reports and Proceedings

Annual Reports of the Board of Visitors of The Citadel, The Military College of South Carolina. Daniel Library, The Citadel, Charleston, S.C.

Annual Reports of the President to The Citadel Board of Visitors. The Citadel Archives and Museum, The Citadel, Charleston, S.C.

Bulletins of The Citadel, The Military College of South Carolina — Catalogues. Daniel Library, The Citadel, Charleston, S.C.

"The Citadel 1982 Self-Study — 1982–1983." Documents in possession of author.

"The Citadel 1993 Self-Study." Documents in possession of author.

"The Citadel War Record — Vietnam Casualties." The Citadel Archives and Museum, The Citadel, Charleston, S.C.

Minutes of The Citadel's Board of Visitors. The Citadel Archives and Museum, The Citadel, Charleston, S.C.

Official Registers of The Citadel. The Citadel Archives and Museum, The Citadel, Charleston, S.C.

Records of the Commandant's Office. The Citadel Archives and Museum, The Citadel, Charleston, S.C.

Records of the President's Office. The Citadel Archives and Museum, The Citadel, Charleston, S.C.

"A Self Study, The Citadel 1972." Documents in possession of author.

Student Publications

The Brigadier, the Newspaper of The Military College of South Carolina. The Citadel Archives and Museum, The Citadel, Charleston, S.C.

The Bulldog. The Citadel Archives and Museum, The Citadel, Charleston, S.C.

The Guidon. Daniel Library, The Citadel, Charleston, S.C.

The Shako. The Citadel Archives and Museum, The Citadel, Charleston, S.C.

The Sphinx. The Citadel Archives and Museum, The Citadel, Charleston, S.C.

Newspapers and Periodicals

Atlanta Constitution
Charleston Evening Post
Charleston Magazine
Charleston News and Courier
Charleston Post and Courier
Charlotte Observer
Columbia Record
Esquire
Florence Morning News
Greenville News
Jet
Life
The Nation
New Orleans Times-Picayune
Newsweek
New Yorker
New York Times
Rockland County Journal-News
The Saturday Evening Post
Saturday Review
Seattle Post-Intelligencer

Southern Living
Sports Illustrated
The State
Time
U.S. News and World Report
Washington Post

Television Shows

West 57th Street (CBS)

Interviews
[All tapes in author's possession unless otherwise noted.]

Bagnal, Richard. Interview by author via phone, 13 January 1998. Tape recording.

Banner, David. Interview by author, 22 January 1998, Florence, S.C. Tape recording.

Barrett, Michael. Interview by author, 14 January 1998, Charleston, S.C. Tape recording.

Bozeman, Michael. Interview by author via phone, 19 October 1997. Tape recording.

Brown, Thomas. Interview by author, 5 February 1999, Atlanta, Ga.

Byrd, Thomas. Interview by author via phone. 13 January 1988.

Cassidy, James. Interview by author, 23 January 1998, Greenville, S.C. Tape recording.

Clarkson, Philip. Interview by author, 10 October 1997, Spartanburg, S.C. Tape recording.

Courvoisie, T. Nugent. Interview by author, 4 October 1997, Mount Pleasant, S.C. Tape recording.

Dawson, David. Interview by author via phone, 27 January 1998. Tape recording.

Eubanks, David. Interview by author, 10 October 1997, Spartanburg, S.C. Tape recording.

Feaster, Kenneth. Interview by author via phone, 9 January 1998. Tape recording.

Ferguson, Larry. Interview by author via phone, 23 January 1998. Tape recording.

Fitzgerald, Albert. Interview by author, 21 December 1997, Greenville, S.C. Tape recording.

Funderburk, Charles. Interview by author via phone, 15 January 1998. Tape recording.

Gantt, Larry. Interview by author via phone, 5 February 1998. Tape recording.

Gilliard, Patrick. Interview by author via phone, 13 December 1997. Tape recording.

Graham, George. Interview by author via phone, 28 January 1998. Tape recording. Tape in possession of Graham.

Gray, George. Interview by author via phone, 25 November 1997. Tape recording.

Grinalds, John. Interview by author, 7 June 2002, Charleston, S.C. Tape recording.

Hoffmann, Philip. Interview by author via phone, 29 October 1997. Tape recording.

Hooper, David. Interview by author via phone, 14 October 1997. Tape recording.

Hughes, Alan. Interview by author, 10 October 1997, Spartanburg, S.C. Tape recording.

Jenkinson, William. Interview by author, 5 October 1997, Charleston, S.C. Tape recording.

Jones, Keith. Interview by author, 9 January 1998, Charleston, S.C. Tape recording.

Jones, Samuel. Interview by author via phone, 16 November 1997. Tape recording.

Kennedy, Henry. Interview by author, 24 October 1997, Charleston, S.C. Tape recording.

Lane, Lucien. Interview by author, 5 February 1999, Atlanta, Ga.

Legare, Herbert. Interview by author, 15 January 1998, Charleston, S.C. Tape recording. Tape in possession of Legare.

Lockridge, James. Interview by author via phone, 26 January 1998. Tape recording.

Mace, Emory. Interview by author, 7 June 2002, Charleston, S.C. Tape recording.

Madding, Scott. Interview by author, 10 October 1997, Spartanburg, S.C. Tape recording.

Marett, Bill. Interview by author, 22 December 2001, Seneca, S.C.

Martin, Charles C. Interview by author via phone, 15 October 1997.

———. Interview by author, 24 October 1997, Charleston, S.C. Tape recording.

McDowell, John. Interview by author via phone, 21 January 1998. Tape recording.

McGinnis, David. Interview by author, 20 January 1998, Charleston, S.C. Tape recording.

Mood, Frank P. Interview by author, 18 May 2002, Columbia, S.C. Tape recording.

Moore, Claude L. Interview by author via phone, 20 January 1998. Tape recording. Tape in possession of Moore.

Moreland, Laurence. Interview by author, 22 October 1997, Charleston, S.C.

Reid, John. Interview by author via phone, 30 October 1997. Tape recording.

Rich, Douglas. Interview by author via phone, 21 January 1998. Tape recording.

Riggs, William. Interview by author via phone, 7 December 1997. Tape recording.

Seabrooks, Norman. Interview by author via phone, 17 October 1997. Tape recording.

Sealey, Reginald. Interview by author via phone, 18 October 1997 and 2 February 1998. Tape recording.

Shine, Joseph. Interview by author, 20 December 1997, Columbia, S.C. Tape recording.

Shine, Joseph. Interview for wcsc News in Charleston, 16 June 1997. Videotape in possession of Shine.

Short, Paul. Interview by author, 6 October 1997, Columbia, S.C. Tape recording.

Stern, Ira. Interview by author via phone, 30 January 1998. Tape recording.

Varner, Adolphus. Interview by author via phone, 20 November 1997. Tape recording.

Vogel, Robert. Interview by author via phone, 17 November 1997. Tape recording.

Yonce, Leon. Interview by author, 14 January 1998, Charleston, S.C. Tape recording.

Books and Articles

Clark, Mark W.. *Calculated Risk*. New York: Harper and Brothers, 1950.

Conroy, Donald Patrick. *The Boo*. New York: The Old New York Bookshop Press, 1970; Mockingbird Books, 1993.

Conroy, Pat. *My Losing Season*. New York: Doubleday, 2002.

Flipper, Henry O.. *The Colored Cadet at West Point: Autobiography of Lieutenant Henry Ossian Flipper*. New York: Homer Lee and Company, 1878. Reprint, New York: Johnson Reprint Corporation, 1968.

Grimsley, James A. *The Citadel: Educating the Whole Man*. Princeton, N.J.: Princeton University Press, 1983.

Hunter-Gault, Charlayne. *In My Place*. New York: Farrar Straus Giroux, 1992.

Malcolm X. *The Autobiography of Malcolm X*. With Alex Haley. New York: Ballantine Books, 1965.

McMillan, George. "Integration with Dignity." In *Perspectives in South Carolina History: The First 30 Years*, edited by Ernest M. Lander and Robert K. Ackerman, 381–391. Columbia: University of South Carolina Press, 1973.

Mace, Nancy, with Mary Jane Ross. *In the Company of Men: A Woman at The Citadel*. New York: Simon and Schuster, 2001.

Roesch, Roberta, and Harry De La Roche Jr. *Anyone's Son: A True Story*. Kansas City: Andrews and McMeel, 1979.

Sass, Herbert Ravenel. "The Citadel: American Epic." *Saturday Evening Post*, March 20, 1943.

Stockdale, Jim, and Sybil Stockdale. *In Love and War: The Story of a Family's Ordeal and Sacrifice during the Vietnam Years*. Annapolis, Md.: Naval Institute Press, 1990.

SECONDARY SOURCES

Addelston, Judi, and Michael Stirratt, "The Last Bastion of Masculinity: Gender Politics at The Citadel." In *Men's Lives*. 4th ed., edited by Michael S. Kimmel and Michael A. Messner, 205–220. Boston: Allyn and Bacon, 1998.

Alexander, Charles C. *Holding the Line: The Eisenhower Era, 1952–1961*. Bloomington: Indiana University Press, 1975.

Ambrose, Stephen E. *Duty, Honor, Country: A History of West Point.* Baltimore, Md.: Johns Hopkins University Press, 1966.

———. *Eisenhower: The President.* 2 vols. New York: Simon and Schuster, 1984.

Andrew, Rod. *Long Gray Lines: The Southern Military School Tradition, 1839–1915.* Chapel Hill: University of North Carolina Press, 2001.

Applebome, Peter. *Dixie Rising: How the South Is Shaping American Values, Politics, and Culture.* New York: Times Books, 1996.

Atkinson, Rick. *The Long Gray Line.* Boston: Houghton Mifflin, 1989.

Bailey, Beth. *Sex in the Heartland.* Cambridge, Mass.: Harvard University Press, 1999.

Baker, Gary R. *Cadets in Gray.* Columbia, S.C.: Palmetto Bookworks, 1989.

Bartley, Numan V., ed. *The Evolution of Southern Culture.* Athens: University of Georgia Press, 1988.

———. *The New South, 1945–1980.* Baton Rouge: Louisiana State University Press, 1995.

———. *The Rise of Massive Resistance: Race and Politics in the South during the 1950s.* Baton Rouge: Louisiana State University Press, 1969.

Bauman, Mark K. "Confronting the New South Creed: The Genteel Conservative as Higher Educator." In *Education and the Rise of the New South,* edited by Ronald K. Goodenow and Arthur O. White, 92–113. Boston: Hall, 1981.

Bederman, Gail. *Manliness and Civilization: A Cultural History of Gender and Race in the United States, 1880–1917.* Chicago: University of Chicago Press, 1995.

Bell, Derrick. *Faces at the Bottom of the Well: The Permanence of Racism.* New York: Basic Books, 1992.

Billingsley, William J. *Communists on Campus: Race, Politics, and the Public University in Sixties North Carolina.* Athens: University of Georgia Press, 1999.

Binkin, Martin, and Mark J. Eitelberg. *Blacks and the Military.* Washington, D.C.: Brookings Institution, 1982.

Bird, Kai, and Martin J. Sherwin. *American Prometheus: The Triumph and Tragedy of J. Robert Oppenheimer.* New York: Alfred A. Knopf, 2005.

Black, Earl. *Southern Governors and Civil Rights: Racial Segregation as a Campaign Issue in the Second Reconstruction.* Cambridge, Mass.: Harvard University Press, 1976.

Bond, Oliver J. *The Story of The Citadel.* Richmond, Va.: Garrett and Massie, 1936. Reprint, Greenville, S.C.: Southern Historical Press, 1989.

Branch, Taylor. *Parting the Waters: America in the King Years, 1954–1963.* New York: Simon and Schuster, 1988.

Brinkley, Alan. "The Problem of American Conservatism." *American Historical Review* 99 (April 1994): 409–429.

Brodie, Laura Fairchild. *Breaking Out: VMI and the Coming of Women*. New York: Pantheon, 2000.

Brundage, W. Fitzhugh, ed. *Where These Memories Grow: History, Memory, and Southern Identity*. Chapel Hill: University of North Carolina Press, 2000.

Burner, David. *Making Peace with the 1960s*. Princeton, N.J.: Princeton University Press, 1996.

Burton, Orville Vernon. "The Effects of the Civil War and Reconstruction on the Coming of Age of Southern Males, Edgefield County, South Carolina." In *Web of Southern Social Relations: Women, Family, and Education*, edited by Walter J. Fraser Jr., R. Frank Saunders Jr., and Jon L. Wakelyn, 204–224. Athens: University of Georgia Press, 1985.

Carroll, Peter N. *It Seemed Like Nothing Happened: The Tragedy and Promise of America in the 1970s*. New York: Holt, Rinehart, and Winston, 1982.

Carter, Dan T. *The Politics of Rage: George Wallace, the Origins of the New Conservatism, and the Transformation of American Politics*. Baton Rouge: Louisiana State University Press, 1995.

Cash, W. J. *The Mind of the South*. New York: Alfred A. Knopf, 1941. Reprint, New York: Vintage Books, 1991.

Caute, David. *The Great Fear: The Anti-Communist Purge Under Truman and Eisenhower*. New York: Simon and Schuster, 1978.

Chafe, William H. *The Unfinished Journey: America Since World War II*, 4th ed. New York: Oxford University Press, 1999.

Chester, Lewis, et al. *American Melodrama: The Presidential Campaign of 1968*. New York: Viking Press, 1969.

Cleaver, Eldridge. *Soul on Ice*. New York: Dell Publishing, 1991.

Cobb, James C. *Away Down South: A History of Southern Identity*. New York: Oxford University Press, 2005.

———. *The Brown Decision, Jim Crow and Southern Identity*. Athens: University of Georgia Press, 2005.

———. "An Epitaph for the North: Reflections on the Politics of Regional and National Identity at the Millennium." *The Journal of Southern History* 66 (February 2000): 3–24.

———. *The Most Southern Place on Earth: The Mississippi Delta and the Roots of Regional Identity*. New York: Oxford University Press, 1992.

———. *Redefining Southern Culture: Mind and Identity in the Modern South*. Athens: University of Georgia Press, 1999.

———. *The Selling of the South: The Southern Crusade for Industrial Development, 1936–1980*. Baton Rouge: Louisiana State University Press, 1982.

Coffman, Edward M. *The War to End All Wars: The American Military Experience in World War I*. New York: Oxford University Press, 1968.

Collins, Elizabeth Ann. "The Post War Boy Scout Handbooks: Manhood for the Atomic Age." M.A. thesis, University of Georgia, 1999.

Conkin, Paul Keith. *Gone with the Ivy: A Biography of Vanderbilt University*. Knoxville: University of Tennessee Press, 1985.

Connell, R. W. *Masculinities*. Berkeley: University of California Press, 1995.

Conroy, Pat. *The Lords of Discipline*. 2nd ed. New York: Bantam Books, 1983.

Cooper, William J., and Thomas E. Terrill. *The American South: A History*. New York: McGraw-Hill, 1991.

Cox, Maxie M. "1963 — The Year of Decision: Desegregation in South Carolina." PhD diss., University of South Carolina, 1996.

Cuordileone, K. A. "'Politics in an Age of Anxiety': Cold War Political Culture and the Crisis in American Masculinity, 1949–1960." *Journal of American History* 87 (September 2000): 515–545.

Dabbs, James McBride. *The Southern Heritage*. New York: Alfred A. Knopf, 1958.

Dalfiume, Richard M. *Desegregation of the U.S. Armed Forces: Fighting on Two Fronts, 1939–1953*. Columbia: University of Missouri Press, 1969.

Daniel, Pete. *Lost Revolutions: The South in the 1950s*. Chapel Hill: University of North Carolina Press, 2000.

Davis, John Walker. "An Air of Defiance: Georgia's State Flag Change of 1956." *Georgia Historical Quarterly* 82 (Summer 1998): 305–330.

Dean, Robert D. *Imperial Brotherhood: Gender and the Making of Cold War Foreign Policy*. Amherst: University of Massachusetts Press, 2001.

DeBenedetti, Charles, and Charles Catfield. *An American Ordeal: The Antiwar Movement of the Vietnam Era*. Syracuse, N.Y.: Syracuse University Press, 1990.

Dittmer, John. *Local People: The Struggle for Civil Rights in Mississippi*. Urbana: University of Illinois Press, 1994.

Donald, David. "A Generation of Defeat." In *From the Old South to the New: Essays on the Transitional South*, edited by Walter J. Fraser Jr. and Winfred B. Moore Jr., 3–20. Westport, Conn.: Greenwood Press, 1981.

Douglas, Susan. *Where the Girls Are: Growing Up Female with the Mass Media*. New York: Times Books, 1995.

Drago, Edmund L. *Initiative, Paternalism, and Race Relations: Charleston's Avery Normal Institute*. Athens: University of Georgia Press, 1990.

Drobney, Jeffrey A. "A Generation in Revolt: Student Dissent and Political Repression at West Virginia University." *West Virginia History* 54 (1995): 105–122.

Dumbrell, John. *The Carter Presidency: A Re-evaluation.* Manchester: Manchester University Press, 1993.

Dudziak, Mary L. *Cold War Civil Rights: Race and the Image of American Democracy.* Princeton, N.J.: Princeton University Press, 2000.

Dyer, Thomas G. "Higher Education in the South since the Civil War: Historiographical Issue and Trends." In *The Web of Southern Race Relations: Women, Family, and Education,* edited by Walter J. Fraser Jr., R. Frank Saunders Jr., and Jon L. Wakelyn, 127–145. Athens: University of Georgia Press, 1985.

———. *The University of Georgia: A Bicentennial History, 1785–1985.* Athens: University of Georgia Press, 1985.

Edgar, Walter. *South Carolina: A History.* Columbia: University of South Carolina Press, 1998.

———. *South Carolina in the Modern Age.* Columbia: University of South Carolina Press, 1992.

Egerton, Douglas R. *He Shall Go Out Free: The Lives of Denmark Vesey.* Madison, Wisc.: Madison House Publishers, 1999.

Egerton, John. *The Americanization of Dixie: The Southernization of America.* New York: Harper's Magazine Press, 1974.

Emilio, John D., and Estelle B. Freedman. *Intimate Matters: A History of Sexuality in America.* New York: Harper & Row, 1988.

Estes, Steve. *I Am a Man! Race, Manhood and the Civil Rights Movement.* Chapel Hill: University of North Carolina Press, 2005.

Evans, Sara. *Personal Politics: The Roots of Women's Liberation in the Civil Rights Movement and the New Left.* New York: Knopf, 1979.

Faludi, Susan. *Stiffed: The Betrayal of the American Man.* New York: William Morrow and Company, 1999.

Farber, David. *The Age of Great Dreams: America in the 1960s.* New York: Hill & Wang, 1994.

Farrell, James J. *The Spirit of the Sixties: The Making of Postwar Radicalism.* New York: Routledge, 1997.

Ferrel, Charles. *Harry S Truman: A Life.* Columbia: University of Missouri Press, 1994.

Fields, Barbara J. "Ideology and Race in American History." In *Region, Race and Reconstruction: Essays in Honor of C. Vann Woodward,* edited by J. Morgan Kousser and James M. MacPherson, 143–177. New York: Oxford University Press, 1992.

Fleming, Thomas J. *West Point: The Men and Times of the United States Military Academy.* New York: William Morrow and Company, 1969.

Foner, Eric. *The Story of American Freedom*. New York: W. W. Norton and Company, 1998.

Foster, Gaines. *Ghosts of the Confederacy: Defeat, the Lost Cause, and the Emergence of the New South: 1865–1913*. New York: Oxford University Press, 1987.

Fraser, Walter J. *Charleston! Charleston! The History of a Southern City*. Columbia: University of South Carolina Press, 1989.

Franklin, John Hope. *The Militant South, 1800–1861*. Cambridge, Mass.: Harvard University Press, 1956.

Frederickson, Kari. *The Dixiecrat Revolt and the End of the Solid South, 1932–1968*. Chapel Hill: University of North Carolina Press, 2001.

———. "'The Slowest State' and 'Most Backward Community': Racial Violence in South Carolina and the Federal Civil Rights Legislation, 1946–1948." *South Carolina Historical Magazine* 98 (April 1997): 177–202.

Freedman, Samuel G. *The Inheritance: How Three Families and the American Political Majority Moved from Left to Right*. New York: Simon and Schuster, 1996.

Gerstle, Gary. *American Crucible: Race and Nation in the Twentieth Century*. Princeton, N.J.: Princeton University Press, 2001.

———. "The Protean Character of American Liberalism." *American Historical Review* 99 (October 1994): 1043–1073.

Gilman, Owen W. *Vietnam and the Southern Imagination*. Jackson: University Press of Mississippi, 1992.

Gilmore, Glenda. *Defying Dixie: The Radical Roots of Civil Rights, 1919–1950*. New York: W. W. Norton and Company, 2008.

———. *Gender and Jim Crow: Women and the Politics of White Supremacy in North Carolina, 1896–1920*. Chapel Hill: University of North Carolina Press, 1996.

———. "Gender and *Origins of the New South*." *Journal of Southern History* 67 (November 2001): 769–788.

Gitlin, Todd. *The Sixties: Years of Hope, Days of Rage*. Toronto: Bantam Books, 1987.

———. *The Whole World Is Watching: Mass Media in the Making and Unmaking of the New Left*. Berkeley: University of California Press, 1980.

Goldfield, David. *Still Fighting the Civil War: The American South and Southern History*. Baton Rouge: Louisiana State University Press, 2002.

Goldman, Eric F. *The Crucial Decade, America 1945–1955*. New York: Knopf, 1956.

Grabavoy, Leann Almquist. *Joseph Alsop and American Foreign Policy: The Journalist as Advocate*. New York: University Press of America, 1993.

Grantham, Dewey W. *Southern Progressivism: The Reconciliation of Progress and Tradition*. Knoxville: University of Tennessee Press, 1983.

Greene, Christina. "'We'll Take Our Stand': Race, Class and Gender in the Southern

Student Organizing Committee, 1964–1969." In *Hidden Histories of Women in the New South*, edited by Virginia Bernhard, Betty Brandon, Elizabeth Fox-Genovese, Theda Perdue, and Elizabeth Hayes Turner, 173–203. Columbia: University of Missouri Press, 1994.

Griffin, Clifford S. *The University of Kansas: A History*. Lawrence: University Press of Kentucky, 1974.

Griffin, Larry J., and Don H. Doyle, eds. *The South as an American Problem*. Athens: University of Georgia Press, 1995.

Hackney, Sheldon. "Southern Violence." *American Historical Review* 74 (February 1969): 906–925.

Hall, Jacquelyn Dowd, et al. *Like a Family: The Making of a Southern Cotton Mill World*. Chapel Hill: University of North Carolina Press, 1987.

Hartmann, Susan. *The Homefront and Beyond: American Women in the 1940s*. Boston: Twayne Publishers, 1982.

Heineman, Kenneth J. *Campus Wars: The Peace Movement at American State Universities in the Vietnam Era*. New York: New York University Press, 1993.

Hennen, John. "Struggle for Recognition: The Marshall University Students for a Democratic Society and the Red Scare in Huntington, 1965–1969." *West Virginia History* 52 (1993): 127–147.

Herring, George C. *America's Longest War: The United States and Vietnam, 1950–1975*, 3rd ed. New York: McGraw-Hill, 1996.

Hoganson, Kristin L. *Fighting for American Manhood: How Gender Politics Provoked the Spanish-American and Philippine-American Wars*. New Haven, Conn.: Yale University Press, 1998.

Holm, Jeanne. *Women in the Military: An Unfinished Revolution*. Novato, Calif.: Presidio Press, 1982.

Horwitz, Tony. *Confederates in the Attic: Dispatches from the Unfinished Civil War*. New York: Vintage Books, 1998.

Jackson, Kenneth J. *Crabgrass Frontier: The Suburbanization of the United States*. New York: Oxford University Press, 1985.

Johnson, Haynes. *Sleepwalking through History: America in the Reagan Years*. New York: Anchor Books, 1991.

Johnson, Lyndon Baines. *The Vantage Point: Perspectives of the Presidency, 1963–1969*. New York: Holt, Rinehart, and Winston, 1971.

Kantrowitz, Stephen. *Ben Tillman and the Reconstruction of White Supremacy*. Chapel Hill: University of North Carolina Press, 2000.

Karabel, Jerome. *The Chosen: The Hidden History of Admission and Exclusion at Harvard, Yale, and Princeton*. New York: Houghton Mifflin, 2005.

Katz, Milton. *Ban the Bomb: A History of SANE, the Committee for a Sane Nuclear Policy, 1957–1985.* Westport, Conn.: Greenwood Press, 1986.

Kearns, Doris. *Lyndon Johnson and the American Dream.* New York: Signet, 1977.

Kessler-Harris, Alice. *In Pursuit of Equity: Women, Men, and the Quest for Economic Citizenship in 20th-Century America.* New York: Oxford University Press, 2001.

Kimmel, Michael. *Manhood in America: A Cultural History,* 2nd ed. New York: Oxford University Press, 2006.

Kirby, Jack Temple. *The Countercultural South.* Athens: University of Georgia Press, 1995.

———. *Media-Made Dixie: The South in the American Imagination.* Athens: University of Georgia Press, 1986.

Lander, Ernest M., Jr., and Richard J. Calhoun, eds. *Two Decades of Change: The South since the Supreme Court Desegregation Decision.* Columbia: University of South Carolina Press, 1975.

Lears, T. Jackson. *No Place of Grace: Antimodernism and the Transformation of American Culture, 1880–1920.* New York: Pantheon Books. 1981.

Lesesne, Henry H. *A History of the University of South Carolina: 1940–2000.* Columbia: University of South Carolina Press, 2001.

Levine, Lawrence W. *Black Culture and Black Consciousness: Afro-American Folk Thought from Slavery to Freedom.* New York: Oxford University Press, 1977.

Lewis, George. *The White South and the Red Menace: Segregationists, Anticommunism and Massive Resistance, 1945–1965.* Gainesville: University Press of Florida, 2004.

Link, William A. *William Friday: Power, Purpose, and American Higher Education.* Chapel Hill: University of North Carolina Press, 1995.

Lipsky, David. *Absolutely American: Four Years at West Point.* New York: Houghton Mifflin, 2003.

Lovell, John P. *Neither Athens nor Sparta? The American Service Academies in Transition.* Bloomington: Indiana University Press, 1979.

Macaulay, Alex. "Discipline and Rebellion: The Citadel Rebellion of 1898." *South Carolina Historical Magazine* 103, no. 1 (January 2002): 30–47.

MacGregor, Morris J. *Integration of the Armed Forces, 1940–1965.* Washington, D.C.: Center of Military History, United States Army, 1981.

MacLean, Nancy. *Behind the Mask of Chivalry: The Making of the Second Ku Klux Klan.* New York: Oxford University Press, 1994.

Manegold, Catherine. *In Glory's Shadow: Shannon Faulkner, the Citadel, and a Changing America.* New York: Alfred A. Knopf, 1999.

Mansbridge, Jane. *Why We Lost the ERA.* Chicago: University of Chicago Press, 1986.

Mathews, Donald, and Jane Sherron DeHart. *Sex, Gender and the Politics of ERA: A State and the Nation*. New York: Oxford University Press, 1990.

Matusow, Allen J. *The Unraveling of America: A History of Liberalism in the 1960s*. New York: Harper and Row, 1984.

May, Elaine Tyler. *Homeward Bound: American Families in the Cold War*. New York: BasicBooks, 1988.

McAdam, Doug. *Freedom Summer*. New York: Oxford University Press, 1988.

McCandless, Amy Thompson. "In a White Man's World: Women at The Citadel." *Women's History Magazine* 52 (Spring 2006): 14–24.

———. *The Past in the Present: Women's Higher Education in the Twentieth-Century American South*. Tuscaloosa: University of Alabama Press, 1999.

McEnaney, Laura. *Civil Defense Begins at Home: Militarization Meets Everyday Life in the Fifties*. Princeton, N.J.: Princeton University Press, 2000.

———. "Gender Analysis and Foreign Relations." In *Encyclopedia of American Foreign Policy*. 2nd ed. Vol. 2, edited by Alexander De Conde et al., 123–133. New York: Charles Scribner's Sons, 2002.

McGirr, Lisa. *Suburban Warriors: The Origins of the New American Right*. Princeton, N.J.: Princeton University Press, 2001.

McLaurin, Melton. "Country Music and the Vietnam War." In *Perspectives on the American South: An Annual Review of Society, Politics and Culture*. Vol. 3, edited by James C. Cobb and Charles R. Wilson, 145–161. New York: Gordon and Breach Science Publishers, 1985.

McNeill, Paul W. "School Desegregation in South Carolina, 1963–1970." PhD diss., University of Kentucky, 1979.

Metcalf, George R. *From Little Rock to Boston: The History of School Desegregation*. Westport, Conn.: Greenwood Press, 1971.

Meyer, Leisa D. *Creating GI Jane: Sexuality and Power in the Women's Army Corps during World War II*. New York: Columbia University Press, 1996.

Miller, James. *"Democracy Is in the Streets": From Port Huron to the Siege of Chicago*. New York: Simon and Schuster, 1987.

Mitchell, Brian. *Women in the Military: Flirting with Disaster*. Washington, D.C.: Regnery Publishers, 1998.

Mohr, Clarence L. "World War II and the Transformation of Southern Higher Education." In *Remaking Dixie: The Impact of World War II on the American South*, edited by Neil R. McMillen, 33–55. Jackson: University Press of Mississippi, 1997.

Mohr, Clarence L., and Joseph E. Gordon. *Tulane: The Emergence of a Modern University, 1945–1980*. Baton Rouge: Louisiana State University Press, 2001.

Morris, Robin M. "Memory and Manhood: The Citadel and the Civil War Centennial 1961." MA thesis, University of Mississippi, 2001.

Mzorek, Donald J. "The Cult and the Ritual of Toughness in Cold War America." In *Ritual and Ceremonies in Popular Culture*, edited by Ray B. Browne, 178–191. Bowling Green, Ky.: Bowling Green University Popular Press, 1980.

Navasky, Victor S. *Naming Names*. New York: Penguin Books, 1981.

Nelson, Jack, and Jack Bass. *The Orangeburg Massacre*. New York: World Publishing Company, 1970.

Nichols, W. Gary. "The General as President: Charles P. Summerall and Mark W. Clark as Presidents of The Citadel." *South Carolina Historical Magazine* 95 (October 1994): 314–335.

Nicholson, Dennis Dewitt. *A History of The Citadel: The Years of Summerall and Clark*. Charleston, S.C.: The Citadel Print Shop, 1994.

Nye, Robert A. "Western Masculinities in War and Peace." *American Historical Review* 112, no. 2 (April 2007): 417–438.

O'Neill, Stephen. "From the Shadow of Slavery: The Civil Rights Years in Charleston." PhD diss., University of Virginia, 1994.

O'Neill, William L. *Coming Apart: An Informal History of America in the 1960s*. New York: Quadrangle, 1971.

O'Reilly, Kenneth. *Nixon's Piano: Presidents and Racial Politics from Washington to Clinton*. New York: Free Press, 1995.

Pach, Chester J., Jr., and Elmo Richardson. *The Presidency of Dwight D. Eisenhower*. Rev. ed. Lawrence: University Press of Kansas, 1991.

Palmer, Bruce. *The Twenty-Five-Year War: America's Military Role in Vietnam*. Lexington: University Press of Kentucky, 1984.

Payne, Charles. *I've Got the Light of Freedom: The Organizing Tradition and the Mississippi Freedom Struggle*. Berkeley: University of California Press, 1995.

Peacock, James. "The South in a Global World." *Virginia Quarterly Review* 78 (August 2003): 581–594.

Peck, Abe. *Uncovering the Sixties: The Life and Times of the Underground Press*. New York: Pantheon Press, 1985.

Polenburg, Richard. *War and Society: The United States, 1941–1945*. Philadelphia: Lippincott, 1972.

Pratt, Robert A. *The Color of Their Skin: Education and Race in Richmond, Virginia, 1954–1989*. Charlottesville: University Press of Virginia, 1992.

———. *We Shall Not Be Moved: The Desegregation of the University of Georgia*. Athens: University of Georgia Press, 2002.

Prince, K. Michael. *Rally 'Round the Flag, Boys! South Carolina and the Confederate Flag.* Columbia: University of South Carolina Press, 2004.

Ransby, Barbara. *Ella Baker and the Black Freedom Movement: A Radical Democratic Vision.* Chapel Hill: University of North Carolina Press, 2003

Reed, John Shelton. *The Enduring South: Subcultural Persistence in Mass Society.* Lexington, Mass.: Lexington Books, 1972.

Roediger, David. *The Wages of Whiteness: Race and the Making of the American Working Class.* New York: Verso, 1991.

Rorabaugh, W. J. *Berkeley at War: The 1960s.* New York: Oxford University Press, 1989.

Roscigno, Vincent, and William Danaher. *The Voice of Southern Labor: Radio, Music and Textile Strikes, 1929-1934.* Minneapolis: University of Minnesota Press, 2004.

Rossinow, Douglas C. "'The Break-Through to New Life': Christianity and the Emergence of the New Left in Austin, Texas, 1956-1964." *American Quarterly* 46 (September 1994): 309-340.

———. *The Politics of Authenticity: Liberalism, Christianity, and the New Left in America.* New York: Columbia University Press, 1998.

Rotundo, E. Anthony. *American Manhood: Transformations in Masculinity from the Revolution to the Modern Era.* New York: BasicBooks, 1993.

Sale, Kirkpatrick. *SDS.* New York: Random House, 1973.

Sarratt, Reed. *The Ordeal of Desegregation: The First Decade.* New York: Harper and Row, 1966.

Schulman, Bruce J. *The Seventies: The Great Shift in American Culture, Society and Politics.* New York: Free Press, 2001.

Scott, Joan W. "Gender: A Useful Category of Historical Analysis." *American Historical Review* 91 (December 1986): 1053-1075.

Simon, Bryant. *Fabric of Defeat: The Politics of South Carolina Mill Workers, 1910-1948.* Chapel Hill: University of North Carolina Press, 1998.

Sitkoff, Harvard. *The Struggle for Black Equality, 1954-1992.* Rev. ed. New York: Hill and Wang, 1993.

Small, Melvin, and William D. Hoover, eds. *Give Peace a Chance: Exploring the Vietnam Antiwar Movement.* Syracuse, N.Y.: Syracuse University Press, 1992.

Smallet, Andrea L. "'I Just Like to Kill Things': Women, Men, and the Gender of Sport Hunting in the United States, 1940-1973." *Gender & History* 17, no. 1 (April 2005): 183-209.

Sosna, Morton. "The GIs' South and the North-South Dialogue during World War II." In *Developing Dixie: Modernization in a Traditional Society,* edited by Winfred

B. Moore Jr., Joseph F. Tripp, and Lyon G. Tyler Jr., 311–326. Westport, Conn.: Greenwood Press, 1988.

———. "More Important than the Civil War? The Impact of World War II on the South." In *Perspectives on the American South: An Annual Review of Society, Politics and Culture.* Vol. 4, edited by James C. Cobb and Charles R. Wilson, 145–161. New York: Gordon and Breach Science Publishers, 1987.

Sproat, John G. "Firm Flexibility: Perspectives on Desegregation in South Carolina." In *New Perspectives on Race and Slavery in America*, edited by Robert H. Abzug and Stephen E. Maizlish, 164–184. Lexington: University of Kentucky Press, 1986.

Stearns, Peter N. *Be a Man! Males in Modern Society.* 2nd ed. New York: Holmes and Meier, 1990.

Strum, Philippa. *Women in the Barracks: The VMI Case and Equal Rights.* Lawrence: University Press of Kansas, 2002.

Sugrue, Thomas J. *The Origins of the Urban Crisis: Race and Inequality in Postwar Detroit.* Princeton, N.J.: Princeton University Press, 1996.

Sweetman, Jack. *The United States Naval Academy: An Illustrated History.* Annapolis, Md.: Naval Institute Press, 1979.

Synnott, Marcia G. "Desegregation in South Carolina, 1950–1963: Sometime Between Now and Never." In *Looking South: Chapters in the Story of an American Region*, edited by Winfred B. Moore Jr. and Joseph F. Tripp, 51–64. Westport, Conn.: Greenwood Press, 1989.

Tindall, George B. *The Ethnic Southerners.* Baton Rouge: Louisiana State University Press, 1976.

Townsend, Kim. *Manhood at Harvard: William James and Others.* New York: W. W. Norton, 1996.

Tyson, Timothy B. "Dynamite and the 'Silent South': A Story from the Second Reconstruction in South Carolina." In *Jumpin' Jim Crow: Southern Politics from Civil War to Civil Rights*, edited by Jane Dailey, Glenda Elizabeth Gilmore, and Bryant Simon, 275–297. Princeton, N.J.: Princeton University Press, 2000.

———. *Radio Free Dixie: Robert F. Williams and the Roots of Black Power.* Chapel Hill: University of North Carolina Press, 1999.

Vagts, Alfred. *A History of Militarism.* Westport, Conn.: Greenwood Press, 1959.

Viorst, Milton. *Fire in the Streets: American in the 1960s.* New York: Simon and Schuster, 1979.

Watts, Trent, ed. *White Masculinity in the Recent South.* Baton Rouge: Louisiana State University Press, 2008.

Weiner, Jon. "Reagan's Children: Racial Hatred on Campus." *The Nation*, February 27, 1989.

Weisbrot, Robert. *Freedom Bound: A History of America's Civil Rights Movement.* New York: W. W. Norton and Company, 1990.

Whites, LeeAnn. *The Civil War as a Crisis in Gender: Augusta, Georgia, 1860–1890.* Athens: University of Georgia Press, 1995.

Whitfield, Stephen J. *The Culture of the Cold War.* 2nd ed. Baltimore, Md.: Johns Hopkins University Press, 1996.

Wilentz, Sean. *The Age of Reagan: A History, 1974–2008.* New York: HarperCollins, 2008.

Wilkinson, J. Harvie. *From Brown to Bakke: The Supreme Court and School Integration, 1954–1978.* New York: Oxford University Press, 1979.

Willingham, Calder. *End As a Man.* New York: Donald I. Fine, 1947.

Wilson, Charles Reagan, and William Ferris, eds. *The Encyclopedia of Southern Culture.* Chapel Hill: University of North Carolina Press, 1989.

Woodward, C. Vann. *The Burden of Southern History.* 3rd ed. Baton Rouge: Louisiana State University Press, 1993.

———. *The Strange Career of Jim Crow.* 2d ed. New York: Oxford University Press, 1966.

Zaroulis, Nancy, and Gerald Sullivan. *Who Spoke Up? American Protest Against the War in Vietnam, 1963–1975.* Garden City, N.Y.: Doubleday & Company, 1984.

Zinn, Howard. *A People's History of the United States, 1492–Present.* New York: HarperPerennial, 1995.

———. *The Southern Mystique.* New York: Alfred A. Knopf, 1964.

Ackerman, Conni, 138–139

American Civil Liberties Union, 196, 202

Anderson, Robert, 62

Andrew, Rod, 2, 12, 108

Army Specialized Training Program (ASTP), 14–15, 16, 17–18

Association of Citadel Men, 120, 157, 170, 182

Baldwin, Sallie, 204–205, 206

Bay of Pigs, 89

Bicentennial (1976), 131–132

Bond, Oliver J., 5

Bozeman, Michael, 67

Bradley, John, 134, 155–156

Brown, Arthur J., 61

Brown v. Board of Education, 53, 54–55, 83–84, 85, 86

Byrd, Harry, 55

Byrnes, James, 36, 53

Capers, Elison, 159

Carter, Hodding, 163

Carter, Jimmy, 111, 132, 135, 147

Cash, Wilbur J., 9–10, 209

Chapman, Angela, 194

Chapman, Harry, 168

Charleston, 9, 47, 61, 76, 79, 89–90

Citadel, The: academics at, 21, 41, 75, 91, 114–115; African American Studies Program at, 213; Afro-American Student Association at, 73, 80–81, 173, 174, 179, 182; athletics at, 20–21, 22, 39, 65, 75; beneficiary cadets at, 5; building construction at, 19, 20, 39–40; during Civil War and Reconstruction, 9, 11, 142; egalitarian ideals of, 5, 26, 62–63, 113; and GI Bill, 18–19; and Great Depression and New Deal, 13–14; Greater Issues lecture series at, 47–48, 54–55, 58, 89, 102, 104; honor system at, 43–46, 80, 106–107, 113, 192, 196; Iranian student-exchange program at, 133–135; origins of, 8, 10–11, 188; postbellum reopening of, 11–13; recognition day at, 126–127; and southern "traditions," 4, 5–6, 28, 57–58, 60, 130, 209–210; student unrest at, 12, 59, 87, 101–103, 104–109, 145–146, 149; and veteran's program, 19–22, 23–24, 47, 91, 112, 118–120, 194–196; World War II's impact on, 2–3, 14. See also Citadel man/men; citizen-soldiers; coeducation; faculty; fourth class system; racial integration; whole man concept

Citadel man/men, 1, 8, 210; and attitudes toward women and coeducation, 1, 31–32, 117–118, 138, 146, 148, 195, 205–207; on Board of Visitors, 169–170; bonds among, 71, 78–79, 84–85, 149, 172–173, 178, 179, 181, 186, 190–191; and Citadel ring, 118–120; and citizenship, 1, 2–5, 7–8, 38, 59–60, 88, 107–108; and Clark, Mark, 37, 38–39, 41, 47, 49–50, 51, 54, 130; and

Citadel man/men (*continued*)
Cold War, 24–25, 28–30, 32–33, 38, 59–60, 89, 107; compared with veterans, 15, 118–120; and Confederacy, 57–58, 185–186; and conformity, 15, 18, 23, 25, 28–29, 50, 88, 107, 211; and fourth class system, 6, 17, 32–33, 93–94, 96, 118, 119–120, 123, 158–159, 193, 204; and Grimsley, 160, 164, 185; and honor system, 46; and Mood Report, 153, 154–155, 161; racial component of, 39, 54, 70, 112, 190, 209; racial divisions among, 78–79, 85–86, 173, 178–179, 186, 190; and segregation, 55; and Stockdale, 148, 149–150; and student movement, 93, 112, 211; and toughness, 6, 32–33, 38–39, 50–51, 92–93, 112, 125, 138, 145, 151, 153; and Vietnam antiwar movement, 93, 112, 211; and World War II, 2, 3. *See also* citizen-soldiers; whole man concept
Citadel Men Foundation, The, 213
citizens' councils, 55
citizenship: and Cold War, 25, 59–60; definitions of, 6–8, 209, 215; and masculinity, 2, 5, 25, 59–60, 112, 146, 160–161, 199, 210; and Vietnam antiwar movement, 107. *See also* Citadel man/men; citizen-soldiers; fourth class system; whole man concept
citizen-soldiers: and coeducation, 114, 118, 146, 149–150; and Cold War, 24–25; definition of, 2–3; and fourth class system, 149–150; and masculinity, 1, 7, 112, 195; and race, 4, 85–86; and southern military tradition, 12; training of, 12, 15; and Vietnam

antiwar movement, 4, 93, 104. *See also* Citadel man/men; whole man concept
civil rights movement, 4, 28, 83, 86, 88, 132–133; comparisons of, with women's movement, 202–203; and school desegregation, 48, 53, 55, 83–84, 86; in South Carolina, 61–62. *See also* segregation
Civil War, 9, 11, 57
Clark, Mark W., 37–38, 129, 130, 132, 164; Cold War ideology of, 38, 47, 51, 58; and honor system, 44–45; immediate impact on Citadel, 38, 39–41, 42–43; and whole man concept, 39, 59–60
— relationship of: with corps of cadets, 43, 89, 90; with faculty, 41–42
— views of: on fourth class system, 51, 52; on integration, 42, 54–55, 62–63; on manliness, 38–39, 47, 49
Clark, Walt, 154
Clemson University, 52, 61–62, 63, 66, 84, 102
Clyburn, James, 184
Cobb, James C., 111
coeducation, 192–211 passim, 213; cadet mockery of, 31, 165; connection of, with racial integration, 169–170, 175–176, 202–203; and low enrollment issues, 92, 114–115, 116–118; and pressure from ERA and women's movement, 136–141; and presumed "destruction" of The Citadel, 112, 117–118, 204, 212; of summer school, 31; of U.S. service academies, 137, 165; and veteran's program, 194–196. *See also* Faulkner, Shannon; fourth class system, and women

Cold War, 25, 30, 46, 55–56, 58–59, 89–90; impact of, on Citadel, 3, 24–29, 38, 47–49, 55–56, 58–59, 92–93; and masculinity, 3, 32, 34, 38, 50–51, 59–60, 92–93

College of Charleston, 103, 113–114

Common Sense, 103

Confederacy, 9, 12; Citadel service to, 11, 13; evocation of, by Citadel personnel, 13, 159, 164, 175–176, 185–188, 191, 208–209; meaning of, to cadets, 81–83, 57–58, 60, 176, 183–184; and neo-Confederates, 2. *See also* Confederate Flag; Dixie

Confederate flag, 74, 176, 184, 190, 191; cadet attitudes toward, 81–82, 185–186, 188, 209; at Citadel football games, 80, 81–83, 175, 183–185, 187, 189; in Citadel yearbooks, 58; and segregation, 57–58; atop South Carolina State House, 183, 184, 210, 213

Conroy, Pat, 51, 66, 92, 118, 197

Converse College, 197, 201–202

Courvoisie, T. Nugent, 66–67, 91

Crabbe, William, Jr., 124–125

Cuban Missile Crisis, 90

Davis, Ossie, 86

De La Roche, Harry, Jr., 142–145

Department of Health Education and Welfare, 73, 74, 76, 167, 168

Dick, Harvey, 145

Dixie, 80, 82, 175–176, 183–189, 190, 191, 209, 212, 213

Dixiecrats, 28

Doucet, Norman, 206

Duckett, James, 105–106, 120–121; and fourth class system, 120–123, 127, 131

Edwards, James, 131

Egerton, John, 110–111

Eisenhower, Dwight David, 37, 40, 48, 56, 90

End As a Man (Willingham), 42–43

Equal Rights Amendment, 136–137, 140–141, 145

Ervin, Sam, 111, 136

faculty, 2, 5, 26, 102, 108, 161; and academic freedom, 41–42; under Clark, Mark, 40, 41–42; and coeducation, 114, 116, 117, 165; and fourth class system, 34, 94, 122, 125–126; and GI Bill, 18; and Great Depression, 13, 14; and honor system, 44, 46; and Nesmith incident, 171, 175, 181–182; and racial integration, 42, 65, 72, 75–76, 78, 82, 167, 188, 189; and uniforms, 115, 117; and veteran students, 19, 20, 21, 196; and World War II, 14–15

Faulkner, Shannon, 1, 196–198, 202–205, 207, 208, 214

Feaster, Ken, 77, 78

Ferguson, Larry, 74, 79, 80–81, 86

Ford, Gerald, 137

Ford, Robert, 187

Foster, Charles, 62, 63–64, 66–70, 72, 79, 203, 207

fourth class system, 16–17, 22–23, 92, 98, 148–151, 158–159, 160, 211; and citizenship, 6, 24–25, 51–52, 60, 112; Cold War's impact on, 32–33, 51, 60; and De La Roche murders, 142–143, 144, 145, 150; and hazing, 33–34, 52, 77, 78, 84, 92–94, 95–99, 120–128, 148–150, 152–154, 190, 192–193, 213–214;

fourth class system (*continued*)
  1972 review of, 123–127; and racial
  integration, 71, 74, 75, 77, 78, 84–85,
  190; and student movement, 93;
  Vietnam War's impact on, 89, 91–93;
  and women, 141, 149–150, 155–156,
  160–161, 192, 199–201, 204–205. *See
  also* Mood Report; Nesmith incident;
  Whitmire Report

Gantt, Harvey, 61–62, 63
GI Bill, 18, 20
Gibler, John, 145
Gibson, William, 175
Gilliard, Patrick, 78
Ginsburg, Ruth Bader, 207
Goldwater, Barry, 56, 90
Graham, Billy, 48
Graham, George, 74–75, 78, 79, 80, 81, 86
Gressette Committee, 53, 54
Griffin, Marvin, 54
Grimsley, James A., 158, 160–161, 170–171,
  181, 184–185, 190, 191; and Citadel
  man concept, 164–165; and Nesmith
  incident, 171–172, 173–175, 176–179
Grinalds, John S., 212, 213
Gulf War, 194

Haggard, Merle, 108
Harris, Hugh P.: background of, 64;
  and fourth class system, 92, 93–94,
  95–96, 97; and racial integration, 66,
  69, 70, 73, 76; racial views of, 64–66;
  and student unrest, 101–103, 123; on
  Vietnam, 107
Harvey, Paul, 46, 48
Hee-Haw, 111
Hollings, Ernest, 197

Hooks, Benjamin, 175
Hooper, Dave, 67, 69
Hoover, J. Edgar, 47
House Un-American Activities
  Committee, 48–49, 90
Hurricane Hugo, 187

Inouye, Daniel, 89
International Days of Protest, 91
Iran hostage crisis, 135

Jackson, Jesse, 174
James, George, 169
Johnson, Lyndon Baines, 91
Johnson, Patricia, 194
Jones, Keith, 77, 79, 85

Kennedy, John F., 62, 89
Kent State, 103–104
Kilpatrick, James, 202
King, Martin Luther, Jr., 75, 180
Kissam, Keller, 185
Korean War, 27, 51

Lacy, Elizabeth, 194
Legare, Herbert, 73, 74, 79
Lockridge, James, 71, 72, 102, 103
Lost Cause, 12, 194
Lucy, Autherine, 55

Mace, Emory, 212
Mace, Nancy, 212
Malcolm X, 86
Manly, Sarah, 194, 197
Marshall Plan, 27
McConnell, Glenn, 187
McDowell, John, 77, 79
Mendoza, Michael, 171

military schools, 12, 162
Mill, Rick, 196
Miss USA Pageant, 132
Monteith, Henrie, 62
Mood, Frank, 152. *See also* Mood Report
Mood, George, 148, 152, 158
Mood Report, 151–157, 158, 159, 160, 161, 178

National Association for the
   Advancement of Colored People
   (NAACP), 55, 56, 61, 174–175, 177
National Organization of Women (NOW),
   137–139
Nesmith, Alonzo, 170–171, 174
Nesmith, Kevin, 171, 174, 176, 178–179,
   190, 206
Nesmith incident, 163–164, 171–179, 190,
   191, 192, 202, 206
New Left, 107–108
Nicholson, Dennis D., 19, 135, 157, 162;
   and censorship of student newspaper,
   101–102; on De La Roche murders,
   142, 144; on fourth class system, 144,
   150; and racial integration of The
   Citadel, 63, 66, 167; on women at The
   Citadel, 140, 164
1964 Civil Rights Act, 63, 193, 195
Nixon, Richard, 111

Oil Embargo (1973), 110, 133–134

Percy, Walker, 111
Portee, Frank, 176
Prioleau, William, 157, 160, 162, 168, 170
Pusser, Buford, 111

racial integration, 4, 48, 53–58, 61–86
   passim, 213; of Board of Visitors,

167–170; and Citadel recruitment
   of African American cadets, 62, 65,
   166–168, 170, 182, 186; comparisons
   of, with gender integration, 202–203;
   of faculty, 181–182; South Carolina
   Human Affairs Commission, 179–181,
   183–184; and unresolved racial
   tensions, 135, 163–164, 175, 181–183,
   188–191. *See also* Confederate Flag;
   Dixie; fourth class system, and racial
   integration; Nesmith incident
Reagan, Ronald, 163–164
Reconstruction, 11, 162–163
Reed, John Shelton, 111, 210
Reilly, Rick, 192
Ridgway, Matthew, 48
Riggs, William, 67, 69, 70, 84
Risher, William, 193
Rivers, Mendel, 89–90
Rosa, John, 213, 214, 215

Sass, Herbert Ravenel, 9, 14
Seabrooks, Norman, 73, 77, 78, 79, 80, 82
Sealey, Reginald, 77, 79, 80
segregation, 28, 59–60, 202; in public
   schools, 42, 83–84; in South Carolina,
   53–55
Seignious, George M.: background and
   career of, 131, 147; Citadel resurgence
   under, 131–132, 133; on coeducation,
   137, 140, 141; and fourth class system,
   141–142, 145–146; support of, for
   Iranian exchange-student program,
   133–134
service academies, 84, 113, 115, 137, 142,
   165; Annapolis, 147, 148, 154; West
   Point, 140
Sheheen, Fred, 170

Shine, Joseph, 70–73, 79, 203
Solomon, James, 62
South: image of, 2, 6–7, 34, 110–112,
  163, 209–210; and masculinity, 53,
  111–112, 132, 210; as "New America,"
  130, 132–133; and New South, 11–12;
  post–World War II changes in, 4, 7,
  53, 111, 209–210; resistance to change
  in, 5–6, 57–58, 91–92, 161
South Carolina colleges and universities,
  61–62, 167–168, 169, 170. See also
  specific schools
South Carolina Commission on Higher
  Education, 169, 170
South Carolina Human Affairs
  Commission, 179–181, 183–184
South Carolina Women's Leadership
  Institute, 201–202
southern colleges and universities:
  desegregation of, 61–62, 84; and GI
  Bill, 18, 20; and New South, 11–12;
  during 1960s, 108–109; and southern
  military tradition, 12, 108; and
  World War II, 4. See also civil rights
  movement; South Carolina colleges
  and universities; and specific
  schools
southern military tradition, 12, 108
Specialized Training and Reassignment
  Program (STAR), 14–15,
  17–18
Spellman, Francis, 47–48
Stahr, Elvis, 89
Stockdale, James, 2, 147–150, 157, 159, 160,
  161, 193; and Mood Report, 151–152,
  154–155, 156, 158
student movement, 4, 90, 93, 101,

102, 107–109, 132–133, 193. See also
  Vietnam antiwar movement
Summerall, Charles P., 13, 36, 129,
  130, 132; and Citadel man concept,
  15, 28, 29, 34; and Cold War
  anticommunism, 26; concerns of,
  over ASTP and STAR, 16; and fourth
  class system, 16–17, 18, 33–34; and
  veteran students, 20
Summerall Guards, 80, 135

Tangerine Bowl, 39
Teague, Eddie, 125–126
Tet Offensive, 99
Thomas, Sandra, 201
Thurmond, Strom, 28, 55, 207
Tillman, Benjamin, 5
Timmerman, George B., 53, 54
Timmerman, James, 114–115
Truman, Harry S, 27–28

United States Justice Department, 193,
  196, 198, 200
University of Alabama, 55
University of Georgia, 84
University of Mississippi, 61
University of South Carolina, 62, 84, 104,
  144

Vergnolle, Ronald, 206
Vesey, Denmark, 10
Vietnam antiwar movement, 4, 132–133,
  193; and Citadel, 87–88, 90–91, 93,
  99–101, 102, 102–104, 107, 108
Vietnam War, 48, 89, 91, 99, 103, 107, 110,
  147
Vigil, 87–88, 102–103

Virginia Military Institute (VMI), 193, 196–201, 204, 207, 209

Vojdik, Val, 200, 201–202, 207

Waltons, The, 111

Waring, Tom, 54–55, 66

Watergate, 110, 111, 112–113

Watts, Claudius E., 186–187, 188, 189, 193, 201

Weiner, Jon, 163

West, John, 122

Whitmire Report, 94–99, 123–124, 136

whole man concept, 210–211; and citizenship, 1, 60; and coeducation, 150, 192, 195; and Cold War, 59–60; definition of, 39, 164–165; and fourth class system, 50, 96, 122–123, 149–150, 153; and race, 85–86, 172–173, 181.

See also Citadel man/men; citizen-soldiers

Willingham, Calder, 42

Winthrop, 52–53, 117

women: cadet attitudes toward, 1–2, 31–32, 52–53, 117, 120, 137–140, 151, 165–166, 191, 195, 203, 204–206; in early Cold War era, 3–4, 30–31, 52; and New Left, 108. *See also* coeducation; Equal Rights Amendment; women's movement

women's movement, 136–138, 140, 145, 149–150, 160, 161. *See also* coeducation

World War II, 2, 9

Yippies, 101

Young, Andrew, 111

9 780820 326511